SPIRITUALITY WITHIN RELIGIOUS TRADITIONS IN SOCIAL WORK PRACTICE

MARY VAN HOOK
University of Central Florida School of Social Work

BERYL HUGEN
Calvin College School of Social Work

MARIAN AGUILAR
Texas A&M International University

AUSTRALIA • CANADA • MEXICO • SINGAPORE • SPAIN • UNITED KINGDOM • UNITED STATES

BROOKS/COLE
THOMSON LEARNING™

Sponsoring Editor: *Lisa Gebo*
Assistant Editor: *Alma Dea Michelena*
Marketing Team: *Caroline Concilla, Tami Strang*
Editorial Assistant: *Sheila Walsh*
Project Editor: *Keith Faivre*
Production Service: *Buuji, Inc.*
Manuscript Editor: *Quica Ostrander*
Permissions Editor: *Sue Ewing*
Cover Design: *Jennifer Mackres*
Print Buyer: *Vena Dyer*
Typesetting: *Buuji, Inc.*
Printing and Binding: *Transcontinental Printing, Inc., Louiseville*

For more information about this or any other Brooks/Cole products, contact:
BROOKS/COLE
511 Forest Lodge Road
Pacific Grove, CA 93950 USA
www.brookscole.com
1-800-423-0563 (Thomson Learning Academic Resource Center)

Printed in Canada

10 9 8 7 6 5 4 3 2 1

Library of Congress Cataloging-in-Publication Data

Spirituality within religious traditions in social work practice / [edited by]
Mary Van Hook, Beryl Hugen, Marian Aguilar.
p. cm.
Includes bibliographical references and index.
ISBN 0-534-58419-5
1. Social service—Religious aspects. 2. Spiritual life. 3. Spirituality.
I. Van Hook, Mary. II. Hugen, Beryl. III. Aguilar, Marian Angela.

HV530 .S69 2002
291.1'783—dc21 2001046472

CONTENTS

Chapter 2

Lakota—Native People's Spirituality 18

Maria Yellow Horse Brave Heart

Chapter 3

Hinduism 34

Ram Singh

Chapter 4

Buddhism 53

Edward R. Canda

PREFACE

With growing recognition of the role that spirituality and religious beliefs, practices, and institutions can play in people's lives, *Spirituality within Religious Traditions and Social Work Practice* is designed to help social workers and other counselors make their practice culturally relevant with respect to the religious traditions of their clients and the communities they serve. Knowledge of these religious traditions can lead to an understanding of how they shape clients' lives and help them construct meaning about the world around them. These sources of meaning influence how events are experienced and determine the nature of the help that is available to clients within the traditions. Furthermore, it is valuable for social workers and other counselors to expand their understanding in order to practice in the United States and other countries where religious diversity is increasing.

To help social workers incorporate this understanding in their assessment and interventions with clients, this book includes essential information about a number of important religious traditions. Although spirituality can be conceptualized and experienced apart from religion, in this book spirituality will be discussed in the context of particular religious traditions and in terms of the sense of meaning and connection that religion can provide. Chapter 1 introduces the conceptual model we will use to understand religious traditions and spirituality; each of the subsequent chapters discusses a specific religious tradition. We recognize that there are a wide variety of religious traditions, and thus any book can only include some of them. Because the goal is to inform social work practice, we have chosen religious traditions that are likely to be followed by the large majority of people who might be seen by social workers or are potentially influential in community life. Furthermore, an analysis of some of the important dimensions of religion can illustrate ways to understand religious traditions that could be useful in social workers' efforts to explore the role of religion in the lives of their clients from other religious backgrounds.

The information about specific religious traditions is organized around the following themes: the history and basic beliefs (master stories) of the particular tradition; the sources of power and resiliency in the religious tradition; the tradition's rituals; views of health and sources of healing; some specific implications for social work practice; and a personal narrative by the author that helps illustrate the religious tradition. Each author will expand on these themes somewhat differently, in part because of the differences among the traditions. The book emphasizes some similarities in the purpose and structure of religious traditions, while at the same time affirming the specific and unique aspects of each. In view of the importance of health (including both mental and physical health) in social work practice and a growing body of research linking religion and spirituality with good health, the final chapter presents a model of how religion can affect health and social work responses.

The religious traditions discussed represent three broad categories: North American Native People's spirituality, Eastern religions (Hinduism, Buddhism, and Confucianism), and the Judeo-Christian/Islamic tradition. Within these categories, specific religions are discussed in chronological order (those that evolved earlier are discussed first). This organization can help the reader understand some of the similar themes as well as the differences among the traditions. We recognize that there are many different traditions among Native People, and a complete treatment of this topic is beyond the scope of this book. The Lakota tradition is included because it represents a major one among Native People. The author of the chapter is a widely recognized expert on the topic. Both Christianity and Islam have common roots within the monotheistic tradition of Judaism. Several groups subsequently separated from the original Christian group that came to be called the Catholic (meaning universal) Church. Among these groups were Protestants and Mormons. Protestantism is discussed before Mormonism because this order reflects the chronology of the divide. Given the diversity within Protestantism and the large number of Protestants, we have included an overview of Protestantism and several examples of Protestant denominations. The Baptist faith was chosen because it is the largest denomination within the Protestant tradition. The chapter on African American Baptists was included because this faith too represents a large number of people as well as a different historical and cultural perspective. The Seventh-day Adventist group was chosen because it represents a large group internationally and plays an important role in many communities in health care systems, as a consequence of its strong emphasis on health. The Seventh-day Adventists also represent a separatist orientation. An understanding of this orientation can help social workers in working with clients from other groups that share such an orientation.

This book is intended for a variety of audiences, including practitioners, program planners, and students at the undergraduate and graduate levels. For practitioners, it can be a valuable reference for working with clients from various religious backgrounds. Program planners can use the book to help design culturally sensitive programs. Students can use the book to learn about the religious traditions of the clients they serve in their internships and to carry out other related assignments. The Council of Social Work Education has recently recognized the importance of educating students to understand the religious and spiritual traditions of clients. Although knowledge of religion can help create a richer understanding of clients and thus shape more effective interventions, dealing with religion in the classroom can sometimes be difficult because of the strong emotions the topic can evoke. This book helps deal with some of the problems faced in addressing religion in class because it helps students create a bridge between their own religious beliefs and experiences and those of clients and other members of the class. The book also provides a conceptual framework for understanding religious perspectives that helps students move beyond their own personal experience of religion. It can thus help focus class discussions and assignments by providing a professional perspective on an issue that can be quite emotionally laden.

The authors are experienced in social work practice and education. Thus, they are aware of the needs of these diverse audiences. The authors are also well grounded in the traditions represented, in that they identify with and participate actively in the life of the tradition.

Several features of the book help it make an especially valuable contribution to the current literature. The authors' personal accounts of their own religious experiences and the ways those have shaped their view of social work and their professional lives help readers understand the traditions from a unique personal perspective and link the traditions to social work. The book supports the strengths perspective on social work through its emphasis on the sources of power and resiliency in the religious traditions. With growing recognition of the need to identify the strengths of clients and the resources available to them, it is important to understand their religious traditions as potential resources for clients, to seek ways to draw on these resources, and to recognize possible barriers to doing so. Religion is discussed in terms of the beliefs and practices that pertain to the life cycle of individuals and families. The life cycle approach is incorporated into courses on human behavior and social work courses and provides a framework for understanding how religion influences various life stages.

The book also includes information about how different religious traditions view health and the appropriate sources for promoting healing.

Information is contained to some degree in the chapters about specific religious traditions and is developed in more detail in a final general chapter on religion and health. Health issues are addressed in the book because many social workers have clients who are coping with issues relating to health. A growing body of research literature linking health to religious beliefs and practices supports the value of becoming aware of religion in the lives of clients. The final chapter also draws on information from the other chapters and gives a framework for understanding the various ways in which religion can influence health in the broad sense of the term.

We would like to thank the following reviewers for their helpful comments and suggestions: Wilma Greenfield, Florida Atlantic University; Romel Mackelprang, Eastern Washington University; Donna McIntosh, Siena College; Ann Nichols, Arizona State University; and Robin Russel, University of Nebraska–Omaha.

Finally, we dedicate this book to our families who have given their ongoing support throughout this project.

INTRODUCTION

BERYL HUGEN

Although the beginnings of the Western concept of the social work profession were rooted within a Judeo-Christian worldview, social work developed largely as a secular profession in the middle of the 20th century. The secularization of the social work profession—the notion that spirituality and religion in both an ideological and institutional sense have little or no part in forming or informing the professional world of social work—has been extensive (Hugen, 1994; Marshall, 1991; Russel, 1998). As a result, many social workers, regardless of their personal religious convictions and affiliations, have been trained to think that their own or their clients' religious involvement or faith has little or no relevance for everyday professional practice. Not surprisingly, a high percentage of social workers report that they lack the knowledge and skills required to integrate religious and spiritual concerns into practice (Canda & Furman, 1999).

Some social workers may occasionally seek answers or reassurances from religious sources, but even for these workers, religion is often a private or personal matter, having relatively little bearing on their professional lives. A significantly smaller number of social workers attack religion as harmful to clients. They view religious beliefs and values as being in direct conflict with the goals and values of the profession. As the profession became increasingly allied with empirical scientific and rationalistic paradigms, many social workers accepted Freud's characterization of religion as illusion and his tendency to reduce religious conviction and practice to psychological processes. Still other social workers, less prominently represented in the literature and possibly fewer in number, give religion a central role in their lives. For this group, the relationship between the sacred and the secular aspects of life is the key question, both personally and professionally.

The general neglect by the profession of the religious and spiritual dimensions of life has resulted in what may be thought of as a "religiousness gap" between the profession and certain religious communities. As a result, some religious groups have developed separate social service programs that rely more on religious sources of help for people's problems.

The process of secularization takes place on different levels. One can distinguish between secularization on the individual level (a decline of religiousness among individuals), and secularization on the societal level (a restriction of the range of influence of religion on society). The latter has affected the professions. This distinction between secularization on the individual level and secularization on the societal level is important, because these two levels of secularization do not necessarily coincide. For example, the secularizing influences related to the modernization and professionalization of society do not mean that individual religious commitment has correspondingly diminished or disappeared.

On the contrary, studies indicate that during the 20th century in the United States, individual religiousness has flourished, with many new religious movements emerging, particularly within the past 30 years. Recent surveys indicate that 96% of Americans believe in God or a universal spirit, 90% pray (the majority doing so daily), and 43% attend religious services weekly or more often (Gallup, 1996; Hastings and Hastings, 1996). In addition to the broad involvement in institutional religion in this country, there is a corresponding belief in the growing role of religion and its increasing importance in public life.

Adding to this situation is the broad diversity of religious traditions social workers now encounter in practice. Since the passage of the 1965 Immigration Act, new immigrants from all over the world have settled in the United States, bringing with them their religious traditions—Islam, Hinduism, Buddhism, Sikhism, Zoroastrianism, and others. They have also brought a new diversity to American Christianity and Judaism. Today, "we the people" of the United States include individuals of many religious traditions, new and old, all contributing to the pluralism that comes with religious freedom. From the white towers of new Hindu temples ornately decorated with images of Hindu deities to celebrations of the end of the Ramadan month of fasting at a new Islamic center, this new religious landscape is apparent in virtually every major city in the United States as well as in many smaller cities in the heartland.

Today, there are 5–6 million Muslims in the United States—more Muslims than Episcopalians or Presbyterians. Within the next decade, there will very likely be more Muslims than Jews. By rough estimates, there are

1 million Hindus and 1 million Buddhists in this country (Gallup, 1996). In Detroit, one is just as likely to see someone reading the Koran as the Bible. There is no denying that the American religious landscape is changing. And one thing is certain: This far more complex, multi-religious America is here to stay. Within this diverse religious environment, the relative inattention of the social work profession to matters of religion and spirituality is striking indeed.

EXPANDING THE ROLE OF SPIRITUALITY AND RELIGION IN SOCIAL WORK

The growing diversity of religious traditions and the increasing personal investment of most Americans in religion represent a new and significant challenge to the profession. As wholistic, empowerment-focused, and culturally appropriate approaches to social work practice become more widely adopted, the ability to integrate spirituality and religion into practice will become a critical professional skill. In addition to a long-standing commitment to the ecological and person-in-situation perspective on social work, many contemporary models of social work and other counseling professions also stress the essential importance of understanding how clients interpret the world around them and their role in it. While the terms vary and reflect a concern for different levels of analysis or theoretical concepts, phrases like "family paradigm," "cognitive schema," and "personal narrative" all share the recognition that human beings are meaning-making creatures. The nature of the meanings is shaped by an individual's past and present experiences of self, family, and social group. Religious traditions and beliefs can and do help shape the meanings of life experiences for many people. In fact, an understanding of religion's place in a particular culture is often essential to offering culturally appropriate services.

Unfortunately, too many social workers have only a sketchy knowledge of the religious beliefs and practices of their clients. Most report that they received little or no education regarding spiritual and religious issues in social work classes (Canda & Furman, 1999; Joseph, 1988). Based on a large national survey of social workers conducted in 1997, Canda and Furman (1999) report that over 73% of respondents indicated that they did not receive any instruction in spirituality or religion in their social work education. Even in courses dealing with human diversity, only about 13% had received such content.

Social work has accepted the professional obligation to enhance the lives of people—as individuals and in families, in groups, and in communities—and to use knowledge and skills that will enable people to make maximum use of their capacities as full and effective participants in society. Because human life clearly has a spiritual and religious dimension, which is significantly interrelated with its other aspects, it is vitally important for social workers to know and to understand this dimension.

IMPLICATIONS FOR SOCIAL WORK EDUCATION

The literature on religious issues in social work has several implications for social work education. The first relates to the need for social workers to become better informed regarding the spiritual dimension of human behavior, religious diversity, and the implications of such knowledge for practice. Several strategies for addressing spirituality and religion in social work education have been proposed (Bullis, 1996; Canda, 1988, 1997; Cornett, 1992; Dudley & Helfgott, 1990; Furman, 1994; Krill, 1990, 1995; Loewenberg, 1988; Ortiz, 1991; Russel, 1998; Sheridan, Bullis, Adcock, Berlin, & Miller, 1992). One purpose of this book, therefore, is to build on these efforts—to help social workers become more aware of the key beliefs and practices of different religious traditions.

A second implication relates to the social worker as an individual. Just as social workers are expected to be reasonably self-reflective regarding their own physical and mental health, they should be expected to have a sense of self-understanding regarding their own spiritual and religious well-being. Religion is a primary motivating force behind many social workers' commitment to serve people through their practice. Social work has become, therefore, a means for expressing fundamental moral imperatives that arise from one's spiritual experiences and convictions.

How is the social worker to secure such knowledge and self-understanding? Religious knowledge accumulates throughout life, deriving from many possible sources, including association with and participation in organized religion and reading and study of the subject. And self-understanding, the process of spiritual self-awareness, is increasingly being recognized as essential for all social workers so that they may respond adequately to the spiritual and religious needs of clients.

In 1961, Sue Spencer outlined the following propositions related to spirituality and religion as suggestions for consideration as appropriate educational objectives for social work education:

- Human beings almost universally have spiritual needs and aspirations, which are discernible, though not necessarily separable, from other needs and aspirations.
- The social worker needs to know and understand and appreciate these needs and aspirations.
- Religious beliefs and practices may play a central and important role in individual, family, and community life.
- Social workers should be able to enter into the client's description of spiritual and religious beliefs, practices, and problems with the same degree of professional understanding, knowledge, and skill as that used in other areas of professional practice.
- Social workers should be prepared to help clients call upon the knowledge and resources of religion, when this is appropriate.

- Without specific professional preparation for helping clients with religious problems, social workers are not generally prepared to carry on professional practice any more than they would be professionally equipped to deal with legal, medical, or psychological problems.

The current Curriculum Policy Statement of the Council on Social Work Education stresses the importance of preparing students to practice with knowledge and skills related to the client's religion (CSWE, 2001). Spencer's suggestions stand today as excellent guidelines for curriculum development in this area.

CHALLENGES AND CONCERNS

Incorporating spiritual and religious content into social work education requires more than simply recognizing spirituality and religion as another dimension of assessment or being tolerant of diversity. It involves a personal engagement with spirituality and religion, through encounter and dialogue, often in the give-and-take of a professional social work relationship. Reflection on spiritual and religious issues with a client can become particularly difficult whenever the practitioner experiences a conflict in beliefs. What practitioners need in such situations is the ability to discern how to be faithful to their own religious beliefs and commitments while continuing to acknowledge the integrity and worth of those of the client.

Social workers, like most people, tend to react to religion from the point of view of the specific religion they know best. They may generalize from their own specific experience or lack of experience with religion to all religions in general. However, such generalizations are problematic in that they are frequently inaccurate. It is important to recognize that just as religions vary, so do individuals' own unique experiences with a particular religious tradition. A particular religious experience may have been damaging or rewarding to one person, but this does not mean that all religious experiences will have a similar impact on others. Religious experiences also vary widely depending on life cycle or other individual life events. Different religious traditions may promote very diverse personal meanings in response to similar problem situations. For example, in people diagnosed with cancer, responses can range from a sense of personal responsibility engendering guilt, to fatalism which may create a sense of resigned acceptance.

Furthermore, religious beliefs and practices within specific religious traditions are not homogeneous or monolithic phenomena. As a result, it is difficult to identify *the* Protestant Christian view or *the* Muslim view on a particular social problem. Just as knowing that someone is Hispanic or Irish or Lakota does not allow one to conclude that he or she will act or believe in a specific way, so drawing conclusions in terms of religion involves a balance between understanding the nature of a specific religious tradition and further exploration of the person involved in that tradition. In effect, the principles and techniques of learning cultural appropriateness must be applied to developing an understanding of spiritual and religious diversity (Raines, 1996; Rey, 1997).

Two by-products of the growing religious pluralism and diversity in American society have been the development of an ethic of tolerance for different religious beliefs and a belief that no religion should offend another (Cuddihy, 1978). Christian theologian Reinhold Niebuhr (1932) argued that the multiplicity of religious positions in America (specifically, the denominationalism and disunity of Protestant Christianity), along with this etiquette of not offending other religious groups, ironically led to the need for a more unifying focus in the social work profession—a focus provided by secularization. Niebuhr believed that the secularization process was probably inevitable, even if it was not desirable from the perspective of many religious groups. The successful reintroduction of religious perspectives will require both personal and professional restraints, such as not proselytizing and not imposing one's own religious values on clients. These restraints, if not respected by religious social workers, may again lead to the disestablishment of religion and spirituality in the profession.

Incorporating spiritual and religious diversity into social work practice raises a challenging question for each social worker of faith: How do I hold my truth to be The Truth, when everyone perceives the truth differently? The professional challenge is to learn to listen intently to another person's explanation of reality, even when that worldview differs significantly from one's own. As practitioners, we need not share a client's view of reality, nor even agree with it. But if we are willing to listen, we will come away knowing clients in new ways—and this knowledge and awareness will not only increase our own cultural sensitivity but also help us demonstrate a genuine respect for clients by truly honoring their religious and spiritual perspectives.

This book is a response to a growing need to bring into the social work literature the divergent beliefs and convictions fostered by several of the major religious faiths represented in contemporary American society. This pluralistic society presents a paradox: It stresses both individuation—the unhampered and spontaneous expression of what is unique—and cooperation, the common pursuit of universal human values. A difficult problem in such a society is to keep these contradictory processes in balance. The attempt to do this presupposes that along with authentic, even at times momentous differences, all religious groups have certain common overarching ends. These common ends frequently find expression in the ultimate and perennial questions that all religions and spiritual traditions address.

The purpose of the book, however, is not to be syncretistic—it is not primarily an effort to show the extent of common ground among religious faiths so as to show how much we all are alike. This book is as much concerned with differences as with common elements. It also attempts to present religious life and tradition within an empowerment and strengths perspective, with the major emphasis on the potential of religion for enhancing life. This is not to downplay the dangers of imposing our own religious values on the people who turn to us for help. Nor is it to fail to recognize that aspects of religious traditions can pose problems for some individuals involved, or that there is a history of discrimination on the basis of religion. However, the dangers of religion have been given more attention and are perhaps better known than are the potential resources religious traditions offer. We hope this book contributes to the social work profession's efforts to increase social workers' understanding of and ability to incorporate religious issues into their work with diverse clients.

REFERENCES

Bullis, R. (1996). *Spirituality in social work practice.* Washington, DC: Taylor & Francis.

Canda, E. R. (1988, Winter). Conceptualizing spirituality for social work: Insights from diverse perspectives. *Social Thought,* 30–46.

Canda, E. R. (1997). Does religion and spirituality have a significant place in the core HBSE curriculum? Yes. In M. Bloom & W. C. Klein (Eds.), *Controversial issues in human behavior in the social environment.* Boston: Allyn & Bacon.

Canda, E. R., & Furman, L. D. (1999). *Spiritual diversity in social work practice: The heart of helping.* New York: The Free Press.

Cornett, C. (1992). Toward a more comprehensive personology: Integrating a spiritual perspective into social work practice. *Social Work, 37*(2), 101–115.

Council on Social Work Education. (2001). Curriculum Policy Statement. Alexandria, VA: Council on Social Work Education.

Cuddihy, J. (1978). *No offense: Civil religion and protestant taste.* New York: Seabury.

Dudley, J., & Helfgott, C. (1990). Exploring a place for spirituality in the social work curriculum. *Journal of Social Work Education, 26*(3), 287–294.

Furman, L. E. (1994). Religion and spirituality in social work education: Preparing the culturally sensitive practitioner for the future. *Social Work and Christianity: An International Journal, 21,* 103–115.

Gallup, G., Jr. (1996). *Religion in America: 1996 Report.* Princeton, NJ: Princeton Religion Research Center.

Hastings, E. H., & Hastings, P. K. (Eds.). (1996). *Index to international public opinion, 1994–95.* Westport, CT: Greenwood Press.

Hugen, B. (1994). The secularization of social work. *Social Work and Christianity, 21*(4), 83–101.

Joseph, M. (1988). Religion and social work practice. *Social Casework, 69*(7), 443–452.

Krill, D. (1990). *Practice wisdom: A guide for the helping professional.* Newbury Park, CA: Sage.

Krill, D. (1995). My own spiritual sojourn into existential social work. *Reflections: Narratives of professional helping, 1*(4), 57–64.

Loewenberg, F. (1988). *Religion and social work practice in contemporary American society.* New York: Columbia University Press.

Marshall, J. (1991). The spiritual dimension in social work education. *Spirituality and Social Work Communicator, 2*(1), 12–15.

Niebuhr, R. (1932). *The contribution of religion to social work.* New York: Columbia University Press.

Ortiz, L. (1991). Religious issues: The missing link in social work education. *Spirituality and Social Work Journal, 2*(2), 13–18.

Raines, J. (1996). Toward a definition of spiritually sensitive social work practice. *Society for Spirituality and Social Work Newsletter, 3*(2), 4–5.

Rey, L. (1997). Religion as invisible culture: Knowing about and knowing with. *Journal of Family Social Work, 2*(2), 159–177.

Russel, R. (1998). Spirituality and religion in graduate social work education. In E. R. Canda (Ed.), *Spirituality and social work: New directions.* Hazleton, PA: Haworth Press.

Sheridan, M., Bullis, R., Adcock, C., Berlin, S., & Miller, P. (1992). Practitioners' personal and professional attitudes toward religion and spirituality: Issues for education and practice. *Journal of Social Work Education, 28*(2), 190–203.

Spencer, S. (1961). What place has religion in social work education? *Social Work, 3,* 161–170.

SPIRITUALITY AND RELIGION IN SOCIAL WORK PRACTICE: A CONCEPTUAL MODEL

CHAPTER I

BERYL HUGEN

The social work profession's attempt to define terms such as *spirituality, religion,* and *faith* mirrors the history of the use of spirituality and religion in social work itself. The profession has long struggled with this definitional dilemma. Recently, discussion has broadened to focus on how to reintroduce religious or spiritual concerns into a profession that has expanded beyond specific sectarian settings and ideologies to include diverse sources of knowledge, values, and skills. The discussion also focuses on how to respond to the needs of a much more spiritually diverse clientele.

DEFINITIONS: SPIRITUALITY, RELIGION, AND FAITH

One of the first social work writers to attempt to define religion and spirituality was Sue Spencer (1961). She defined *spirituality* as "those aspects of individual feelings, aspirations and needs which are concerned with man's effort to find a purpose and meaning in life experiences, and which may occur without the individual's being related to an organized church body or his making use of a systematized body of beliefs and practices" (p. 161). The term *religion* is used to signify a "systematic body of beliefs or practices or an organized group of people who believe in certain doctrines concerning the nature of the universe and of man in relation to the universe" (p. 161). Religion thus incorporates cultural, structural, and historical elements as well as personal spirituality.

Addressing this same definitional dilemma, numerous other writers (Brower, 1984; Canda, 1988a, 1988b, 1989; Denton, 1990; Dudley & Helfgott, 1990; Joseph, 1988; Sheridan, Bullis, Adcock, Berlin, & Miller, 1992; Siporin, 1982, 1985) all advocate an understanding of spirituality that includes a wide diversity of religious and non-religious expressions. Such an inclusive understanding of spirituality would enable social workers to reflect on their clients both within and outside of particular institutional religious settings and ideologies.

From this beginning, Canda (1988a, 1988b) further developed a concept of spirituality for social work that incorporates insights from diverse religious and philosophical perspectives. He identified three components of spirituality—values, beliefs, and practice issues—"all serving the central dynamic of a person's search for a sense of meaning and purpose, developed in the context of interdependent relationships between self, other people, the nonhuman world, and the ground of being itself" (Canda, 1988a, p. 43). In this definition, spirituality is distinguished from religion: "Religion involves the patterning of spiritual beliefs and practices into social institutions, with community support and traditions maintained over time" (Canda, 1997, p. 173).

In a similar vein, the work of James Fowler, known more for his model of faith development, is particularly instructive. Fowler (1981) states that in order to understand the "human quest for relation to transcendence," the key phenomenon to examine is not religion or belief, but *faith* (p. 14). According to Fowler, who draws on the ideas of religionist Wilfred Smith, *religions* are "cumulative traditions," which represent the expressions of faith of people in the past (p. 9). Included in a cumulative tradition are such elements as "texts of scripture, oral traditions, music, creeds, theologies," and so forth. *Belief* refers to "the holding of certain ideas or assent to a set of propositions" (p. 13). Faith, according to Fowler, differs from both religion and belief. Fowler describes faith as a commitment, "an alignment of the will . . . in accordance with a vision of transcendent value and power, one's ultimate concern" (p. 14). One commits oneself to what is known or acknowledged and lives loyally, with life and character being shaped by that commitment. Defined in this way, faith is believed to be a universal feature of human living, recognizably similar everywhere, and in all major religious traditions.

What then does faith consist of? Fowler describes three components of faith. The first he terms *centers of value,* the "causes, concerns, or persons that consciously or unconsciously have the greatest worth to us." These are what we worship, things and persons that give our lives meaning (p. 277). The second component of faith is described as *images of power,* the "power with which we align ourselves to sustain us in the midst of life's contingencies" (p. 277). These powers need not necessarily be supernatural or transcendent. This concept of images of power can be especially valuable in identifying clients' potential strengths and resiliency. Finally, faith is composed of the *master stories* that we tell ourselves and by which we interpret and respond to the events that affect our lives. Essentially, our master stories reveal what we believe to be the fundamental truths, "the central premises of [our] sense of life's meaning" (p. 277).

In discussing faith and spirituality, Fowler and Canda both emphasize its pervasive, all-encompassing nature in an individual's life. Neither faith nor spirituality is a separate dimension of life or a compartmentalized specialty, but rather an orientation of the total person. Accordingly, Fowler's three components of faith—centers of value, images of power, and master stories—and Canda's three components of spirituality—values, beliefs, and practices—exert "structuring power" in our lives, shaping our characters and action in the world, including our work. Faith and spirituality are defined here as the essence of religion. Faith and spirituality take on a religious meaning when the centers of value, beliefs, images of power, practices, and master stories of one's faith—the central dynamic of one's search for a sense of meaning and purpose—are grounded in the creeds, texts of scripture, rituals, and theologies of a particular religious tradition.

RELIGION: SOCIAL AND COMMUNAL FACTORS

What are missing, or not given much recognition in Fowler's or Canda's definitional concepts, are the social or institutional aspects of religious life. A person who has a religious experience by definition participates in a community. In contrast, although some people may feel a need to share their spirituality and faith, these can also be experienced individually. The sociological perspective on religious studies (the Durkheim/Weber tradition) has identified a number of different social functions of religion:

- Religion serves an integrative function by establishing norms and values, making for moral character and for ethical relations with others.
- Religion serves a social control function by fostering order, discipline, and authority.
- Religion provides the individual believer with emotional support when needed.
- Religion confers on believers a sense of identity.
- Religion can serve as a source of positive physical and mental health. It can contribute to happier, more stable families, marriages, and communities.

A number of social dysfunctions of religion have also been identified, including the following:

- Religion may promote fanaticism, intolerance, and prejudice.
- In a pluralistic society, religion no longer serves an integrative function, but has become a socially disruptive force, dividing society into believers and nonbelievers.

- Religion, directly or indirectly, supports the establishment by directing attention away from social injustices. In this way it tends to perpetuate these injustices. (Loewenberg, 1988, p. 35)

The focus on the social or communal nature of religion also allows for some generalization based on an identification of a person's religion. This can be helpful in guiding the religious/spiritual assessment process with clients. For example, Christianity implies a belief in the divinity of Jesus. Buddhism implies a search for enlightenment. Using such generalizations, however, always carries the danger of stereotyping the members of a religious group. It is important to remember that even though religion is a social and group experience, individual people often interpret the value and belief systems of a particular religious tradition quite differently. In other words, a religion may imply a set of beliefs, values, and rituals, but these must not automatically be assumed to fit every member of a religious community.

TOWARD DEFINITIONAL CLARITY

The differences in the definitions of *religion, spirituality,* and *faith* are becoming solidified within the social work profession. *Religion* refers to the outward form of belief, including rituals, dogmas, and creeds, denominational identity, and ecclesiastical structures. For example, a Christian might identify herself as a United Methodist and believe in a historic statement of belief such as the Apostles Creed.

Spirituality refers more to inner feelings and the experience of the immediacy of a higher power. These feelings and experiences are not always easily conformable to the formulations of statements of creed or to theological discriminations. Spirituality, by its very nature, is eclectic, inclusive, and generally described with broad definitions. The concept of spirituality has been more widely endorsed in the social work literature than that of religion. Clearly it is more inclusive and comprehensive, and given some of the dysfunctions of institutional religion, it is perceived as less potentially offensive.

However, such a broad definition often fails to convey what faith and spirituality really mean to those who adhere to a religious tradition. It also fails to deal adequately with the various social functions that religious institutions fulfill in society, particularly that of binding people together in communities of faith. Another problem with such broad definitions is that they make it difficult, if not impossible, to determine the strength of religiousness of a given person or specific group. Psychologist Abraham Maslow (1970) reported that he once attended a conference with theologian Paul Tillich, who defined religion as "concern with ultimate concerns" (p. 45). Maslow, an avowed secular humanist, defined humanistic psychology in exactly the same way and then wondered whether there was really any difference between a supernaturalist and a humanist. In his book *Spirituality in Social Work Practice* (1996), Bullis defines spirituality as "divinely focused altered states of consciousness." Given such a broad definition, what then is the difference between a religious person and a secular person?

Historically, institutional religion and individual spirituality and faith were predominately one and the same. Only recently have the two been differentiated. Most people still connect the two aspects—living out their faith and spiritual life in the context of faith communities and religious institutions. For them, participation in organized religion and its accompanying rituals is a spiritual experience.

We therefore have chosen a definition of religion that emphasizes an intrinsic religious propensity (often called religiousness)—the degree and manner of expressions of a person's spirituality within religious institutional contexts—but one that is broad enough to include all formal religious groups. This book defines a person as religious if he or she *belongs to or identifies with a religious group; accepts and is committed to the beliefs, values, and doctrines of the group; and participates in the required practices, ceremonies, and rituals of the chosen group*. This definition incorporates both the personal and the sociological aspects of religious and spiritual life.

LIFE-CYCLE EVENTS AND HEALTH

To help identify specific implications for social work practice, each contributor to this book was asked to address how the personal and social aspects of her or his religious tradition assist in carrying out family life-cycle tasks. Important religious beliefs, rituals, and social structures can play key roles as individuals and families move through the life cycle. For example, the impending birth of a child raises issues regarding the role of new life within the family and ways to protect this life. Religious rituals such as baptism and circumcision reflect important beliefs about the ongoing life of the family. Religious beliefs shape the parent-child relationship and the socialization of children. Family members induct children into the beliefs and practices of their religious community and thereby seek to maintain family cohesiveness and religious traditions. As individuals enter young adulthood, religious codes can influence their perceptions of appropriate future partners and life vocations.

Religion can affect how disruptions in families such as divorce and unemployment are interpreted and can inform appropriate responses and provide support networks. If family members become ill, disabled, or near death, key religious beliefs and rituals can become activated to help people find a sense of meaning and comfort in suffering. Family decisions regarding whom to include in religious rituals can also give valuable information about family roles and relationships.

In addition to addressing personal and social aspects of his or her religious tradition, each contributor was asked to address the implications of faith for basic health concerns, both physical and mental. Religious issues play an important role in conceptions of health: what constitutes health, what helps maintain good health, and what resources are available and appropriate when one becomes ill. When illness strikes, members of some groups may view it appropriate to offer a prayer; others may seek healing through a specific sacrifice to make amends or restore right relationships. Religious groups can mandate what medical procedures are acceptable and what types of problems are amenable to standard medical care. Since many social workers become involved with individuals and families when physical or mental health issues arise, an understanding of how religious groups view health concerns can be important in assessing the meaning of these issues and the availability of potential resources.

A MULTICULTURAL PERSPECTIVE

The range and complexity of spiritual and religious diversity in the United States is staggering. There are hundreds of different religions with many denominations, along with variations of spirituality based on race, ethnicity, gender, and many other aspects of human diversity. Almost every religion exhibits a continuum of belief perspectives ranging from fundamental to liberal. In addition, each person, family, and religious community develops a distinctive pattern of spiritual and religious activity, by drawing on all these influences and by searching out personal paths of meaning and practice.

Chapters in the book were chosen to represent this religious diversity and to reflect the current religious landscape of American society. More than 90% of Americans identify with a specific religion (Gallup, 1996, 1998). The United States remains predominantly Christian (85%), and 57% of Christians consider themselves Protestant. The largest Protestant denominational affiliations are Baptist (19%), Methodist (9%), Lutheran (6%), Presbyterian (4%), Episcopalian (2%), and Pentecostal (1%). Twenty-six percent of American adults are Roman Catholic, 2% are Mormon (Church of Jesus Christ of Latter-Day Saints), and 1% are Orthodox Christians.

Six chapters in this book address Christian religious traditions. Marian Aguilar addresses Catholicism in Chapter 7, and Dennis Haynes investigates Mormonism in Chapter 13. In Chapter 9, Mary Van Hook presents an overview of the Protestant perspective and describes a faith journey that includes several denominational affiliations (Methodist, Christian Reformed, and Presbyterian). T. Laine Scales describes her Baptist tradition in Chapter 10, and Darlene Grant writes about the African American Baptist tradition in Chapter 11. Seventh-Day Adventism, representing one of many relatively small and unique Protestant traditions, is described by Curtis VanderWaal and Daryl McMullen in Chapter 12.

The non-Christian proportion of the United States population has been rapidly increasing, from 10% in 1970 to 15% in 1995 (Gallup, 1996). Two percent of Americans identify themselves as Jewish. Bruce Friedman writes about the Jewish tradition in Chapter 6. Five percent follow other religions: Islam, Hinduism, and Buddhism, each currently at 1%. Buddhism is the fastest-growing Eastern religion in the United States. Others identify with the

Sikh, Bahai, Shinto, and Confucianism faiths. Of the traditions within the Eastern religions, Hinduism is described by Ram Singh in Chapter 3, Ed Canda writes about Buddhism in Chapter 4, and Douglas Chung describes Confucianism in Chapter 5. A strong revival of First People's spiritual traditions has also been occurring, particularly among younger generations. Maria Yellow Horse Brave Heart writes about a major Native People's spiritual tradition, Lakota, in Chapter 2. Islam, a very rapidly growing religious tradition in the United States and other countries, is described in Chapter 8 by Aneesah Nadir and Sophia F. Dziegielewski.

Religion is intertwined with race and ethnicity. Ethnicity influences religious preference, yet it is crucial that we not reflexively link religion with ethnicity. Although most Irish Americans are Catholic, those from Northern Ireland may well be Protestant. Contrary to popular belief, only about one-third of Arab Americans are Muslim; many are Christian. Refugees from the former Yugoslavia are not only Serbian, Croatian, Bosnian, or Kosovar, but also Orthodox Christian, Catholic, or Muslim. In almost all of the chapters, contributors identify how their ethnic identity is interwoven in the religious tradition being discussed.

Among African Americans, 73% are Protestant, 10% are Catholic, and a growing number are Muslim. Although Hispanics are commonly assumed to be Catholic, in fact, 25% are Protestant, with a growing number turning to Pentecostal churches. Hispanics and Blacks frequently tightly interweave cultural influences into all aspects of their traditional Christian spiritual experience. Two chapters in the book specifically highlight cultural perspectives within larger religious traditions—Hispanic culture and Roman Catholicism (Chapter 7) and Black culture and the Baptist tradition (Chapter 11).

Patriarchy, an ancient and enduring cultural pattern embedded in most religious traditions, has been a dominant force and powerful legacy. Today, voices across the religious spectrum have been calling for women's rights and equality. Still, within many religious groups, women continue to support traditional role relations, adhering to their faith convictions and valuing the respect they receive for their centrality in family life as mothers and caregivers. Six of the twelve chapters were written by women, and these authors address how they personally relate to gender issues within their respective religious traditions.

SUGGESTED CHAPTER TOPICS

Each contributor, though representing a different religious tradition, was asked to work with a list of topics that reflect the conceptual model of spirituality and religion outlined earlier. The list of topics was intended not as a rigid outline but rather as a guideline for each contributor to follow in expressing the individual character of a particular religious tradition. Contributors were allowed to approach each of the topics in their own style and format. The suggested topics are as follows:

- *Master stories.* Give a brief history and description of your religious tradition.
- *Contributor's personal story.* Religion is a primary motivating force behind many social workers' commitment to serve people through social work. Social work has become, therefore, a means for expressing fundamental moral imperatives that arise from personal spiritual experiences and convictions. Relate how your religious tradition influenced your motivation to enter the social work profession and/or sustains your participation in the profession.
- *Meaning of major life events.* How does your religious tradition answer life's big questions? What is the purpose of life? How are suffering and death understood?
- *Sources of power.* What are the spiritual resources (personal and communal) of your religious tradition—the beliefs, books, texts, and persons that provide strength and facilitate empowerment?
- *Rituals and practices.* What are some of the rituals and practices of your religious tradition (prayer, meditation, stories, scripture study, etc.), and how are they used in problem solving and helping relationships?
- *Family life-cycle transitions.* Identify several life transitions (birth, marriage, death, divorce, relocation, miscarriage) and describe how your religious tradition provides assistance, strength, and meaning for people going through these transitions.
- *Conception of health.* Identify your tradition's concept of health (physical and mental) and explain the importance of understanding the religious meaning of this concept.
- *Implications for practice.* What are several implications for social work practice of your religious tradition?

REFERENCES

Brower, I. (1984). The 4th ear of the spiritually sensitive worker. Dissertation Information Service. Ann Arbor, MI: University Microfilms International.

Bullis, R. (1996). *Spirituality in social work practice.* Washington, DC: Taylor & Francis.

Canda, E. R. (1988a, Winter). Conceptualizing spirituality for social work: Insights from diverse perspectives. *Social Thought,* 30–46.

Canda, E. R. (1988b, April). Spirituality, religious diversity and social work practice. *Social Casework,* 238–247.

Canda, E. R. (1989). Religious content in social work education: A comparative approach. *Journal of Social Work Education, 25*(1), 36–45.

Canda, E. R. (1997). Spirituality. In Richard L. Edwards (Ed.) *Encyclopedia of social work, 19th edition supplement* (pp. 299–309). Washington, DC: National Association of Social Workers.

Denton, R. T. (1990). The religiously fundamentalist family: Training for assessment and treatment. *Journal of Social Work Education, 26*(1), 6–14.

Dudley, J., & Helfgott, C. (1990). Exploring a place for spirituality in the social work curriculum. *Journal of Social Work Education, 26*(3), 287–294.

Fowler, J. (1981). *Stages of faith.* San Francisco: Harper & Row.

Gallup, G., Jr. (1996). *Religion in America: 1996 report.* Princeton, NJ: Princeton Religion Research Center.

Gallup, G., Jr. (1998). *Newsletter of the Princeton Religion Research Center.* Princeton, NJ: Princeton Research Center.

Joseph, M. (1988). Religion and social work practice. *Social Casework, 69*(7), 443–452.

Loewenberg, F. (1988). *Religion and social work practice in contemporary American society.* New York: Columbia University Press.

Maslow, A. (1970). *Religion, values and peak experiences.* New York: Viking.

Sheridan, M., Bullis, R., Adcock, C., Berlin, S., & Miller, P. (1992). Practitioners' personal and professional attitudes toward religion and spirituality: Issues for education and practice. *Journal of Social Work Education, 28*(2), 190–203.

Siporin, M. (1982). Moral philosophy in social work today. *Social Service Review, 56*(4), 516–538.

Spencer, S. (1961). What place has religion in social work education? *Social Work,* 161–170.

2 CHAPTER LAKOTA—NATIVE PEOPLE'S SPIRITUALITY

MARIA YELLOW HORSE BRAVE HEART

INTRODUCTION

Interventions with Native clients should incorporate historical and cultural perspectives. This requires an understanding of Native spirituality. This chapter examines the traditional beliefs and values of one Native culture, the Lakota (Teton Sioux), as well as Lakota life-cycle issues, concepts of power and relationships, historical trauma theory, views of bereavement, and definition of illness. The chapter concludes with an examination of implications for social work assessment and practice. Brief illustrations of interventions with Lakota clients are offered as examples. However, although these examples are somewhat generalizable to other tribal cultures, the uniqueness of each Native culture must be respected and practice must be modified accordingly.

Empowerment practice is based on maintaining egalitarian relationships with clients, viewing the client as an expert in her or his culture, valuing the client's culture, and raising the client's consciousness of external sociopolitical forces that impinge on his or her life, while simultaneously attending to emotional and psychological issues (Cox & Parsons, 1994). Acknowledging the inherent wisdom of indigenous spiritual practices is consistent with an empowerment perspective. Traditionally, Natives utilize diverse methods for healing physical conditions as well as emotional turmoil. Healing ceremonies are empowerment strategies in that they involve extended kinship networks, thereby fostering integration and social support for the client (see Cox & Parsons, 1994).

THE LAKOTA: AN EXAMPLE OF ONE NATIVE CULTURE

American Indians, referred to in this chapter as Natives, are a diverse collective of indigenous nations. In this chapter I describe Lakota culture, the nation with which I am affiliated and within which I actively participate spiritually. My descriptions of Lakota spirituality and culture are general and are intended only to counter misperceptions and ultimately to be helpful to Native clients; there are a number of references that the reader can examine for further information. I also ask that the reader respect the privacy and integrity of Native spirituality and recognize that our sacred ceremonies are intended for our own community.

Contrary to the popular myth that Natives are "pagan," indigenous spiritual tenets are congruent with other religious traditions that assert the existence of one God or Creator, which Natives refer to as the Great Spirit, Mystery, or Sacred One. There is no traditional belief in a Devil, no fallen angels, and no true evil. However, as a result of colonization, Christianity now permeates and influences Native worldviews. A traditional Lakota explanation of this modern dilemma is that the mind has created the concept of evil and has projected this belief, resulting in an experience of evil or the Devil by the individual who so believes (Birgil Kills Straight, personal communication, August 28, 1992).

For the Lakota and many other Native peoples, spirituality is an integral part of culture and of one's sense of self and worldview. Lakota spirituality is based upon the Seven Sacred Rites brought by the White Buffalo Calf Woman (see Black Elk & Neihardt, 1972). Inherent in this spiritual tradition are the sacredness of women, the sacred relationship with the Buffalo Nation, the values manifested in the ceremonies of self-sacrifice for the good of others, and the importance and sacredness of relationship with all of creation. The Seven Laws (*Woope Sakowin*) of the Lakota include generosity; compassion; humility; respect for all of creation; the development of a great mind through observance, silence, and patience; bravery in the face of adversity in order to protect the nation; and wisdom. The Lakota embrace principles of non-interference and tolerance and value interdependence. Traditionally, all decisions are made with the next seven generations in mind.

PERSONAL REFLECTIONS

As a Lakota, I first became painfully conscious of our historical trauma in the late 1970s. I recall sitting on my living room floor, looking at some historical photos and sobbing. I had an overwhelming sense of massive grief, which I knew was much larger than my own personal grief. I was mourning for all Native trauma and loss, across generations. At the time, I was immersed in clinical social work training. I had heard of the emerging work on children of Jewish Holocaust survivors, and the parallels struck me. This experience stands out in my mind as transformational and deeply spiritual.

My historical trauma work is sacred to me. I share some of my own personal experience with the expectation that the reader will respect the sacredness of this information. I also have permission from one of the Lakota spiritual interpreters to share this information. We are cautious about what we share so that we may protect that which is sacred; sometimes, sacred information is supposed to be shared to increase understanding or to help our people. We use discernment in what we share.

When I reflect back on my own past, I remember childhood dreams that I now understand as related to the role I would come to take in trying to help my people heal from our historical trauma. In 1981, I was told during a Lakota ceremony that the Spirit of Spotted Elk would be with me and would help me to help our people. Later, a Lakota spiritual healer further interpreted that message to me. He told me that the spirit was that of Sitanka (Big Foot), who was also known as Spotted Elk, and that the message was related to the historical trauma work I had already begun. The spiritual interpreter advised me that I should share this information so that our people would know that such work is sacred. The Takini Network, a collective of Lakota traditional spiritual leaders and service providers formed to address healing from historical trauma for all Native people, was formed in 1992. Each of us in the Takini collective had already been on a Lakota spiritual path, and we continued to have ceremonies both collectively and individually to pray for spiritual help with our work. We feel the spiritual presence of our ancestors Sitting Bull, White Lance, and Crazy Horse helping us. Over the years, I have deepened my own spiritual development. Each member of The Takini Network has participated as often as possible in as many of the Seven Sacred Rites as feasible.

The work of The Takini Network is both supported by my Lakota spirituality and inspires me to deepen my Lakota spiritual growth. Both are lifelong processes that also reach back into past generations as well as into the future seven generations. The other sacred way I reach into the future and heal the past is through being a mother to my daughter. I pray for her, for The Takini Network, for the Buffalo Nation, for my relatives, and for all of creation daily; in that way, I renew my commitment as a Lakota, my commitment to the sacred.

THE LAKOTA LIFE CYCLE

Birth is viewed by the Lakota as the return of a spirit to earth and a gift from the Creator. Children are considered sacred and are placed at the center of the Nation. Historically, pregnancies were spaced to provide time for the mother–child bond. Children were raised in a nurturing environment. There was no corporal punishment; children learned through the use of stories and metaphors as well as by modeling. The body was viewed as a container for the spirit.

Women were sacred and valued in traditional Lakota society. While gender roles were clearly defined, exceptions were also permitted; women were the primary caretakers, but men would assist with child care when not out hunting (Standing Bear, 1928/1975,1933/1978). There was gender complementarity. Most Lakota were monogamous. Men often took a second wife, typically the widowed sister of the wife, not as a sexual partner but until she could be married again. This was done with the first wife's consent. Only in the last hundred years, with the influence of European views of women and children as property, was sexual union with a second wife likely to take place. However, this still required the consent of the first wife (Birgil Kills Straight, personal communication, February 1, 1996; Powers, 1986). Sex was viewed as a sacred act through which the spirits were connected; abstinence outside of marriage was valued. With the impact of colonization and the ensuing social problems, women and children have been devalued, and many now experience abuse and neglect similar to that occurring in non-Native communities.

Transexuality among the Lakota was uncommon but was less stigmatized than in the dominant culture; the transgendered individual held a socially prescribed functional role in society. For example, a *winkte* (a transsexual or transvestite who may or may not have been gay) performed naming ceremonies for newborns, adolescents, or adults at times of transition, adoption, or honoring accomplishments. One was deemed a winkte only after having had a specific dream that had to be spiritually interpreted.

After rearing children and contributing to the well-being and protection of the Nation, elders maintained a vital role in the community. They were revered and acknowledged as the culture carriers and wisdom keepers. Menopausal women were able to devote more time to their own spiritual development as well as maintaining close relationships with younger members of the community. Death was not viewed as a finite state but rather as a transition to a different status. The Lakota maintained active relationships with the spirit world, and ancestors' spirits might be called upon to help the living.

LAKOTA CONCEPTS OF POWER AND RELATIONSHIPS

The following quote describes the Lakota view of power and relationships:

> In Lakota culture, all life dimensions are included in empowering an individual to function as an integral part of creation. Gaining or developing power, one definition of empowerment (Cox & Parsons, 1994), is viewed by the Lakota as securing help from the spiritual and natural world for a higher purpose than the individual self—to benefit the *Oyate* (Lakota Nation). The sense of self is developed in relation to the *Oyate*, the natural world, and all of creation. Empowerment practice facilitates influencing

> institutions affecting one's life (see Cox & Parsons, 1994). Historically, the Lakota invoked supernatural help to influence the natural world and life events. With such cataclysmic events like the 1890 Wounded Knee Massacre (see McGregor, 1940/1987; "Wounded Knee remembered," 1990), genocide altered this capacity to affect life and the government-regulated environment. A return to traditional empowerment promises restoration of a sense of self and a healthy sphere of influence. Collective goals—a cornerstone of empowerment practice—can be fostered, based on the natural collectivity inherent in Lakota culture. Traditional Lakota culture can offer a model for egalitarian gender roles and relationships and provide protective factors against domestic violence and child abuse (Brave Heart, 2000).

In Lakota creation stories, the Lakota Nation emerges from the Black Hills and is related to the Buffalo Nation. Hence, the spiritual connection with the animal world is critical. Therefore, hardships resulting from the decimation of the buffalo and the loss of free access to the land continue to be a source of trauma and grief for the Lakota. All of creation is thought to possess a spirit. We are not owners but rather caretakers of the land. One recent song to the Creator by Earl Bullhead about the Lakota responsibility to protect the Black Hills, which were confiscated by the United States in violation of an 1868 treaty, is loosely translated as "Grandfather, I am having a hard time protecting the Black Hills; I am doing the best I can." (Bullhead, 1995, track 1)

The Lakota ideal (Brave Heart, 1998) is a generous and interdependent person who holds the welfare of the Nation above her or his own welfare, can endure suffering for the good of others, values the sacredness of women and children, communes with the spirits, and respects the animal world. Ideal behavioral qualities include deliberation, politeness, deference, the capacity to listen to all opinions without interrupting, and reserve in front of strangers.

Among the Lakota, the extended kinship network, or *tiospaye* (collection of related families), provides extensive social and spiritual support as well as obligations. One of the seven sacred rites of the Lakota is the *Hunka* (making of relatives) ceremony, a traditional adoption ceremony that binds the participants' spirits, creating a relationship that is considered more sacred than biological kinship. This ceremony extends the tiospaye and the potentially powerful support system, providing alternative psychological, emotional, and physical resources if immediate kin are embroiled in dysfunctional patterns. Further, Hunka relatives provide surrogate families for people who have lost members of their biological family or are estranged from them. If the members of a tiospaye, either biological or Hunka, embrace the Woope Sakowin (Seven Laws), they will participate in a reciprocal relationship that incorporates generosity and respect. However, massive generational trauma has tended to erode the Woope Sakowin and created an imbalance within the tiospaye system: Some members adhere to the traditional mores, while others are enmeshed in dysfunctional behavior.

Consequently, the former are burdened with family obligations and yet receive little family support.

HISTORICAL TRAUMA THEORY AND LAKOTA CULTURE

One cannot examine traditional Lakota culture and spirituality and discuss modern manifestations of that culture without an understanding of our history as victims of genocide and oppression, including spiritual persecution, and our responses to that legacy. The theory of historical trauma evolved among the Lakota from qualitative and quantitative research, clinical experience, and observations (Brave Heart, 1998, 1999a, 1999b, 2000; Brave Heart-Jordan, 1995). Historical trauma theory explains the existence of modern psychosocial problems (see also Manson et al., 1996; O'Nell, 1996; Robin, Chester, & Goldman, 1996).

Historical trauma is the intergenerational emotional and psychological injury that results from Native genocide (see Legters, 1988; Stannard, 1992; Thornton, 1987) and their ongoing oppression. The *historical trauma response* is a constellation of features associated with massive group trauma that is cumulative across generations and within the individual's lifespan (Brave Heart, 1998, 1999b, 2001a, 2001b). This response is analogous to traits identified among Jewish Holocaust descendants (Danieli, 1998; Kestenberg, 1990) and includes anxiety, depression, self-destructive behavior, substance abuse, poor affect tolerance, survivor guilt, intrusive trauma imagery, identification with ancestral pain, fixation to trauma, somatic symptoms, and elevated mortality rates (Brave Heart, 1998, 1999b). The *historical unresolved grief* emanating from generational trauma leads to impaired mourning (Brave Heart, 1998).

Traditional Lakota Bereavement and Historical Trauma

Lakota mourning differs from European American grief. *Decathexis* (detachment) from the deceased, a part of the universal human mourning process, according to the grief literature (Pollock, 1989), is distinctly different among the Lakota, who maintain relationships with ancestor spirits. Further, the loss of a close relative, among the Lakota, is experienced as the loss of part of the self, exhibited by cutting the hair (Brave Heart, 1998). Native bereavement is compounded by massive group trauma resulting from the genocide of indigenous people and current elevated mortality rates, which have impaired normative grief processes. The frequency and quality of losses have reduced time for traditional mourning practices. Federal prohibition of Native spiritual practices also restricted bereavement; the prohibition resulted in unresolved grief across generations, manifested in various symptoms such as depression and self-destructive behavior (Brave Heart, 1998).

ADDITIONAL CULTURAL CONSIDERATIONS

There are varying degrees of cultural affiliation and tribal-specific vs. pan-Indian identification, as well as conflict between Christian religions and traditional spirituality. Historically, Native children were placed in boarding schools operated by the federal government and various Christian denominations (Noriega, 1992). The practice of Native spirituality was prohibited not only in the schools but also on the reservations. Natives were forced to adopt Christian religions. However, some families maintained their traditional beliefs and secretly practiced traditional spirituality. Practitioners of traditional spirituality and participants in indigenous ceremonies were subject to arrest.

Sitting Bull's assassination and the Wounded Knee Massacre in 1890 were results of spiritual persecution that occurred in response to the *Wanagi Wacipi* (Ghost Dance). At a time of mass starvation, loss of lives, and the decimation of the buffalo, the Lakota began practicing a new spiritual movement—the Wanagi Wacipi—that promised reunification with deceased relatives as well as a return of the buffalo and the old way of life. However, there was a federal ban against such ceremonies, and the federal authorities were threatened by the empowerment that the Wanagi Wacipi provided for the Lakota. Sitting Bull was erroneously accused of encouraging the Wanagi Wacipi and was assassinated by government police (Vestal, 1932/1957). Then, hundreds of unarmed men, women, and children were massacred at Wounded Knee (McGregor, 1940/1987; "Wounded Knee remembered," 1990). In the aftermath of the massacre, many Native spiritual practices were either eliminated or went underground. People feared for their lives. Included in the prohibited ceremonies were indigenous mourning practices; their prohibition contributed to impaired grief resolution, resulting in historical unresolved grief. All of this served to limit the degree of indigenous cultural identification.

Originally, the Wanagi Wacipi, which was started by a Paiute named Wovoka, had Christian overtones, as it predicted the return of a Messiah. However, the Lakota interpretation focused instead on reunification and cultural resurgence, suggesting that it may have been a manifestation of an acute grief reaction (Brave Heart, 1998). Nonetheless, Christianity did have some influence among the Lakota in addition to the impact of the Christian boarding schools. The Native American Church (NAC), to which some Lakota individuals belong, is considered by some to represent a blending of Christianity and traditional Native practices. Others claim that the Christian overtones were used only as a vehicle to permit the practice of a Southwest Native ceremony. Nonetheless, one sees varying degrees of Christian influence among Native communities. Some both worship within Christian denominations and participate in traditional indigenous ceremonies; others practice either Christianity only or traditional ceremonies exclusively.

CULTURAL DEFINITION OF ILLNESS

According to Lakota tradition, illness indicates a lack of balance and harmony within the person's environment and with the natural world. Traditional ceremonies are performed to restore functioning and harmony. The DSM-IV (American Psychiatric Association, 1994) delineates only some of the Native "disorders" in the glossary of culture-bound syndromes.

ASSESSMENT, INTERVENTION, AND NATIVE SPIRITUALITY

Spiritual manifestations in Native clients might be misinterpreted as visual or auditory hallucinations or delusions, leading to misdiagnosis. Consulting with community informants can facilitate more accurate assessment. Such informants can reveal if the person is seen by peers as spiritually gifted rather than pathological (Brave Heart, 2001a, 2001b). The clinical social worker must examine the individual's overall functioning within the cultural context. The following case illustrates the role of spirituality in social work practice:

> Robert, a 27-year-old recovering alcoholic with a history of violent behavior and poor object relationships, presented with avoidant eye contact and guardedness; some paranoid ideation was evident. However, traditional spiritual practices seemed to help him not only to maintain sobriety, thereby limiting violent acting out, but also provided a context in which to contain his psychotic thinking and visual hallucinations. Spiritual interpretation of the content of his hallucinations brought his psychotic features into a more socially congruent context. His involvement in ceremonies also afforded him ego enhancement and a sense of mastery and competence. Due to his resistance to medication, the lack of command hallucinations, the lack of danger to self or others, and the fact that he had been able to maintain sobriety for over one year with the help of ceremonies, he was not placed on psychotropic medication. The treatment plan included supporting his involvement in the spiritual traditions. (Brave Heart, 2001a, 2001b)

Traditional spirituality and indigenous cultural practices can provide healthy coping strategies and defense mechanisms. Traditional activities can facilitate sublimation of longing for the past as well as grief resolution. The abilities to delay gratification and to control impulses—healthy ego functions—are evident in traditional Lakota ceremonies, which require commitment, physical hardship, deprivation (such as fasting), as well as endurance for a higher purpose and transcendence (Brave Heart, 2001a, 2001b). Traditional values also incorporate altruism, another high-level defense. Many modern Lakota participate in the Sun Dance, which involves fasting and physical endurance, in order to pray for sick relatives and community members or sometimes for their own healing and spiritual growth. Traditional spirituality and culture can foster healthy ego functioning and mastery of trauma and can be effective therapeutic interventions for Posttraumatic Stress Disorder (Silver & Wilson, 1988). Spiritual oppression and genocide caused the practice of Native healing to diminish across generations, but there has been a spiritual and cultural resurgence.

Clinical social work practice with Native clients is challenging when the clinician is of European descent, because of the negative historical legacy of genocide and persistent oppression of Natives (Brave Heart, 2001a, 2001b). Trust issues are paramount, and there will always be some cultural distance between the client and the social worker. Native clients are coping with varying degrees of taboo about sharing spiritual information with outsiders or outside of a ceremony. Dreams are sometimes shared only after they have been spiritually interpreted, when they are no longer thought to lose their power upon disclosure. The typical European American style of direct communication is often experienced by the Native client as intrusive; the Native client is more likely to be comfortable with an indirect communication style (see Brave Heart, 2001a, 2001b).

For many Natives, European American clinicians represent the perpetrators of genocide. The War Department was originally home to the Bureau of Indian Affairs, which is now responsible for social services and is the progenitor of the Indian Health Service, under which mental health services are provided. The social worker whose clients are Native people must always be aware of this historical legacy and the related complex cultural issues. Additionally, the social worker of European descent must recognize her or his own legacy of prejudice toward Native people as "savage" and must guard against projection and victim blaming (see Berkhofer, 1979; Brave Heart, 2001a, 2001b).

Some Native clients are more assimilated into European American culture and will be assertive, maintain a great deal of direct eye contact, and may request more directive interventions; others will behave in a more traditional fashion, with less eye contact and more indirect communication. The social worker must be prepared to alter his or her intervention style accordingly (see Brave Heart, 2001a, 2001b). Further, the social worker should be ready to facilitate a client's involvement in traditional ceremonies while respecting the client's right to choose such a course and to decide on its timing. Many clients may be resistant to or conflicted about traditional ceremonies. The following case illustrates this point:

> Joel is an 11-year-old, attractive, full-blood, dark-skinned Lakota male with short dyed blonde hair and glasses. He presented with exaggerated feminine behavior and associated almost exclusively with female peers. Joel was referred because of poor grades, problematic behavior, and pregnancy fantasies. Joel would attend late night alcoholic parties. In a histrionic effeminate style, Joel boasted about his precocious escapades and attempted to impress the clinician with his cognizance of the latest reservation scandal.
>
> Joel avoided discussing his past history, particularly his neglectful alcoholic mother, whose current whereabouts were a mystery. He was being cared for

> by his overwhelmed but well-meaning grandmother, Mrs. A, who was a boarding school survivor. Joel was sexually abused at the age of nine by a gang of older boys at a boarding school . . . . After that, Mrs. A brought Joel home to attend a reservation day school.
>
> Taught that she needed to abandon her Lakota culture, language, and spirituality through strappings at boarding school, Mrs. A embraced Catholicism and consulted with the local priest who was advising her to send Joel to a Catholic boarding school to "straighten him out." However, Mrs. A's Lakota belief system still presented itself with some tenacity and she wondered if Joel could be a winkte [a transsexual]. (Brave Heart, 2001a, 2001b)

In this family, an ambivalent relationship with a Christian denomination has undermined traditional values and practices, and the client was coping with a myriad of issues, including boarding school experiences (see Irwin & Roll, 1995), maternal alcoholism and abandonment, internalized oppression (Brave Heart & DeBruyn, 1998; Freire & Ramos, 1992) manifested by the dyed blonde hair symbolizing a wish to be Caucasian, and the possibility of being a winkte. From a Lakota perspective, a traditional ceremony may have empowered Joel and provided a more socially acceptable manner for resolving his gender identity (Brave Heart, 2001a, 2001b). However, the family followed the advice of the priest, and Joel was sent away again to a Catholic boarding school.

Invitations to Native ceremonies require sensitive handling. The Lakota are traditionally very inclusive as a result of the belief that all of creation is related. Once a client develops more trust, she or he is likely to invite a non-Native social worker to ceremonies. If the social worker's own spiritual beliefs prohibit attendance, this must be skillfully communicated to the client while recognizing that a refusal entails the risk of irreparably damaging the relationship (Brave Heart, 2001a, 2001b). If the social worker does attend the ceremony, maintaining professional neutrality while participating is important. The non-Native social worker can attend to this by limiting his or her prayers, requesting help only for the client and other participants and not for himself or herself (Brave Heart, 2001a, 2001b). Native social workers, in contrast, will be expected to participate actively in a ceremony and must cope with more fluid professional/personal boundaries. Non-Native social workers who work with Native people on a long-term basis will experience Native acculturation and may ultimately be required to develop more fluid professional /personal boundaries. Recalling that traditional ceremonies provide safe affective containers for clients as well as facilitating cathartic release of emotions (Brave Heart-Jordan, 1995; Silver & Wilson, 1988) will help the non-Native social worker understand the importance of promoting the availability of these ceremonies for clients, even in an urban area (Duran & Yellow Horse-Davis, 1997). Although doing so may be a challenge, non-Native social workers must depend on Native contacts to make arrangements for such ceremonies, particularly where a Native client may feel isolated or estranged from family who otherwise would help him or her arrange a ceremony.

Another issue that a social worker may face concerns medication. Depending upon the client's level of acculturation, the social worker can seek the help of an indigenous healer in gaining the client's acceptance of medication. Many healers support Native use of both Western medicine and traditional healing, including the use of insulin and, at times, surgery. Hospitals serving Native clients are increasingly undertaking consultations with Native healers. However, in some instances ceremonies eliminate the need for medication. For example, a Lakota woman diagnosed as schizophrenic was placed on antipsychotic medication. After a traditional ceremony, she was able to stop taking her medication and has remained symptom-free. A Lakota male complained of suicidal impulses following his abusive mother's death, and anti-depressants were prescribed. Following a ceremony, without the help of the anti-depressants, all suicidal ideation disappeared (Brave Heart, 2001a, 2001b).

CONCLUSION

Traditional Native culture and spirituality can be empowering vehicles for Native clients. Social workers must respect the wholistic view of Native culture whereby spirituality is integrated throughout one's worldview. Our churches are the earth and all of its inhabitants. All of creation, including the hallowed ground on which we walk, has a spirit. Social workers must be aware of the impact of historical trauma and comprehend the varying degrees of cultural conflicts in order to intervene effectively with Natives. Moreover, social workers should be aware of the continuing spiritual persecution and spiritual genocide against Natives and the struggle of Natives to regain the caretaking function for sacred sites, such as the Black Hills in South Dakota. Social work practitioners can also find the elaboration of Native culture useful in planning community interventions and conducting research in Native communities.

There are a number of community resources to which social workers can turn for help (Duran & Yellow Horse-Davis, 1997). The Takini (Survivor) Network is one national and regional resource. The Takini Network is conducting research (Brave Heart, 1998, 1999a, 1999b), community education, and community healing, as well as training service providers. The Network incorporates indigenous spirituality in all aspects of its work and advocates cultural resurgence as an empowerment strategy. The Network strives to foster respect for all of creation, based on the traditional Lakota phrase *Mitakuye Oyasin:* We are all related.

REFERENCES

American Psychiatric Association. (1994). *Diagnostic and statistical manual of mental disorders* (4th ed.). Washington, DC: Author.

Berkhofer, R. F., Jr. (1979). *The white man's Indian: Images of the American Indian from Columbus to the present.* New York: Vintage, Random House. (Original work published 1978)

Black Elk, & Neihardt, J. G. (1972). *Black Elk Speaks.* New York: Pocket Books. (Original work published 1932)

Brave Heart, M. Y. H. (1998). The return to the sacred path: Healing the historical trauma and historical unresolved grief response among the Lakota. *Smith College Studies in Social Work, 68*(3), 287–305.

Brave Heart, M. Y. H. (1999a). Gender differences in the historical trauma response among the Lakota. *Journal of Health and Social Policy, 10*(4), 1–21; and in Day, P. A., & Weaver, H. N. (Eds.), *Health and the American Indian* (pp. 1–21). New York: Haworth.

Brave Heart, M. Y. H. (1999b). *Oyate Ptayela:* Rebuilding the Lakota Nation through addressing historical trauma among Lakota parents. *Journal of Human Behavior in the Social Environment, 2*(1/2), 109–126; and in Weaver, H. N. (Ed.), *Voices of First Nations people: Human services considerations* (pp. 109–126). New York: Haworth.

Brave Heart, M. Y. H. (2000). *Wakiksuyapi:* Carrying the historical trauma of the Lakota. *Tulane Studies in Social Welfare,* 21–22, 245–266.

Brave Heart, M. Y. H. (2001a). Clinical assessment with American Indians. In R. Fong, & S. Furuto (Eds.), *Cultural competent social work practice: Practice skills, interventions, and evaluation* (pp. 163–177). New York: Longman.

Brave Heart, M. Y. H. (2001b). Clinical interventions with American Indians. In R. Fong, & S. Furuto (Eds.), *Cultural competent social work practice: Practice skills, interventions, and evaluation* (pp. 285–298). New York: Longman.

Brave Heart, M. Y. H., & DeBruyn, L. (1998). The American holocaust: Historical unresolved grief among native American Indians. *National Center for American Indian and Alaska Native Mental Health Research Journal, 8*(2), 56–78.

Brave Heart-Jordan, M. Y. H. (1995/1996). The return to the sacred path: Healing from historical trauma and historical unresolved grief among the Lakota. (Doctoral dissertation, Smith College School for Social Work, 1995). *Dissertation Abstracts International,* A 56/09, p. 3742. Copies available from The Takini Network for a donation of $35.00, made payable to The Takini Network, PO Box 4138, Rapid City, SD 57709-4138.

Bullhead, E. (1995). "Black Hills Song." *Track 1 of Keeper of the Drum* [CD]. Albuquerque, NM: Sound of America Records.

Cox, E. O., & Parsons, R. J. (1994). *Empowerment-oriented social work practice with the elderly.* Belmont, CA: Brooks/Cole.

Danieli, Y. (Ed.). (1998). *International handbook of multigenerational legacies of trauma.* Plenum Publishing.

Duran, E., & Yellow Horse-Davis, S. (1997). Final research evaluation report—Evaluation of family and child guidance clinic hybrid treatment model. Report to the Indian Health Service. Washington, DC: U.S. Department of Health and Human Services.

Freire, P., & Ramos, M. (1992). Pedagogy of the oppressed. New York: Continuum.

Irwin, M. H., & Roll, S. (1995). The psychological impact of sexual abuse of Native American boarding-school children. *Journal of the American Academy of Psychoanalysis, 23*(3), 461–473.

Kestenberg, J. S. (1990). Survivor parents and their children. In M. S. Bergmann & M. E. Jucovy (Eds.), *Generations of the Holocaust* (pp. 83–102). New York: Columbia University Press. (Original work published 1982)

Legters, L. H. (1988). The American genocide. *Policy Studies Journal, 16*(4), 768–777.

Manson, S., Beals, J., O'Nell, T., Piasecki, J., Bechtold, D., Keane, E., & Jones, M. (1996). Wounded spirits, ailing hearts: PTSD and related disorders among American Indians. In A. J. Marsella, M. J. Friedman, E. T. Gerrity, & R. J. Scurfield, (Eds.), *Ethnocultural Aspects of Posttraumatic Stress Disorder* (pp. 255–283). Washington, DC: American Psychological Association.

McGregor, J. (1987). *The Wounded Knee massacre: From the viewpoint of the Sioux*. Rapid City, SD: Fenske Printing. (Original work published 1940)

Noriega, J. (1992). American Indian education in the United States: Indoctrination for subordination to colonialism. In M. A. Jaimes (Ed.), *The state of Native America: Genocide, colonization, and resistance* (pp. 371–402). Boston: South End Press.

O'Nell, T. D. (1996). *Disciplined hearts: History, identity, and depression in an American Indian community.* Berkley: University of California Press.

Pollock, G. H. (Ed.). (1989). *The mourning-liberation process, Vol I.* Madison, CT: International Universities Press.

Powers, M. (1986). *Oglala women.* Chicago: University of Chicago Press.

Robin, R. W., Chester, B., & Goldman, D. (1996). Cumulative trauma and PTSD in American Indian communities. In A. J. Marsella, M. J. Friedman, E. T. Gerrity, & R. M. Scurfield (Eds.), *Ethnocultural Aspects of Posttraumatic Stress Disorder* (pp. 239–253). Washington, DC: American Psychological Association.

Silver, S. M., & Wilson, J. P. (1988). Native American healing and purification rituals for war stress. In J. P. Wilson, Z. Harele, & B. Hahana (Eds.), *Human adaptation to extreme stress: From the Holocaust to Viet Nam* (pp. 337–355). New York: Plenum.

Standing Bear, L. (1975). *My people the Sioux.* Lincoln, NE: University of Nebraska Press. (Original work published 1928)

Standing Bear, L. (1978). *The land of the spotted eagle.* Lincoln, NE: University of Nebraska Press. (Original work published 1933)

Stannard, D. (1992). *American Holocaust: Columbus and the conquest of the new world.* New York: Oxford University Press.

Thornton, R. (1987). *American Indian Holocaust and survival: A population history since 1492*. Norman, OK: University of Oklahoma Press.

Vestal, S. (1957). *Sitting Bull: Champion of the Sioux*. Boston: Houghton Mifflin. (Original work published 1932)

Wounded Knee remembered. (1990, December). *The Lakota Times* (Special Edition).

ADDITIONAL RESOURCES

Book and Articles

Brave Heart, M. Y. H. (Spring, 1998). Premenstrual Dysphoric Disorder among American Indian Women: A preliminary exploration, *Rural Community Mental Health*.

Brave Heart-Jordan, M., & DeBruyn, L. (1995). So she may walk in balance: Integrating the impact of historical trauma in the treatment of American Indian women. In J. Adelman & G. Enguidanos (Eds.), *Racism in the lives of women: Testimony, theory and guides to antiracist practice* (pp. 345–368). New York: Haworth Press.

Brave Heart, M. Y. H., & Spicer, P. (1999). The sociocultural context of American Indian infant mental health. In J. D. Osofsky & H. E. Fitzgerald (Eds.), *World association of infant mental health handbook of infant mental health*. New York: John Wiley & Sons.

Duran, E., Duran, B., & Brave Heart, M. Y. H. (1998). Native Americans and the trauma of history. In *Studying Native America: Problems and prospects of Native American Studies* (pp. 60–76). New York: Social Science Research Council.

Duran, E., Duran, B., Brave Heart, M. Y. H., & Yellow Horse-Davis, S. (1998). Healing the American Indian soul wound. In Yael Danieli (Ed.), *International handbook of multigenerational legacies of trauma*. New York: Plenum.

Weaver, H., & Brave Heart, M. Y. H. (1999). Examining two facets of American Indian identity: Exposure to other cultures and the influence of historical trauma. *Journal of Human Behavior in the Social Environment*, 2(1/2), 19–33. Reprinted in H. Weaver (Ed.), *Voices of first nations people: Considerations for human services*. New York: Haworth.

Music

Bullhead, E. (1995). "Black Hills Song." Track 1 of *Keeper of the Drum* [CD]. Albuquerque, NM: Sound of America Records.

Web Site

www.csp.org/communities/native-american.html

Address

The Takini Network
PO Box 4138
Rapid City, SD 57709-4138

GLOSSARY

Black Hills An area of sacred land in Western South Dakota to which the Lakota never relinquished title. A 1982 Supreme Court decision validated that the Black Hills were illegally confiscated by the United States in violation of the 1868 Treaty of Fort Laramie. However, the Supreme Court did not rule that the land should be returned, but instead offered a monetary settlement that the Lakota have refused, in spite of great poverty.

Boarding school A residential school established in 1879 for the education of Native children. The initial federal policy included the forced removal of children to the school and their separation from parents and tribal communities in residential schools sometimes as far as 1,000 miles away, with no contact with family for years at a time. Eventually, boarding schools were built closer to reservation communities and more family visits were allowed. In the schools there was rampant physical neglect and abuse of children. They were beaten for speaking Native languages and forced to wear non-Native clothing. Boarding schools were often overcrowded and were implicated in tuberculosis epidemics up until the 1950s. Modern boarding schools still exist, although they are much improved, and many Native children now attend day schools and live at home.

Bureau of Indian Affairs & Indian Health Service The BIA is a division of the U.S. Department of the Interior that is responsible for monitoring and providing educational and social services to tribes as well as land management and other dealings for tribes. The BIA originated as part of the War Department, but in 1824 was transferred to the Interior Department. Although health care services were originally provided by the BIA, the Indian Health Service was moved to the Department of Health and Human Services.

Crazy Horse A traditional Lakota leader, who fought in the Battle of Little Big Horn, and was a contemporary of Sitting Bull. He was killed in 1877.

Decathexis A term developed by Freud to indicate a process of detachment of emotional investment, as in decathexis from a deceased relative.

DSM-IV The *Diagnostic and Statistical Manual* of the American Psychiatric Association, utilized in mental health settings and in clinical social work assessment.

Empowerment The development of power and efficacy by individuals and communities.

Historical trauma Cumulative psychological and emotional wounding across generations, including life-span trauma; a concept developed by M. Y. H. Brave Heart (1998).

Lakota The traditional name for the Teton or Western division of the Great Sioux Nation. The Lakota reside in North and South Dakota and comprise seven bands, all speaking the Lakota dialect of the Sioux language.

Mitakuye Oyasin A Lakota expression used in prayer, which means "We are all related."

Native A general term for all the indigenous inhabitants of the land area now known as the United States. This term is synonymous with Native American, American Indian, First Nations, and indigenous.

Native American Church A faith that incorporates aspects of Christianity in some interpretations and the use of an indigenous plant, peyote, as a medicine to induce spiritual experiences and enlightenment. Although NAC is practiced by a variety of tribal members from different regions, its origins are more Southwestern and it is more popular in the Southwest.

Oyate A Lakota word meaning Nation or the People.

Seven Sacred Rites Seven Lakota ceremonies brought to the Lakota by White Buffalo Calf Woman, among which is the Sun Dance.

Sitting Bull A Hunkpapa Lakota traditional spiritual and political leader who was assassinated in 1890.

Spiritual interpreter A Lakota "medicine man," or healer.

The Takini Network A Lakota organization formed in 1992 to address historical trauma healing and research among Native people. The address is PO Box 4138, Rapid City, South Dakota, 57709-4138, (605) 399-2554, email: takininet@aol.com

Tiospaye A Lakota word meaning extended kinship network.

Wanagi Wacipi The Ghost Dance, a spiritual movement and practice that emerged in 1890 during a time of mass starvation and severe reservation conditions. The Ghost Dance promised the return of a traditional way of life, the buffalo, and reunification with deceased relatives, according to the Lakota interpretation of this ceremony. It was practiced in many forms among some other tribes and originated with the prophecy of Wovoka, a Paiute.

White Buffalo Calf Woman The spiritual figure who brought the Sacred Pipe and the Seven Sacred Rites to the Lakota.

White Lance A Lakota leader, a cousin of Sitting Bull, who survived the Wounded Knee Massacre. Descendants and relatives of White Lance live primarily in the Medicine Root District in Kyle, South Dakota on the Pine Ridge Indian Reservation.

Winkte A Lakota term for a transsexual.

Woope Sakowin The Seven Laws of the Lakota, including the values of generosity, humility, and respect.

Wounded Knee Massacre The massacre in 1890 by United States troops of hundreds of unarmed men, women, and children in South Dakota on the Pine Ridge Indian Reservation.

3 CHAPTER HINDUISM

RAM SINGH

Hinduism is a pre-historic religion. Its origin is quite different from that of other major religions of the world. It evolved through centuries as a wholistic philosophy of life. Sometime between 8000 and 2000 B.C., a group of enlightened Aryans (the Sanskrit word for "civilized people")—the early settlers of India—began to engage in deep meditations and spiritual discussions. These were compiled into what came to be called the Vedas, the most sacred books of the Hindus. The Vedas emphasized the harmonious relationship of individuals, society, nature, and supernatural forces. The hymns of the Vedas pray for the welfare of all humanity and all of nature. The daily prayers of the Aryans, still repeated by Hindus around the world, clearly convey this ideal:

> Om! O Lord! Let every one be happy, let every one be without affliction . . . O Lord! Let us all live together; let us all share our food together, . . . May there be welfare to all beings; . . . Peace, Peace, Peace.

The concepts of peace and the innate divinity of each human being are so central to Hinduism that each prayer begins with "Om" and ends with "Peace." "Om" symbolizes divinity within and all around. The entire social and spiritual structure of Hinduism reflects an effort to elevate humans to a higher level of existence, helping them to realize their higher selves. One may ask, " If humans are divine, then why do they suffer?" Hindus respond that people suffer because of a narrow outlook and an ignorance of their true identity. Broadening one's worldview is Hinduism's fundamental objective. In this aim, Hinduism meets all four directives of a global ethic postulated by Hans Kung (1996): (1) commitment to a culture of non-violence and respect for life; (2) commitment to cultural solidarity and a just economic order; (3) commitment to tolerance and truthfulness; and (4) commitment to equal rights and partnership between men and women.

Starting with Alexander the Great in the 2nd century B.C. through Muslim invasions in the 10th century A.D. and the establishment of British rule in the 17th century, India suffered a series of foreign invasions and rulers (Knipe, 1991). During these thousands of years, India witnessed the destruction of great temples, educational institutions, and libraries containing thousands of books on spirituality, astrology, astronomy, social and physical sciences, and so on. In response to frequent invasions and foreign rule, Hindus adopted many adaptive and defensive survival mechanisms. As a result, the Hindu culture, in contrast to many ancient cultures that disappeared long ago, managed to survive. It is now the oldest continuous culture on earth. It has a unique socio-spiritual strength and resiliency that permeates every aspect of its functioning. Over 2000 years ago, Alexander the Great, whose powerful army could not be resisted by the mightiest kings, was forced to retreat from India when he was confronted by a Hindu saint. Gandhi also used the strength of Hindu spirituality and its tradition of non-violence in his *Satyagraha* (struggle for truth) movement to win freedom for India from the British Empire. It was in response to such invasions and socio-political challenges that Hinduism produced several social reformers in the 19th century (Klostermaier, 1994).

MY PATH TO HINDU HUMANISTIC PHILOSOPHY

Writing this chapter has been a pleasant and exciting exercise that has encouraged me to explore my childhood stories and the family religious and social influences that have deeply embedded humanistic values within me. Swami Vivekananda said that religion is character that grows through early childhood experiences. What we learn about religion in the family has a greater influence on shaping our worldview than the religious books we follow. Most of the Hindu gurus and saints encourage an aspirant to go through a deep self-examination through meditation.

I was born in a Hindu family in India. My mother was religious; she observed many Hindu festivals, fasted on auspicious days, and was a vegetarian. She never turned down a poor person or a pious monk seeking alms. She regularly performed *puja* (worship) at an altar at home. She kept idols and pictures of many gods (Vishnu, Ram, Krishna, Kali, Hanuman, Ganesh, Swami Rama Krishna Paramhamsa, Swami Vivekananda, Buddha) in our home. What I liked the most about this worship was the fragrance of incense, the sweet chimes of the bell, a rhythmic chanting of some melodious mantras and prayers, and most importantly, the delicious sweets (*prasad*) given to all of us and also to the neighbors after the puja was done.

While in high school, I was sent to a local Christian missionary school. One day, quite influenced by a sermon at the school, I brought a picture of Jesus Christ and put it on the altar. My mother did not say a word. In the evening I was flabbergasted to notice that my mother was worshipping Jesus Christ along with the other idols and pictures. When I asked, her answer was that all these idols and pictures are just to help us concentrate. God is one, but there are many means.

One day I went to an Arya Samaj temple. A picture of Swami Dayananda, the originator of this path, was hanging on the wall. There were no idols, as Arya Samajis do not believe in idol worship. I told my mother about this temple. She just nodded her head, saying everyone has a right to his or her own belief system. "And they are correct too," she added. "These idols and pictures are just stones or papers. They are powerful symbols for those who know how to use them to elevate their minds to a higher level of concentration beyond the worldly reality. Even the written words are nothing else but symbols. They convey a message to a person who can read. But for a person not exposed to that language, they are just meaningless scribbles."

My father told me the story of Swami Vivekananda. The swami was invited to the World Parliament of Religions in Chicago in 1892. He asked a Hindu king to finance his trip. The king was highly critical of idol worship. Swami Vivekananda did not say a word. He saw a picture of the king on a wall. He brought it down and placed his shoes on it. The king screamed "How do you dare insult me?" "I respect you a lot, my honor! This is just your picture, not you." Swami explained that in the same way idols are only symbols, they are not God in themselves.

One day someone in my school made fun of Hinduism, saying that Hindus are weak, as they do not eat beef, while millions of people starve and many old and neglected cows roam on the streets. My mother answered, "People have a right to their belief system. It is not a matter of who is right or who is wrong, but it is just a matter of individual comfort and emotional satisfaction. We all grow up on cow's milk, and, therefore, we treat her like our mother." My father, who heard this dialogue, explained the tremendous respect mothers command in Hindu religion. Today, it makes sense that I found myself so attracted to the Mother's Trust/Mother's Place, a women's spirituality center in Ganges, Michigan. Gauri Ma, the sannyasini of the center, is an embodiment of women's spirituality, whose clear message is to look for divinity in each woman.

The respect for women is epitomized by Sri Rama Krishna's marriage, arranged by his parents at a very early age, as they feared that he might denounce worldly life. His bride asked him, "How do you look upon me?" Sri Rama Krishna replied, "I look upon you as the embodiment of the Divine Mother." The two never consummated their marriage, and Rama Krishna worshipped her as the divine mother.

Hinduism has a deep respect for women's spirituality. The main force behind every god is a woman. All the three aspects of God in the Hindu trinity—Brahma, the creator, Vishnu, the protector, and Shiva, the facilitator of the universal cycle through destruction—get their strength from their consorts: Saraswati, the goddess of wisdom, Lakshmi, the goddess of wealth, and Durga, the goddess of power.

One of the greatest values that I learned from my family was the tremendous respect and love that was to be bestowed upon a guest. Any guest could walk in any time and would be offered tea, food, and a bed if he wanted to stay. A very special annual visitor to our house was a swami who lived somewhere in the foothills of the Himalayas in Kashmir and went on a tour all over India every year. His visits were intensely spiritual days for my mother and many of our neighbors. My mother would prepare the best vegetarian meals. I asked her why she and the swami did not eat meat of any kind. She had already explained about the cow, but what about the goat and the sheep? They are not our mothers. One of our neighbors, who visited our house almost every day, cited the example of Gandhi: "He drank goat milk and was totally vegetarian and see how much spiritual strength he had. God has given us plenty of food. Why do we have to kill animals?" She had heard me talking about starvation in India. "India is not a poor country," she exclaimed with excitement, "just imagine a country being systematically exploited and a religion being massacred by foreign invasions for thousands of years. Moreover, recently highly fertile chunks of land in Punjab, Sindh, and Bengal have been carved out to create a new country, named Pakistan." My uncle, who had been in the British army, added, "The worst famine I have ever seen in India was in 1942. It was mainly because the Britishers while engaged in the Second World War diverted all the food grains to feed the army. All they cared was to win the war, not to feed the people. Now that we are free the situation will change." Now, while reminiscing, I see how correct my uncle was. Today, India is not only self-sufficient but also exporting food and technology to other countries and gradually emerging as a great world power with vast industrial development.

THE HINDU WORLDVIEW: A WHOLISTIC PERSPECTIVE ON DIVERSITY

Hinduism is not based on the teachings of a single spiritual leader. It developed out of thousands of years of dialogues between great philosophers and saints. Religion for a Hindu, therefore, means a process of exploring the mysteries of the external universe as well as the universe within each individual. Hindus do not view religion as separate from philosophy, culture, epistemology, physics, chemistry, math, astrology, and art. The Vedas deal with almost all branches of knowledge and practices concerning human life and beyond. A reader who wants to understand and appreciate the true essence of Hinduism and its concept of human welfare must transcend Western linear, dualistic, and uni-dimensional thinking. Hinduism's great contribution to science and civilization consists in its emphasis on maintaining a balanced state of mind through yoga, self-discipline, wholistic thinking, and positive attitude (Machve, 1994).

The core of Hindu thinking is a worldview emphasizing that (1) the universe is permeated by a spiritual power; (2) the divine life is present in all beings; (3) since all human beings represent a spark of the divine, they all belong to the same family; (4) true happiness can be achieved by a cooperative commonwealth that ensures the welfare of all beings; and (5) all religions are but partial approaches to finding the ultimate reality (Singh, 1990). The Hindu worldview conceptualizes the existence of innumerable universes, all going through a cyclic process of creation, condensation, and re-creation for eternity (Smith, 1991). The Vedas assert that there was no time when the universes did not exist or will not exist.

HINDU WORLDVIEW AND SOCIAL WELFARE

Basic Assumptions

Since Hinduism has no set beginning date or originating leader, Hindus call their belief system *Sanatana dharma*—an eternal set of principles and assumptions about human life that have guided the entire universe since eternity (Bharti Krishna Tirtha, 1964). *Dharma* (translated as "religion" in English) means being good to each other by following the principles that facilitate spiritual growth within a well-functioning society. Dharma is a set of principles, attitudes, and behaviors beneficial to the individual and the society (Joshi, 1996).

The Hindu sages, knowing the limitations of the human mind and language, encouraged each individual to experience God within, in a manner suitable to his or her own disposition, rather than following a doctrine blindly. Aryans assumed that the ultimate reality that cannot be described through words can only be experienced through deep meditation. This assumption led them to emphasize the importance of sharing spiritual experiences with great spiritual leaders and having dialogues between the aspirants. It led to the development of an enormous collection of spiritual literature, unsurpassed by any other civilization. Thousands of years of such dialogues and spiritual revelations (called *Sruti*) were compiled in the four Vedas (the books of knowledge)—the Rig, Yajur, Sama, and Atharva—and in dozens of *Upanishads* (a word literally meaning "sitting near a guru and exploring spiritual knowledge"). These intellectual explorations were explained and illustrated in the 18 *Puranas* (old stories) with the help of thousands of folk tales, historical as well as mythological. One Purana, Sri Mad Bhagvatam (and the Bhagavadgita, a part of the epic Mahabharata) constitute the main source of inspiration for the Hare Krishna movement around the world. The two great epics, Ramayana and Mahabharata (the latter is the longest epic in the world) describe the ideals and conflicts of life and God's incarnation on earth as Rama and Krishna to save the world from injustice and develop an ideal society called *Rama Rajya* ("Rama's ideal kingdom"). The creation of a utopian society has always been a great source of inspiration for Hindus. However, as the Indian society became more complex and more defensive following invasions, a few Smritis (the books of social and moral laws) were written. The most famous among these is the *Manusmriti,* written by Manu, described as the first sociologist in the world. It was during Manu's time that many social institutions were established, within the framework of the Hindu organismic theory of society (i.e., the idea that a society functions as a whole, or as one organism). One of the most controversial of these institutions was the caste system, which turned into a rigid system determined on the basis of birth rather than on the quality and actions of a person, as Krishna had described in the Gita (Chidbhavananda, 1994).

The Hindu circular worldview looks at the universes as being without a beginning or an end. The universes, Hindus assume, have been going through a circular process of expansion and contraction forever. One of the most significant aspects of the Hindu circular worldview is its theory of birth and rebirth. According to this view, human beings can go through thousands of births before achieving *moksha,* or salvation. Re-birth could be in the form of a human or an animal or a tree or any living thing. The theory establishes an essential affinity between humans, animals, and the entire natural realm.

The Hindus' circular thinking led to their belief in *Karma.* This is based on the everyday observation that each action has a reaction and that by controlling an action, the reactions can be controlled. We have no control of others' behavior, but we do have control of our actions, and we can act so as to modify others' reactions. Emphasizing the moral and physical laws of cause and effect, Karma aims to motivate individuals to create their own future by planning, setting goals, and accepting responsibility and accountability (Venkateswaran, 1995). This theory, however, has been widely misinterpreted and criticized as deterministic. Karma is not a pre-set destiny based on the past actions (for example, a homeless individual's situation cannot be attributed to his past karma), but rather a process of building one's future. The theory emphasizes task-oriented (*Arjita Karma*) action, which will eventually lead to relief from the pains of life. Krishna states in the Gita that we have control of actions, but not of results. However, if we follow a method, the results will come. He advises Arjuna not to refrain from action but to detach himself from expectations. Krishna's encouragement to Arjuna to take charge of his life and then surrender to Him can easily be compared with the twelve steps of Alcoholics Anonymous.

The theory of karma has been a source of motivation to Hindus to engage in moral behavior and promote social welfare and social justice. Kindness and acts of helping others bring good karma. Unkindness yields bad karma. The accumulation of bad karma by not helping the needy and inflicting pain is a sin. Hinduism gives a social welfare twist to the concept of sin, emphasizing purity, devotion, humility, and charity as the four keys to good conduct (Subramuniyaswami, 1993).

The Hindu concept of God (Brahman) is not simplistic. Being aware of limitations of language, the Vedic saints encouraged each individual to experience God within through meditation and self-righteous behavior rather than to follow a great leader blindly. God as Brahman is the ultimate reality, the absolute power beyond human conception and description. We must elevate ourselves beyond linguistic and anthropomorphic definitions. Brahman, being absolute, is called He, She, or It, and it makes no difference to Hindus. Along with this absolute conception of God, a Hindu also wants to establish a personal relationship with God. Brahman, as creator and caretaker of the universes, is also perceived as Ishvara, who incarnates on earth in different forms from time to time to help devotees and salvage society. Different incarnations of Ishvara establishing direct relationships with humans and other creatures are various aspects of one God. Hinduism, therefore, is neither polytheistic nor monotheistic but henotheistic—it allows the worship of one god without denying the existence of other gods (Smith, 1991). Hindus see God as perfect goodness, love, truth, and bliss. God is neither vengeful nor wrathful and does not punish wrongdoers. It is the karma (action) of an individual that brings good or bad consequences. Karma, however, is not deterministic but can be modified through devotion to God and righteous actions. Moreover, a person can earn God's grace through devotion and total surrender (Subramuniyaswami, 1993).

Based on the observation that the same physical destination can be reached by many paths, a Hindu assumes that spirituality can be attained by following the path that is the most suited to one's growth (Singh, 1990).

The Hindu theory of society, emphasizing interdependence, is intrinsically organismic. Nature demonstrates a delicate interdependence between the trees, insects, animals, and so on. Destruction follows when this balance is lost. The *Taittareya Upanishad,* in its description of creation, uses the analogy of a spider weaving a web from the thread that emanates from within. Thus did Brahman create the universe from within. "Sarvam khalvidam Brahman"—everything around us is Brahman. Krishna declares "Having entered into the earth with my life-giving energy I support and uphold all the life forms (Chidbhavananda, 1994).

The Meaning of Life

The purpose of life and the way to ultimate liberation (moksha) are questions that have haunted every religion and society. Hinduism considers that the world is covered by *Maya.* Since Maya has been misinterpreted as "illusion," Hindus have been criticized as being otherworldly, apathetic toward life and the world in general. Maya is actually the outer appearance of the reality within. A piece of gold, for example, can be melted and formed into jewelry. Melt it again, and the jewelry is gone. That is Maya. In contrast to the Real, which is changeless and immutable, Maya is something that is subject to constant change (Vivekananda, 1963). Keeping this in mind, Hindus conceive of four aims of life: Dharma, living a righteous life; *Artha,* personal and social well-being; *Kama,* enjoyment of worldly pleasures; and finally, moksha, salvation from the miseries of life. Hindus are advised to maintain a balanced attitude in fulfilling all these aims and finding meaning of life.

Sources of Suffering

Humans, being a part of the divine, are blessed with eternal joy and bliss, *Ananda.* However, they subject themselves to suffering for many reasons. One of the most significant of these reasons is humans' ignorance of their true identity and over-involvement with the worldly senses of pleasure and pain. The Gita mentions uncontrolled desires, anger, and undue attachment to the world as the main sources of suffering. Two other major reasons for suffering are peoples' inability to balance the four aims of life at different developmental stages and their tendency to become attached to their actions in a narcissistic manner rather than doing their duty.

Sources of Power

The ancient Hindus, preoccupied with understanding human behavior and improving social conditions, emphasized the significance of spirituality for the wholistic development and empowerment of the individual as well as the society (Miller, 1999). They tried a large-scale social experiment, dividing society into four groups based on people's predispositions and skills. They wanted a well-balanced society, with equal emphasis on spirituality, social protection, prosperity, and maintenance of cleanliness. This division later developed into four major castes: Brahmin, Kshattriya, Vaishya, and Shudra. The caste system emphasized division of labor, role complementarity, and expertise in specific trades by specific groups. However, this division of labor turned into a social stratification, with the Shudras, being the least powerful group, called "untouchables." This label became institutionalized, leading to their isolation from the mainstream of life. Gandhi re-labeled this group *Harijans,* or the children of God in need of special attention to improve their social and financial conditions. The Indian Constitution granted them and other minority groups financial assistance, scholarships, and employment, and their condition has been improving.

One of the hallmarks of Hindu spirituality is that it empowers humans by reminding them of the divinity within each of them. Since Hindus conceive of Brahman as the only final and ultimate reality and everything else as Maya, they emphasize finding the eternal truth beyond Maya. The Upanishads encourage the seekers to look for divinity within each human being, in animals, birds, and the entire nature (Taittiriya Upanishad, 1:11). Hinduism encourages a relentless search for unity and for connection with the highest of human potentials (Emmons, 1999).

From the earliest Vedic age, the Hindus did not conceive of this world as the center of the universe. The Vedic seers were aware of the existence of the millions of stars and galaxies in the universe and theorized an eternal cyclic process for their evolution and devolution. Hinduism encourages seekers to explore their true identities and empower themselves by establishing a relationship with the cosmic order and its creator. There are various ways to accomplish this:

One may seek the help of a competent guru, who, after evaluating the seeker's strengths, guides the seeker in choosing the approach that best fits him or her and leads him or her to the way to divinity. Hindus recognize the great saints of all other religions as gurus.

Hinduism encourages total freedom in choosing one or many paths toward spirituality. Broadly speaking, these paths fall into four major categories: (1) Karma Yoga, or non-attached selfless action; (2) Bhakti Yoga, total surrender to God and seeing God in all; (3) Jnana Yoga, the development of intellectual ability to find the ultimate reality beyond worldly delusions; and (4) Raja Yoga, the experience of altered states of consciousness to get deeper into the human subconscious (Singh, 1990).

Hindus view spiritual life as a journey. While traveling, one may want to rest a while and enjoy the beauty of the surroundings. Different approaches to spirituality are viewed as resting places where a seeker can relax for a while. The only caution is that the traveler should not lose sight of the destination.

Because of its circular thinking, Hinduism does not see any danger for a seeker in starting at any point that she or he may choose, because eventually the seeker will complete the circle in the same way as others did.

There is an element of truth in each belief system. One can reach the top of a mountain from many directions. What is important is persistence in climbing it despite the slippery stones and thorny bushes.

Since Brahman is both the primordial and constituent cause of this universe, all objects and beings are merely different manifestations of the same original energy that is Brahman, the energy that grows and multiplies and becomes many. A Hindu invariably sees unity in multiplicity and diversity in unity.

The Life Cycle

With a view to balancing the four aims of life, Hinduism conceived of four stages of life which are reminiscent of Erik Erikson's eight stages (1964): Brahmacharya, from birth to age 25, is the period dedicated to learning self-discipline and formal education; Grihastha, from 25 to 50, is the period of living a householder's life, supporting family and social institutions through work and donations and taking care of the indigent and the needy; Vanprastha, from 50 to 75, is the stage of gradual retirement dedicated to social welfare; and Sannyasa, from 75 on, is the stage of gradual detachment from the world, with full dedication to God and humanity. In order to facilitate a smooth transition from one stage to another, Hindus have developed a range of ceremonies and rituals in which the entire family and clan participate with great enthusiasm. These ceremonies aim at strengthening the family bond and the fulfillment of "social dharma"—one's duties and responsibilities to the family, community, and the world at large (Subramuniyaswami, 1993). They prepare people for the cyclic stages of life from birth to death.

One major difference between Erikson's stages and those of Hinduism is that the Hindu conceptualization is not necessarily uni-dimensional but circular; for example, Hindus see aspects of childhood in old age, and vice versa. Old age is seen as preparation for another childhood after re-birth. Erikson called old age "the second childhood"; Hindus see the regressive childlike behavior of an old person as a kind of preparation for the next childhood. This gives a new perspective to caretakers, who can view their task as helping the elderly to a brighter future rather than just accepting death. Such a paradigm shift helps them to see an elderly person as a future child, enkindling a great motivation to help build his or her future life. It was this kind of comparison of the stages of development in the West and in India that inspired Erikson to study the life of Gandhi, a man who basically defied the Western way of looking at the stages of life.

THE HINDU VIEW OF HEALTH AND WELL-BEING

The question of the health and well-being of all has been a major concern of Hindus. The ancient Indian science of medicine, *Ayurveda,* focuses on treating mind and body through mind training, yoga, meditation, herbal/natural remedies, diet and a balanced life. For the last three decades, there has been a great amount of research in the West exploring connections between body, mind, and spiritual values (Benson, 1996; Gartner, Larson, & Allen, 1996; Pargament, 1997; Richards and Bergin, 1997). The Ayurveda had discovered the alliance between body, mind, and spirit thousands of years ago.

THE HINDU THEORY OF SOCIAL WELFARE

Hinduism, from the Vedic age to current times, has been highly oriented toward social welfare. Since everything is spiritual, Hindus see social welfare as spiritual. Dharma is defined as a set of principles that promote the welfare and happiness of all, and its purpose is to facilitate an individual's and society's growth. That is one of the primary reasons Hindus do not have a formal method of conversion. Their main focus is conversion to a broader worldview, not to an organized religion.

The main objective of Hinduism has been to develop an ideal society conducive to everyone's growth and welfare. The dream of Rama-rajya—an ideal state run by Rama, an incarnation of God, where truthfulness, honesty, and equal justice for all are preserved—has stayed with Hindus for thousands of years. Many countries in Southeast Asia share this vision by re-enacting the story of Rama every year. The Hindu concept of social welfare differs from the Western view in many ways. The Western approach is problem-focused and individualistic, the Hindu approach is social-organismic and interdependent. Hinduism has no Western concept of duality and conflict between good and evil, mind and body, or man and nature. The Hindu concept of social welfare is wholistic. Social welfare is not separate from Dharma, philosophy, epistemology, art, and science. Each of these, in one way or the other, is related to social welfare.

The Wholistic Concept of Dharma

As mentioned earlier, Hindus don't consider following a particular leader or book as Dharma. For them, giving donations to a poor and needy person, entertaining humanistic thoughts, going to holy places and meeting with holy people, and realizing one's inner potentials to their fullest by getting rid of Maya are all part of Dharma. A Hindu is supposed to donate 10% of his income for the purpose of Dharma and universal social welfare.

Dharma, being the central essence of Hinduism, has been conceived and classified in a variety of ways. One classification specifies four kinds of Dharma: human Dharma is showing love and respect for humanity as a whole; the personal Dharma emphasizes self-improvement and spirituality leading to salvation; social Dharma aims at fulfilling social obligations, including helping the poor and the needy; universal Dharma encourages actions conducive to the welfare of all of nature (Subramuniyaswami, 1993).

There is also the concept of *chaturdharma,* i.e., the four religious laws governing life: Rita, the universal laws; Varna dharma, the social obligations; Asrama dharma, the responsibilities of the four stages of life; and Svadharma, a set of personal principles and practices that one should follow. Following these laws is crucial for one's psychological and spiritual growth. It is because of its emphasis on the psychological aspects of human functioning that many scholars view Hinduism more as a psychological theory than a religion (Aurobindo, 1995).

Hinduism encourages a universalistic worldview and individual choices. Unlike Western religious traditions, it does not discriminate between "religious" and "secular" and does not see any conflict between the two concepts (Subramuniyaswami, 1993).

The Cyclic Theory

The entire universe is engaged in a whirling flow of change and movement symbolized in dancing Shiva. Galaxies soar in movement; atoms swirl in movement (Subramuniyaswami, 1993). In its emphasis on cause and effect, the cyclic theory is related to Karma theory. The cyclic theory has great significance for the Hindu concept of social welfare. First, it emphasizes positive changes and alerts one to negative changes in life. Since change is the law of nature, you never stay at one point in life. If you are poor today, you may become rich tomorrow. And if you are rich, thank God, but don't be arrogant. Be prudent and care for the poor, as you might be poor tomorrow. The cyclic theory, like systems theory and the law of entropy, assumes that any closed system tends to decay, including a closed religion. That is why Hindus rarely resent religious reforms and are able to integrate diverse concepts.

The cyclic theory brings the entire universe closer, emphasizing a state of balance and interdependence. The theory highlights the need for self/other balance in interpersonal relationships. Similarly, problems and solutions are related in a cyclic fashion. What may be perceived as a solution to one problem may also be a genesis of another problem. New problems need new solutions. For example, a divorce, as a good solution to a messy marriage situation, might create new problems for parents and/or children.

The Karma Theory

As mentioned earlier, Karma is one of the most significant theories affecting Hindu thinking and behavior in everyday life. Karma has three popular meanings: it can be an act or deed, the principle of cause and effect, or the consequences of an act. Each action has a reaction. A good act will bring positive reactions and a bad act will bring negative ones. The theory lays the ground for moral laws of cause and effect and encourages people to engage in good deeds. Selfish acts or making others suffer will bring negative results (karma). It encourages an individual to create his or her own destiny by accepting responsibility and accountability for his or her own words, thoughts, behaviors, and actions and take appropriate steps to produce positive Karma (Venkateswaran, 1995).

Gandhi's strategy of using non-violent means to fight the British in a way was based on the principle of karma. It was Gandhi's genius to closely examine the cyclic processes in human minds and to understand how a violent reaction evokes hostility, insecurity, and retaliation. Non-violent reactions to a violent situation, on the other hand, provoke a sense of guilt, responsibility, pity, self-condemnation, and remorse on the part of the perpetrator of violence. Gandhi discovered the psychological power of non-violence. And the whole world has seen how correct he was.

The Hindu theory of karma also looks at karma as the cause of bondage. The moment I do a favor for someone, I expect thanks. Hinduism encourages doing good to others out of a sense of duty without attachment and expectations. This is the main theme of the Bhagavadgita. Krishna advises Arjuna that fighting for social justice is his sacred responsibility, i.e., Dharma. The Hindu theory of suffering is also based on this concept of action-reaction. Usually three kinds of reactions lead one to suffering: overreacting to an unwanted situation, which wastes energy that could otherwise have been used to find its solution; ignoring possible ways that one might be responsible for creating a negative situation; and expecting others to change but refusing to improve one's own behavior. The moment one rises above these three reactions, the misery disappears. Gita calls this *Nishkama karma*—acting with objective detachment.

Nature worship is an integral part of Hinduism. Many mountains, rivers, trees, plants, animals, and birds are considered holy. Hindus believe that humans are guests on the planet and must show respect to nature. The Vedas and other literature are full of prayers to different aspects of nature. The Aryans visualized different aspects of nature as gods. They saw nature as the source of life for humans. The mother earth, the provider of all resources, has a very special place in Hinduism.

The Organismic Theory of Society

No other civilization launched such a large-scale social experiment as the Hindus did, in the form of division of responsibilities in society, which later on developed into the caste system. Hindus wanted to create a well-integrated society, each individual complementing each other and working as a team to fulfill the various needs of the society.

One of the significant aspects of the caste system was the importance of the skills associated with different professions of each caste. The contributions made by each segment of the society were so vital that people did not want their trade secrets to die if their children moved to a new occupation (Klostermaier, 1994). They passed their family trade secrets from generation to generation, but when India faced invasions, the system became rigid and inflexible.

The Importance of Sacrifice and Charity

Hindus call charity *yajna*. Yajna is any act of selfless sacrifice and fulfillment of one's life duties. It is any pious or devotional work or any deed done with a sense of dedication and with the welfare of others in mind without any kind of selfish motive.

In the Gita, Krishna describes life as a yajna. There are various kinds of yajna:

- Dravya yajna is the construction of wells, tanks, temples, and public houses for free lodging of travelers, providing food, clothing, water, medicine, and books to the starving, afflicted, invalid, helpless, and ailing.
- Tapah yajna is sacrifice in the form of penance, going through hardship in order to help others without desire for reward.
- Yoga yajna is rigorous practice of yoga (Goyandaka, 1978).

The great Indian social reformers like Gandhi, Vinoba Bhave, Swami Vivekanada, and Swami Dayananda Saraswati treated their lives as a yajna and changed the face of India and the modern world in many ways.

As both social welfare and spiritual growth were interwoven with the four stages of life, the family and the extended family system were considered crucial for socio-spiritual purposes. The extended family took care of the indigent, the disabled, and the unemployed.

There are also many Hindu social institutions that take care of the needy and the indigent. Temples have been providing shelter and food to people for thousands of years. The Ashrams of the rishis are always open for needy people to stay and eat and gradually put their life together. The places of pilgrimage take care of the poor. In the temples and public places *Bhandaras* distribute food, clothes, medicine, and even cash. This is not something new in India. For example, Ashok, a great king in India in the 2nd century A.D., constructed a 2000-mile road from north to south, now called the Grand Trunk Road, and had hundreds of shelters built along it, which provided free food and water to all, irrespective of their caste or creed.

GENDER ISSUES

Hindus visualize God as both male and female and also as beyond any gender. But the respect and worship of God as mother holds a very special position. As a great philosopher and yogi of the 20th century, Sri Aurobindo put it, "The mother is the consciousness and force of the Divine, or, it may be said, she is the divine in its consciousness force" (Aurobindo, 1928).

It was this concept of feminine divinity that led the Vedic Aryans to have many women scholars, including Maitreyi, Gargi, and Katyayani. Patanjali had many female students of grammar and philosophy (Machwe, 1994). The verses and mantras of at least twenty women scholars and saints are part of the Vedas. Women were not discriminated against for initiation into priesthood or education. It was because of their systematic molestation by invaders that women withdrew from public life, only to re-emerge as powerful partners in social growth after India gained independence.

IMPLICATIONS FOR SOCIAL WORK PRACTICE

The strength that Hinduism has shown in surviving as a major religion despite thousands of years of systematic efforts to annihilate it is intrinsically embedded in each Hindu client, no matter how impoverished or physically disabled he or she happens to be. A social worker must be aware of and have respect for various aspects of Hinduism when helping a Hindu client:

- Respect for the client's right to self-determination in solving problems, through seeking family support, offering prayers to God, paying respect to ancestors, offering fire sacrifices, making trips to sacred places, and so on.
- Respect for the client's family system, the close relationships between parents and children, husband and wife, and other close interpersonal

relationships with friends and neighbors. Respect for parents and the elderly and age-old family traditions. (For example, it is considered a sign of respect to address elderly people as "uncle," "aunt," or "grandparent," rather than addressing them by name.) Any social work intervention that violates the sanctity of these close bonds could be counterproductive.

- Respect for the age-old Hindu philosophy that acknowledges the immense nature of this universe and the cyclic, action-and-reaction (karma) theory of life. The karma theory could be used to engage a Hindu in philanthropic and social welfare projects, to help others improve their current lives and sow seeds for a better future life for himself during the next birth.
- Respect for Hindu symbolism. The complexity of the Hindu worldview, as noted above, called for a range of symbolism, including idol worship, the theory of reincarnation, and so on, which a social work practitioner must respect as a means of mental concentration, meditation, and inner development for a Hindu.
- Respect for the Hindu practice of personal hospitality. A social worker might find himself or herself being offered tea, coffee, or gifts by the client.

Since a Hindu client would prefer to have a personal relationship rather than a professional one, the social worker must be careful to maintain a fine balance between the two.

- Any intervention by the social worker must make sense in terms of each individual's personal growth, as the very essence of Hinduism consists in encouraging each individual's personal growth rather than following religion as a social institution.
- Respect for spirituality as a way of life and for Hinduism's lack of distinction between spirituality and a secular life. Since Hinduism by its very nature is all-inclusive, it is hard to discriminate between what is spiritual or religious and what is secular. Hinduism encourages individual experimentation to explore the spirituality within and looks at life as a process of attaining spirituality. Any effort at problem solving must keep in perspective the individual's striving for his or her spiritual growth, and the solution must fit into the client's spiritual worldview.

CONCLUSION

As the world is becoming more interconnected, the need for social work education that prepares students to understand and integrate concepts from different religions so that they can work effectively with clients from different religious-spiritual backgrounds cannot be overemphasized (Miller, 1999). This chapter has explored some of the social and spiritual ideals and practices of Hinduism and explains its broader emphasis on human welfare and universal ecology, to illustrate how its age-old traditions and practices can be used in helping a client with Hindu background.

As discussed earlier, the Hindu concept of social welfare encompasses a very broad perspective, covering various dimensions of human existence. Hindus view reality on three levels: *Bhautic,* or worldly reality; *Adhi Bhautic,* the higher reality beyond sensual perception; and *Adhi Daivic,* the highest reality, the divine spirituality. The concept of social welfare also, therefore, covers the above three dimensions.

In its broad approach to life and humanity, the Hindu social welfare system emphasizes a balance of psychological, ecological, and spiritual welfare for all. Hinduism emphasizes every aspect of human functioning, including dharma (righteous living), artha (materialistic prosperity), kama (fulfillment of worldly desires), and moksha (desire for salvation). Hinduism has a unique respect for nature and all creatures inhabiting the universe. It emphasizes achieving a state of mind of eternal joy and bliss and encourages people to act as psychological supports to each other. Hinduism looks at every aspect of life and every phenomenon in the universe as divine. It emphasizes attaining a tranquil state of mind, which leads to an individual's liberation in this life, i.e., "living liberation," rather than liberation after death (Fort and Mumme, 1996). It is possible to summarize the Hindu approach to social welfare in one sentence: Hinduism aims to help each individual to realize and get in touch with the divinity within and all around and to treat everyone on this earth as the member of one family.

REFERENCES

Aurobindo, Sri. (1928). *Essays on the Gita.* Pondichery, India: Sri Aurobindo Ashram.

Aurobindo, Sri. (1995). The secret of the Veda. Twin Lakes, WI: Lotus Light Publications.

Benson, H. (1996). *Timeless healing: The power and biology of belief.* New York: Scribner.

Bharti Krishna Tirtha, S. (1964). *Sanatana dharma.* Bombay, India: Bharti Vidya Bhavan.

Chidbhavananda, S. (1994). *The Bhagavad Gita.* Tirupparaitturai: Sri Ramakrishna Tapovanam, IV:13, V:10, XV:13.

Emmons, R. A. (1999). *The psychology of ultimate concerns.* New York: The Guilford Press.

Erikson, Erik. (1964). *Childhood and society.* New York: Norton.

Fort, Andrew O., and Mumme, Patricia Y. (Eds.) (1996). *Living liberation in Hindu thought.* Albany: State University of New York Press.

Gartner, J., Larson, D. B., & Allen, G. D. (1996). Religious commitment, mental health, and prosocial behavior: A review of the empirical literature. In E. Shafranske (Ed.), *Religion and the clinical practice of psychology* (pp. 187–214). Washington, DC: American Psychological Association.

Goyandaka, J. (1978). *Srimad Bhagavadgita.* Gorakhpur, India: Gita Press.

Joshi, T. L. (1996). *Critique of Hinduism and other religions.* Bombay: Popular Prakashan.

Klostermaier, K. K. (1994). *A survey of Hinduism.* Albany: State University of New York Press.

Knipe, D. M. (1991). *Hinduism, experiments in the sacred.* San Francisco: Harper.

Kung, H. (Ed.) (1996). *Yes to a global ethic.* New York: Continuum.

Machve, P. (1994). *Hinduism: Its contribution to science and civilization.* New Delhi: Machwe Prakashan.

Miller, R. M. (1999). Diversity training in spiritual and religious issues. In W. R. Miller (Ed.), *Integrating spirituality into treatment.* Washington, DC: American Psychological Association.

Pargament, K. I. (1997). *The psychology of religion and coping.* New York: Macmillan.

Richards, P. S., & Bergin, A. E. (1997). *A spiritual strategy for counseling and psychotherapy.* Washington, DC: American Psychological Association.

Singh, K. (1990). *Essays on Hinduism.* New Delhi: Ratna Sagar Pvt Ltd.

Singh, R. N., and De Lange, J. (1992). Perception and reality: The cognitive approach and Vedanta philosophy. *The Indian Journal of Social Work,* LIII:4, 661–668.

Smith, H. (1991). *The world's religions.* San Francisco: Harper.

Subramuniyaswami, S. S. (1993). *Dancing with siva.* Kapaa, Hawaii: Himalayan Academy.

Venkateswaran, T. K. (1995). Hinduism, a portrait. In J. D. Beversluis (Ed.), *A sourcebook for earth's community of religions.* New York: Global Education Associates.

Vivekananda, S. (1963). Inspired talks. In *The complete works of Swami Vivekananda.* Calcutta: Advaita Ashrama.

ADDITIONAL RESOURCES

Addresses

Vedanta Press Books
Vedanta Society of Southern California
1946 Vedanta Place
Hollywood, CA 90068-3996

Vedanta Society of Northern California
2323 Vallejo St.
San Francisco, CA 94123
Phone: (415) 922-2323

RamaKrishna Monastery
1440 Upas St.
San Diego, CA 92103
Phone: (619) 291-9377

Vivekananda Vedanta Society
5423 South Hyde Park Blvd.
Chicago, IL 60615
Phone: (773) 363-0027

Mother's Trust/Mother's Place
Interfaith Educational Community
6676 122nd Ave.
Ganges, MI 49508
Phone: (616) 543-3951

The Rama Krishna-Vedanta Society
of Massachusetts
58 Deerfield St.
Boston, MA 02215
Phone: (617) 536-5320

Vedanta Society of St. Louis
205 South Skinker Blvd.
St. Louis, MO 63105
Phone: (314) 721-5118

RamaKrishna Vedanta Center
17 East 94th St.
New York, NY 10028
Phone: (212) 534-9445

Vedanta Society
34 West 71st St.
New York, NY 10023
Phone: (212) 877-9197

Vedanta Society of Western
Washington
2716 Broadway East
Seattle, WA 98102
Phone: (206) 323-1228

Vedanta Center of Greater
Washington D.C.
3001 Bel Pre Road
Silver Springs, MD 20906
Phone: (301) 603-1772

For Sri Aurobindo Centers and
Study Groups around the country,
contact
Auroville Internationale USA
P.O. Box 877
Santa Cruz, CA 95061

California Institute of Integral
Studies
1453 Mission St.
San Francisco, CA 94103
Phone: (415) 575-6100

South Asia Books
P.O. Box 502
Columbia, MO 65205
Phone: (573) 474-0116

Web Sites

www.hindunet.org/
www.hinduism.co.za

GLOSSARY

Aryans The early settlers of India.

Ayurveda The ancient medical science of India.

Bhandaras Places where free food is distributed for the poor.

Brahman The ultimate power/energy behind the entire universe, the Highest Reality.

Chatur-dharama The four laws related to the cosmic universe, society, the four stages of life, and one's personal life.

Dharma The Hindu concept of religion that focuses on personal spiritual integration and development.

Guru A personal spiritual teacher.

Ishvara The personal aspect of the Brahman who takes care of the universe and all its beings.

Maya The outer appearance of inner reality.

Om The symbol of divinity at all levels of existence in the universe.

Puja A Hindu worship ceremony.

Prasad The sweets distributed after a worship ceremony.

Puranas Mythological stories illustrating moral behavior.

Sanatana Dharma A name for the Hindu belief system that signifies its eternal nature.

Sannyasini A female ascetic.

Sattyagraha The term coined by Gandhi for non-violent resistance based on spirituality.

Smriti The Hindu books of moral laws.

Swami A male ascetic, a self-realized person.

Upanishad Deep spiritual literature based on dialogues between teachers and their disciples.

Vedas The most ancient sacred books of the Hindus.

BUDDHISM

EDWARD R. CANDA

CHAPTER 4

HISTORY AND GENERAL CHARACTERISTICS OF BUDDHISM

Buddhism is a religious tradition that originated in the area of present-day Nepal and India about 2500 years ago (Gethin, 1998; Harvey, 1990; Nielsen et al., 1993). Buddhism is more properly known as the *Buddha Dharma* (Sanskrit),[1] meaning "the teaching or way of the Buddha, the Awakened One." This name highlights the core concern of Buddhism: to wake up to the true nature of the human condition and reality.

Thanks to Hae Kwang Zen Master (Stanley Lombardo, Ph.D.) of the Kansas Zen Center and Professor Daniel Stevenson, Ph.D., of the University of Kansas Department of Religious Studies, for helpful suggestions regarding this chapter

[1]Most Buddhist philosophical terms originated from the classical languages of the scriptures of South Asia, i.e., Sanskrit and Pali, as well as other Asian languages such as Chinese. In this chapter, the pronunciation of Buddhist terms derived from Asian languages will be rendered in English letters and the original language will be specified at first use of the term.

[2]Historical dates will be given in the style commonly accepted for comparative religious studies. B.C.E. means "before the common era," which the Gregorian calendar begins 2001 years ago. For example, 566 B.C.E. equals 2567 years ago. C.E. means "in the common era." For example, 500 C.E. (or 500) equals 1501 years ago.

The founder of the Buddha Dharma, *Siddhartha Gautama*, lived from about 566 (or 563) to 486 (or 483) B.C.E.[2] According to common belief, he was the son of a local king. As will be described later, he renounced the privileged and sheltered life of royalty in order to find out for himself what human existence is about. When he woke up to reality, he came to be called the Buddha, which means the Awakened (or Enlightened) One. The Buddha spread his insights widely for about 45 years until his death. His teachings became the foundation for an extremely diverse range of types of Buddhism that vary in cultural and philosophical nuances. However, all the types of Buddhism share the belief that if human beings are to be truly fulfilled, they must wake up from egocentric illusions and attachments.

In the first century of the development of Buddhism, the Buddha and his disciples spread the teachings, refined the spiritual disciplines of meditation and lifestyle, and organized communities of monks, nuns, and laypeople in various regions of India (Schuhmacher & Woerner, 1994). For the next few centuries, rival interpretations of doctrine and practice developed within the oldest branch of Buddhism, called *Theravada* (Pali), "the Way of the Elders." Between the first and the seventh centuries C.E., a second major branch developed as the Buddha Dharma spread through China, Korea, and Japan. It is called *Mahayana* (Sanskrit), "the Great Vehicle" of Buddhism. Mahayana developed with major influences from Chinese Taoism and Confucianism and other local religious traditions of East Asia. After the 7th century CE, as Indian Buddhism spread to Tibet and central Asia, a third major branch, *Vajrayana* (Sanskrit), "the Diamond Vehicle," formed. Vajrayana incorporated aspects of Tibetan shamanism and Indian *tantra* (Sanskrit) practices. Tantra practices involve meditation and ritual disciplines intended to generate spiritual energy and insight. After the 13th century C.E., Buddhism declined significantly in India but flourished throughout East and Southeast Asia.

Followers of the Theravada branch pride themselves on remaining closest to the original Indian forms of Buddhism (Gethin, 1998). There are now over 100 million followers, mainly in Sri Lanka, Burma, Thailand, Cambodia, and Laos. The Theravada branch uses scriptures in the Pali language. It emphasizes the ideal of the *arahat* (Pali), a person who has extinguished all illusions and egoistic attachments and enters *Nibbana* (Pali) or *Nirvana* (Sanskrit) at death. In this sense, nirvana means "cessation": the extinction of personal ego-bound identity through realization of oneness with all. The historical Buddha is honored as one who achieved full enlightenment and showed the path for others to achieve it. He is not regarded as a deity formally, but some folk traditions treat him as such.

The Mahayana branch of Buddhism flourishes today, with 500 million to 1 billion followers, mainly in China, Taiwan, South Korea, Japan, and Vietnam. It emphasizes scriptures in the Sanskrit language as well as scriptures and commentaries developed by revered teachers or attributed to Buddhas in local languages, such as Chinese. The Mahayana ideal is the Bodhisattva (Sanskrit), which means "Enlightenment Being." A Bodhisattva is a being who cultivates enlightenment, not only for one's own salvation, but also for the compassionate service of all beings. There are also various kinds of Buddhas (fully enlightened beings) recognized in addition to the historical Buddha. While the Vajrayana tradition utilizes the Tibetan and Sanskrit languages and has certain distinctive attributes, it shares with Mahayana an emphasis on doctrine and ritual and is sometimes considered a subtype of it.

Since one of the most influential types of Buddhism in social work and psychotherapy is Zen, it should be noted that Zen Buddhism is a school of Mahayana. The term *Zen* is an English adaptation from the Japanese language. However, this school of Buddhism developed in China (where it was named *Ch'an*) around the 5th or 6th century. Ch'an spread to Korea (where it is called *Son*) and Japan. The term Ch'an comes from the Sanskrit *dhyana,* which means "deep meditation" (Gethin, 1998). Hence, the various versions of Zen all emphasize that practitioners should emulate the historical Buddha by engaging in rigorous meditation intended to yield direct insight into the nature of reality, rather than relying only on religious doctrines.

In Mahayana and Vajrayana, certain highly realized beings, such as Buddhas and Bodhisattvas, are represented anthropomorphically in iconography and ritual. Some practitioners relate to these beings as deities through prayer and worship. However, they are more formally regarded as symbolic representations of various aspects of the true nature of the universe and of human beings. For example, there are numerous Buddhas in addition to the historical Buddha. These Buddhas are fully awakened beings dedicated to particular qualities of enlightenment. One of the most popular in East Asia is Amitabha Buddha (Sanskrit), the Buddha of Infinite Light. In the Pure Land sect, which has numerous followers in East Asia and the United States, Amitabha is regarded as lord of the Western Heavenly Paradise, who oversees a place of bliss for the souls of the deceased. Adherents believe that devoted chanting of Amitabha's name will lead to rebirth in the Western Heavenly Paradise. Another popular Buddha is Maitreya (Sanskrit), who waits in *Tusita* (Sanskrit) Heaven for the appropriate time to come to earth to usher in a new era of spiritual awareness.

Among Bodhisattvas, perhaps the most popular is Kwan Shi Yin (Chinese), the Bodhisattva of Compassion (Blofeld, 1988). Kwan Shi Yin literally means, "perceiving the sound of the universe." This Bodhisattva has the power to perceive the cries of suffering of all beings and to reach out to help them. Some Mahayanists take this being literally and pray to her or him. Kwan Shi Yin can be represented in male, female, or androgynous form. But in typical Mahayana style, Bodhisattvas are also understood to be metaphors for aspects of truly enlightened human nature. Thus, everyone who is dedicated to compassion for all beings can be considered as manifesting Kwan Shi Yin's quality. Every act of compassion can be regarded as Kwan Shi Yin in action. Thus, Buddhas and Bodhisattvas serve both as ideals to which people may aspire and as representations of aspects of humanity's already present true nature of wisdom, compassion, and correct action.

Buddhism in the United States

Buddhism began to grow in the United States during the middle to late 19th century C.E., fueled by immigration from China and Japan to the West coast and Hawaii as well as by the European American transcendentalist and theosophical movements (Fields, 1992; Morreale, 1998; Prebish, 1999; Prebish & Tanaka, 1998). During the 1950s and 1960s, counter-cultural groups such as beatniks and hippies stimulated more interest in Asian philosophies and religions as alternatives to established American religions that were deemed too much part of the status quo. This was also a time when Buddhist monks and scholars from Asia were rapidly increasing their teaching and establishment of Buddhist centers that were focused on attracting non-Asian members. After 1975, the influx of more than 800,000 refugees from Southeast Asia brought a rapid increase of Theravada practitioners. Baumann (cited in Prebish, 1999, p. 272) estimated that by the mid 1990s, there were 3 to 4 million Buddhists in the United States, including about 800,000 European American adherents. During the past decade, the number of Buddhist practice centers has grown most quickly (Morreale, 1998). As of 1997, Morreale identified 1062 Buddhist centers representing four major orientations (423 Mahayana, 352 Vajrayana, 152 Theravada, and 135 polydenominational).

Many observers note a contrast between Buddhist communities that are primarily made up of Asian immigrant and refugee populations and those that are primarily European American in membership (Prebish & Tanaka, 1998). These are by no means mutually exclusive communities, however, as membership and participation cross these lines. Further, the founding teachers of the mainly European American Buddhist centers were usually Asians. The primarily Asian American Buddhist communities in the United States tend to be rooted in particular cultural and linguistic traditions (e.g., Cambodian, Chinese, Japanese, Korean, Lao, Vietnamese, etc.). They also tend to provide a wide array of community support services and activities integrated with the daily family life of members (Canda & Phaobtong, 1992; Furuto, Biswas, Chung, Murase, & Ross-Sherif, 1992; Timberlake & Cook, 1984). The primarily European American communities tend to focus on meditation practice. As they have been maturing in development, many of these centers have been making attempts to formalize rituals for the life cycle and to offer a wide range of social support for members, especially suited to the urban, post-industrial lifestyle. These centers have also been active in broadening Buddhists' concern with women's rights, social activism, environmental protection, and gay and lesbian issues.

As this brief overview reveals, there is tremendous diversity within Buddhism, both globally and within the United States. Any social worker working with a Buddhist client would have to start by understanding the particular form and social context of Buddhism embraced by that client.

THE CENTRAL GUIDING STORY OF BUDDHISM

The story of the life of Siddhartha Gautama provides an exemplary guide for followers of all forms of Buddhism. There are many different versions of this story, including events from his previous incarnations. This recounting will summarize elements that are common to most versions of his life as founder of Buddhism (Gethin, 1998; Hahn, 1991; Harvey, 1990; Herold, 1954; Schumacher & Woerner, 1994; Zo, 1975).

It is said that Siddhartha's mother, Mayadevi, dreamed that a divine being took the form of an elephant and magically entered her side, presaging an auspicious birth. Siddhartha was born into the Sakya clan, which was headed by his father, Suddhodana. The birth occurred while Mayadevi was traveling through a forest, the Lumbini grove, on the way to give birth at the home of her relatives. It is said that Siddhartha emerged from her side as a young boy, already able to speak. He proclaimed that he was supreme because, in this life, he would attain enlightenment and liberation from death and rebirth. Lotus blossoms sprang up where he stepped. Unfortunately, his mother died 7 days later. Siddhartha was raised by his aunt, the second wife of Suddhodana.

Soothsayers foretold that this amazing baby would grow up to be either a great ruler, expanding his father's domain, or a great sage, bringing truth to the world. Siddhartha's father was pleased by the auspicious signs that surrounded his son. But he wanted to be sure that his son became a great king rather than a sage detached from the world. So he kept Siddhartha confined to the palace to live in protected luxury.

At the age of 16, Siddhartha married Yashodhara and 5 years later, their son Rahula was born. Though Siddhartha enjoyed life with his family, two big questions continued to nag him: What is life like outside this little world of mine? What is the meaning of life? At the age of 29, he convinced his charioteer to take him outside the palace on four occasions. During the first three excursions, he saw what life was like for most people. He witnessed a severely ill person, an aged and decrepit person, and a corpse. He realized that his sheltered life had obscured the facts of the common lot of people: sickness, old age, and death. On the fourth excursion, Siddhartha saw a monk who had renounced worldly attachments to pursue the answer to the meaning of life. Some say that these four people were really manifestations of Hindu deities who appeared to him to guide him onto his spiritual path. Siddhartha could no longer be satisfied with the comforts of palace and family, which came to seem like a gilded cage. So he set out on the way of the monk. Leaving his wife and son was difficult, but his personal preferences were outweighed by his commitment to understand the reason for human suffering and to help others with the answer.

He studied with a variety of ascetic practitioners of meditation and yoga, trying to pierce through to the essential truth about life. Although he found that extreme ascetic practices provided some insights, they did not yield the answers he sought. Finally, at the age of 35, he took up residence in the Bodhgaya forest and meditated under a tree, determined to persist until he understood the cause of human suffering. He continued for 49 days, overcoming numerous distracting desires and temptations. On the last day, he overcame the temptations of the evil one, Mara, and stretched out his hand to touch the earth, receiving its affirmation of his spiritual merit. Upon seeing the morning star rise, he attained complete enlightenment.

For a while he remained in silent meditation, knowing that the truth revealed to him could not be communicated in words. However, several spiritual practitioners who had been his previous companions were impressed by his radiance and obvious attainment. They convinced him to share his insight with others. For a period of 45 years, he taught others and established the first communities of Buddhist monks and nuns. He propounded a Middle Way, which did not succumb to the extremes of harsh asceticism or indulgence in inappropriate desires. Indeed, his wife and son became a nun and a monk under his teaching. Siddhartha died at the age of 80, after eating some spoiled mushrooms. While he was dying, the Buddha exhorted his followers, "Pursue the path of enlightenment by your own diligent and unrelenting effort."

The Buddha's core teaching can be summarized in the Four Noble Truths. The first truth is that existence is characterized by physical and mental suffering related to pain and decay in the body, unattainable desires, unwanted afflictions, and dissatisfaction with the transitory nature of the world. The law of impermanence is such that everything held onto with desire will pass away at some point, giving a sense of loss. Health, wealth, relationships, and life itself all pass away. The second truth is that this suffering is caused by inappropriate desires that cause one unwittingly to cling to the cycle of death and rebirth. The third truth is that suffering can be eliminated by stopping all egoistic desires and attachments. The fourth truth is that egoistic desires and attachments can be discarded by following a lifestyle based on the Eightfold Path. This path consists of eight "perfections" that can be summarized as aspects of correct perception, correct conduct, and correct meditation.

Though not all Buddhists take the magical contents of Buddha's life story literally, the essentials of the story serve as a model for all followers of the Buddha Dharma. We are not to be distracted by inappropriate desires or aversions. Each of us is challenged to wake up to the truth of who we really are. What this is cannot be put in words, but it can be realized through diligent effort.

This story opens up several other key insights shared by Buddhists and refined from the Hindu context in which the Buddha lived (Gethin, 1998; Harvey, 1990; Schuhmacher & Woerner, 1994; Williams, 1989). The Buddha broke the bonds that held him into the cycle of death and rebirth, which involves numerous types of suffering. These bonds are held together by *karma* (Sanskrit), which literally means "action." The law of karma is that one's actions (and especially their intentions) sow the seeds for future results that affect oneself. Actions of compassion generate spiritual merit and propel one toward a better rebirth. Actions motivated by greed, hatred, and delusion destroy one's spiritual merit and propel one toward a rebirth of more suffering. The law of karma is considered a natural operation of the cosmos, rather than a matter of reward or punishment by a divine being. Meditation can yield insight into the karmic patterns (habits of thought and behavior, for example) that are harmful to oneself and others. Karmic knots can be untied, behaviors can be changed for the better, and spiritual merit can be increased. Finally, when one achieves complete enlightenment, like a Buddha, karma no longer traps one in an involuntary cycle of suffering and rebirth.

Karma is not just an individual matter, though. All things come into existence through mutual influence and causation. All things are woven together in a web of interconnectedness. Even to think of oneself as a separate individual is a fundamental delusion at the root of selfishness and harmful actions. This insight is similar to the wholistic perspective of dynamic systems theory in social work (Macy, 1991; Robbins, Chatterjee & Canda, 1998). Thus, everyone's patterns of karma and merit interpenetrate. Some Buddhist practices involve accumulating spiritual merit for oneself and transferring it to others, to alleviate their suffering and to assist them toward enlightenment.

As a person realizes that all beings are interconnected and also that one has shared their form of existence at some point in countless previous lifetimes, the sense of empathy naturally deepens. Empathy generates compassion, or *karuna* (Sanskrit), a sense of loving and caring put into skillful action to benefit others (Blofeld, 1988; Brandon, 1976; Canda, 1995; Eppsteiner, 1988; Keefe, 1975; Williams, 1989). The Buddha sought enlightenment not only for his own sake, but so that he could teach and help others. In the Mahayana and Vajrayana traditions, compassion is the supreme virtue, embodied by the Bodhisattvas who purposely remain within the cycle of death and rebirth in order to continue helping all other beings to attain enlightenment. A primary commitment made in all traditions of Buddhism is to further the well-being and enlightenment of all.

MY PATH INTO BUDDHISM AND ITS INFLUENCE ON MY APPROACH TO SOCIAL WORK

A recent national survey of NASW practitioner members indicated that about 10% of religious adherents combined more than one spiritual affiliation. The most common of these combinations was Christian with Buddhist. "Five percent of Christians affiliated with Buddhism, accounting for 48% of Buddhist respondents" (Canda & Furman, 1999, p. 94). I too have multiple spiritual affiliations. My relation to Buddhism is not typical of most Buddhists in the world, in that I am an American Zen practitioner whose roots are Christian. However, Buddhism everywhere generally has been open to coexistence and combination with the pre-existing spiritual traditions of the cultures it contacts. So in this sense, my experience reflects a recent manifestation of a very old Buddhist pattern.

I grew up in a very devout Catholic family and attended Catholic elementary and high schools. Our cultural style of Catholicism was influenced by our Czech immigrant history. Christian spirituality infused all aspects of our life at church, home, and work. I was inspired by the mystical tradition within Catholicism to learn practices of prayer and meditation that would enhance awareness of God.

By the time I reached high school, I had begun self-taught meditation practices and the study of many different religious traditions, including Buddhism. I was especially attracted to the writings of Thomas Merton, a Trappist monk who was a contemplative social activist and an admirer of Zen. Accordingly, I became involved in peaceful student protest against social injustice and war and volunteered for social service in a Veterans psychiatric hospital and a residential treatment facility for people with autism and mental retardation.

While an undergraduate major in anthropology, I focused on the study of East Asian cultures and religions. I was offered an opportunity to go to South Korea immediately after graduation in order to study East Asian philosophy at a Confucian oriented university. Later, while completing an M.A. degree in comparative religious studies in the United States, I felt an intense call to greater social service, in order to apply the insights of religious teachings and practices to help people directly. So in 1980 I began working toward my M.S.W. degree.

In 1981, I met Korean Zen Master Seung Sahn at a 3-day retreat in California that combined intensive meditation and chanting. I did more retreats with Buddhist teachers in the international Kwan Um School of Zen, founded by Zen Master Seung Sahn. This Zen school is nonsectarian in the sense that participation does not necessarily exclude any other religious affiliation. Its priority is meditation practice rather than doctrinal adherence or debate. I also continued scholarly study and meditation training with other Mahayana and Vajrayana teachers, as well as with teachers in other religious traditions. In 1989, I moved to Lawrence, Kansas and soon became involved with the Kansas Zen Center. I am currently a Dharma Teacher-in-Training in the Kwan Um School of Zen.

My development as a Zen practitioner and my development as a social worker have been complementary and mutually beneficial. Zen practice has helped me to keep centered and focused when relating with clients, students, and colleagues, even during stressful times. It has also helped me to cut through the veil of confusing and conflicting religious differences and conflicts by seeing life more directly and simply. Zen practice has enriched my Catholicism by deepening the Christian contemplative experience and by helping me keep a sense of freshness and vividness regarding the teachings and example of Jesus. Indeed, among Christian denominations, Catholicism is one of the most actively involved in dialogue with Buddhism (e.g. Graham, 1963; Johnston, 1976; Waldenfels, 1980). Since becoming a professor of social work in 1986, I have dedicated most of my effort to promoting mutual understanding and cooperation in social welfare activity among people of diverse spiritual perspectives. Zen practice has aided that by helping me to relate on the basis of our common human heart of compassion.

SPIRITUAL RESOURCES

Committed Buddhists—laypeople and monastics alike—acknowledge their gratitude to the spiritual resources of Buddhism through the following affirmation: "I take refuge in the Buddha, the Dharma, and the *Sangha*" (Sanskrit). These are known as the "three treasures" because they provide a base of support and guidance through which one can seek enlightenment (Harvey, 1990). By taking refuge in the Buddha, one gives respect to the founder of the spiritual tradition for his great effort, profound insight, and generous teaching. By extension, one also honors the inherently enlightened nature of oneself and all other beings, and reinforces one's commitment to actualize this enlightenment. In Mahayana and Vajrayana traditions, one may take refuge in a Buddha other than the historical Buddha (for example, Amitabha Buddha in the Pure Land sect, as mentioned previously).

By taking refuge in the Dharma, one gives respect to the body of teachings that have followed from the Buddha and the Buddhist tradition. By extension, this refuge signifies one's commitment to practice this spiritual path diligently in order to realize directly the truth to which the teaching points. In the largest sense, Dharma is the true way or order of the universe, the ultimate reality.

The Buddhist Dharma is explicated in numerous scriptures, commentaries, and other writings in original sacred languages such as Pali and Sanskrit, and also in vernacular and local languages. The Pali scriptures alone are about eleven times longer than the Bible (Mascaro, 1973). These scriptures are collectively known as the *Tipitaka*, or "Three Baskets" (Pali); they include the *Vinaya Pitaka* (on rules for the life of monastics), the *Sutta Pitaka* (teachings of the historical Buddha), and the *Abhidhamma Pitaka* (scholarly and philosophical writings) (Wilson, 1991).

One of the most widely read Pali scriptures is the *Dhammapada,* which means "the path of the Dharma." The opening twenty verses convey a central concern of Buddhism: If a person speaks or acts with an unclear mind, suffering will follow, just as the wheels of a cart follow the beast that pulls the cart. But if a person speaks and acts with a clear mind, then joy follows. If a person's words and actions are free of selfish passion, hate, and delusion, then that person's life is and will be one of holiness (Mascaro, 1973).

The Diamond Sutra is one of the most influential Mahayana scriptures (Price & Wong, 1969). Sections three and four convey a common Mahayana caution about attaching to anything, including enlightenment. These sections teach that even when innumerable beings have attained Nirvana through the help of Buddha, no individual being has really been liberated. This is because true Bodhisattvas do not cling to the idea of a separate ego-identity. Furthermore, a Bodhisattva's nonattachment should be such that he or she practices compassion to all without regard to any appearances or qualities.

By taking refuge in the Sangha, one gives respect to all those who are committed to Buddhist spiritual practice, especially monastics and highly realized people who serve as teachers and guides. By extension, one honors all one's fellow spiritual seekers and commits to mutual help. In the largest sense, Sangha refers to the universal community of all beings on the path to enlightenment.

Consideration of the Sangha is of particular importance for social workers with Buddhist clients. Buddhists in the United States, whenever possible, establish temples and meditation centers that provide mutual aid for members. Well-established Buddhist communities, such as among Southeast Asian–American Buddhists, offer a wide range of supports such as material aid, psychological counseling, social support, community celebration, traditional culture-specific approaches to healing, preservation of religious and ethnic traditions, and teaching of meditation and ritual practice (Canda & Phaobtong, 1992; Morreale, 1998; Prebish, 1999; Timberlake & Cook, 1984). There is also an extensive global *cybersangha* (a term coined in 1991 by Gary Ray) on the World Wide Web (Prebish, 1999). One can find extensive information about many types of Buddhism in the United States and around the world by entering key Buddhist words used in this chapter into an Internet search engine.

BUDDHIST SPIRITUAL PRACTICES

The particulars of Buddhist spiritual practices vary significantly, depending on the sect, although they all include forms of scripture study, meditation, and ritual. A description of some practices that have been standardized in the Kwan Um School of Zen will illustrate the Mahayana tradition, as this school adapts practices from Zen, Pure Land, and other sects for international use. My description draws from standard teaching texts of the school as well as from my own experience (Fraser, 1994; Mitchell, 1976; Sahn, 1987, 1997).

All types of Buddhism encourage meditation to calm and clear the mind. Meditation can be done alone, but often it is performed in groups for brief periods or at intensive prolonged retreats for days, months, or years. Traditionally, strict seated meditation practice was mostly for monastics, but there have always been lay practitioners of meditation. Contemporary Buddhism has increased emphasis on lay practice. In the Kwan Um Zen style, the meditator usually sits on a cushion cross-legged. The spine is kept straight but not rigid. The gaze is directed gently through half-open eyes toward the floor about 3 feet ahead. The hands are placed in the lap, left palm resting on right, with thumb tips lightly touching to form an oval over a spot a few inches below the navel. This spot is the lower *tan t'ien* (Chinese), a concentration point for the vital energy of the body (Schuhmacher & Woerner, 1994). Attention is kept clear and open to the moment. Posture can be adapted to the practitioner's physical condition.

Usually, the meditator practices to remain aware of the inward and outward flow of the breath, which is taken in and released from the tan t'ien. The out breath is about three times longer than the in breath. Sometimes a *mantra* (Sanskrit) is used as another focus. A mantra is a brief significant word or phrase. In this case, the mantra is silently repeated in the mind in harmony with the breath. Another technique is to use a brief question in the same way as a mantra. This question should be significant and strong enough to compel attention, such as "What am I?"

Meditation can also be done while walking silently or while chanting sutras or mantras. This approach helps to integrate a clear mind with physical movement and promotes clarity in all daily life activities. The clear mind fostered by meditation is the basis for all other spiritual practices, such as bowing and rituals.

Bowing and prostration mean different things to different Buddhists. Generally, one bows as a sign of greeting and respect to fellow practitioners and especially to teachers and monastics. One also customarily does three prostrations upon entering a temple, in honor of the Buddha, the Dharma, and the Sangha. In the Kwan Um Zen style, bowing and prostration in front of a statue of the Buddha or another religious image signify respect for the ideal represented by the image, commitment to attain that ideal oneself, and recognition of one's own original true nature. Most Zen practitioners do not intend these actions as supplication to or worship of a personal deity in the Judeo-Christian sense.

Some Mahayana and Vajrayana Buddhists engage in practices of devotion to Buddhas and Bodhisattvas as anthropomorphic deities. Some may even supplicate and ask for material blessings. But officially, most long-established Buddhist sects view these "deities" as manifestations of the true Buddha nature that all beings ultimately share. Some enlightened beings, like Amitabha Buddha, may be understood to exist literally and be able to help those who approach in the right way. But Amitabha's purpose is ultimately to help a person attain awareness of his or her own Buddhahood (de Bary, 1969).

The Kwan Um School adapts the practice of dharma interviews (*kongan,* Korean; *koan,* Japanese) from Korean Zen. In kongan practice, an authorized teacher presents the practitioner with a traditional brief story from the Zen tradition that illustrates some key point of Buddhist teaching. The story includes some apparently paradoxical or challenging situation. The student is expected to respond to this situation in a lively manner that displays clear understanding of the situation and correct action in response to it. The student must "get unstuck" from assumptions and intellectualizations in order to respond spontaneously. These situations can be seen as prototypes of real-life situations; by responding to them, the practitioner learns to apply clear, spontaneous, and compassionate action in daily life.

There are also many rituals for various aspects of the personal and community life cycle. For example, in the Kwan Um Zen style, there are rituals for the community to celebrate the birth and enlightenment days of the historical Buddha, the opening of a new Zen center, and the installation of a new abbot, guiding teacher, or Zen master. For individuals and families, there are rituals for taking precepts, or vows, in commitment to the Buddha Dharma as laypeople or monastics, for repenting to the community for misdeeds, for celebrating a new baby 100 days after birth, for marriage, and for commemorating the deceased at a funeral.

Some Buddhist traditions emphasize careful intellectual study and debate of scriptures and commentaries, especially for those who will be formal teachers of the Dharma. All traditions emphasize the moral dimension of practice, which hinges on the cultivation of compassion and wisdom in action. The moral dimension should permeate all the other spiritual practices mentioned. For example, many people beginning a formal commitment to Buddhism take five vows: to abstain from killing, stealing, lustful conduct, lying, and taking of intoxicants. In the Kwan Um School style, these precepts are regarded as guides to a correct lifestyle that does no harm to self or others and encourages compassion. However, they should be applied flexibly according to the situation, with compassion being the paramount consideration.

DHARMA THROUGHOUT THE LIFE CYCLE

Since the Buddha Dharma adapts its forms to each cultural context, there are Buddhist rituals to mark key turning points in the life cycle, as understood within local customs. These culturally prescribed ways of marking life cycle events (e.g., birth, marriage, death) are given significance within the context of the Buddhist concern for using these turning points as part of the process of seeking enlightenment for oneself and promoting the well-being of loved ones and all other beings.

It is said that to attain a human birth is rare, to hear of the Buddha Dharma is rarer still, and to find a teacher who can help one on the Way is even more difficult (Gethin, 1998; Harvey, 1990). Thus, human life is considered precious as a means to attain enlightenment. However, existence is not considered to be positive per se, since it is characterized by suffering. The Buddha Dharma can be used as a means to liberate oneself from the bonds of karma that hold one in the suffering cycle of countless deaths and rebirths. Buddhist traditions have special rituals to mark a person's commitment to practice the Dharma and seek enlightenment. As mentioned previously, beginners may take the Five Precepts to mark formal commitment to the Buddha Dharma. For monastics, and more recently for laypeople as well, there are rituals for more advanced precepts and for testing and certifying the level of spiritual awareness and gaining permission to teach others.

The Buddhist perspective on death is that it is not the end of the life cycle, but rather a transition (Evans-Wentz, 1960; Kapleau, 1989; Sogyal, 1993). For most people who are not fully enlightened, death begins a process of transformation of consciousness in preparation for rebirth, as determined by one's karma. In many Buddhist traditions, the time of transition between a death and rebirth is believed to be 49 days. Many Buddhists prefer cremation of the body, so there is a special funeral ceremony at the time of cremation. There may be daily ceremonies thereafter for the 49 days, with a larger ceremony each seventh day. These ceremonies are intended to help the person make best use of the state in between death and life so that she or he can move toward a more auspicious rebirth or attain enlightenment. Many believe that the deceased person can still hear soon after physical death. In the Tibetan tradition, for example, a monk or loved one may stand near the corpse and gently propound teachings on how to move through the transition period, or *bardo* (Tibetan). This 49-day period also helps the bereaved to process their grief and to continue a supportive communication with the deceased through ritual. Given the importance of the after-death period, many Buddhists are uncomfortable with treatments of the body that may disturb the consciousness of the deceased, such as autopsy or organ transplant. However, if these actions can benefit other beings and be performed respectfully, they may be considered acceptable.

The fully enlightened person stops going through the cycle of involuntary life, death, and rebirth. In the Theravada tradition, this status of the "non-returner" is an ideal, though one that is rarely achieved (Harvey, 1990). In the Mahayana and Vajrayana traditions, a person may aspire to become a Bodhisattva, one who is no longer chained to the illusion of individual existence, but who can voluntarily use physical incarnations or rebirths in non-physical realms in order to help all beings attain enlightenment.

CONCEPTIONS OF HEALTH

Buddhists prefer good physical and mental health, as anyone does. Indeed, some Buddhists view their religion primarily in terms of reliance upon Buddhas and Bodhisattvas for blessings to support their own comfort and success and those of loved ones. Buddhists may also use whatever methods of healing are available in their culture, both through Buddhist adepts (such as traditional healers and ritualists who are monastics) and through practitioners of other culture-specific and Western science-based forms of medicine. Thus, it is necessary to inquire of a Buddhist client what particular types of healing he or she may utilize.

Practitioners committed to seeking enlightenment use aids to health because good health provides a foundation for spiritual practice and for helping others. Many Buddhists may be cautious about the use of medications that dull awareness, such as some pain-control medicines, because they can interfere with the clarity necessary for meditation and for dealing with crises, such as the death passage. Medications that are obtained through violence against animals or humans may also be problematic.

But everyone becomes sick and dies, no matter what recourse to medications and other healing practices they may have. Physical health and mental health are not the primary indicators of good health in the most significant sense. Good health is indicated by dedication to spiritual practice and compassion. Even sickness and death can be used as means to grow spiritually and to help others. In fact, the most fundamental forms of illness are considered to be anger, selfishness, and delusion, which trap one into the cycle of suffering. Thus, the historical Buddha is sometimes referred to as the Medicine

Buddha, or the Great Physician, because through the Four Noble Truths he diagnosed the fundamental illness (human suffering), proclaimed the cure (cessation of inappropriate desire), and explained how to administer the cure (the Eightfold Path).

IMPLICATIONS FOR SOCIAL WORK PRACTICE

The beliefs and practices described in this chapter should be considered only a general introduction and orientation to possible views of Buddhist clients and communities. It is most important to learn from clients and community representatives directly.

Since Buddhism is one of the fastest-growing religious traditions in the United States, it will be increasingly common for social workers to encounter Buddhist clients. Immigration from Asian countries has brought many varieties of Buddhism to this country. Social workers working with Asian immigrants, Asian visitors, Asian Americans, and others who are Buddhist need to ascertain the particular cultural and denominational form that is relevant. If the client is an active member of a Buddhist temple community or meditation center, it is especially important to understand the person's spiritual resources, beliefs, and practices (Canda & Phaobtong, 1992). Buddhist clergy, traditional healers, and community leaders can be important allies for collaboration and referral.

Social workers who assist recent Buddhist immigrants and refugees may need to help them address tensions and difficulties that relate to making the transition into a culture that is predominantly Christian (Canda & Furman, 1999). For example, Southeast Asian Buddhist refugees may have been sponsored and resettled with the assistance of Christian churches. Some of them have reported experiencing unwanted pressure to convert to Christianity. Some Buddhist immigrants and refugees are comfortable combining Christian and Buddhist practices and may seek ways to honor and appreciate the religion of their Christian supporters while also maintaining Buddhist practice. Some may wish to become Christian and then need to work through this change with their Buddhist loved ones and community members.

Sometimes the Buddhist belief in karma is misused to claim that a person who has been victimized by war, violence, or injustice has brought this on himself or herself by previous bad behavior in this or an earlier life (Sam, 1987). Oppressors might misuse the teaching of karma to rationalize unjust circumstances, saying that the disadvantaged deserve their bad fortune. Some people may inappropriately blame themselves for their hardship, just as Christians sometimes exhibit inappropriate guilt or self-blame. In these cases, social workers may need to help clients investigate the deeper meaning of karma and develop empowering strategies to change their circumstances.

Another area of tension arises for many contemporary Buddhists who wish to challenge Buddhist customs rooted in cultures that institutionalize hierarchy of authority and male privilege (De Silva, 1995; Prebish, 1999; Prebish & Tanaka, 1998). Some Buddhist teachers in the United States have used their authority to exploit members. Many American Buddhist communities have responded by creating means for ethical review of teachers and developing more democratic and egalitarian ways of organizing. While these changes may be valuable, they may also bring confusion or consternation for Buddhist traditionalists. When people feel caught in the middle of these controversial situations, they might seek help from social workers who are open to Buddhism but who are not part of the clients' Buddhist community.

Some social workers have begun to draw on Buddhist insights to innovate within social work theory and practice (Brandon, 1976; Canda & Furman, 1999; Keefe, 1996; Nakashima, 1995). Brandon has emphasized the importance of keeping one's mind fresh, clear, and present in the moment so that social work practice reflects a spontaneous and empathetic helping relationship. Keefe has described the nonsectarian adaptation of Buddhist meditation practices to enhance empathy and alleviate stress for both worker and client. Canda and Furman have incorporated Buddhist insights, along with insights from many other religious and nonreligious perspectives, into a comprehensive framework for spiritually sensitive theory and practice. They suggest that the Buddhist understanding of the interdependence of all and compassion for all can extend social work's person-and-environment conception to include a commitment to the well-being of all beings. Nakashima has described the importance of Buddhist influences in preparing her for hospice-based social work, given Buddhism's special concern about the nature of life, death, and rebirth. Further implications pertaining to mental health and clinical practice can be found in the rapidly expanding fields of Buddhist psychology and psychotherapy, socially engaged Buddhism, and transpersonal theory (e.g., De Silva, 1995; Eppsteiner, 1988; Imamura, 1998; Macy, 1991; Robbins, Chatterjee, & Canda, 1998; Rothberg, 1998, Tarthang, 1975; Wilber, 1995).

In conclusion, a common Mahayana portrayal of the Bodhisattva of Compassion is apropos to social work (Blofeld, 1988; Canda & Furman, 1999). The main head of the Bodhisattva displays an attitude of composure and detached compassion for all beings. Eleven faces above the head refer to diverse appropriate ways to perceive and respond compassionately to all suffering beings. A thousand hands and eyes stretching in all directions symbolize the ability to perceive the distress of all beings in all situations and to respond skillfully to them. Indeed, Korean Buddhist social workers use this image to represent the ideal for enlightened social work (Canda, 1995; Canda & Canda, 1996; Canda, Shin & Canda, 1993). If we look beyond the particular religious imagery into the deeper meaning, we can find a way of life that benefits all.

REFERENCES

Blofeld, J. (1988). *Bodhisattva of compassion: The mystical tradition of Kuan Yin.* Boston: Shambhala.

Brandon, D. (1976). *Zen in the art of helping.* New York: Delta/Seymour Lawrence.

Canda, E. R. (1995). Bodhisattva, sage, and shaman: Exemplars of compassion and service in traditional Korean religions. In H. Kwon (Ed.), *Korean cultural roots: Religion and social thoughts* (pp. 31–44). Chicago: Integrated Technical Resources.

Canda, E. R., & Canda, H. J. (1996). Korean spiritual philosophies of human service: Current state and prospects. *Social Development Issues, 18*(3), 53–70.

Canda, E. R., & Furman, L. D. (1999). *Spiritual diversity in social work practice: The heart of helping.* New York: Free Press.

Canda, E. R., & Phaobtong, T. (1992). Buddhism as a support system for Southeast Asian refugees. *Social Work, 37*(1), 61–67.

Canda, E. R., Shin, S. I., & Canda, H. J. (1993). Traditional philosophies of human service in Korea and contemporary social work implications. *Social Development Issues, 15*(3), 84–104.

de Bary, T. (Ed.). (1969). *The Buddhist tradition in India, China and Japan.* New York: Vintage Books.

De Silva, P. (1995). Human rights in Buddhist perspective. In A. A. An-Na'im, J. D. Gort, H. Jansen, & H. M. Vroom (Eds.). *Human rights and religious values: An uneasy relationship?* (pp. 133–143). Grand Rapids, MI: Eerdmans.

Eppsteiner, F. (Ed.). (1988). *The path of compassion: Writings on socially engaged Buddhism.* Berkeley, CA: Parallax Press.

Evans-Wentz, W. Y. (Trans.). (1960). *The Tibetan book of the dead* (3rd ed.). London: Oxford University Press.

Fields, R. (1992). *How the swans came to the lake: A narrative history of Buddhism in America.* Boston: Shambhala.

Fraser, M. (Ed.). (1994). *Dharma mirror: Manual of practice forms.* Cumberland, RI: The Kwan Um School of Zen.

Furuto, S. M., Biswas, R., Chung, D. K., Murase, K., & Ross-Sherif, F. (Eds.). (1992). *Social work practice with Asian Americans.* Newbury Park, CA: Sage.

Gethin, R. (1998). *The foundations of Buddhism.* Oxford, England: Oxford University Press.

Graham, D. A. (1963). *Zen Catholicism.* New York: Harcourt, Brace & World, Inc.

Hahn, T. N. (1991). *Old path, white clouds: Walking in the footsteps of Buddha.* Berkeley, CA: Parallax Press.

Harvey, P. (1990). *An introduction to Buddhism: Teachings, history and practices.* Cambridge, England: Cambridge University Press.

Herold, A. F. (1954). *The life of Buddha.* (P. C. Blum, Trans.). Tokyo: Charles E. Tuttle.

Imamura, R. (1998). Buddhist and Western psychotherapies: An Asian American perspective. In C. S. Prebish & K. K. Tanaka (Eds.). *The faces of Buddhism in America* (pp. 228–237). Berkeley: University of California Press.

Johnston, W. (1976). *Silent music: The science of meditation.* New York: Harper & Row.

Kapleau, P. (1989). *The wheel of life and death: A practical and spiritual guide.* New York: Doubleday.

Keefe, T. (1975). A Zen perspective on social casework. *Social Casework, 56*(3), 140–144.

Keefe, T. (1996). Meditation and social work treatment. In F. J. Turner (Ed.). *Social work treatment: Interlocking theoretical approaches* (4th ed.) (pp. 434–460). New York: Free Press.

Macy, J. (1991). *Mutual causality in Buddhism and general systems theory.* Albany: State University of New York Press.

Mascaro, J. (Trans.). (1973). *The Dhammapada.* New York: Viking Penguin.

Mitchell, S. (Ed.). (1976). *Dropping ashes on the Buddha: The teaching of Zen Master Seung Sahn.* New York: Grove Press.

Morreale, D. (Ed.). (1998). *The complete guide to Buddhist America.* Boston: Shambhala.

Nakashima, M. (1995). Spiritual growth through hospice work. *Reflections: Narratives of Professional Helping, 1*(4), 17–27.

Nielsen, N. C., Jr., et al. (1993). *Religions of the world* (3rd ed.). New York: St. Martin's Press.

Prebish, C. S. (1999). *Luminous passage: The practice and study of Buddhism in America.* Berkeley: University of California Press.

Prebish, C. S., & Tanaka, K. K. (Eds.) (1998). *The faces of Buddhism in America.* Berkeley: University of California Press.

Price, A. F., & Wong, M. L. (Trans.). (1969). *The Diamond sutra and the sutra of Hui Neng.* Boulder, CO: Shambhala.

Robbins, S. P., Chatterjee, P., & Canda, E. R. (1998). *Contemporary human behavior theory: A critical perspective for social work.* Boston: Allyn & Bacon.

Rothberg, D. (1998). Responding to the cries of the world: Socially engaged Buddhism in North America. In C. S. Prebish and K. K. Tanaka (Eds.), *The faces of Buddhism in America* (pp. 266–286). Berkeley: University of California Press.

Sahn, S. (1987). *Ten gates: The kong-an teaching of Zen Master Seung Sahn.* Cumberland, RI: Primary Point Press.

Sahn, S. (1997). *The compass of Zen.* Boston: Shambhala.

Sam, Y. (1987). *Khmer Buddhism and politics 1954–1984.* Newington, CT: Khmer Studies Institute, Inc.

Schuhmacher, S., & Woerner, G. (1994). *The encyclopedia of eastern philosophy and religion.* Boston: Shambhala.

Sogyal Rinpoche (with Gaffney, P. & Harvey, A.) (Eds.).(1993). *The Tibetan book of living and dying.* San Francisco: HarperSanFrancisco.

Tarthang, T. (Ed.). (1975). *Reflections of mind: Western psychology meets Tibetan Buddhism.* Emeryville, CA: Dharma Publishing.

Timberlake, E. M., & Cook, K. O. (1984). Social work and the Vietnamese refugee. *Social Work, 29*(2), 108–114.

Waldenfels, H. (1980). (J. W. Heisig, Trans.). *Absolute nothingness: Foundations for a Buddhist-Christian dialogue.* New York: Paulist Press.

Wilber, K. (1995). *Sex, ecology, spirituality: The spirit of evolution.* Boston: Shambhala.

Williams, P. (1989). *Mahayana Buddhism: The doctrinal foundations.* London: Routledge.

Wilson, A. (Ed.). (1991). *World scripture: A comparative anthology of sacred texts.* New York: Paragon House.

Zo, Zayong, (Ed). (1975). *The life of Buddha in Korean paintings.* (J. Strom, Trans.). Seoul, Korea: Kwangmyong Printing Company.

ADDITIONAL RESOURCES

Books

Blofeld, J. (1998). *Bodhisattva of compassion: The mystical tradition of Kuan Yin,* Boston: Shambhala.

Canda, E.R., & Phaobtong, T. (1992). Buddhism as a support system for Southeast Asian refugees. *Social Work 37*(l), 61–67.

Eppstiner, F. (Ed.) (1998). *The path of compassion: Writings on socially engaged Buddhism.* Berkley, CA: Parallax Press.

Glethin, R. (1998). *The foundations of Buddhism.* Oxford, England: Oxford University Press.

Harvey, P. (1990). *An introduction to Buddhism: Teaching, history and practices.* Cambridge, England: Cambridge University Press.

Prebish, C.S. (1999). *Luminous passage: The practice and study of Buddhism in America.* Berkeley, CA: University of California Press.

Sahn, S. (1997). *The compass of Zen.* Boston: Shambhala.

Web Sites

For information on the Kwanum School of Zen and Korean Buddhism: www.kwanumzen.com

For information on the Zen Peacemaker Order: www.peacemakercommunity.org/zpo/index.html

For information on the Buddhist Peace Fellowship: www.bpf.prg/index.htm

For information on socially engaged Buddhism: www/dharmanet.org/engaged.html

For listings of many online resources: buddhanet.net and http/ccb.ntu.edu.tw/BWF

GLOSSARY

Amitabha (Sanskrit) In Mahayana Buddhism, the Buddha of Infinite Light, who is an enlightened being presiding over the Heavenly Western Paradise, a pure and blissful state of consciousness promoting complete enlightenment.

Arahat (Pali; also **arhat,** Sanskrit) In Theravada Buddhism, the ideal of a person who has attained enlightenment, free of all attachments and illusions, and who will exit the cycle of rebirth at death, thus ceasing to exist as a separate ego-bound entity.

Bodhisattva (Sanskrit) In Mahayana Buddhism, the ideal of an enlightened being who is liberated from attachments but chooses out of compassion to continue to be reborn in order to help all beings toward enlightenment.

Buddha (Sanskrit and Pali) A fully awakened or enlightened being that is liberated from all cravings, aversions, and delusions. In the present age of human history, the preeminent Buddha was Siddhartha Gautama, the founder of Buddhism.

Dharma (Sanskrit; also **dhamma,** Pali) The teaching of the Buddha that leads to enlightenment through understanding the true nature of reality in keeping with cosmic law.

Eightfold Path A summary of the guidelines for living prescribed by Gautama Buddha to lead to enlightenment; the fourth of the Four Noble Truths. The eight aspects of this path are correct understanding, correct intention, correct speech, correct conduct, correct livelihood, correct effort, correct awareness, and correct meditative concentration.

Four Noble Truths The essence of Gautama Buddha's teaching about the nature of human existence and the way to attain enlightenment. First, life is characterized by suffering. Second, suffering is caused by inappropriate desires, aversions, and the delusion of separate ego identity. Third, people can stop suffering by ceasing inappropriate desires, delusions, and aversions. Fourth, this can be accomplished by following the Eightfold Path.

Karma (Sanskrit; also **kamma,** Pali) Literally, "action." The cosmic law of moral cause and effect by which good actions generate beneficial consequences and bad actions generate harmful consequences for the one responsible. Karma shapes the quality of a person's future in the current life and in later lives.

Kwan Shi Yin (Chinese; also **Avalokitesvara,** Sanskrit) In Mahayana Buddhism, the Bodhisattva of Compassion. The name literally means "perceive the sound of the universe." This Bodhisattva perceives the suffering of all beings and reaches out in all directions to help them. It represents the quality of compassion in the true nature of human beings.

Mahayana (Sanskrit) A major branch of Buddhism that developed in Central and East Asia through a combination of Indian original teachings and regional customs and philosophies. The name means "great vehicle," signifying that it is a spiritual way broad enough to carry all beings to enlightenment. The Bodhisattva ideal is characteristic of Mahayana.

Nirvana (Sanskrit; also **nibbana,** Pali) The name means "cessation or extinction," referring to the cessation of inappropriate desires, aversions, and the delusion of separate ego identity that comes with enlightenment. Nirvana is liberation from the wheel of death and rebirth and the bonds of karma. At death, the enlightened person may enter nirvana, thus ceasing to exist as a separate ego-bound entity. Nirvana is not nihilism, however, but rather a state of being that transcends the limits of egoism, thinking, and verbal expression. In Mahayana Buddhism, nirvana can be realized in the midst of the suffering world.

Sangha (Sanskrit; also **samgha,** Pali) The Buddhist community of monks, nuns, and novices. By extension, it includes lay followers. By further extension, it includes all beings on the path to enlightenment. Along with Buddha and Dharma, Sangha is one of the Three Treasures of Buddhism to which Buddhists give formal respect.

Siddhartha Gautama (Sanskrit; also **Siddhatta Gotama,** Pali) The historical founder of Buddhism and the preeminent Buddha of this age of human history. He was born in a noble family of the Shakya clan in what is now Nepal. He lived from about 566 or 563 B.C.E. to 486 or 483 B.C.E.

Theravada (Pali) A major branch of Buddhism common in South and Southeast Asia that can be traced back to the original formation of Buddhism in Nepal and India. The name means "teaching of the elders." It is also known as Hinayana, "the small vehicle," which technically refers to a set of original schools of Buddhism of which Theravada is the only survivor. Since the term Hinayana is sometimes used with negative connotations by followers of the Mahayana (Great Vehicle) branch, followers of Theravada usually do not use it. The arahat ideal is characteristic of Theravada.

Zen (Japanese; also **ch'an,** Chinese) A style of Mahayana Buddhism prevalent in China, Japan, Korea, Vietnam, and increasingly common in the West. The name is short for *zenna,* which is the Japanese derivation of the Chinese *ch'anna,* itself derived from Sanskrit *dhyana.* The term refers to meditative concentration that cuts off artificial categories of thinking and opens one to the true nature of reality. There are various Zen sects, but they all hold in common an emphasis on the practice of meditation for direct realization of truth rather than reliance only on teachings and rituals.

CONFUCIANISM

DOUGLAS K. CHUNG

CHAPTER 5

INTRODUCTION

Confucianism is a philosophy with a religious function. It is named after Confucius, whose teachings on ethical behavior have been adopted as a national development model throughout Chinese history. Currently, Confucianism has a strong influence in China, Korea, Taiwan, and the countries of Southeast Asia, as well as among people of Far Eastern descent living around the world. An increasing number of Westerners are able to appreciate Confucianism through international contacts and literature. Confucianism includes some elements of traditional Chinese religion, such as reverence for heaven and the worship of ancestors. It does not assert the existence of a deity, although it recognizes and promotes synchronization with *Tien* (Heaven, the Ultimate, or Tao) through harmonious relationships with others and the environment. Most Chinese view Confucianism as a philosophy or a practical way to reach an ideal world rather than as a religion. Because Confucianism provides a vision of an ideal world and knowledge about how to achieve this world, it has been used by most Chinese rulers to establish new dynasties and facilitate governance.

HISTORY OF CONFUCIANISM

Confucius (551–479 B.C.) is renowned as a philosopher and educator, but little attention is given to his roles as researcher, statesman, change agent, social planner, social innovator, enabler, and spiritual advocate. He is said to have spent nearly 30 years touring various states in China, advising local rulers on social reforms but finding no real opportunities to actualize his political and social vision. It is widely believed that in his old age, Confucius went back to his home and committed himself to education. As a devoted teacher, he had 72 disciples and some 3000 students during his lifetime. Confucius was a philosophical and spiritual teacher but not a religious scholar. He was a humanist in the sense that his main concern was people and their environment and relationships. It is widely believed that during his old age, Confucius edited several ancient works that later formed the basic canon of Chinese scholarship. Five of the works are extant: *The Book of Odes (Shi-Ching), The Book of History (Shu-Ching), The Book of Rites (Li), The Book of Changes (I-Ching),* and *The Spring and Autumn Annals* (a book of history). The transformational method he developed offers a means to change individuals, families, communities, and nations into a harmonious universal society.

Since the second century B.C., Chinese political, social, and intellectual life have been strongly influenced by Confucianism. Two leading philosophers of this ancient school were Mencius and Hsun Tzu. Although the ideas of Confucius are considered the most central to the school, they are captured in what can at best be described as jottings by students that record memorable quotations from his lectures and anecdotes of time spent in his presence. The writings of Mencius (390–305 B.C.) and Hsun Tzu (340–245 B.C.) are much more complete and, because of their sheer volume and comprehensiveness, have served to articulate more fully many Confucian ideas and values.

When the Chinese Confucians came into contact with Indian Buddhism around the first century C.E., they developed a spiritual discipline called *Ch'an* (meditation). Ch'an was eventually adopted in Japan, around 1200 C.E., where it was known as Zen. Zen is thus a unique blend of the philosophies and idiosyncrasies of three different cultures. It is typical of Japanese life, and yet it reflects the Buddhism of India, the Taoists' love of nature, and the pragmatism of the Confucian mentality.

Since the 11th century, Buddhism and Taoism have been better known for their religious content rather than as schools of philosophy. Confucians were forced to find metaphysical and epistemological foundations for their ethics. Two major schools of Neo-Confucianism eventually emerged: the rationalists, who emphasized the "inner world" (philosophy), and the idealists, who emphasized practical learning in the "outer world" (social science). The leading exponent of the rationalists was Chu Hsi (1033–1107 C.E.); the idealists' exponent was Wang Yang-Ming (1472–1529 C.E.). The rationalists held that reason is inherent in nature and that mind and reason are not the same thing.

The idealists held that reason is not to be sought from without; it is nothing other than the mind itself.

Ever since Christian missionaries brought Western philosophy to China, Confucians have been challenged to accommodate Western thought. Many scholars translated Western books into Chinese. They also adopted Western inductive logic and classification methods to decipher the phonological system of ancient Chinese in order to study ancient texts. Their efforts set a precedent for positivist research.

Through this process, Chinese scholars incorporated Western concepts and methods into their studies. Western and Eastern cultures have been integrated, resulting in some rather eclectic systems of thought, among them three major schools in modern Chinese philosophy. The first is the school of comprehensive synthesis, represented by the work of Thome H. Fang (1899–1977), which takes any philosophical view it finds useful and profound and offers insights into cosmic existence and human nature. Metaphysics and philosophical anthropology are the main foundations of this school. The second is the school of contemporary Neo-Confucian synthesis, represented by Tang Chun-Yi and Mou Tsung-san. They emphasize the idealist school of inquiry into the "mind," in the tradition of Mencius and Wang Yang-Ming. They also accommodate the German idealism of Kant and Hegel. The third is the Chinese scholastic synthesis school, represented by Wu Ching-Hsing and Lo Kuang. Lo Kuang connected the formal ontology of the scholastic philosophers with the "doctrine of becoming" of Chinese philosophy, laying the foundation for a philosophy that could encompass both ethical and religious aspects of life. His principal concept is benevolence, through which a person is capable of endless development.

The overall vision connecting the different strands of thought within Confucianism is the goal of revitalizing the human virtue of *te* (an ethical code of loving and caring) through educating people to meditate, to search for truth, to be self-motivated, and to be self-controlled. Confucianism seeks to enable people to assume responsibility for carrying out the dual aim of cultivating the individual self and contributing to the attainment of an ideal harmonious society.

MY PERSONAL EXPERIENCE OF CONFUCIANISM

I come from Taiwan, where Confucianism was taught in the middle and high school curricula. We had to memorize texts such as *The Great Learning, The Doctrine of Mean,* and *The Analects.* I personally did not care much about them—they were simply required courses. Like many Sunday school students, I memorized them without much understanding or serious consideration.

In 1973, I earned my M.S.W. degree in the United States and taught social work courses in Taiwan for 5 years. I found that many of the social work theories that I learned in my M.S.W. program were not applicable in Taiwan, so

I came back to the United States for Ph.D. training. One year after I gained my doctoral degree in social work, I was in a car accident. I was forced to rest at home for 2 weeks. During that period, I re-read *The Great Learning, The Analects,* and *The Doctrine of Mean.* The Ph.D. training had really opened my eyes. I practiced Confucian meditation to calm my energy systems, increase my self-awareness and sensitivity, promote my own health, and understand the counterforces within myself and in all personal and social conflicts. Truth searching within myself made me fall in love with qualitative and quantitative integrated research activities in my academic life. I was able to recognize the various theories described by Confucius and his followers and fully appreciate the depth of Confucianism. In 1989, I made a study trip to Korea to visit a Korean Confucian institute and learned that sincerity and equality are the core of Confucianism. This insight enabled me to commit myself to developing culturally sensitive models for various ethnic groups, such as Christians, Muslims, Buddhists, Jews, and others. My Confucian Model of Transformation is based on the Confucian global vision and mission (Chung, 1992a). The Chung Model of Family Conflict Management (Chung, 1993a) was inspired by the Tao image in the Yin/Yang diagram. The Confucian Role Approach and Yin/Yang theory were developed in response to the challenges of Asian refugee families in cultural transition and poverty (Chung, 1993b, 1994). I became a contemporary Confucian agent prescribing Confucian situational approaches and theories for human needs. Through meditation, I internalize my energies to connect the past, the present, and the future.

MEANING OF MAJOR LIFE EVENTS

Confucius considered life a process of transformation. Although there are individual differences, every life goes through the same developmental stages. Each stage has its own task to be achieved. Confucius reviewed his own life journey and implied the following life developmental stages (Cheng, Y., 1988).

Birth as a Continuation of the Life Force

Confucianism considers the self as a here-and-now link in a chain of existence from the past to the future. Everyone should have descendents to continue the family tree. To have no children (thus, to discontinue the family tree) is considered the most unforgivable thing. Having a child to carry on the family name, particularly a boy in traditional societies, is very important.

Therefore, when a new baby is 1 month old, the family gives a party for the extended family and friends to announce and celebrate the new family member. The mother receives a month off to take care of the baby and recover from the delivery. It is the family's responsibility to take care of the mother's needs, to reward her production and contribution to the family. Her family status increases accordingly.

Children at home are taught to follow the ethical code: honor parents, love brothers and sisters, respect elders, trust friends, and be loyal to the family. Life is considered to be a great potentiality, a creative source of energy. This creative life energy is bestowed by Heaven (the Ultimate) and has attributes of originality, development, perfection, and consumption. That is, life as a creative vital force has originality connected with the Ultimate. It can be perfect. The substance of development and consumption depends on the particular individual and environment (Cheng, 1988).

Age of Young Adulthood

Females are considered to reach young adulthood by the age of 14, and males by the age of 16. Both males and females start to dress differently at this stage. The social symbols of adulthood are given with the expectation that the individuals will learn to perform their roles adequately through individual and family education. The young adults participate in social activities and assume related responsibilities, which extend the ethical code of obedience to society. Self-searching, self-awareness, self-acceptance, identity development, acceptance of others, and synchronicity with the environment are expected tasks. At this stage, one prepares the self in obscurity while awaiting the proper time to act.

Age of Independence and Life Establishment: Age 30

People carry on a journey of self-searching from age 16 to age 30. Confucius believed that a person who has reached the age of 30 should be an independent professional. A person should have career and family established by that age and should have achieved basic personal self-development. During this stage, it is important to bring one's inner qualities outward in order to understand and develop the self.

Age of Mental Maturity: Age 40

Confucius asserted that a person who has reached the age of 40 should have a determined personality, no longer struggling with trial and error. One indicator of mental maturity is a lack of regret about oneself and one's decision making.

Age of Spiritual Maturity: Age 50

Confucius believed that a person who reaches 50 years of age should be spiritually reconnected with the Ultimate, knowing Heaven's endowment and being synchronized with it. A mature person should have answers to the questions "Where did I come from?" "Where am I going?" "What is the purpose of my life?" "What are my talents and strengths?" "Who am I?" These spiritual questions facilitate reconnection with originality, nature, Tao, and the

Ultimate, for transformation into another life stage. During this stage, synchronizing one's energies with the systems' needs is the key. Real life is just beginning, not ending, at this stage. One should transform sexual energy into spiritual energy and utilize this to start a second life.

Age of Acceptance: Age 60

Confucius believed that only a person who has gone through a spiritual journey and knows who he or she is will be able to actualize the self spiritually. Spiritual maturity facilitates acceptance of diversity and thus respect for different opinions. During this stage, one may advance into a position of leadership where one can appreciate and utilize diverse strengths for collective accomplishments. Detachment from the ego is an important task.

Age of Unification: Age 70

Confucius taught that after the age of 70, one can purify his or her mind and free the self from negative thoughts. The inward, real self becomes outwardly apparent after it reconnects with the Ultimate and accepts the self and others. Any internal wishes or intentions that are expressed do not violate the positive principle, a code of loving and caring. During this stage, retirement and detachment may be beneficial. If you attach to situations, you may have regrets.

SOURCES OF POWER: THE CONFUCIAN WORLDVIEW

Confucians believe that *Tai Chi* is the Ultimate, an integrated energy of Yin and Yang, which can be transformed into various forms, including nothingness (*Wu Chi*). The Ultimate source of all substance, energy, and knowledge is the *Tao,* which is a continuum without boundaries in time and space, infinite, formless, and luminous. Therefore, Tao has descriptive and non-descriptive attributes.

In Confucian philosophy, the system of Yin and Yang was conceived as a way of explaining the universe. It is a purely relativist system; any one thing is either Yin or Yang only in relation to some other object or phenomenon, and all things can be described only in relation to each other. The Yin and Yang are the negative and positive principles of the Universal force, and are pictorially represented by the symbol of Tai Chi. The Yin and Yang together constitute the Tao, the eternal principle of Heaven and earth, the origin of all things human and divine, and therefore finally produce the *chi (qi).*

The following assumptions from Confucian literature outline the Confucian worldview (Cheng, 1988; Chung, 1992a; Liu, 1985):

- From all eternity was Tao, which is the cause, the reason, the principle, the way that cannot be walked, the name that cannot be named, the unknowable.

- In the beginning was Wu (nothing, in which Tao was not), the great emptiness, non-existence, no limit (which reason can find).
- From this emanated Hun-Tun, or chaos, which is synonymous with Tai-Chi, the Great Ultimate (a mingled potentiality of form, breath, and substance).
- Hun–Tun underwent a great change, and that was the beginning of Hsing (life form).
- Two primary forces—Yin, the negative principle, and Yang, the positive principle—followed this. Yin and Yang are two complementary opposites in Chinese cosmology that together comprise the essential elements of all phenomena and events in the universe (Rose & Yu Huan, 1999). Yin is the receptive, inward, contracting principle and Yang is the active, outward, and expansive principle (Eden, 1999). It is believed that an imbalance in the Yin/Yang dynamic causes illness or organizational dysfunction.
- Yin/Yang interaction produces four symbols, leading to eight trigrams. This interaction, the coming together of the forces, and the trigrams permeating the Yin and Yang resulted in everything (*Wan Wu*), including human beings *(jen)*.

In contemporary terms, the Yin/Yang theoretical worldview can be defined as a school of transformation that is research-oriented and employs a multidimensional, cross-cultural, multilevel, and comprehensive approach. This worldview is applicable to both micro and macro systems. It is a way of life that aims to synchronize the systems of the universe to achieve both individual and collective fulfillment.

Four major principles describe changes in environmental systematic interrelationships can be used to empower clients:

- Change is easy, because the Tao, which is its source, exists in everything and every moment of daily life. Simply synchronize with daily life and enjoy it.
- Change is a transforming process, because of the dynamics of Yin and Yang. Any change in part of Yin or Yang will lead to a change in the system and its related systems. If one member gets hurt, the whole family suffers. The transforming process has its own cycle of expansion and contraction. Everything has its beginning and ending point. As a result, one can be hopeful that things will change and that good fortune may follow a time of bitterness.
- Change implies the notion of constancy and changelessness—change itself is unchanging. One should expect change and be ready for it.
- The best transformations are those that promote growth and development of the individual and the whole at the same time, leading toward excellence for all portions of an interdependent network. The best way to solve a problem is to help your counterpart to achieve the common goal.

Any intervention that attempts change should involve the client, and the client and social worker should jointly consider the following intervention factors:

- *The status of the client within his or her interdependent networks.* What is the client's role and position? What is his or her social status? What are his or her rights and duties? Have the client's basic rights been violated? Did the client do his or her duty?
- *The timing of change.* What are the attitudes of others in the client's interdependent networks with regard to a potential change? Is it good timing to initiate change at the present moment?
- *The mean (moderation, or mu) position.* This position is considered the most strategic one for dealing with change. Tao (truth) exists in the mean (*chung*). The most acceptable solution to a problem is one that satisfies all parties—a win-win solution.
- *The interaction between counterforces (Yin and Yang forces).* Are opposing parties willing to discuss and compromise to achieve co-existence and integration?
- *The integration of parts and whole.* The client should evaluate his or her situation with regard to social processes (that is, economic dynamics, or *Ti Tao;* political dynamics, or *Jen Tao;* and cultural dynamics, or *Tien Tao*). Decision making is contingent on the interrelationships of these factors.

Individual existence implies a network of interdependent and interconnected relationships at all levels (from individual through family and state to the world). The whole is dependent upon the harmonious integration of all the parts (sub-systems), while the parts require nurturance from the whole. The helping professional should help the client reframe his or her self-perception and assume his or her social role(s) accordingly. The self, in the Confucian view, is understood to be shaped by the way an individual performs roles in daily life. One's humanity is achieved only with and through others. A meaningful life is achieved only through sharing loving energies with people that one encounters. Individual and social transformations are based on self-cultivation, the personal effort to search for truth and to become a life-giving person. Searching for and finding the truth will lead you and your client to originality and creativity in problem solving and development. Followers of Confucianism believe that wisdom (truth), love, and courage are non-separable concepts in reality. Helping clients to locate and develop these internal assets will help them overcome their problematic situations.

The Confucian code of ethics is based on the family concept (from nuclear family to national family). Loving and caring start in the immediate family circle and extend to the larger society. Family well-being can be reached or reestablished when family members find and stay with the truth: Existence is an interconnected whole. Methods that assume and take account of connections work better with Confucians than methods that focus on isolated elements. Family or organizational effectiveness can be improved through rearrangement of relationships between family members or workers. These are culturally sensitive interventions for Confucians and most Asian Americans.

In other words, a balanced and harmonious development of the interdependent network is the most beneficial for all. Self-actualization and collective goals should be integrated, according to Confucianism. Many similarities exist between this Transformation Model, the ideas of Gordon's General Systems (1979), and those of Germain and Gitterman's Life Model (1980). Like systems theory, the Transformation Model assumes that there is an interdependent relationship between the parts and the whole. Guided by the above values and knowledge, Confucianism prescribed various social transformation methods and skills, or strategies and approaches, to reach the ideal caring society.

There are various sources of empowerment in Confucianism. The most important source of empowerment is meditation. Meditation can revitalize the internal inborn virtue (te), which can be reconnected with the Ultimate (Tao) so the self can reach unification. In other words, internalization of energy (through meditation) can lead to balance among energy systems, self-awareness, self-empowerment, self-discipline, self-development, moral courage, and truth finding. These qualities will empower the individual to cultivate and expand the self and regulate family relationships so that they reach an orderly state, which will contribute to peace and equality in the world. Each step can be a source of empowerment. Since energy exists in interrelated systems, the individual should pay attention to his or her internal energy systems at all times. In addition, a person should observe others. Confucius considered that people could learn from anyone. If someone does good, certainly I can model it. If someone does not behave correctly, this provides me with an opportunity to review my own behavior.

CONFUCIAN RITUALS AND PRACTICES TODAY

Birthday Celebration: Noodles for Long Life

For a child's first birthday, a birthday party is held among the extended family. Both eggs (a symbol of life) and noodles (a symbol of longevity) are prepared and served. Family members and friends are encouraged to eat these foods as a blessing for the child's long and happy life. This celebration confirms the status of both the child and the mother in the family. Many parents also offer different gifts to the child during the party to test his or her talents or areas of interest for future education. Whatever gifts the child grabs are interpreted as indicators of the child's talent(s) or interests.

Li: Proper Behaviors

Confucianism created various norms and customs called *Li,* which prescribes certain behaviors in particular situations. Li ranges from a bow to an elder, to taking off shoes before entering a house, to being silent and respectful to elders, to bringing a gift to the host, to writing thank-you notes. The purpose is to help an individual to express proper caring relationships. For example, it is inappropriate to smile during a memorial service.

It is the helping professional's responsibility to educate the client about Li (proper behaviors) in the problem-solving and development process. For example, you can make clear to your client the norms of your agency and the laws and regulations of the community. A professional must also observe Li. For example, if a Chinese female client bows to you, you may bow back. You may shake hands with Chinese male client to greet him, instead of bowing.

Teachers' Day

An elaborate ceremony is held at Taipei's Confucian Temple on September 28 to honor the birthday of Confucius. His birthday has been dedicated to honoring all teachers, and Teachers' Day is a national holiday in Taiwan. Music and dance are performed to honor Confucius and all teachers.

Helping professionals are considered life teachers of their clients. The professional might mark this day by asking a client to write a progress note or follow-up report. This is a good means of reinforcing the helping relationship and redefining the relational boundary.

Honor the Ancestors

Confucians promoted ancestor worship by burning paper money and offering fruits and food to show respect for the root of life during the spring. April 5 is a Chinese memorial day, when people go to graveyards and honor their relatives. It is also a day to clean up the graveyard and the environment. These rituals not only show respect for ancestors but also educate the younger generations. Helping professionals may empower clients by connecting them with their life roots, thus honoring and improving the self.

CONFUCIAN HEALING AND DEVELOPMENTAL MODEL

Historically, the Chinese had been ruled by Confucian scholars who intended to actualize the ideal society prescribed by Confucius as the Great Commonwealth of the world. They followed the Confucian transformation model (Chung, 1988). Most Confucian scholars practiced Confucian *qigong,* or meditation. This section analyzes and describes how these historical Confucian scholars, through micro and macro qigong practice, put

Confucianism (therapeutic and developmental concepts) into practice in an effort to reach universal unification and world harmony.

The Confucian transformation model starts with individual meditation, goes through personal enhancement, self-discipline, personality integrity, family integration, and state governance, and reaches the excellence of a universal commonwealth. Individual meditation starts with learning to rest the energy (*chu chu*), in order to be stabilized (*ting*), be still and calm (*ching*), reach peace (*an*), and be mindful (*li*). A mindful energy is ready to learn the truth and reveal the virtue (te) (Liu, 1985). This is achieved through Confucian meditation (qigong)—sitting still to free oneself from ego and get in touch with the real self. Qigong aims to internalize and calm down the energy (qi) in order to calm the mind, body, and spirit. It is a mind, body, and spiritual training process to regain control of the self/mind and prepare for further training and development for *Tien jen* unification (micro and macro unification). In "Mental Fasting" in *Chuang Tzu,* Confucius prescribed a five part meditation method (Lee, 1982):

1. Concentrate your mind. Focus or rest your mind on a point.
2. After your mind is focused, use your mind rather than your ears to listen to your breath.
3. "Don't listen with the mind but listen with qi." With practice, the mind and breath/qi will gradually be integrated. The practice can be described as "using qi to listen qi." The integration of mind and body calms the energy and leads to an internal peace.
4. "Physical listening ends at the ears, while mental listening (concentration) ends after the mind and body (breath) integration has been reached." Detach your physical ears' listening after you can listen with your mind. While you are making progress, detach your mindful breathing after your mind and breath are well integrated, and move on to the next step—a process of detaching from the ego. The egoless state will facilitate spiritual reconnection and growth.
5. "Qi is a kind of emptiness to contain objects; only Tao holds emptiness. The purpose of mental fasting (meditation) aims to achieve emptiness." That is, the goal of meditation is to move from the mind/body integrated condition into the mind, body, and spirit integrated condition, which has no intention, no ego. The empty self becomes a part of the macro self and reaches unification.

Confucians called this meditation *Chou Won. Chou* means "to sit," *Won* means "to forget (the self)." It is an essential mean to detach the ego attachments and reach mental freedom. It is an important mental training to reach emptiness (egolessness) for mental health, self-awareness, self-enhancement, self-discipline, truth finding, self-actualization, and social change. This is a cornerstone of the Confucian transformation method.

Mencius described Confucian meditation (qigong) as cultivating *Hao zan zhi qi* (moral righteousness or courage, which is intrinsically connected with universal qi). Universal qi can be fostered and developed, which may transform the individual into a righteous person with great moral courage and integrity. This universal moral righteousness can be gained only through morally correct means (positive mentality and constructive methodology). Mencius clearly stated that qi is governed by the mind under the individual's will or intention. The practical method he prescribed to cultivate qi is *jiyi*, which means constantly perform good deeds. Helping others on daily basis will foster personal integrity and moral courage.

These mental processes aim to revitalize the internal virtue (te, or moral consciousness) through mindfulness of Tao's image, which leads to insight about the real self and awareness of the universal interconnection of energy. Meditation trains an individual to become a highly self-disciplined, self-initiated, moral, harmonious, and universal (Tao-connected) personality. This simple meditation method aims to integrate mind, body, and spirit for wholistic healing, including disease prevention, healing, and development of one's human capacity. Therefore, it can serve as an empowerment tool for clients and help both the helping professional and the client with stress management and prevention of burnout.

The Concept of Social Development

Confucius prescribed seven steps in a general social transformation method (strategy) to achieve the ideal society, based on the individual discipline of meditation (Chung, 1992a). *The Great Learning* provides one of the best examples of Confucian qigong practice for social change and forms the gate by which first learners enter into virtue. The Confucian transformation model, as outlined by Chung (1988, 1992a), starts with investigation of individual things (variables) until the whole kingdom is made tranquil and happy. The model (shown in Figure 5.1) consists of the following seven general transformational steps, or processes:

1. *The investigation of things.* Finding out the way things are and how they are related.
2. *The completion of knowledge.* Finding out why things are the way they are and the ways in which they are related.
3. *The sincerity of thoughts.* Establishing a sincere attitude and a commitment to excellence and truth.
4. *The rectifying of the heart.* Assuring that the motivation for change is a right one, good for the self as well as the whole.
5. *The cultivation of the person.* Developing integrity between the knowledgeable self (achieved in steps 1 and 2) and the moral self (achieved in steps 3 and 4) through self-discipline and self-improvement.
6. *The regulation of the family.* Applying the principle of self-discipline to one's own family—honoring parents, loving children, respecting the spouse, and caring for brothers and sisters.
7. *The governance of the state.* Establishing a state that provides education, honors the elderly, cares for the vulnerable, has policies rooted in public opinions, and selects virtuous and capable persons for public officials and employees.

The Confucian social transformation model brings about both individual and social change leading to individual and collective excellence and a harmonious world. Moral consciousness exists in all social relationships.

FIGURE 5.1 | CONFUCIUS ECOLOGICAL-SYSTEMS PERSPECTIVE OF SOCIAL TRANSFORMATION

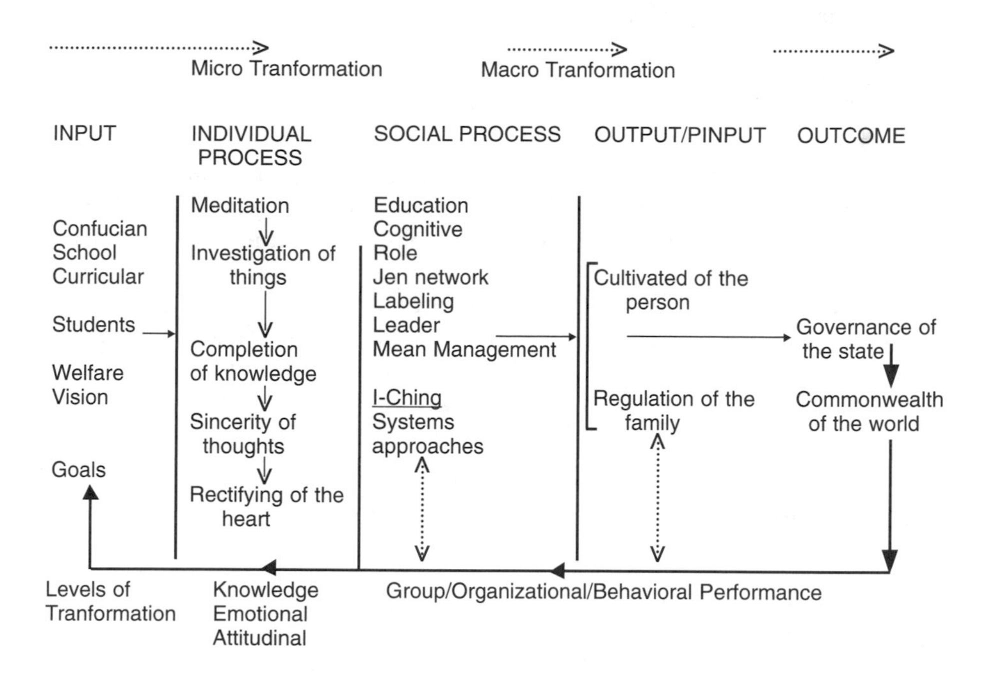

Confucian qigong is rooted in moral consciousness, cultivated from individual meditation and lifelong searching for truth, mental reframing, behavioral change, and development of potential, and then expanded to family, community, state, and the world.

The Concept of Yang-Sheng: Health Maintenance and Promotion

Confucius used various strategies for health maintenance and promotion. First, he promoted a simple lifestyle that included light food and a positive attitude. According to Confucius, food must not only be fresh and wholesome, it must also be prepared and taken in certain styles and manners (Chou, 1995). Confucius also emphasized using the right sauce for different kinds of food. According to *Huang-ti Nei-ching* ("The Yellow Emperor's Inner Classic," the earliest Chinese medical text), the Yin essence of the human body is derived from the five tastes (i.e., sour, bitter, sweet, hot, and salty). If there is disharmony in the tastes of food, it will harm the five organs that harbor the Yin essence. Confucius insisted on being served proper sauces and always used gingers to balance the five tastes in his food for good circulation of qi and longevity.

Confucius had a clear concept of energy management in different stages of life. He said:

> There are three things which the superior man guards against. In youth, when (his) physical energy (*hsueh chi*) is still blooming, he guards against lust. When he grows up, his physical energy is full of vigor, he guards against quarrelsomeness (fighting). When he is old, his physical energy is decayed, he guards against covetousness. (Confucius, 1971).

In other words, Confucius prescribed abstention as a form of energy management for three stages of the life cycle. For teenagers, he prescribed sexual abstention. For adults, he warned against physical fighting. For the elderly, he advised detachment.

Confucius believed that perfection in moral life is the first step toward longevity (Liao, 1993). This implies that a morally integrated personality facilitates the achievement of inner peace and harmony—a coherence of mind, body, and spirit leads to health and longevity. Confucian meditation is the key for health promotion, mental transformation, and spiritual unification.

The Concept of Tao (Tai Chi, the Ultimate) in the Movement of the Mean

There is a regularity to change that people can observe. For example, as illustrated by the seasons, everyone receives equitable treatment from nature: People live half in the daytime (Yang) and half in the nighttime (Yin), but this equity achieved at the end of the yearly cycle. The concept of the mean (chung), therefore, implies a fair, equal treatment of all at all times. It also implies that mean positions are changing all the time in a dynamic way, so that fair or equal treatment can only be perceived at the end of the cycle. If one only looks at part, treatment may appear unfair. For example, people complain that the weather is too cold or the days are too dark (too much Yin) in the winter.

The Chung (Mean) Model, or the Way of Chung Yung, means sincerely following the course of the Mean, the Way, the Tao, the Truth. By following the Tao, one will be able to reach the highest excellence. The human mind in its state of chung is in its state of absolute correctness, excellence, or harmony (Lee, 1982). Since the Tao exists in everything, people should observe their surrounding environment to learn the Tao through following and synchronizing with environmental changes (Tao's function).

MEAN MANAGEMENT UNDER THE DYNAMICS OF YIN AND YANG FORCES

Figure 5.2 (Chung, 1993a) illustrates that there may be different options for solving a situational conflict using the dynamics of the mean. One may approach conflict through finding common ground between opposing parties (coalition strategy). One may diffuse boundaries for negotiation by

FIGURE 5.2 | CHUNG MODEL OF FAMILY CONFLICT MANAGEMENT

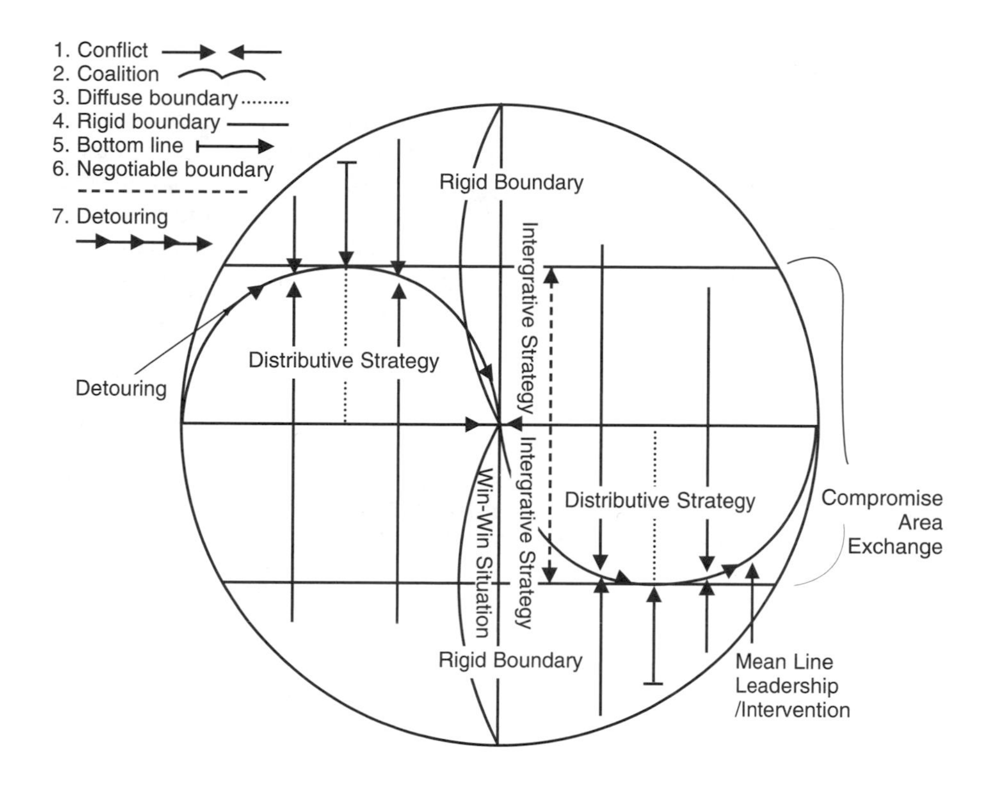

encouraging giving and taking (distributive strategy), such as the husband honoring the wife more at home and the wife respecting the husband in social occasions. One may define both parties' bottom lines and avoid crossing these rigid boundaries (a strategy of respecting and honoring). One may search for the (truth) in terms of finding a common goal and identifying areas of compromise without crossing the rigid boundaries. Or one may combine any two or more of the above approaches to solve conflict. Finally, both parties may separate from the system and form new systems, if they fail to solve conflict through these alternatives.

Any client's conflict solutions and/or development goals must dynamically integrate love (jen), justice, freedom, and faithfulness (the image of Tao). Justice will be achieved by the end of the cycle under perfectly equal treatment. The client can exercise freedom by voluntarily participating in negotiation and compromise—maintaining the flexibility of the mean line and the possibility of forming new systems. Faithfulness is reached by the stability, repeatability, and accountability of leadership and/or revealed by the natural laws. The core image of the Tao—love, justice, freedom, and faithfulness—is integrated in the dynamics of conflict resolution by management by the mean. Role equity and role change, therefore, are core implications of the Yin/Yang Theory.

Concept of Role

The Confucian approach to roles (Chung, 1993b, 1994) is based on the assumption that lawlessness and social problems arise from uncultivated individuals, normless social structures, and lack of adequate relationships between individuals and society. A role is the way a person acts out her or his culturally defined status, such as parent, child, teacher, student, employer, or employee. In order to solve the social problems encountered during his time, Confucius prescribed five role sets. His definition of the five social relationships forms the basis of Chinese and other Asian social structures and relationships. His influence in these areas is still profoundly felt by many Asians in their daily lives.

In Confucian influenced societies, the traditional social structure is based on five fundamental interpersonal relationships: superior-subordinate, parent-child, husband-wife, sibling-sibling, and friend-friend (Chung, 1992b). These relationships reflect a hierarchical order of position and status. Thus, social relationships are more vertical in Asian culture than in American culture. For example, the superior-subordinate relationship requires that loyalty be given to the government or to one's superior on the job. In return, the government or employer takes care of subordinates' needs. Second, the parent-child relationship requires filial piety: children should obey, honor, and respect their parents, and parents should love their children. The husband-wife relationship prescribes that the wife be submissive to the husband and that the husband love the wife. Young brothers should respect elder brothers, while elder brothers should love the younger ones. Between friends, righteousness and trust are the rule. Confucianism prescribes family relationships and indicates the degree of intimacy and social distance as well as obligations. Anyone who is within this network of relationships is considered part of the family. Otherwise, he or she is an outsider. As a member of the family, one enjoys membership privileges such as trust, intimacy, and sharing.

One must also fulfill family obligations and make contributions (such as getting good grades in school to increase the family's reputation and not making trouble for the family). Social institutions (schools or employers) thus become extensions of the family, requiring the same respect for the elderly and for authority. Self-control is expected for maintaining social harmony.

Role Confusion and Role Expansion

According to the original teachings of Confucianism and the Yin/Yang theory, each individual should perform his or her role in an excellent way with a sincere attitude. However, after thousands of years of Confucian role practice, the ideal of role equity has been violated, and role change becomes rigidity. The original spirit of mean philosophy and Tao image is being lost. Sincerity may no longer exist in relationships. Studies indicate that many Asian Americans are suffering the effects of role conflict in their daily life. Many Asian Americans are playing the American cultural role during the day and the Asian Confucian role during the evening at home. Many are suffering maladjustment due to the cultural transition. Song-Kim (1992) reported that of 115 Korean women respondents, 60% reported being battered, a clear indicator of dysfunctional Confucian roles.

A helping professional may help a client reframe ambiguous or conflicting roles as the first step in role conflict resolution. The next step, balancing relative merits and sanctions for each of the two roles as Yin/Yang counterforces, then becomes a task of mean management. The third step is redefining and expanding one of the roles to include the other. Thus, role conflict due to a fixed and vertical structure may be transformed by role expansion, equity, and other positive coping strategies under the implications of Yin/Yang dynamics.

The Concept of Daily Review

Confucian daily review allows daily confrontation with conflicting roles and forces an individual to be open to different points of view, to be more flexible, and to expand sources of information for personal transformation. Confucian daily review can be described as a model of mental reframing for adjusting the perception of reality, which modifies and shapes interpersonal relationships and behaviors and group performance. The major focus of the daily review technique is reframing negative thinking, prejudice, or other dysfunctional thinking to lead to attitudinal, emotional, and behavioral changes for both the individual and the group.

The daily review covers three dimensions of role performance: professional accountability, faithfulness of interpersonal relationships, and positive mentality. The daily review establishes developmental goals and objectives to prevent problems and actualize the self. Daily review may be more powerful when integrated with daily meditation. Helping professionals may practice Confucian meditation and daily review for personal stress management as well as for client consultation.

The Concept of Labeling

Finding the truth through the integration of intuitive (right brain/meditation) and logical (left brain/investigation) approaches is an important process in Confucianism. The next step is to label a thing (subject or variable) according to the methodology of problem solving. Then the personal and social issues are defined clearly in terms of individual and social development. For example, "Is abortion a right or a killing to be prohibited?" "Should helping professionals facilitate life termination for their clients who wish to end their suffering?" Confucianism promotes intuitive and logical social investigation to find out the truth and officially label such issues through public lawmaking.

The Concepts of Religion and Spirituality

According to Confucians, spiritual development comes after physical, emotional, and mental development. One must first learn to know oneself and to respect and honor oneself in performance of one's daily roles. As Confucius said, "If you don't know how to live as a person, how can you serve the spirit?" Confucianism stresses being spiritual, not being religious.

The Concept of Jen as Loving Relationship

Jen is a proper relationship between two parties, a loving and caring relationship that reflects humanity. Meditation is considered a cornerstone of the search for self and truth and the achievement of individual and collective goals.

The Concept of Harmony

A central feature of Confucianism is harmony between people and their environment (nature), or Tao. An example of the idea of harmony with the environment is the symbol of Tai Chi (the Yin/Yang diagram). The idea of harmony is also applied to the concepts of health/energy (qi/chi), balance for disease prevention and healing, and the development of human potential.

This core value of Confucianism has had negative effects in Chinese history and became quite detrimental to women and children. The ruling class used this value orientation to maintain its class interest. Many Chinese women were expected to commit suicide to "accompany" their husbands into death and gain the "women's virtue" during the 17th, 18th, and 19th centuries. The younger generations were not allowed to express their opinions before the elders. Conflict and confrontation are still prohibited. As a result, many Asian Americans have difficulty dealing with their employers. Women and children who are abused are still expected to be submissive. Social workers and helping professionals must understand the hidden cultural dynamics to deal with the roots of problems during the helping process. The concept of harmony should be clear during counseling.

The Ideal Welfare Society

Confucius used a general method to transform individuals, families, communities, and nations. His multilevel approach is in accord with the growing emphasis in social work on social systems networks, self-help, volunteerism, social support, and social care. Beneficial social change in post-industrial society implies that people must care for and about each other.

While therapeutic models are readily found in the social work literature, models of practice that describe implementation of social care ideas are not as well articulated. This may result from the fact that social work has difficulties reconciling relationships between helping individuals and the surrounding community (Harrison, 1989). Since there is an intrinsic relationship between social change and social planning, it is crucial for the social work profession to address some existing problems in social planning (Lauffer, 1987).

IMPLICATIONS FOR SOCIAL WORK PRACTICE

The implications for social work practice of the Confucian healing and development model are many. First, the model asserts that the unique, unequal, and diversified world is receiving an equal treatment from nature, or Tao. The revealed natural laws can imply equality in social policy and public laws.

Second, Confucianism provides various practical methods—including meditation for physical relaxation and mental transformation, education, the role approach, the mean philosophy, and conflict resolution—to create an ultimate Great Commonwealth where justice and quality are achieved. These approaches are effective means for prevention of discrimination and promotion of social justice.

Third, Confucian concepts of birth and life provide a very positive orientation. Confucians treat life and death as realities, and accept them positively. They welcome life, engaging and challenging themselves daily. This mentality and attitude shape a positive behavior pattern and personality by breaking through an individual's limitations.

Fourth, Confucians positively and creatively engage in investigations and studies to find the truth and solutions to problem situations so as to achieve their ultimate social welfare goal. They accept the chaos of social disorder and social problems as developmental opportunities for creation and transformation. Confucius prescribed the five sets of roles to build and maintain social relationships and social structure and created Li, a code of ethics, to be integrated with other social strategies for achieving social welfare.

Fifth, Confucianism prescribes the nature of the relationship between the person and the environment at various levels: the individual, family, group, state, nation, and world. It defines the core of the social environment: We are the environment, and the environment is us. We shape individuals; we shape the environment. In turn, the environment shapes us through different developmental stages.

The Confucian healing and development model shapes the individual and the environment (micro and macro) at the same time through its comprehensive approaches. It offers a historical case of macro social transformation for all human service professionals to examine and learn from.

Confucianism assumes a positive human interaction that encourages the progressive forces in human nature and human growth at various levels of practice. It helps both clients and practitioners to view human motivation in a positive way by identifying progressive forces and removing blocks and obstacles in development processes. It allows workers to be free from the fear of creating dependency in the helping process. Actually, the Confucian model views each person as a constituent, an equal partner in an interdependent society, rather than a "client." "Clientizing" people by nonequal relationships is dehumanizing and should be replaced with the concept of clients as "constituents" (Harrison, 1989).

Confucianism perceives that the cause of human dysfunction is found in both the individual and the social environment. Thus, any social treatments must not only prescribe methods of individual internal change and adaptation, but also offer ways of changing the environment and the transactions between individuals and their environment.

The Confucian model can be used by the helping professional because it is a multilevel, culturally sensitive, and strengths-based approach to problems that emphasizes individual human development. This model may also serve as an international social work model that can further world peace and human well-being because of its assumption of virtue and, systems interrelatedness and its ultimate emphasis on human welfare.

Confucius took the role approach because of situational needs. During that period of time, social disorder was the key social problem. Defined social roles would help to settle the social order. Therefore, his role approach was an excellent social strategy to achieve desired social goals. The implication of the approach is that a change agent choice depends on the situation encountered. One must study the reality of the situation—the underlying contradictions or the way things are—and then respond. Absolute freedom to choose the strategy or approach does not exist: One only has a temporary and situational choice. This situational approach, which is the *I Ching's* approach, may be the appropriate leadership and management approach for social work practice with Asian Americans as well as for universal social work practice.

REFERENCES

Cheng, Y. (11th century). I Ching: The Tao of Organization. (T. Cleary. trans. 1988). Boston: Shambhala.

Chou, R. J. Confucianism and the concept of Yang-sheng in ancient China. *Journal of Wen Shu Hsueh Po,* No. 42, pp. 105–152.

Chung, D. (1988, Oct.). *Transformation model for cross-cultural social work practice.* Paper presented to the Continuing Professional Education Sessions of the NACSW Training Conference, San Antonio, TX.

Chung, D. (1992a). Confucian model of social transformation. In Furuto, S. M., Biswas, R., Chung, D., Murase, K., & Ross-Sheriff, F. (Eds.). *Social Work Practice with Asian Americans.* Newbury Park, CA: Sage.

Chung, D. (1992b). Asian Cultural Commonalities: A Comparison with mainstream American culture" in Furuto, S. M., Biswas, R., Chung, D., Murase, K., & Ross-Sheriff, F. (Eds.), *Social work practice with Asian Americans.* Newbury Park, CA: Sage.

Chung, D. (1993a, August). *Chung model of family conflict management.* Paper presented at the Second International Symposium on Families East and West, Indianapolis: IN.

Chung, D. (1993b, August). *Using Confucian role approach and Yin Yang theory to understand and help Southeast Asian refugee families in cultural transition.* Paper presented at the Second International Symposium on Families East and West. Indianapolis, IN.

Chung, D. (1994). *Overcoming poverty by Confucian role approach and Yin Yang theory.* Paper presented at the 40th Annual Program Meeting, Council of Social Work Education in Atlanta, GA.

Confucius (1971). *Confucian Analects, the Great Learning, and the Doctrine of the Mean* (J. Legge, Trans.). New York: Dover Publications.

Eden, D. (1998). *Energy medicine: Balance your body's energies for optimum health, joy and vitality.* New York: Penguin Putnam.

Germain, C.B. and Gitterman, A. (1980). *The life model of social work practice.* New York: Columbia University Press.

Harrison, W. D. (1989). Social work and the search for postindustrial community. *Social Work, 34*(1), 73–75.

Hearn, G. (1979). General systems theory and social work. In F. J. Turner (Ed.), *Social work treatment.* New York: Free Press.

Lauffer, A. (1987). Social planners and social planning in the United States. In F. M. Cox, J. L. Erlich, J. Rothman, & J. E. Tropman (Eds.), *Strategies of community organization* (pp. 311–326). Itasca, IL: F.E. Peacock.

Lee, L. C., Ed. (1982). Mental Fasting. In *Shien Shui Mou Shiun (Selected articles on qigongology)* (pp. 63–65) Taipei, Taiwan: Truth, Goodness, and Beauty Publishers.

Liao, K., (1993). *Tsu-yang Chih-tao.* Taipei, Taiwan: Ming-wen Shu-chu.

Liu, S. C. (1985). *A new view of the Chinese Philosophy.* Taipei, Taiwan: World Book.

Song-Kim, Y. I. (1992). Battered Korean women in urban United States. In S. M. Furuto, R. Biswas, D. K. Chung, K. Murase & F. Ross-Sheriff (Eds.), *Social work practice with Asian Americans* (pp. 213–226). Newbury Park, CA: Sage.

ADDITIONAL RESOURCES

Books

Basic Writings of Mo Tzu, Hsun Tzu, and Han Fei Tzu. (1967). (B. Watson, Trans.). New York: Columbia University Press. (Original work published circa 500 B.C.)

Cheng, Y. (1988). *I Ching: The Tao of organization.* (T. Cleary. trans.). Boston: Shambhala. (Original work written in the eleventh century A.D.)

Chung, D. (1992a). Confucian model of social transformation. In Furuto, S.M., Biswas, R., Chung, D., Murase, K., & Ross-Sheriff, F. (1992). *Social work practice with Asian Americans.* Newbury Park: Sage.

Chung, D. (1992b). Asian cultural commonalities: A comparison with mainstream American culture. In Furuto, S.M., Biswas, R., Chung, D., Murase, K., & Ross-Sheriff, F. (1992). *Social work practice with Asian Americans.* Newbury Park: Sage.

Confucius (1971). *Confucian Analects, the Great Learning and the doctrine of the mean.* (J. Legge, Trans.). New York: Dover Publications. (Original work published circa 500 B.C.)

Confucius (1967). *Li Chi.* (J. Legge, Trans.). New York: University Books. (Original work published circa 500 B.C.)

I-Ching Mandalas: A program of study for The Book of Changes. (1989). (T. Cleary, Trans.). Boston: Shambhala. (Original work published circa first century A.D.)

Ou-I, Chih-Hsu. (1987). *The Buddhist I Ching.* (T. Cleary, Trans.). Boston: Shambhala.

The Tso Chuan: Selections from China's oldest narrative history (722 to 468 B.C.). (1992). (B. Watson, Trans.). New York: Columbia University Press.

Yi, T'oegye (1988). *To become a sage.* (M.C. Kalton, Trans.). New York: Columbia University Press.

Web Sites

http://www.enteract.com/~geenius/Kongfuzi

www.easternreligions.com/confucius-n.html

www.religioustolerance.org/confuciu.htm

GLOSSARY

Acceptance Confucians accept the way things and people are.

Ancestor Forefathers or family members who have died. Confucians promote fidelity and ancestor worship to show respect for their roots of life. April 5th is a memorial day for Chinese to respect their ancestors.

The Analects Lun Yu, one of what are known as *The Four Books, or Ssu Shu.*

Birth The creation of a new life. The purpose of birth is to continue family life by living here and now by linking the chain of family existence from the past to the future.

Code of Ethics The Confucian code of ethics is based on the family (from the nuclear family to the national family). Five role sets prescribe a loving and caring network starting from the small family circle to larger society.

Confucius (551—479 B.C.) Renowned as a philosopher and educator, he was also considered a researcher, statesman, change agent, social planner, social innovator, enabler, and spiritual advocate. He is said to have preserved and recreated Chinese culture.

Confucianism A life philosophy based on Confucius' teaching. It consists of some elements of traditional Chinese religion such as reverence toward heaven and the worship of ancestors. It does not assert the existence of a deity, although it recognizes and promotes synchronization with Tien (Heaven, the Ultimate, or Tao) through harmonious relationships with others and the environment. Confucianism teaches a practical way to reach an ideal world through management of energy at various levels.

Daily review Confucians promote professional, family and personal transformation through daily review of role performance in professional accountability, faithfulness of interpersonal relationships, and positive mentality.

The Doctrine of Mean Chung Yung, one of *The Four Books, or Ssu Shu.* It prescribes the mean (moderation) philosophy for management of life forces.

Empowerment Confucians utilize meditation to empower the self for personal, professional, family and social development. Internalizing the energy is the key for self-awareness, insight, and empowerment.

The Great Learning Ta Hsueh, one of *The Four Books, or Ssu Shu.*

Hao zen zhi qi Moral righteousness or courage, cultivated by daily meditation. It is intrinsically connected with universe qi.

I-Ching *The Book of Changes,* is one of the Five Classics of Confucianism.

Ideal welfare society Confucians promote an ideal welfare society prescribed in Li Chi as their ultimate goal of social transformation.

Jen Loving and caring; the cornerstone of all fundamental relationships promoted by Confucians.

Labeling Confucians promote truth finding through the integration of intuitive (right brain/meditation) and logical (left brain/investigation) approaches, which allow a problem or an issue to be labeled, so as to promote communication, development, and problem-solving.

Li Proper behavior in a certain situation. Confucians create various norms and customs of Li to guide people in fulfilling expected roles.

Life stages Confucians consider life as a transformation process with different developmental stages. Each stage has its own task and process to be achieved.

Mean management Confucians believe that Tao exists and moves in the Mean Way. Therefore, all energy management in meditation, personal life, family, business and social administration should follow the Mean for effectiveness, efficiency, and accountability.

Meditation A starting point of energy management for personal, family, and social transformation.

Mental Fasting A chapter in *Chuang Tzu* where Confucius prescribed five stages of meditation in order to physically relax, mentally forget self-attachments, and reach spiritual freedom.

Mental maturity The life stage of a person who has reached 40 years old and who has matured into a determined personality, no longer struggling with trail and error.

Person in the environment Confucians consider that we are the environment and the environment is us. Individuals shape the environment, in turn, the environment shapes us through developmental stages.

Qi Energy or life force that enables the blood to circulate and maintain life.

Ritual Confucians promote many rituals to facilitate adequate role performance, such as birthday celebration, Li, teachers' honor day, and ancestors' memorial day.

Role Confucians prescribed five role sets (superior-subordinate, parent-child, husband-wife, sibling-sibling, and friend-friend) to define personal, interpersonal, and social relationships.

Self Confucians consider the self as a here-and-now link in a chain of existence from the past to the future. The self is very important for carrying on the family tree.

Social development Confucians prescribe seven steps of social transformation to achieve the ideal society, with meditation as the starting point.

Sources of power Confucians believe that Tai Chi is the Ultimate, the integrated energy of Yin and Yang, which can be transformed into various forms of being. The Ultimate source of all substance, energy, and knowledge is called Tao in Chinese.

Spirituality Confucianism stresses being spiritual, not being religious. Spiritual development comes after physical, emotional and mental development.

Spiritual maturity The stage of life when a person is spiritually reconnected with the Ultimate and knows Heaven's will.

Synthesis Synthesis of the elements of the universal interdependent energy network (the Way of Tao) will yield unification and an ideal society.

Systems Confucians believe that Yin/Yang counter forces exist in all interrelated systems. Systems balance or harmony can be reached through meditation and mean energy management.

Systems theory Confucians operate under the Yin/Yang theory, or systems theory.

Tai Chi Confucians believe that Tai Chi is the Ultimate, an integrated energy of Yin and Yang that can be transformed into everything.

Tao God, the Ultimate, or Tai Chi.

Taoism A life philosophy prescribed by Liao-Tzu in the *Tao Te Ching*.

Te Virtues or moral principles and conduct that can be seen in daily life. It is the function of Tao. The individual can revitalize the internal virtue (te) through meditation (synchonize with the Tao for unification).

Teacher Confucians consider that anyone can be a teacher or role model.

Tien jen unification Confucians promote a systemic energy balance in a changing world that is an endless interrelated universal system. How individuals (jen) synchonize and unify with Tien (Nature, Heaven, or the Ultimate) to follow the Way of Tao is the core concern of Confucianism.

Transformation Change from one form of energy to another form of energy, such as physical health, emotion, attitude, behavior, and material.

Ultimate God, the Tai Chi, the Truth, the Way, or the First Cause of the universe.

Unification Achieving awareness of and becoming a part of the whole in an interdependent energy network.

Yang-sheng Health maintenance and promotion through a simple life, a positive attitude, adequate food intake, and energy management.

Yin and Yang The negative and positive principles of Universal force, or counter forces that are in conflict with yet complement each other and create tension in all systems for change and creation.

Zen The Japanese name for the spiritual discipline of Ch'an (meditation), a unique blend of the philosophies and idiosyncrasies of three different cultures. It is a typical way of Japanese life, and yet it reflects the Buddhism of India, the Taoists' love of nature, and the pragmatism of Confucianism.

6 CHAPTER | JUDAISM

BRUCE FRIEDMAN

When I was asked to write this chapter about Jewish spiritual and religious tradition and social work practice, I thought hard about whether there was a single Jewish tradition. Judaism, especially American Judaism, is very complex. There are a number of divisions within American Judaism, including Humanistic, Reform, Reconstructionist, Conservative, Traditional, Orthodox, and Hasidic. I would refer to these divisions as political divisions rather than spiritual divisions, because a person can express his or her spirituality through participating in any of them. In addition to divisions defined on religious lines, there is room in Judaism for secular and Zionist divisions as well. Thus, it becomes difficult to define Judaism as a single tradition.

I think of Judaism as having a single foundation built on three bases: God, Torah, and Israel (people or community) (Friedman, 2000). A Jewish person functions in a universalism that is built on the oneness of the universe (one God), with a legal system that prescribes a value orientation (Torah) that is sanctioned by a community (Israel). The interaction of these three components and their relationship to spirituality and helping will be discussed later in this chapter. It is important, though, that these three elements work together, for the least number of legs needed for stability is three, and these three provide that stability. This chapter will provide an overview of how these three bases are evident in Judaism and how they relate to social work practice. It will also provide a historical overview of the American Jewish community, describe basic beliefs and ritual practices, and touch on sources of power, problem resolution, and helping within the Jewish tradition.

HISTORICAL BACKGROUND

Jewish tradition is built upon the Torah, or the first five books of the Old (First) Testament. Although written as a historical journey beginning with the creation of the world and going through the death of Moses, the Torah is more than a historical account of the evolution of the Jewish people. The Torah presents these stories as a way to help Jews begin to learn the values and ethics that relate to their development as a people. In essence, the historical narratives of the Torah are a way to assert God's reaching out to humanity to accept value and truth. "Torah must be seen as a record not of man's spiritual genius, but of God's will communicated to mortal and finite man" (Donin, 1972, p. 25). For the Jewish person, Torah is the law on which the tradition of Judaism is built. Although it begins with the Five Books of Moses, there are oral traditions and commentaries that are just as important. These include the Prophets, the Writings, the Talmud, and the Shulchan Aruch. Jewish people in each generation look at these writings and adapt them to the current context of their particular time and society.

Let me briefly explain each of these books to illustrate how Judaism has not stagnated but has adapted the Five Books of Moses during each generation to provide meaning. The Torah, or the Five Books of Moses, ends with the death of Moses before the people of Israel can enter the Promised Land. The story continues with the Books of the Prophets, in which the Jews enter the Promised Land through the building of the two Temples. The Books of the Prophets describe various kings, the destruction of the first Temple, the exile and return to the Promised Land, and a change in religious practices from sacrifice to prayer. Written at the same time as the Books of the Prophets, the Writings include a variety of theoretical books, such as Job and Ecclesiastes, that try to explain life and issues of good and evil. The Talmud was developed between the third and fifth centuries C.E. The Talmud consists of two books, the Mishnah and the Gemara. Each presents case law discussions by leading rabbis. These are written like Supreme Court decisions, presenting arguments on the interpretation of law as defined in the Torah and outlining how the Torah relates to the time period when a particular rabbi was living. The Shulchan Aruch is a compilation and interpretation of the laws identified in the Talmud as they related to the Jews during the 16th century. Commentary and interpretation of the Torah and the other books continue today, and important figures throughout Jewish history have made major contributions to Jewish thought and practice. In general, when a Jew refers to the Torah, he or she may be referring to any one of these books even though the Torah is actually only the Five Books of Moses.

The Jewish person tries to apply the Torah to current times. For example, the single most important event in Jewish history is the Exodus from Egypt. It is the Exodus that established the Jewish people as a people. So important is the Exodus from Egypt that it is traditional to relive the Exodus each year through the celebration of Passover. In their Exodus from Egypt, the Jewish people stopped at Mt. Sinai and received the Ten Commandments. It is the spiritual reliving of the Exodus from Egypt that unites one generation of Jews to another and binds together the almost 5800 years of Jewish history. That is not to say that Jewish history stopped with the Exodus from Egypt, but rather that everything else in Jewish history relates to the Exodus. The joy of emerging from slavery into freedom is something that is applicable in every generation. It is this concept that makes the Exodus the paramount event within Jewish life.

The task of being a Jew is to integrate the concept of freedom into one's life, thus bringing the Exodus into current times. For example, after wandering in the wilderness for 40 years and living a semi-nomadic lifestyle, the Jewish people settled in their homeland of Canaan, a land that had been purchased by Abraham before his great-grandchildren went to Egypt. Once they settle in Canaan, the Jewish people changed to an agrarian society, and their form of worship also changed. The prophets took the lessons of the Torah and tried to help the people change from honoring God through sacrifice to using prayer as a mode of worship.

Following the destruction of the first Temple and exile to Babylonia in 586 B.C.E., prophets such as Jeremiah convinced the people to follow God through worship rather than sacrifice. This practice lasted until the return to Israel (land) in 539 B.C.E. and the reconstruction of the Second Temple in 516 B.C.E. During the period of the Second Temple, people worshipped God through a combination of prayer and sacrifice. But this soon ended with the destruction of the second Temple in 135 C.E. and the exile of the people from Israel.

During the period of exile (*galut*) from the land of Israel, the focus continued to be on God and Israel (the land). Laws were interpreted to relate to the practices of the time. For example, since Jews in Spain were mainly merchants, Maimonides adapted Torah to address the specific form of trade in which they engaged. He created a formula for giving that focused on monetary equivalence rather than on land, as was described in the Torah. Thus, in each generation, rabbis and community leaders study the Torah and adapt it to the current situation. This has led to the major religious divisions within Judaism: Humanistic, Reform, Reconstructionist, Conservative, Traditional, Orthodox, and Hasidic.

AMERICAN JEWISH RELIGIOUS MOVEMENTS

Humanistic Judaism

In the 1970s, Rabbi Sherwin Wine broke from his Reform roots to form Humanistic Judaism. The emphasis is on the celebration of people rather than belief and praying to a deity. This approach helped many people who were questioning God's role in the Holocaust. There are two types of laws: those between people and God and those between people. Humanistic Judaism focused on the values and traditions of the laws between people and on those commandments relating to ethical treatment of other people and the world in which we live.

Reform Judaism

Reform Judaism had its beginnings in Germany in the early 19th century as a reaction against what some Jews regarded as Orthodox rigidity and backwardness, and as a response to Germany's new, more liberal political climate (Telushkin, 1991, p. 230). Based on the writings of Moses Mendelssohn, Reform Judaism began the practice of not automatically accepting tradition as truth, but rather studying it and accepting it only if it made sense. The focus was on how to reform Judaism to make it relevant to the time.

In the United States, Reform Judaism took a radical departure from traditional Jewish practices. Both the Pittsburgh Platform (1885) and the Columbus Platform (1937) (Telushkin, 1991) established a Reform Jewish movement that sought to adapt to the American community. It changed the major day of prayer from the traditional Saturday to Sunday, to conform with American religious practices. Over the past 30 years, there has been a widespread reversal to bring more traditional practices back into the Reform movement (Bial, 1971). However, Reform Judaism continues to offer a more liberal interpretation of Torah law that relates to the circumstances of the period.

Reconstructionist Judaism

In a break from his Orthodox and Conservative Jewish roots, Mordecai Kaplan founded the Reconstructionist Jewish movement in the middle of the 20th century. Struggling with traditional concepts of a personal, transcendent God and Jews as the chosen people (Kaplan, 1962; Telushkin, 1991), Kaplan established a movement that continued to observe many of the familiar traditions, but within a larger, more scientific context. Kaplan was a proponent of egalitarian measures within Jewish tradition. It was the Bat Mitzvah of Kaplan's daughter that began the widespread tradition of such ceremonies for girls. Prior to Kaplan's daughter's Bat Mitzvah, ceremonies for 13-year-olds entering adulthood were for boys only. (The ceremony and its symbolism will be discussed later in the chapter.) Kaplan also was a firm believer in the need for community centers where Jews could meet for reasons other than prayer (Telushkin, 1991).

Conservative Judaism

In response to the growing Reform movement in the United States, a Jewish Theological Seminary was established in 1887 (Telushkin, 1991). The intent was not to create a new Jewish denomination but rather to offer a traditional alternative for more liberal-minded Jews.

Conservative Judaism strikes a middle road between Reform and Orthodox Judaism (Telushkin, 1991). Conservative Judaism feels bound by Torah rituals yet free to be innovative in interpreting Jewish law. Some of these innovations have come in response to the changing demographic nature of the community. For example, the Conservative movement has permitted driving a car on the Shabbat but only to transport oneself to and from the Synagogue.

Traditional Judaism

Orthodox and Conservative leaders have come together to create Traditional Judaism. The practices within this movement take a middle road between the liberalism of Conservative Judaism and the practice of Orthodox Judaism. The movement began gathering initiative as the Conservative movement moved toward an egalitarian perspective by ordaining women as rabbis in 1972.

Orthodox Judaism

Many different institutions have contributed to Orthodox Judaism. Many communities have independent *yeshivot* that produce rabbis who serve in Orthodox congregations. Throughout history, yeshivot were strictly Jewish schools of study with no secular studies. However, in 1928, Yeshiva College was founded. There it became possible for a student to earn a Bachelor of Arts degree in the pursuit of rabbinical studies (Telushkin, 1991).

Although a number of different yeshivot in both the United States and Israel train rabbis, and they differ in religious and political affiliation, a unifying factor is a strong focus on Torah law and practices. People affiliate with Orthodox congregations because of the close adherence to Torah law and practices. However, specific congregations vary according to the rabbi's interpretation of Torah law, including observances relating to Shabbat and *Kashrut* (keeping kosher).

Hasidic Judaism

Although many who see the earlocks, beards, and black coats of Hasidim may refer to them as an ultra-orthodox group, their origin is far from it. Hasidic Judaism emerged in the middle of the 18th century in Eastern Europe in response to the Orthodox Jews known as *Mitnagdim* (Telushkin, 1991). The Mitnagdim followed the practices of the Vilna Gaon, who stated that the only good Jewish person was a yeshiva student. However, the founder of the Hasidic movement, Israel Ba'al Shem Tov, countered that one could be a good Jew without having to experience the rigors of Jewish study. Israel Ba'al Shem Tov used parables as a way of conveying the Torah to his followers (Ben-Amos & Mintz, 1972). A wealth of stories emerged about the rabbis of the time and how they dealt with issues. These stories were used to teach people about moral behavior and to explain the meaning of Torah. The Hasidim also placed a heavy emphasis on the joys of Judaism, based on Isaiah 6:13, "The whole world is full of His glory." They accomplished this by incorporating song and melodies, called *nigunim,* into the service. Many Hasidic services today are filled with song and dance.

Israel Ba'al Shem Tov had a number of disciples. Each of these disciples came from a different community, and these groups later became the sects of Hasidism known today. Thus, each sect acquired its name from its community of origin. The largest Hasidic group is the Satmar, who originated from Satmar (St. Mary's), Poland. The next largest group is the Chabad Lubavitch, from White Russia and Lithuania (Hellman, 1967). A very influential Lubavitch Rebbe (leader) was Menachem Mendel Schneersohn, who until his death in 1998 was believed by many of his followers to be the Messiah. These groups migrated to the United States to escape religious persecution in Eastern Europe during the late 19th and early 20th centuries. Today, new Hasidic groups are forming, each following a different spiritual leader (rebbe). For example, a group called the Bostoner Hasidim follows the Bostoner Rebbe.

ISRAEL AND ITS RELATIONSHIP TO JUDAISM

Around the end of the 19th and beginning of the 20th centuries, a group of Jews wanted to have Israel (the people) return to Israel (the land). The Zionist convention was charged with finding a homeland for the people. Although the British government offered other locations, the only place acceptable to the Jewish people was Israel. For almost 5800 years, the concepts of exodus and return to Israel have symbolized freedom for the Jewish people. It is the acquisition of freedom through exodus and return that is celebrated in the Passover service each year.

Prior to 1948, the Jewish people were said to be in the Diaspora. However, since the United Nations created the State of Israel in 1948, there has been a change in terminology; now, Jews who do not live in the State of Israel are said to be in exile (galut). This change reflects the idea that there now is a Jewish homeland, but it is a person's individual choice whether to return to that land, Israel. Thus, the concept of returning continues to be an important theme throughout Jewish ritual practice. For returning to land means more than just a physical return; it also refers to a spiritual return, relating to the concept of freedom. Because some Jews choose to remain outside of Israel, there are additional observances that are introduced into religious practice to assist the individual in coming closer to the spiritual plane that would be achieved by being in Israel.

The concept of exodus and return to Israel is represented through a developmental process in the Torah. The Torah does not begin with the Exodus but talks about the transition from idol worship to monotheism through Abraham. Throughout this history the Jewish people begin to see the relationship between man and God and between man and his fellow man. There is a tradition of learning how to interact and live together as stewards of the earth.

TENSIONS WITHIN JUDAISM

I have referred to the divisions in Judaism as political divisions, because all continue to be based on the foundation of God-Torah-Israel. Tension arises because each division feels that its interpretation of the foundation is the correct one for this time. This creates a sense that Jews who do not follow particular practices are not good Jews. Goodness relates to the spiritual and truly comes from within. In fact, Judaism does permit individual choice. Thus, the issue of rightness relates more to a political and functional approach to maintaining the distinctiveness of a particular division.

Consider a real-life example of this issue of rightness. The State of Israel was founded as a Jewish state. Theodor Herzl, one of the founders of the First Zionist Congress, did not care where the Jewish state was as long as there was one. However, he was overruled by others who said that it had to be in Palestine. Once the State of Israel was established, the rule of law became that of the more Orthodox Jews. There is a provision that any Jew can come to Israel and declare immediate citizenship. This raises a problem in the definition of a Jew. Orthodox Judaism defines a Jew as anyone who was born of a Jewish mother or who has converted to Judaism. Yet, there is a restriction on who performs the conversion, as the Orthodox will not recognize conversions done by the other divisions. In addition, the Reform and Reconstructionist movements have decided that if one parent is Jewish (either the mother or the father), and the parents raise the child as Jewish, then the child is Jewish. The Israeli government would not allow this child to become an automatic citizen, because its Orthodox laws do not define the child as Jewish. These are political issues and not spiritual ones.

CUSTOMS AND CEREMONIES

Regardless of the tensions within Judaism, there are customs and ceremonies that are universal for all groups. The customs and ceremonies relate back to the Exodus and its theme of moving from slavery to freedom. These customs and ceremonies are carried out both on particular days during the Jewish year and in connection with certain events in the lives of individual Jews.

THE JEWISH CALENDAR

Shabbat

The most important holiday in the Jewish calendar is the Shabbat (the Sabbath). It is also the holiday that happens most often, as it occurs each week, on Saturday. (The Jewish Shabbat begins at sundown on Friday and ends at sundown on Saturday.) Shabbat is the most important day because of the fourth of the Ten Commandments (the Decalogue):

> Remember the Sabbath day to sanctify it. Six days shall you work and accomplish all your work but the seventh day is Shabbat to Hashem, your God; you shall not do any work, you, your son, your daughter, your slave, your maidservant, your animal, and your convert within your gates—for in six days Hashem made the heavens and the earth, the sea and all that is in them, and He rested on the seventh day. (Exodus 20:8–11)

This fourth commandment is a change from the first three, which focus on belief in God. The fourth commandment orders Jews to emulate God through the observance of the Shabbat.

Modern American practices reflect various interpretations of how one should remember the Sabbath. The Traditional or Orthodox view is to avoid doing any type of "holy" work, or work that involves creating and destroying. These are perceived as the types of work that God did in creating the world. The Reform observance of Shabbat differs. Since the Reform movement emphasizes an individualistic approach to tradition and practice, it is solely up to the individual how the holiday is observed. Some may choose to follow strict Orthodox guidelines; others may want to differentiate the day from the rest of the week by doing something special. The key is to differentiate Shabbat from the rest of the week. The Conservative movement is somewhere in between the others. On one hand, Conservative Judaism places importance on practicing most of the laws of Shabbat prescribed by the Orthodox; on the other hand, there is the recognition that not everyone can live that lifestyle. So Conservative Judaism recognizes some of the modern practical concerns that face many American Jews. For example, there is the recognition that most Jews do not live close to a synagogue, so there are allowances for driving.

Aside from these differences, Shabbat observance is truly the ideal for Jews. Shabbat takes precedence over every act in Jewish life (except saving a life). The week revolves around Shabbat: The spirit of the previous Shabbat will carry a person through Sunday, Monday, and Tuesday, and the anticipation of observing Shabbat helps the individual get through Wednesday, Thursday, and Friday. Some explain it as a psychological and physical dynamic. The whole week (Sunday through Friday) can be viewed as preparation for the coming Shabbat (Siegel, Strassfeld, & Strassfeld, 1973, p. 105).

Metaphors about Shabbat are too numerous to discuss here. One metaphor that is worth noting, however, is that Shabbat should be celebrated as though one is honoring a queen. This means, for example, using the best linen tablecloths and silver for dinner. The traditional practices surrounding Shabbat are also very symbolic. One begins 18 minutes before sundown with the lighting of the candles. These candles provide a utilitarian purpose of lighting one's dining room table. Some people follow the practice of lighting one candle for every member of the household (with a minimum of two). The lighting of the candles is to be the last fire that one lights until the conclusion of Shabbat. Traditional observers of Shabbat do not use any type of electrical appliance.

In many households, the women stay home and light the candles while the men go to the synagogue to say the evening prayers that usher in Shabbat. Once the family returns home and the candles are glowing, it is customary for the head of the household to bless the children. The woman of the house is then honored with the saying of the "Woman of Valor" poem. Following the recitation of the poem, the *kiddish,* or blessing over the wine, is said. While the wine is being blessed, the two loaves of twisted bread, *challah,* are covered. After drinking the wine, family members wash their hands, uncover the challah, and say the blessing over the bread. There are two loaves of challah, to symbolize the double portion of manna that the Jewish people received on Shabbat as they wandered through the wilderness following the Exodus from Egypt. The loaves are covered so as not to offend them by saying the blessing over the wine before the blessing over the bread. For bread symbolizes the actual beginning of the meal, and nothing should come before it. However, the blessing of the wine is important to set Shabbat apart from the rest of the week.

Once the blessing over the challah is completed, everyone eats the first Shabbat meal. Shabbat observance becomes a time for family and family interactions. The meal is a lavish meal—remember, you are serving a queen—and is accompanied by singing around the table. It is customary not to hurry through the meal but to stretch it out. When dessert is finished, the grace after meals is said.

On Saturday morning, the family goes to the synagogue. This is a long service, involving the customary morning service as well as reading from the Torah, and an additional service called *musaf*. This added service represents the additional sacrifices that were brought to the holy Temple to honor Shabbat.

After the service, the family goes home for a second meal. Again, this is a lavish meal, beginning with wine and then the blessing over the challah, but there are some restrictions. As cooking is not permitted on Shabbat, all the food has to be prepared ahead of time. Hot foods are kept over low heat until served. A stew called *cholent* (which can be made in advance and keeps well) was developed to address the special restrictions of Shabbat. The second meal is also accompanied by singing and followed by the grace. Following the meal, Shabbat afternoon is a time for rest and contemplation. Many people study the Torah or other books. The family gets together to talk; people visit their neighbors. It is a time for the community to come together.

As sundown approaches, there is the preparation for the afternoon service, the third meal, and then *havdallah*—the service that symbolizes the conclusion of Shabbat and the return to daily activity. There is the blessing over the wine, spices (to carry the sweet smell of Shabbat into the rest of the week), and the blessing over the candle. Just as Shabbat was ushered in with the lighting of candles, havdallah uses a candle as a way of saying goodbye to Shabbat until next week (a braided candle so it burns brighter than one with a single wick). Finally, the candle is extinguished in wine.

Shabbat practices form a standard for many of the holidays throughout the Jewish calendar. Though other celebrations are not as extensive, many of the same practices are followed to a lesser extent.

Holidays, Holy Days, and Festivals

The Jewish calendar distinguishes between holidays, holy days, and festivals. Since the Jews were a semi-nomadic and then an agrarian culture, the holidays were celebrations that were tied to the land, and it was customary to bring sacrifices to the Temple in Jerusalem. There is a lot written about the holidays in the Torah. The three holidays of Passover, Shavuoth, and Succoth are described in more detail below. Holy days are briefly mentioned in the Torah but have become the focus of much of American Jewry. These are days of repentance and introspection, when it is customary to ask for forgiveness for both individual and community sins committed throughout the year. The two holy days are Rosh Hashanah and Yom Kippur. The festivals do not have a basis in the Torah but are commemorations of military victories by the Jewish people over adversaries. The festivals of Chanukah and Purim are usually celebrated joyfully, though they have little religious value. There are also a number of fast days throughout the Jewish calendar. These days commemorate different atrocities suffered throughout Jewish history.

Passover

The first Jewish holiday is Passover. Passover occurs on the 15th day of the first month of the Jewish calendar. Passover has a very important significance to the Jewish people. Since it represents the Exodus from Egypt, it is the holiday that symbolizes the beginning of the Jewish people as a people.

There are two parts to the 8-day Passover holiday. The first 2 days (or the first day, in Israel) are holy days and are celebrated very much like Shabbat, except that one can cook on those days. The first of these days is used to remember the Passover and the Exodus from Egypt, while the second day begins the celebration of Matzah. The evening meal is called *Seder,* which means "order," and during the meal people retell the story of the Exodus from Egypt. There is a lot of symbolism associated with Seder, which is too extensive to detail here.

The rest of the holiday is celebrated by saying additional prayers and having special readings from the Torah. The entire 8 days (7 in Israel) is celebrated by the eating of unleavened bread, *matzah*. Beginning with the second day of Passover, one begins counting the *omer,* which is a countdown to the next holiday.

Shavuoth

The second Jewish holiday is *Shavuoth*. The word *Shavuoth* means "weeks," and the holiday occurs exactly 7 weeks after Passover. The holiday celebrates Moses' receiving the Ten Commandments at Mt. Sinai. The historical account in the Torah states that it took the Israelites exactly 7 weeks from the time of the Exodus from Egypt to reach the foot of Mt. Sinai. However, Moses took a long time on top of the mountain, and the Israelites became restless and built a golden calf as an image of God. This angered Moses, who broke the tablets when he saw what the Israelites had done. The celebration of Shavuoth is influenced by the creation of the golden calf. On other holidays, it is customary to eat meat; however, as a result of the golden calf incident, it is customary to eat dairy foods during the two days of Shavuoth. A folk legend says that when the Jews received the Torah, they learned that meat was not kosher and symbolized the golden calf; so they ate dairy products (Telushkin, 1991). Thus, Shavuoth is nicknamed "the cheesecake holiday." Like Passover, Shavuoth is celebrated by following many of the practices of Shabbat, except that one is allowed to cook during Shavuoth. Shavuoth is also tied into the first harvest of the season and is sometimes called "the holiday of the first fruits."

Succoth

The third holiday is Succoth, which is celebrated 2 weeks after Rosh Hashanah. It was traditionally celebrated by building a thatch-roofed hut, called a *sukkah,* in the yard and dwelling in the hut for the 7 days of the holiday. The sukkah symbolized the relationship between people and God, because it removed people from the comfort of home and exposed them to the elements. The sukkah became a symbol of the Exodus, since it is a reminder of the interdependence between man and God. Succoth is also the fall harvest holiday, and the celebration of the holiday includes eating meals that use many fall fruits and vegetables and giving thanks for the abundant harvest. This is the Jewish version of Thanksgiving.

The seven days of Succoth are followed immediately by two more holidays, *Shimini Atzeret* and *Simchat Torah*. Shimini Atzeret finalizes the end of the harvest. It is traditional to say a prayer for rain so that the ground will become ready for the spring planting. Simchat Torah is a joyous day, as it commemorates the end of reading the Torah and beginning to read it all over again. Like other holidays, Succoth, Shimini Atzeret, and Simchat Torah are celebrated with a modified observance of Shabbat.

Rosh Hashanah

Although *Rosh Hashanah* is translated as the "head of the year," it actually occurs on the first day of the seventh month. The Jewish calendar differentiates between when the world was created and when the Jewish people became a people. So Rosh Hashanah is considered the celebration of the birth of the world and Passover is the beginning of Jewish peoplehood.

Rosh Hashanah begins a 10-day period of repentance and reflection that ends with *Yom Kippur.* Rosh Hashanah is noted by the sounding of the ram's horn, or *shofar,* to awaken the soul and to call Jews to think about forgiveness. It is also a time when Jews perform rituals to symbolize the throwing away of sins and ask others to forgive them. As in other holidays, food and family are very important. A modified Shabbat celebration is observed. The challah used is usually round rather than braided, to symbolize the roundness of the world and to remind us of repentance.

Yom Kippur

The 10-day period of repentance ends with *Yom Kippur.* Yom Kippur is a major fast day that runs from sundown to sundown (25 hours). Whereas other holidays are very social occasions and times when people are outgoing, Yom Kippur is a day for introspection. It is a day to reflect on the wrong one has done and to ask God for forgiveness. It is called the "Holy of Holies."

Usually the day of Yom Kippur is spent in the synagogue in prayer. The day involves a process of confession *(vidui)* of one's and the community's sins. Following the confession, there is repentance. These are separated because repentance does not come automatically with confession, a lag gives the individual time to reflect on what was confessed. At the end of the day, the shofar is sounded one last time for the season, and then people congregate to break the fast.

Chanukah

Despite a common misperception among non-Jews, *Chanukah* is not a religious holiday. Rather, it is a festival to celebrate a military victory of the Jews over the Assyrians in 167 B.C.E. The victory was possible because a miracle occurred, allowing 1 day's worth of oil to last for 8 days. To commemorate this miracle, it is customary to light lamps and to eat fried foods during this festival.

Purim

The other Jewish festival is *Purim,* which also symbolizes a military victory of sorts. The heroine of the story is Esther, who married the king of Persia. With the help of her uncle Mordecai, Esther defeated the wicked Haman, one of the king's courtiers, who wanted to destroy the Jewish people. Because of the joyous nature of this festival, it is customary to dress up in costume and to give food baskets to others. This festival takes place exactly 4 weeks before Passover.

JEWISH LIFE CYCLE

Just as the Jewish calendar focuses on the sense of becoming free, so do the rituals that mark the life cycles of the people within the community. Beginning with birth and moving through death, a number of rituals tie the individual to the community, as part of a personal exodus and movement to freedom.

Birth

Children are very important in the Jewish tradition. The Torah refers to God as the Father and the people as God's children. People are made in God's image, so Jews are expected to procreate and bring new life into the world. Jews are not to miss the incredible joy, contentment, and pure satisfaction from having a child (Strassfeld & Strassfeld, 1976, p. 11). Thus, birth and procreation are vital to Jewish life.

Jews observe a number of traditional practices that focus on birth. For Jewish males, there is the *brit,* or circumcision ceremony. Brit represents more than just circumcision within the Jewish tradition. It became a sign between God and the Jewish people of the covenant that exists between them. The brit ceremony is held on the eighth day after the child is born and supercedes every other religious practice. Thus, if the child is born on Shabbat, the brit will take place on the following Shabbat. Regardless of the day of the week, the brit takes precedence (Strassfeld & Strassfeld, 1976).

Since Genesis 17:10–11 states that it is Abraham's obligation to perform the brit on his children, it is customary for the father to be the agent and not the mother. Of course, most fathers are not willing or trained to perform the medical procedure, so a trained individual, a *mohel,* acts on behalf of the father. The ritual of the brit involves the godparents handing the child to the father, who then holds the child while the mohel performs the operation. Following the operation, there is usually a feast to celebrate the entry of the new life into the covenant.

If a baby is a girl, it is customary to have a public baby naming. Traditionally, this takes place on one of the days when the Torah is read publicly (Monday, Thursday, or Shabbat) within the first week after the baby girl is born. Since it is a public celebration, a feast follows the naming ceremony. Some individuals have adapted the brit ceremony for their baby girls.

If a baby boy is the first child, a ceremony called *pidyon ha-ben* is performed. This is a direct reference to the Passover and Exodus from Egypt. Because God spared the Jewish first-borns during the tenth plague, it is deemed that the first-born child in a Jewish family belongs to God and fulfills that obligation by being in the service of God. To redeem the child (to release him from this obligation), there is a ceremony on the 31st day after the birth, during which the father gives the priest (the *Cohen*) five silver dollars (Telushkin, 1991).

A number of customs relate to the raising of the child. For example, some believe that one should not cut a child's hair until the third year. There is also a celebration when the child is weaned based on Genesis 21:8, which describes Abraham having a feast on the day that Isaac was weaned (Strassfeld & Strassfeld, 1976).

Bar Mitzvah and Bat Mitzvah

A custom that has received a lot of attention in the United States has been that of Bar Mitzvah. Traditionally, it signifies when a boy becomes an adult member of the community and is responsible for accepting the observance of the commandments. It coincides with puberty. In simplest terms, becoming an adult member of the community is a right of passage and occurs with the 13-year-old boy being called to the Torah. One of the responsibilities following that event is the wearing of *tefillin* (phylacteries) (Telushkin, 1991). A bar mitzvah can take place any of the three days of the week (Monday, Thursday, and Saturday) when the Torah is read in public. In the United States, becoming a Bar Mitzvah has been marked with a lot of celebrity and has gone over and above minimal requirements. The custom has become that the Bar Mitzvah boy is called to the Torah and then reads a section from the Prophets at a Shabbat service. The section from the Prophets that is read is one that reflects the content in *Torah* section that had been read. This custom of reading from the Prophets was added to the service during the Roman occupation of Israel.

The responsibility of wearing *tefillin* comes from the section of the Torah that mentions a person should have a sign on his hand or between his eyes to remember the commandments. *Tefillin* are the straps that one wraps around one's arm (usually left if right-handed) and on the head. Boxes connected to the straps contain sections from the Torah. The *tefillin* are worn during the week but not on Shabbat. Following the Bar Mitzvah, the boy is then counted as an adult member of the community (*minyan*).

As mentioned earlier, the ceremony of *Bat Mitzvah* did not come into existence until Mordecai Kaplan performed the ceremony for his daughter. Since then, it has taken on a significance for girls similar to that of the Bar Mitzvah for boys. It coincides with puberty and involves the girl being called to the Torah and reading a section from the Prophets. In some congregations, the Bat Mitzvah girl is then counted as part of the adult congregation needed to create community (*minyan*).

Marriage

The Torah mentions the importance for an individual of leaving the home of his or her parents and making a life of his or her own. Leaving home is usually accompanied by taking a partner and creating a family of one's own. Thus, when God told Abraham to leave his father's home, Abraham took Sarah and began a family.

Although no formal marriage ceremony is described in the Torah, a very brief and simple marriage ritual has been handed down for generations. The ceremony takes place under a wedding canopy (*chupah*). It is customary (but not mandatory) for the bride to circle the groom seven times. Following that the groom gives the bride a ring and says that she is sanctified onto him under the laws of Moses and Israel. The person performing the ceremony then reads the marriage contract and the seven benedictions; the readings are followed by the drinking of wine and the breaking of the glass (Telushkin, 1991). It is not necessary for a rabbi to perform the ceremony (all that is needed is two witnesses); however, in American Jewish culture, it has become common practice to have a rabbi perform the ceremony.

Following the wedding ceremony, the community celebrates the event. In some communities, different people prepare meals for the newlywed couple for the week immediately following the wedding.

The wedding ceremony marks the beginning of another set of practices relating to family purity. Although these rituals are too complicated to describe in detail here, it is important to mention their existence. Jewish purity practices are tied to the woman's period. Approximately 1 week after the end of the period, the woman goes to the ritual bath to purify herself. She then informs her husband that it is permissible for them to have sex. This practice is followed by Orthodox and others who choose to follow it. Additional information can be obtained from books such as *A Hedge of Roses* (Lamm), *How to Run a Traditional Jewish Household* (Greenberg), or *The Second Jewish Catalogue* (Strassfeld & Strassfeld).

Divorce

Divorce has become an aspect of Jewish life as well. There are a few references in the Torah about divorce. Deuteronomy 24:1 states that if a woman finds no favor in her husband's eyes, he shall write her a bill of divorce and give it to her. In other words, divorce, like marriage, has been recognized for centuries as a part of life, as something that does happen. As a result, ceremonies have been designed to represent the end of the marriage contract.

Death

Just as they do to celebrate a birth, members of the Jewish community gather to support the loved ones of a person who has died. A number of Jewish practices relate to the death of a family member. First, it is important that the body be buried as soon after the death as possible. This is done to show respect to the dead and also to help the healing process for the survivors. Second, following the funeral, the first-degree relatives of the departed sit *shiva,* which is the practice of not doing anything for oneself but permitting others in the community to come into the home, provide for all the basic needs, and soothe the sorrow of the loss. The shiva period is the most intense period of mourning, when the mourners stay in the home and venture out only for Shabbat. Usually mirrors are covered so the mourners do not have to worry about their appearance. Third, following the shiva period, there is another period of 30 days called *sheloshim,* when the family continues to mourn, but not as intensely as during the shiva period. During the sheloshim period, one is permitted to return to work and to perform normal daily routines, but continues to remember the departed by attending synagogue. The mourning period ends with sheloshim, except in the case of the death of a mother or father, when it continues for an additional 11 months. During this period, the mourner will continue to attend daily synagogue services to recite the mourner's *kaddish.* The mourner's kaddish is a prayer that does not mention death but reaffirms one's belief in God. This can only be recited in the presence of a *minyan* (at least ten adults). Thus, the community is crucial to the re-emergence of the mourner following a death.

SOURCES OF STRENGTH IN JUDAISM

This chapter has stressed the importance of God-Torah-Israel (community) as the foundation of Judaism. It is the combination of these three bases that provides Jews with a source of strength. These three relate to Maimonides' Principles of Faith. Maimonides was a rabbi, physician, and scholar who was born in Spain in the 12th century. Maimonides contributed a great deal of commentary to Jewish literature. Much of his work helped those in the Jewish community integrate the Torah into their daily experience. (As the Torah reflected the experiences of a semi-nomadic people and Maimonides lived during a period when Jews were primarily merchants, it was important to relate the teachings of the Torah to those times.) One of his works was a discussion of the principles of faith within Judaism. Maimonides acknowledged the existence of a Creator, one that is the cause of all oneness, whose unity is neither potentially nor actually physical, one that is absolutely eternal with no thing existing before it, and is rightfully worshipped, magnified, and obeyed (Twersky, 1972). Defining God in this manner implies that God is a force outside of oneself. A person can use God to achieve solace. God is a forgiving God, a force to which an individual can pray to ask for forgiveness. Maimonides also acknowledged that people are not perfect and do make mistakes. Thus, it is important to be able to acknowledge those mistakes and to be able to ask for forgiveness.

The sixth through tenth principles in the Maimonides formula describe the Torah as being given by God, and thus all that is said in the Torah is holy.

Maimonides also acknowledged that there are prophets or other persons who carry the word of Torah with them. The Torah is a legal prescription for how Jewish people should live. Rather than providing a prescription of do's and don'ts, however, the Torah uses narratives. It is through these narratives that the individual begins to learn how to reframe a situation. For example, the book of Genesis is filled with a number of stories that may appear from the outside to describe dysfunctional families. Yet, it is through studying the meaning of these stories that one begins to find truth and understanding.

As an example, consider the story of the binding of Isaac, which is defined as a test of Abraham's love for God. A few chapters earlier, God appears to Abraham to tell him that it is important for him to move out of his father's house and to set up a home of his own. There is a striking similarity between how God approaches Abraham in that story and how God approaches Abraham to tell him to take his son to be sacrificed. The story raises the question (since Isaac was 37 at the time) of whether the test was for Abraham alone or whether it was also to help Abraham tell Isaac he needed to be on his own. Thus, the narrative can be used to help the individual reframe stories and learn life lessons from them. The goal is to seek to understand and that becomes the application of the Torah to everyday life. Thus, each Jew is given the task of studying the Torah to find meaning in it to relate to modern times.

The last three of Maimonides' thirteen principles of faith focus on the nature of community and the messianic period. Here Maimonides refers to the people of Israel, not only in his own time, but also throughout the millennium. Thus, one person cannot go out on his or her own without it having an effect on the rest of the Jewish community. This relates to the importance of community in Jewish life.

The combination of God-Torah-Israel is thus the foundation of Jewish belief and practice. Although there may be differences between the divisions within Judaism, the thread that pulls these differences together is an ability to have a common understanding about God, to know that the legal system and its interpretation come from the Torah, and to have a community that will support those interpretations.

PROBLEM RESOLUTION WITHIN THE JEWISH TRADITION

Throughout Jewish history, there has been no shortage of problems to be resolved. During each period of this history, new issues and concerns need to be addressed. It is the belief in the foundations of Judaism that helps Jews address these problems, both on a communal level and on an individual level.

For example, when a problem confronts the community, there is a search through the Torah to see if there can be an application to modern times. During Maimonides' time there was concern as to how to help the poor. The Torah addressed ways to help the poor in an agrarian society, and Maimonides adapted those practices for a mercantile society. He created his eight degrees of charity, with the highest level being self-sufficiency. Each lower level represents a way that the donor contributes and the recipient receives, while trying to maintain the integrity of each. Thus Maimonides demonstrates how the Torah can be used as a living document to be interpreted for his time and ours.

Modern-day rabbis have used the Torah to reframe a number of issues. For example, with an increasing number of Jews choosing to marry outside the faith, rabbis have looked at Torah to be able to reframe the problem. They recommend accepting the convert rather than describing him or her as dead, as Tevye did in *Fiddler on the Roof.*

Individuals also find strength in the Torah by reframing its narratives to make sense out of their lives. Jews are not immune to personal problems such as substance abuse or family problems. By reframing the stories in the Torah, it is possible to accept that problems exist and try to understand them. Then one can turn to God and community in order to gain forgiveness and acceptance. The story of Noah becoming intoxicated and then embarrassed by his son Ham is a good example of a story in the Torah that may lead to an understanding of the family implications of alcoholism. When Lot's daughters think that there is no one left on earth following the destruction of Sodom and Gemorrah, they get their father drunk and sleep with him. This provides a starting point for discussing issues of incest in the family. Thus, the Torah does not try to sugarcoat our ancestors but presents them in real-life situations. By studying and understanding the narrative, it is possible to accept human imperfections and then forgive.

IMPLICATIONS FOR SOCIAL WORK PRACTICE

One of the things that has struck me about Judaism is that it is very cerebral. Its focus has always been on study as a path to understanding something. Once, while in class, a student asked me why I did not answer a question directly. I replied that I did not want to influence their decisions and wanted them to think for themselves. At the Passover seder, the youngest child at the table asks four very specific questions that relate to not eating bread, dipping food in salt water, eating bitter herbs, and reclining at the dinner table. However, the answer does not address any of them—it only states that we were slaves and now we are free. The story then continues with the Exodus from Egypt. As a Jewish person growing up, I was never taught to answer a question directly. Rather, I was acculturated to learn and understand through study.

This heritage has many implications for social work. For example, it may be hard for some Jews, who have been acculturated to focus on the intellect, to focus on their feelings in a situation. Jews are taught to use study as a way to understand their feelings. This does not mean that one is to avoid feelings, but rather to bring feelings into an intellectual form to gain some understanding. In some respects, is this not the nature of therapy, to find meaning? Thus, there is a lot of commonality between the therapeutic process and the coming to meaning through the study of Torah. The difference is what is being studied. In the study of Torah, one looks at the narratives in the written and oral traditions to gain some meaning. In therapy, the narratives come from an individual's own life story. For a Jewish client, it may be useful to begin with the Torah narratives as a reference point for the individual's own life stories.

Another important aspect of the therapeutic process is the notion of forgiveness. I referred earlier to Maimonides' notion that God is a God of forgiveness. This idea is represented through the annual celebration of Yom Kippur, when each Jew goes through a process of asking for forgiveness. This is done by first confessing (*vidui*) and then repenting (*teshuvah*). Thus, one element of Jewish tradition is the movement toward forgiveness.

A third component within Judaism that relates to social work is the importance of family and community. Many rituals are linked to relationships within the family, and the holidays are connected to the community. The concept of needing a minyan for public prayer solidifies the importance of community within Judaism.

Because of their sense of community, many Jews will seek help from their own rather than going outside the community. Jews usually only seek outside help after they have exhausted all resources within the community. For example, about 30 years ago, there were no Jewish resources for substance abuse problems (Friedman, 1980). When a Jewish person went for help for substance abuse, the community denied the existence of the problem, stating that Jews don't become dependent (Friedman, 2000). However, as substance abuse began to be accepted as a problem in the community, AA programs began to emerge in synagogues. The Jewish community finally acknowledged the problem and did something to resolve it. The same holds true for other previously ignored groups of individuals—for example, single adults, divorced individuals, gays and lesbians, the developmentally delayed, and immigrants. Jewish agencies exist within the community to develop services and programs for these people. Thus, the emphasis on seeking help from within the community before turning for help outside the community becomes an important consideration for social work.

In working with a Jewish person, it is essential to keep in mind the importance of family and community for that person. Sometimes an individual may feel estranged from the community, but it is important to make that connection. In addition to community, ritual also plays an important role. Judaism is very much oriented toward rituals, which can help the individual with issues of freedom and forgiveness.

CONCLUSION

Judaism is built on a foundation of God-Torah-Israel (people) that is essential to Jewish life. Much of a Jew's existence relates to this combination. Jewish practice and ritual build on this combination, which is also a source of strength and support. So important is the community to Jewish life that there are a number of institutions that have been created to provide not only a religious but also a social outlet for God-Torah-Israel in the Jewish person's life.

The Jewish person uses this foundation in his or her own therapeutic process. Stories, parables, and narratives can be used to help explain many problems and concerns. Although there are many differences within the Jewish community, the unifying concept of God helps to bring community together.

The ability to accept different interpretations of the same narrative is a strength of Judaism. The ability to accept different interpretations becomes a tool in working with a Jewish individual or family to reframe a situation and see it another way. Since God is a forgiving God, it is possible to use the reframing of the problem to help the individual or family move from acceptance to forgiveness. Since no person is perfect, it is possible to forgive. The ability to accept human imperfections helps move the individual or family to a point of forgiving. The acceptance of imperfections gives the person or family permission to be human and to look at the choices that are being made. The hope is to become able to learn from the mistakes and make choices that fall within the guidelines of God-Torah-Israel.

REFERENCES

Ben-Amos, D., & Mintz, J. R. (1972). *In praise of the Baal Shem Tov.* Bloomington: Indiana University Press.

Bial, M. D. (1976). *Liberal Judaism at home.* New York: Union of American Hebrew Congregations.

Donin, H. H. (1972). *To be a Jew.* New York: Basic Books.

Friedman, B. D. (1980). Developing awareness of Chemical Use of the Jewish Community. *Journal of Jewish Communal Service, 57*(2), 185.

Friedman, B. D. (2000). Building a spiritual based model to address substance abuse. *Social Thought, 19*(3), 23.

Greenberg, B. (1997). *How to run a traditional Jewish household.* New York: Jason Aronson.

Hellman, C. M. (1967). The Rebbe of Lubavich bests Count Uvarov. In L. S. Dawidowicz (Ed.), *The Golden Tradition.* Boston: Beacon Press.

Kaplan, M. M. (1962). The meaning of God in modern Jewish religion. New York: Reconstructionist Press.

Lamm, M. (1969). The Jewish way in death and mourning. New York: Jonathan David.

Lamm, N. (1966). *A hedge of roses.* New York: Philipp Feldheim.

Scherman, N. (1993). *The Chumash.* Brooklyn, NY: Mesorah Publications, Ltd.

Siegel, R., Strassfeld, M., & Strassfeld, S. (1973). *The Jewish catalog.* Philadelphia: The Jewish Publication Society of America.

Strassfeld, S., & Strassfeld, M. (1976). *The second Jewish catalogue.* Philadelphia: The Jewish Publication Society of America.

Telushkin, J. (1991). *Jewish literacy.* New York: Morrow.

Twersky, I. (1972). *A Maimonides reader.* New York: Behrman House, Inc.

ADDITIONAL RESOURCES

Books

Overview of Maimonides

Twkerski, I. (1972). *A Maimonides reader.* New York: Behrman House.

Overview of Judaism

Tlushkin, J. (1991). *Jewish literacy.* New York: William Morrow.

Customs and Practices

Siegel, R., Strassfeld, M., & Strassfeld, S. (1973). *The Jewish catalog.* Philadelphia: The Jewish Publication Society of America.

Strassfeld, S., & Strassfeld, M. (1976). *The second Jewish catalog.* Philadelphia: The Jewish Publication Society of America.

Web Sites

Links to information about Judaism: www.jewish-religion.com/

Global Jewish information network: www.jewishnet.net/

Information and links to information about Judaism: www.judaismunlimited.com/

GLOSSARY

Bar Mitzvah A ceremony for boys to denote that they have become responsible for observing the commandments.

Bat Mitzvah A ceremony for girls to denote that they have become responsible for observing the commandments.

Brit Circumcision ceremony that is done on the eighth day after birth.

Challah Braided bread that is part of the Jewish celebratory meal.

Chanukah The Festival of Lights, which symbolizes a military victory by the Jews over the Romans and the rededication of the Temple.

Cholent A stew that is prepared on Friday and left to cook overnight, then eaten on Shabbat. It consists of beans, barley, potatoes, onions, and meat bones.

Chupah Wedding canopy.

Cohen Priest.

Galut Hebrew for "exile;" a term that is used to refer to all Jews living outside the State of Israel.

Havdallah The concluding service of the Sabbath day.

Kaddish Prayer for the departed.

Kiddish Blessing over the wine.

Maimonides A 12th-century Jewish philosopher, rabbi, and doctor who was born in Spain and adapted the Torah to a mercantile society that existed there in his day. He is known for his 13 Principles of Faith.

Matzah Cracker that is eaten on Passover.

Minyan Ten people needed for public prayer.

Mohel The person who performs a brit.

Passover Holiday that symbolizes the Exodus from Egypt and the beginning of the Jewish people as a free people.

Pidyon ha-ben Ceremony of reclaiming the first-born son.

Purim Festival commemorating Esther's defeat of the evil Haman on behalf of the Jews.

Rebbe Spiritual leader of a Hasidic sect.

Rosh Hashanah The Jewish New Year, a joyous time that opens with the sounding of the ram's horn, or shofar, to begin a period of introspection.

Shabbat Saturday and the end of the week for Jewish people. It is a holy day when one refrains from working.

Shavuoth Harvest holiday that also commemorates the receipt of the Ten Commandments by Moses.

Sheloshim The 30-day period following the death of a loved one.

Shimini Atzeret The final day of Succoth.

Shiva A period (usually a week) following a funeral when people pay their respects to the survivors of the departed person.

Shofar Ram's horn that is blown on Rosh Hashanah.

Shulchan Aruch A compilation of Jewish law completed in the 16th century.

Simchat Torah The day that follows Shimini Atzeret and is the time when the reading of the Torah is completed and started over again.

Succoth Fall harvest holiday.

Talmud Two books of oral case law called the Mishnah and the Gemara. The Mishnah was begun during the Roman occupation and consisted of six books. The Gemara expands on the Mishnah and was completed around 500 C.E.

Tefillin Phylacteries—straps that hold small boxes containing verses from the Torah, worn during the daily prayer service.

Teshuvah Forgiveness prayer said on Yom Kippur.

Torah Literally, the first five books of Moses. In later times, Torah has been expanded to refer to some of the oral law and encompasses the books of the prophets, Writings, the Talmud, and the Shulchan Aruch.

Vidui Confessional prayer said on Yom Kippur.

Yom Kippur A day of fasting and introspection that follows Rosh Hashanah. It is a time when one customarily asks for forgiveness, not only from God but also from other individuals.

7 CHAPTER CATHOLICISM

MARIAN A. AGUILAR

INTRODUCTION

Catholicism and the Catholic faith are increasingly being defined by the lived faith of those who have recently become residents or citizens of the United States. As theologian Orlando Espin (1997) has pointed out, "religion is the socialization of the experience of the divine." He elaborates that this view necessitates a two-sided approach to the study of religion and spirituality, one that focuses both on the historical dimensions of the faith and on the experience(s) of the divine by believers. These two aspects of faith, he says, ultimately explain why people believe. Using this approach, he believes, allows a dialogue between social scientists and theologians. One of the most positive aspects of this approach is the recognition that appreciation of culture increases appreciation of the universal and spiritual truths of the Catholic faith. In other words, since particularity mediates universality, culture mediates the universal church's faith (Espin, 1997). While the addition of the cultural variable of ethnicity confounds issues, it can also serve to enlighten practitioners. Religion is part of culture; it is not separate from it.

The Catholic religion is not unlike most other Western religions based on the life and teachings of Christ. Catholics believe that Jesus founded the church upon the apostles, calling for it to be one, holy, catholic (universal), and apostolic. Its body of knowledge is the teachings of Christ as found in the Scriptures. Catholicism as a religion refers to the experiences shared by those Christians who are in communion with the church in Rome. St. Ignatius of Antioch first used the Greek word *katholikos* to refer to the whole, or universal, church (Glazier & Hellwig, 1994, p. 143). Catholics are united in faith by their belief in the death and resurrection of Jesus Christ.

My own perspective on Catholicism arises from my Hispanic heritage, and from 30 years' experience working in ministry with Mexican Americans as a member of a religious order, as a social worker, and as an educator. As a young adult, I attended many conferences on liberation theology (described later). This perspective shape's this chapter's discussion of Catholicism.

A BRIEF OVERVIEW OF CATHOLICISM

Christ gave his twelve apostles the authority to preach, teach, and heal in his name. Christ gave Peter leadership over the newly established community, and Peter presided as the first leader, or pope, after the death and resurrection of Christ. The church teaches that the authority given by Jesus to his apostles has been handed down by him in a chain referred to as *apostolic succession.*

Early Christian communities chose leaders from among themselves. Eventually the church hierarchy took over most of the leadership positions in the church, and the worshipping community became more passive participants. The hierarchical structure of the church consists of the pope as head of the church, the college of cardinals, the bishops, and the clergy. Departments of the Vatican called *congregations,* each headed by a cardinal, assist the pope. According to *The Catholic Encyclopedia* (online), cardinals "are officially the chief collaborators of the sovereign pontiff in the administration of the affairs of the Universal Church." The Catholic Church is not a structure but a community of people. Since Vatican II (1962–1965), the church has taken care to ensure that the laity reclaim their leadership in the church (see *The Catholic Encyclopedia,* online).

The first Christian communities were founded in larger towns and were presided over by a bishop and subordinate clergy. As the people in the country were converted, churches were erected in those rural areas. The priest or clergy in these rural churches were directly dependent on the bishop and the cathedral of residence of the bishop. Sometime in the 6th or 7th century the terms *diocese* and *parish* came into use. *Diocese* originally signified management of a household. The Romans used the term to identify a territory dependent upon a city for its administration. Eventually the territory presided over by a bishop came to be known as a diocese. The territories over which pastors presided were known as parishes. Christians supported their churches through tithes (*The Catholic Encyclopedia,* online, 1997; Catholic-pages.com)

Catholics are pluralistic about their approach to truth. Besides the Scriptures, Catholics turn to tradition, grace, nature, faith, and works. The church believes that its tradition is expressed in the canonical Scriptures, creeds, the seven sacraments, liturgy, and teaching of the magisterium. Christian beliefs are sometimes referred to as *dogma,* although more recently this term has come to refer to a declarative statement that discloses revealed truth; *doctrine* refers to an explanation of how a truth can be understood. The tradition of the church encompasses the sense of the faithful, the scholarly work of theologians, the prophetic voices that have arisen throughout history, and the voices of the bishops. The code of canon law is the official guide of the church. Encyclicals also give direction to the laity and clergy.

The Catholic Church recognizes seven sacraments: Baptism, Confirmation, Eucharist, Matrimony, Holy Orders (ordination of priests), Reconciliation, and Anointing of the Sick. The code of canon law describes these sacraments as signs and means by which faith is expressed and strengthened, God is worshipped, and humankind is sanctified and united as one in an ecclesiastic community.

According to Sanders (1994), devotions are prayers, religious practices, or exercises that demonstrate reverence for a particular aspect of God, Jesus, Mary, or a saint. Neither Mary nor the saints are worshipped, but rather commemorated, honored, or reverenced. Performing novenas, praying the rosary, lighting candles, and singing hymns are examples of devotional practices. The Catholic Church also uses many symbols—for example, the use of water at Baptism—to demonstrate realities that may not be directly perceivable. Water is a symbol of the washing away of sin and of the new life one enters as a member of the Christian community. *Sacramentals* are sacred signs such as the cross, the rosary, holy water, and the stations of the cross. Parental blessing of children, the distribution of ashes, and the blessing of the throat are other examples of sacramentals (Craghan, in Glazier & Hellwig, 1994).

PROFILE OF CONTEMPORARY AMERICAN CATHOLICS

Through the early years of this nation, members of religious orders founded many schools in the United States for the education of Irish, Polish, Italian, and other Catholic immigrants. Most of the schools staffed by women of various religious orders (sometimes referred to as *nuns* or *sisters*) were coeducational or were for the education of girls. *Brothers* (men who take vows and belong to a religious order of men) and priests of various religious orders founded many of the Catholic schools for boys. Since most of the social life of Catholic immigrants centered around the parish, most schools were connected to parishes. For many of the early ethnic immigrants, the parish church served not only as a source of solace and support but as an avenue for social and educational activities. In some parts of the United States, the Catholic Church continues to provide support for many new immigrants through funding from the U.S. Conference of Catholic Bishops and through diocesan social ministry offices.

In 1999, Catholics in the United States numbered 61.5 million, about 23% of the total population. There was one diocesan priest for every 1,945 Catholics. The number of parishes with a resident priest is declining, while the number of Catholics is increasing. Because of the shortage of priests today, permanent deacons, religious sisters or brothers, or laypeople staff nearly 400 parishes. Table 7.1 gives some other statistics on Catholicism in the United States at the end of the 20th century (National Conference of Catholic Bishops, 2000).

The *Catholic Almanac* estimates that 80% of the Hispanics living in the United States, or about 18.4 million people, are Catholic. The largest Hispanic populations are found in New York, Los Angeles, Chicago, San Antonio, Houston, El Paso, San Diego, Miami, Dallas, and San Jose. The Hispanic population has experienced a growth rate of 59% compared to 20% among African Americans and 8% among the rest of the U.S. population. Based on these figures, projections indicate that by the end of the 21st century, the Catholic Church will very likely be 50% Hispanic (National Conference of Catholic Bishops, 1998).

CONTEMPORARY ISSUES

A number of issues concern the Catholic Church today, as revealed by the results of a survey of American Roman Catholics conducted in 1999 by a team of sociologists and funded by a grant from the Louisville Institute and the *National Catholic Reporter.* One of the major goals of the survey was to examine what American Catholics found most central to being Catholic, in

TABLE 7.1 | STATISTICS ON CATHOLISM IN THE UNITED STATES AT THE END OF THE 20TH CENTURY

Diocesan priests	30,940
Priests in religious orders	15,465
New ordinations (1999)	463
Religious brothers	5,736
Religious sisters	81,161
Catholic colleges and universities	235
Students enrolled	701,240
Catholic high schools	1,347
Students enrolled	660,583
Catholic elementary schools	7,150
Students enrolled	2,000,000
Enrollment in religious education programs	
High school	1,000,000
Elementary school	3,500,000

order to help describe more precisely what the actual lived experience of Catholics is and how it fits with official Catholic teachings (D'Antonio, 1999; Hoge, 1999). The survey included questions encompassing six elements of being Catholic: the sacraments, spirituality, personal growth, church involvement in working for social justice and helping the poor, the Catholic Church's teachings about Mary, the spirit of community among Catholics, and the teaching authority claimed by the Vatican (Hoge, 1999). Respondents indicated that the most important element of being Catholic was the sacraments; the least important element was the teaching authority claimed by the Vatican. When asked whether a person could be a good Catholic without performing certain actions, 77% of respondents said that a person could be a good Catholic without going to church every Sunday, and 72% believed that it was not necessary to obey the church hierarchy's teaching on birth control. Sixty percent believed a person could be a good Catholic without obeying the church hierarchy's teaching on divorce and remarriage, and close to 60% of the respondents also believed that someone could be a good Catholic without obeying the church hierarchy's teaching regarding abortion. On the other hand, the majority of Catholics believed that a person could not be a good Catholic without believing in the resurrection of Jesus and in the Eucharist.

The survey also captured a sample of Latino Catholics to see how they differed from other White Catholics and found that weekly attendance at mass was less important to them than to White Catholics. By a small margin, they were less likely than White Catholics to believe that the locus of moral authority should rest with church leaders on issues regarding divorce, remarriage without annulment, use of birth control, choice regarding abortion, homosexual behavior, and extramarital sex. They were also more likely to be in favor of women becoming priests. They were, however, less likely to be in favor of more democratic decision-making at the parish and diocesan levels than White Catholics. The Latino respondents were younger than the White Catholics surveyed and were more likely to have only a high school education (or less).

The survey also captured generational differences and found that 18–39-year-olds were more likely than older respondents to believe that they could be good Catholics without attending weekly mass and marrying in the church. Only 39% felt that the church was among the most important parts of their life. On the other hand, 66% of those age 59 or older believed that the church was among the most important parts of their life and that Church attendance was important. Interestingly, the difference between age groups on the issue of having a final say on abortion was not as great: 52% of those aged 18 to 39, 48% of those aged 39 to 58, and 40% of those 59 or older (Hoge, 1999). There were also slight gender differences. Women were slightly more likely than men to respond that the church was among the most important parts of their life (48% versus 39%) and that attending mass once a week or more was important (43% versus 31%). Women were also slightly more likely to respond that one could be a good Catholic without obeying church teachings on birth control (73% versus 71%) and abortion (56% versus 50%). They were also more likely to say that the laity should participate in deciding whether women should be ordained (64% versus 62%). Men were slightly more likely than women to say that the laity should participate in selecting priests for their parishes (74% versus 73%) (D'Antonio, 1999; Hoge, 1999).

Though they may be slight in some cases, gender, ethnic, and generational differences do have implications for the Catholic Church and for service providers. A major implication of the 1999 survey results is that, compared to results of two earlier surveys, the gap between what the church teaches and what followers actually practice was wider in 1999. This is an issue of great concern to the church.

MOVEMENTS WITHIN THE CATHOLIC CHURCH TODAY

There are two major renewal programs within the Catholic Church in which substantial numbers of Hispanics have been involved. One of these is the *cursillista* movement, and the other is the charismatic renewal movement. The *cursillo,* or short course in Christianity, is a 3-day renewal retreat in which participants rededicate themselves to Christian ideals through study and sharing their lives in Christ. One of the prime objectives in the early years of the movement was to revitalize the church by bringing people back into its activities. The goals of the Catholic charismatic renewal movement are personal conversion and fostering personal receptivity to the person and power of the Holy Spirit, the reception and use of spiritual gifts, the work of evangelization, and ongoing growth in holiness. Both movements have resulted in the spiritual renewal of many couples, young adults, youths, and families.

Another movement of Latin American origin is the liberation theology movement, which is based on the belief that the Christian Gospel demands a "preferential option for the poor." One outcome of this movement was *comunidades de base,* or base Christian communities, formed to study Scripture and fight for social justice (*The Columbia Encyclopedia,* 2001). This movement has benefited many Latino communities but is not well-established in the United States. When liberation theology was first introduced, theologians espousing its concepts were sanctioned by the church hierarchy. The practices of liberation theology would have a phenomenal impact on the entire Catholic community in the United States.

Hispanic Catholicism is often referred to as popular Catholicism and, according to Espin (1997), "is probably one of the most distinctive and pervasive elements of the country's Latino cultures." The practice of religion through one's culture is seen as a cultural strength.

RELIGIOUS TRADITIONS AMONG MEXICAN AMERICAN CATHOLICS

One of the best definitions of religious tradition is found in Dues's (1998) book on Catholic customs and traditions, where traditions are described as being like "memorial stones." According to Dues (1998), these stones "mark the particular place, moment in time or part of human life made sacred by the meeting of the mystery of God with the mystery of the human creature." People remember this meeting by visiting sacred places, celebrating particular days, keeping certain rituals, saying certain prayers, or eating special foods. Because traditions are human creations, they are changeable and their expressions vary by culture, race, ethnicity, and country.

In the Catholic Church, the most important celebrations commemorate the various feasts of Christ or the Blessed Virgin. The penitential seasons of Lent and Advent serve as a preparation for these feasts. The liturgical year in the Catholic Church begins with Advent, followed by Christmas, the Epiphany, Lent, Easter, and Pentecost. In between are various feasts celebrating special events in Christ's life, the various feasts of Mary, and of the saints.

For Hispanic Catholics, the Feast of Our Lady of Guadalupe, All Souls day, Lent, and Easter are especially ritualized. In Latin America, the population of an entire city will celebrate the feast of the patron saint whose name the city bears. In some cities, workers are given a holiday. Besides the celebration of the liturgy, there are processions and dancing through the streets. The saint or the Virgin may be carried in procession through the streets and sometimes serenaded, and firecrackers explode in the sky in the evening. Food and religious celebrations often go hand in hand. For the feast of the Epiphany and for All Souls Day, special bread is baked to commemorate the occasion. On All Souls Day, there are picnics at gravesides to commemorate the lives of those who have died. During Lent, in commemoration of the Passover, Mexicans eat *nopalitos, capirrotada, albóndigas,* and lentils during Friday meals. *Tamales* are always served at Christmas and *buñuelos* on New Year's Day. Prayer novenas are held in homes before Christmas (the *posadas*) to commemorate the journey of Mary and Joseph that ended with Christ's birth in a manager. The Feast of the Three Magi is celebrated with the laying of the infant Jesus in a crib. This is the day when most of Latin America has traditionally celebrated Christmas—the day that Christ's revelation was first introduced to the gentiles.

Some of these customs are Judeo-Christian and others are a mix of Mexican Indian and Spanish Christian (*mestizo*) traditions. (The biological and cultural mixing of racial and/or ethnic groups is referred to as *mestizaje*. An individual of mixed race is called a *mestizo*. According to Espin [1997], this term has commonly been applied exclusively to cases of intermarriage between Europeans and Amerindians, Spaniards and Africans, or Spaniards and Amerindians.

Religious traditions and practices all assist Christians in staying in touch with the spiritual part of their being. Growth toward holiness is a lifelong process.

SPIRITUALITY

According to Coll (1994) "spirituality is a way of living that arises from an appreciation of human life." Accordingly, it encompasses the whole of an individual's life, including convictions, hopes, emotions, feelings, behaviors, and patterns of thought. It has more to do with being "embodied spirits" than "enspirited bodies." For many people, spirituality is a validation and a celebration and is manifested in its incarnational, relational, prophetic, and empowering characteristics. Hispanic spirituality is rooted in the convergence of the religious spirit of the indigenous pre-Columbian and African people with the Christian faith of the Spanish evangelizers.

According to Aquino (1999), theology is the language through which a person seeks to understand the faith that is lived, celebrated, and proclaimed by the community, whereas spirituality is the experience of the "believing community in seeking the meaning of faith and the direction of its journey of hope lived in the context of charity" (p. 26). Latino spirituality is influenced by its historical context, the way God is perceived, how the perception was arrived at, the community's choice of the most important moments of Jesus' life and message, and how the community relates to Jesus and God as a result of the previous dimensions and also of an individual's options and lifestyle (Espin, 1997). According to Rodriguez (1994) Our Lady of Guadalupe is integral to the development of the spirituality of Mexican American women because as marginalized women and *mesitzas,* religion has been a "significant dimension of their experience" (p. 59).

MEANING OF MAJOR LIFE EVENTS

Religious values and traditions are intertwined with life events among Hispanics, especially Mexican Americans. Life events are celebrated with religious rituals. Most family celebrations begin in the church and are then carried to the home.

One often hears it said that Hispanics are "nominal Catholics," because they have a tendency to attend services to celebrate life events (marriages, baptisms, confirmations, and funerals) but not to participate in regular Sunday services. Often, what older Hispanics know about their religion was passed on to them by their parents or gleaned from a sermon they heard when attending church for a special event or gathered from a few years of attendance at religious education classes.

The reasons for this situation are buried deep in history. If one studies the early church in the Southwest, one finds that American Catholics were not friendly toward and even discriminated against Mexican and Mexican American Catholics. In one parish in which I ministered, the Mexicans in the community were only peripherally involved in the church. Very few attended church on Sundays. Before 1965, the Mexican Catholics of that parish had to sit in the back of the church. Their children could not make Communion with the children of the American Catholics, nor were they allowed in the Catholic school. They could not be baptized in the same baptistery, nor could their dead be buried on the same side of the cemetery. The Mexican Americans waited for a priest on horseback to come every 6 months to have their children baptized and their marriages blessed and to receive the other sacraments. As a result of the church's unwelcoming stance, Mexican Americans kept the faith in their own way. Mexican American Catholics living as a minority in small, rural American communities had similar experiences.

The scenario was different if the church was located in a predominantly Hispanic neighborhood or community. In the early days of the 20th century, Hispanic Catholics preferred to send their children to Catholic schools, not merely to pass on Catholic traditions but also to protect children from the discrimination and racism encountered in the public schools. An example of this was an experience my father had. At the end of his second day in first grade at public school, boys chased him home yelling obscenities and pelting him with stones. He arrived home with a concussion, his clothes drenched in blood. Fearing for his life, my grandparents moved their family to the safety of a Hispanic neighborhood with a predominantly Hispanic Catholic church and school.

Today the church is more welcoming, but the historical memory of past experiences has not died easily. Children are sent to religious education classes to learn about their religion so that they can make First Communion and participate in other sacraments. A small percentage of Hispanic Catholics send their children to religious education classes for all 12 years of their schooling, and an even smaller percentage send their children to Catholic schools. These Catholic parents believe that Catholic schools not only afford the continuity of Catholic traditions but also provide their children with high-quality education that better prepares them for college. Young couples attend marriage preparation classes in order to be able to marry in the church.

Many older Catholics maintain altars or niches in their homes on which they place images of the Virgin or a saint, and before which they light candles and pray. They also attend church and participate in organizations such as the Holy Name Society, the *Guadalupanas,* the Altar Society, and other activities sponsored by the parish.

As the beginning of life is celebrated through the initiation of the infant into the Catholic Church at Baptism, the end of life is also celebrated. Besides taking a body to church for mass, families hold a novena of rosaries in the family home. In a sense, this tradition serves a dual purpose: It allows people to pray for the deceased person and to complete the grieving process in the comfort of God, friends, and relatives.

What nourishes the faith of many Hispanic Catholics has not been attendance at Church but rather their sense of communion with a universal church. They realize that the church will always be there when they need it. This sense of universality gives Hispanic Catholics confidence that the church is wherever they are or wherever they choose to pray.

SOURCES OF POWER

Catholics believe that God is the source of love. Love is the basis of Christian life. Because religion is communal or other-centered, the love of community members for each other is a source of power and transformation. Prayer is a source of strength for many Hispanic Catholics. The Eucharist, the sacraments of Reconciliation and Anointing, and Scripture are other sources of strength in times of stress or trouble. Catholics believe that Mary and the saints are favored by God; therefore, he will be more likely to hear them. Catholics pray to the Virgin or to a saint to intercede to God on their behalf. Cuban Americans and Puerto Ricans pray to the *Virgen del Cobre.* Mexican Americans give devotion to the Mother of God under two names: *Nuestra Señora de Guadalupe* and *Nuestra Señora de San Juan de los Lagos.* According to Mexican Catholic history, there were few converts to the Catholic faith among Mexico's Indians until the apparition of Our Lady of Guadalupe. Her dress and bearing were very symbolic to the Indians. Her image stood in front of the sun and on top of the moon—meaning that she was greater than their sun or moon gods. They saw her as lifting them from the oppression of their conquerors. The Virgin wore a cincture, a symbol of pregnancy, which the Nahua Indians interpreted as a symbol of a new life for them. To this day many Mexican Catholics pray to her in time of need. She is a symbol of strength. Her feast on December 12 is celebrated with *mananitas,* novenas, prayers, pilgrimages, and *fiestas.* The theologian Espin (1997) explains that the apparition of Our Lady of Guadalupe appeared to be the "inculturation of Christianity in colonial Mexico" and today is a sign that the Christian gospel was both announced and accepted at that time.

Catholics also give honor to various patron saints, depending on the need. For example, St. Jude is considered the saint of the impossible, and St. Joseph is the patron of a happy death.

FAMILY LIFE-CYCLE TRANSITIONS

Infancy and Early Childhood: Baptism

Among Hispanics, the family is a source of strength and support. Children are a blessing, a source of pride and joy. In the past, Hispanic Catholics used to give a newborn the name of the saint whose feast was celebrated on the day the child was born. An infant was baptized and initiated into the life of the Catholic Church shortly after birth. Today infants are not necessarily named after a saint, and the christening may take place anywhere from 1 week to over a year after birth.

My father came from a devoutly Catholic family of eleven, and baptisms were particularly significant in my upbringing. The signaling of membership through Baptism in the church was a significant family event. The family processed from the church to the home with the newly baptized baby, family members, and *padrinos* (godparents), and everyone shared a festive meal. Traditionally, the godparents furnished the christening dress for the infant. Godparents were expected to assume the responsibility of raising the children according to Catholic traditions if the parents did not do so or if the parents died. My godparents were particularly important in my life. They literally looked out for me throughout my childhood. They took the role assigned to them at Baptism seriously. Not only did they bring me gifts on birthdays and at Christmas, they visited often and took care to provide advice. They served a mentoring role.

With Baptism, the infant begins the life of shared religious values and traditions that are bequeathed by parents. It is at this stage of life that a child develops a first impression of God. If the parents teach that God is a God of love, then the child will pick this up. On the other hand, if the parents teach about a God of fear, that will be the child's first impression of God. The child's faith and spirituality will be grounded in this first impression of God.

Childhood: First Communion and Reconciliation

Catholics believe that Christ becomes present in the bread and wine during the consecration at the Eucharist. Children prepare for the day when they can partake of the Eucharist by attending religion classes and by participating in the sacrament of Reconciliation. The church teaches that at this age, children can distinguish between right and wrong, can understand the idea of Christ's presence in the Eucharist, and can prepare for the sacraments of Reconciliation and Eucharist. When I was a child, children were often dressed in white for the celebration of First Communion. Girls wore veils. A godparent supplied the wardrobe, rosary, candle, and prayer book. It was an event that I, like most children, looked forward to. It meant that I now had privileges: asking for forgiveness in the sacrament of Reconciliation and partaking of the Eucharist. Probably the most difficult sacrament was Reconciliation, since it meant revealing my sins to a priest. At first there was apprehension, but when it was over, there was relief. There was a sense that a burden had been lifted. The feeling of having been forgiven was exhilarating. Although, the sacrament of Reconciliation can be a positive experience or a negative experience (depending on whether a child perceives God as someone to be feared or loved), the experience of First Communion is generally a positive one. Somehow knowing that Christ was in me gave me a sense of security and a belief that I had someone I could count on.

Adolescence: Confirmation and Quinceañera

Once they reach adolescence, children move beyond family into groups with other values and traditions. At this time, faith and religious beliefs can provide cohesiveness and meaning. Confirmation is the initiation of an adolescent into Catholic adulthood. The coming of the Spirit assists the individual in living a Christian life. It is the Spirit that one receives at Confirmation that renews, transforms, and inspires. Often adolescents preparing for the sacrament of Confirmation are expected to begin to assume their adult Christian role and undertake activities to help or empower others. The *Quinceañera* is a rite of initiation, the introduction of a 15-year-old girl to society. Parents escort their daughter to the church on her 15th birthday to dedicate her to the Virgin and ask God's blessing on her young adult life. Feasting and dancing follow the ceremony. Both rites signal the coming of age—Confirmation in a spiritual sense, and the Quinceañera in a social sense.

My own adolescence reflected a mix of cultures and the constant presence of the church. Although my cousins and I attended many Quinceañeras, most of us chose not to have such a celebration. We were involved in youth groups and in choirs. The parish where my family lived was predominantly Mexican American. At home and in our own parish we spoke Spanish and were involved in Hispanic activities. My mother, who grew up in a rural community surrounded by Ku Klux Klan (some of whom were Catholics), became involved in parish activities as her children reached school age. However, because my parents wanted us to have a good education, they made the sacrifice to send us to a predominantly White Catholic school outside of our home parish. At school the language was English and the culture was White middle- or upper-class.

Early Adulthood

Young adulthood is often a period of examining the spiritual dimensions of life. The young adult searches for meaning and moves toward making learned values and traditions his or her own. This is a period when an individual distinguishes between religion as church attendance and religion as spirituality. Sometimes a young adult who has stopped attending church returns with a renewed sense of the spiritual. The findings of a recent survey of Catholics sponsored by the *National Catholic Reporter* indicated that young adults between the ages of 18 and 39 for the most part do not consider the church among the most important parts of their lives. Seventy-one percent said that they could be good Catholics without marrying in the church, and 81% percent said they could be good Catholics without attending mass (Hoge, 1999). It is difficult to interpret these findings. In the past, although not all young adults attended church, most implicitly believed that failure to attend was a sin. Some of my cousins and siblings stopped going to church when they entered young adulthood and only returned when they married and became parents themselves. Some only attended services on special occasions. Based on the survey, young adults now seem to be saying that attendance at services is not what makes one a Catholic.

Matrimony

When two individuals contract to marry each other, they come to church to have their marriage blessed. The church maintains that marriage lasts forever. The rite of marriage signals the beginning of a new family. Marriage is seen as both a covenant and a contract based on mutual consent. Marriage is considered sacred and therefore a marriage blessed by the church will be graced and secure. My father came from a large family of 11 siblings. As each prepared for marriage it was customary to bring the fiancé to meet the family. The family informally judged whether the intended would fit in with the family. The family was very close knit and my grandmother was the heart of the family. All children married in the Catholic church. This has not been the case for the next generation. Some of my siblings and cousins have married in the church and others have not. While only one of my father's 11 siblings wound up divorce, a number of cousins have been divorced.

Although the church does not condone birth control, over half of all Hispanic women use some form of birth control. There is a widening gap between the church's beliefs and the practices of Hispanic Catholics. The decision to engage in family planning is never an easy one for Catholic women. Abortion is considered murder. Abortion is extremely painful for a Hispanic woman because neither the culture nor the church accepts it. Blea (1997) wrote that Hispanic women "like music, dancing and laughter . . . they value marriage, celebrate births, baptism, first communion, and confirmation and . . . they also mourn divorce, drugs, alcohol abuse, domestic and gang violence, and death."

Mid-Life

Many adult Catholics who become involved in the church do so for the family, especially the children. They believe that religion keeps a family united and that the morals and values that the church teaches help children become adults who are disciplined, have positive values, respect life, and have a sense of community.

Many couples in mid-life become involved in marriage encounters, in *cursillo,* or in other church groups. For example, some of my cousins were involved in the choir, as ushers, with the St. Vincent de Paul society, and as catechists. Others, become involved in community and neighborhood associations.

Mid-life is a time when an individual reassesses the goals and meaning of life. A person may recognize the limitations of religion, yet still embrace and respect it. It is a time when adults can deepen their personal, marital, and spiritual lives and can serve as mentors.

The Older Adult

For Hispanic elderly, attendance at church usually serves both a social and a spiritual function. Involvement in service activities in the church satisfies the communal needs of Hispanic elderly. When the elderly are not able to come to church because of illness or age, they have the benefit of having the priest, deacon, or other member of the parish bring them Communion or visit with them.

Anointing of the Sick

The priest administers the sacrament of Anointing when a person is very ill or dying. The reception of these rites may enable a sick individual to heal or may help an individual to die in peace.

SOURCES OF SUPPORT IN THE CHURCH

Catholicism is communal in nature; the church teaches the importance of taking care of those in need. Besides various secular and religious education programs available to Catholics, many other sources of support are available, depending on the resources of a particular parish or diocese. Catholic charities exist in almost every diocese. There are a number of service societies in every parish. Some parishes have social ministers, volunteer nurses, and counselors who offer self-help groups, social services, and senior services. The St. Vincent de Paul Society in a parish provides both in-kind and monetary assistance to those in need. The Knights of Columbus often undertake social projects. Many support groups such as singles groups, divorce groups, widows' groups, and AA groups meet in parishes. Older adults, especially those in Hispanic churches, often gather for adult day care, social activities, and nutritional services. Senior citizens feel safe in coming to a parish church to socialize and share meals with their peers. Many dioceses in the United States support and sponsor social services, soup kitchens, homeless shelters, or adoption agencies. Orders of nuns provide shelter for abused women or children, run hospitals and clinics, and participate in organizations that address community needs such as housing, safety, education, and issues of justice.

CONCEPTIONS OF HEALTH

Hispanic spirituality is incarnational, in that the *whole* person is considered; the person is not dichotomized into body, mind, and spirit. Hispanics celebrate and embrace all that is contained in life (including death) in their fiestas. This sense of the unity of body, mind, and spirit is at the center of healing, whether physical, emotional, or spiritual. Illness can have either external or internal causes. When they perceive imbalances in body, mind, or spirit, Hispanics sometimes turn to faith healers (*curanderos* or *santeros*), because such healers take all factors into consideration. Besides faith healers, Hispanics also consult *sobadoras* (massage therapists), *yerberas* (herbalists), and *parteras* (midwives). Family and issues of relationship and the personal and communal sense of sin and evil are factors that can affect health and healing. Hispanics sense that the absence of the Spirit produces hatred, jealousy, envy, greed, lust, and despair. The sacraments of Reconciliation, Eucharist, and Anointing are recognized as sources of healing (Rodriguez, 1994). None of these aspects can be ignored in the provision of services in a health-care setting. Emotional illnesses or mental retardation may be perceived as physical illness, a punishment for sin, possession, or the result of someone's wishing evil on the person who is emotionally distressed. Whether services are sought from a priest, a physician, or a *curandero* depends on a person's perception of the root of the emotional illness.

Another spiritual cultural aspect is the use of *dicho* (proverbs or sayings), music, and stories, both to teach a lesson and to reinforce psychological realities. These can be used in therapy with clients of various ages. For example, many elders are familiar with *dichos,* while young folks may be familiar with certain types of music that can touch their spirit and help them recognize a need for change.

Hispanic Catholics believe in miracles and believe that Mary and the saints intercede for them and often grant their requests. When a request is granted, resulting in healing which medical science cannot explain, it is considered a miracle. A *manda* is a promise an individual or family makes to the Virgin Mary or to a saint to go in pilgrimage to the appropriate shrine to give thanks for a healing or miracle experienced by a member of their family. Sometimes a *manda* requires extensive travel and much sacrifice. Hispanics do not mind, because they are grateful for the favor of health bestowed on a loved one.

FAITH TRADITIONS THAT INFLUENCED ME TO ENTER THE SOCIAL WORK PROFESSION

The richness of my Hispanic religious heritage—the numerous celebrations of births, baptisms, and weddings in the context of church and family—greatly influenced my sense of appreciation and celebration of life. Religion taught me to look for the good in every human being. My grandparents and parents taught me that God made us all equal and that he loves me. Throughout my life they reinforced this through stories, sayings, and their own lives. The church also served as safe harbor. Attending Catholic school sheltered me from discrimination until I reached college. In my Catholic home, a good healthy sense of self-esteem was nurtured, which later served as a buffer in the face of discrimination and racism.

My Catholic mother used to say, "What is the use of going to church every Sunday if it does not make a difference in your life?" She said that she saw many people going to church Sunday after Sunday and then coming home and mistreating spouses or children. She believed that religion ought to make a difference in the way one lived one's life—that it ought to show in action. This is probably the greatest lesson I learned from my mother. This other-centeredness of my religious and cultural heritage and my sense of justice and indignation eventually drew me to the profession of social work. I worked with diverse groups, including undocumented immigrants, migrant workers, persons with disabilities, the elderly, the poor, children, parents, perpetrators of child sexual abuse, women with cancer, and other seriously ill persons. My motivation to pursue a Ph.D. was based partly on my observation of how people I worked with were treated by social workers and other professionals because they were poor, from a minority group, or elderly.

IMPLICATIONS FOR SOCIAL WORK PRACTICE

The Use of the Spiritual Dimension in Practice

Those who have not come to terms with the role God does or does not play in their lives are uncomfortable with a discussion of the spiritual dimensions of their lives. Clearly, in working with Hispanic Catholics, it is important to understand not just the religious dimensions of their lives, but also the cultural dimensions, as both have spiritual aspects. This knowledge will allow the social worker to understand how these factors affect clients' lives. A major finding from a study of 300 state adult protective social workers was that caseworkers did not make use of information about a particular cultural group to improve their interventions with clients of various ethnic groups, nor did they use experts from an ethnic or racial community to improve their services to these populations (Aguilar, 1999). The problem was not that they did not have knowledge about Hispanic or Black culture but that their attitudes kept them from utilizing this knowledge for the benefit of their clients. The majority indicated that they already knew all there was to know about Hispanics or Blacks. Unfortunately, changes in attitudes require a change of heart. Without that, knowledge does not necessarily translate into good social work practice.

Culture, Values, and Traditions

Both the Church and Hispanic culture have provided Hispanics with strengths. Families, spiritual values, hope, generosity, a spirit of community are all strengths. Traditions nurture both faith and culture. The remembering of traditions with clients is important in social work practice, because traditions have positive associations. They can be used in intervention or as a point of beginning, as can stories.

Hispanics have an expression that can be interpreted either positively or negatively: "*si Dios quiere*" (if God wills it or wants it). Mainstream American culture interprets this as fatalism. Hispanics interpret it as "God knows what he is doing and we trust that whatever he does or allows is for the best."

Dysfunctional Aspects of Religion

Catholicism is sometimes associated with the negative aspect of *machismo*. The more positive interpretation of *machismo* reflects the scriptural belief that the male is the head of his household. He is responsible for the care and support of his family and takes pride in doing this. The negative interpretation is that the male controls his spouse and she must be obedient and submissive to him. The part of Scripture that is left out by those who attempt to justify such domineering behavior is that a man must love and respect his spouse as he loves and respects the church. Leaving the last part out can be quite detrimental to a spouse and children.

In 30 years of working either in parishes, in agencies, or with social work students at a university level, I have heard countless Mexican American women reveal that their priests have insisted they remain in a marriage even when violence and substance abuse were occurring and they and their children were suffering. Marie Giblin (1999) stresses that religion plays a "formative role in expectations of marriage." She further states that the church does not seem to see the relationship between the belief system of the church and family violence. The Hispanic Catholic woman finds it very difficult to leave an abusive spouse because of church laws. Annulment—whereby a tribunal judges that a marriage never existed and therefore annuls the marriage—is possible in theory, but sparingly utilized. A Hispanic man once told me that he was going to have as many children as God gave him. This man had just brought his wife to the emergency room. She was 7 months pregnant, totally malnourished, and dying of tuberculosis. The attending physician was appalled to see this poor emaciated woman pregnant with her seventh child—while her husband used God to meet his own personal needs. There is a tendency at times to interpret Scripture literally to justify and maintain relationships that are violent and abusive. Another Hispanic man said to me, "Women are like cows!" When I asked him to explain, he said that women had to be kept on a leash; they could not be given too much love or freedom or they would take advantage of a man's love. This man was battering his wife and was sent for counseling because he had sexually abused two small girls, ages 5 and 7.

It has been my experience that Hispanic males at times use the church's teaching on birth control to keep a woman pregnant, under control, and in poverty rather than seeking natural methods of family planning or other activities to reduce family stress and create family unity. As noted earlier, Catholic women are sometimes counseled by their priests to remain in abusive relationships. While the majority of priests might not espouse this view, it is extremely disappointing for a woman whose priest does take this view to find that the church supports her husband. One woman related that her husband was a pillar of the church—a Sunday lecturer and an exemplary Catholic—but she came to church with sunglasses on so that parishioners would not see her blackened eyes. If this woman could not find safe harbor in the church, where would she be able to find it? Giblin (1998) asserts that the church does not always recognize the relationship between violence and church practices. It would be helpful for a social worker handling such a case to find a way to rebuild the woman's faith so that she would one day be able to turn to the church for safety. Faith is critical to the healing process and for forgiveness when violence has taken place.

Intoxication among Hispanic males often leads not only to family violence but also to poverty, emotional abuse, and physical illness. The church indirectly has sanctioned the use of alcohol. As a child growing up, I remember attending many parish *jamaicas,* or festivals. The booth that brought in the most money was always the beer booth. Liquor is culturally acceptable in all celebrations, but alcohol misuse among Hispanic males is a serious problem. Because drinking is socially acceptable, a veil of denial often covers the problem, making intervention difficult. Recognizing the problem, many parishes today have cut out the sale of liquor at parish fundraisers.

The Communal Aspect of Religion and Social Justice

The communal aspect of faith recognized by Hispanics can be called forth by social workers who want to make changes in the community. For example, if a parent's sense of community is awakened because she or he has recognized that the education of her or his children is substandard or that the community is not safe for them, that parent will be more likely to support efforts that help children and the community.

Because they have been oppressed or discriminated against for their religion or ethnicity, some Hispanic Catholics have been reluctant to acknowledge these aspects of themselves. Hispanic parents have begun to realize that in protecting their children from discrimination, they devalued their native language and cultural and religious heritage for their children. Knowing that one has roots and that one belongs gives a person a sense of self-esteem and worth. If children have poor self-esteem, a good way to begin to strengthen it is to focus on their religious and cultural heritage.

Gender and Relationships

The Catholic Church as been historically male-dominated and, like many social institutions, sexist. Men hold most of the positions of power in the church. For example, in 2000, a nun was removed as the secretary to the U.S. Conference of Bishops because she was a woman. She was replaced by a priest.

During the Vatican council, Mary's role in the church and as a figure of the church was affirmed (excerpts from *Lumen Gentium,* 1964). She was given a place in Vatican II. At the same time, women were for the first time invited to audit the council proceedings. Encyclicals, letters, and catechesis written after Vatican II held that the figure of Mary in the Gospel provides "a model of authentic emancipation for women according to God's plan." The new theology affirmed that Mary's presence in scripture demonstrated that

God had such esteem for women that "any form of discrimination was without theoretical basis." A statement made by the Fathers at the conclusion of Vatican II stated that the "hour is coming, in fact has come, when the vocation of woman is being achieved in its fullness, the hour in which woman acquires in the world an influence, an effect and a power never hitherto achieved." The church has recognized that the figure of Mary is a valid response to woman's desire for emancipation since she "fulfilled God's plan of love for humanity." And as a result every woman shares in Mary's dignity (John Paul II, 1995).

Since the ecumenical council of 1962–1965 (Vatican II), the place and role of the Virgin Mary have provided a window of opportunity for women to assume some leadership roles. The founders of many Catholic schools and universities were religious. However, there have been few Hispanic women serving in positions of authority in the church. Young female respondents in a study of Hispanic women and achievement conducted a few years ago indicated that their role models had been the women helping in the church, making and selling tamales or staffing booths at parish festivals (Aguilar, 1996).

Many Hispanic women writers have been openly critical of what they believe has been the church's role in the oppression of women. Catholic Hispanic women do not always recognize this oppression, especially if they see their role within the parish as functional. In social work practice with Hispanic Catholic women, it is important to find out where they are in the gender relations continuum. This knowledge will help guide the social worker's intervention in cases of spousal abuse, child abuse, alcoholism, teen pregnancy, or unwanted pregnancy. Criticizing the Catholic heritage is not appropriate—but recognizing the dysfunctional aspects of religion will help.

Recognizing the functional aspects of Catholicism is also helpful. For example, the concept of authority can lead a client toward self-direction and responsibility. Religion can offer a sense of identity and rootedness. Religion has also served as a socializer and keeper of values and setter of moral standards. Religious symbols and rituals give meaning to life transitions (Joseph, 1987). Begin where the client is. Consider what has been positive about his or her religion. How has religion been an asset? Develop an intervention that indicates that you understand both the client's culture and his or her religion. Use what the client knows to help the person make decisions that are growth-producing. Use the person's own tools and not your own religious or cultural tools.

SUGGESTIONS FOR WORKING WITH CATHOLICS

- Study Catholic practices and beliefs if the clients you work with are predominantly Catholic. If they are from a particular ethnic group, study the relationship between religion and that culture.
- Begin where the client is with respect to religious beliefs and practices.

- Respect the client's position. Realize that clients occupy a continuum—that not all Catholics or Hispanic Catholics use the same symbols or have the same understanding of religious beliefs and concepts. Note that there are generational differences in both religious practices and beliefs.
- Use the positive aspects of religion to develop an intervention. Use spiritual aspects when the client needs hope, has suffered a loss, or needs help with self-determination or overcoming oppression.
- When working with a Hispanic community, remember that "resistance to social, cultural, political, and spiritual domination is a struggle for space, a place in society that is not always at the lowest rung of the social ladder" (Blea, 1997). Social workers involved in community development need to understand that the resistance to domination is not meant to hamper community improvement but to gain recognition of the right to exist and the right to respect for communal strengths.
- There are two things that Hispanic women treasure: their family and their community. Drawing on this love can lead to more effective interventions on behalf of children or to improve the quality of life of the whole community.

CONCLUSION

It is impossible to cover all the aspects of spirituality and religious practices of all groups of Hispanic Catholics. This chapter has been an effort to inform practitioners about those religious aspects of a person's life that may give meaning to his or her existence and can serve as the basis for effective intervention. Everyone is made up of body, mind, and spirit, and if our approach to practice is to be wholistic, then we cannot neglect the cultural and spiritual aspects. For Hispanic Catholics, religion and spirituality are intertwined with everyday life, whether they attend an institutional church or not. To ignore this aspect of life is to ignore many positive tools that can be used by the practitioner to foster growth and change.

REFERENCES

Aguilar, M. A. (1996). Promoting the educational achievement of Mexican American Young Women. *Social Work in Education, 18*(3), 145–157.

Aguilar, M. A. (1999). *An evaluation of diversity training needs of adult protective service workers.* Texas Department of Protective and Regulatory Services, Adult Protective Services.

Aquino, M., (1999). Theological method in U.S. latino/a theology. In O. Espin and M. Diaz (Eds), *From the heart of Our People: Latino/a exploration in Catholic systematic theology.* Maryknoll, NY: Orbis.

Blea, I. (1997). *U.S. Chicanas and Latinas within a global context.* Westport, CT: Praeger.

Boudinhon, A., & Fanning, W. (Transcribed by Bobie Jo M. Bilz). (1913). *Parish. The Catholic Encyclopedia.* Retrieved from the World Wide Web: http://www.newadvent.org/cathen/TheCatholicEncyclopedia

Catholic-pages.com. *Cardinals & Bishops.* The Catholic Pages. Page Design & Layout (1996–1999) Paul McLachlan.

Coll, R. (1994). *Christianity and Feminism in Conversation.* Mystic, CT: Twenty-third Publications.

The Columbia Encyclopedia (2001). *Liberation Theology.* Retrieved July 16, 2001, from the World Wide Web: http://www.bartleby.com/65.li.liberati .html

D'Antonio, W. (October 29, 1999). *The American Catholic laity in 1999. National Catholic Reporter.* Retrieved on July 6, 2001, from the World Wide Web: http://www.natcath.com/NCR_Online/archives/102999/102999i.htm

D'Antonio, W. (October 29, 1999). *Latino Catholics: How different? National Catholic Reporter.* Retrieved on July 6, 2001, from the World Wide Web: http://www.natcath.com/NCR_Online/archives/102999/102999p.htm

Davidson, J. (October 29, 1999). *Generations have different views of the church. National Catholic Reporter.* Retrieved on July 6, 2001, from the World Wide Web: http://www.natcath.com/NCR_Online/archives/102999 /102999o.htm

Dolan, J. P. & Figueroa-Deck, A. (Eds.). (I 994). *Hispanic Catholic culture in the U.S.: Issues and concerns.* Notre Dame, IN: University of Notre Dame Press.

Dolan, J. P., & Hinojosa, G. M. (Eds.). (1994). *Mexican Americans and the Catholic Church: 1900–1965.* Notre Dame, IN: University of Notre Dame Press.

Dues, G. (1998). *Catholic customs and traditions: A popular guide.* Mystic, CT: Twenty-Third Publications.

Espin, O. (1997). *The faith of the people: Theological reflections on popular Catholicism.* Maryknoll, NY: Orbis.

Foster, T. (1993). *The catholic experience of renewal.* Retrieved on July 16, 2001, from the World Wide Web: http://www.garg.com/ccc/articles/Foster /Foster_001.html

Giblin, M. (1999, Winter). Catholic Church teaching and domestic violence. *Listening: Journal of Religion and Culture.* Retrieved June 14, 2001, from the World Wide Web: http://www.listeningjournal.org/article_4.htm

Glazier, M., & Hellwig, M. (Eds.). (1994). Catholicism. *The Modern Catholic Encyclopedia.* Collegeville, MN: Liturgical Press.

Hoge, D. (October 29, 1999). *What is most central to being Catholic? National Catholic Reporter.* Retrieved on July 6, 2001, from the World Wide Web: http://www.natcath.com/NCR_Online /archives/102999/102999j.htm

(John Paul II, 1995). The Pope's catechesis on Mary and the value of women at the General Audience of November 29, 1995, was the seventh in the series on the Blessed Mother. Retrieved from the World Wide Web on July 14, 2001: http://www.cco.caltech.edu/~newman/women-cp/emancipat .html

Johnson, E. (1992). *She who is*. New York, NY: Crossroads.

Joseph, M. (1987). The religious and spiritual aspects of clinical practice: A neglected dimension of social work. *Social Thought, 18*(1), 12–23.

National Conference of Catholic Bishops/United States Catholic Conference. (2000). *A statistical profile of the church in the United States 1789–1999*. Retrieved June 11, 2001, from the World Wide Web: http://www.nccbuscc .org/comm /profile.htm

National Conference of Catholic Bishops/United States Catholic Conference. Hispanic Affairs. *Demographics*. Retrieved September 14, 2000, from the World Wide Web: http://www.nccbuscc.org/hispanicaffairs/demo.htm

National Conference of Catholic Bishops/United States Catholic Conference. *A statistical profile of the church in the United States 1798 to 1998*. Retrieved September 14, 2000, from the World Wide Web: http://www.nccbuscc.org /comm/profile.htm

The National Cursillo Center (2001). *What is Cursillo?* Retrieved on July 16, 2001, from the World Wide Web: http://www.natl-cursillo.org/whatis.html

Rodriguez, J. (1994). *Our Lady of Guadalupe. Faith and empowerment among Mexican-American women*. Austin, TX: University of Texas Press.

Ruether, R. (1998, May). *Crises and challenges of Catholicism today*. Foundation Documents. Paper given at CTA Wisconsin meeting. Retrieved June 14, 2001, from the World Wide Web: (http://www.cta.usa.org/founda tiondocs /foundruether2. html

Sanders, T. (1994). In Walsh, M. (Ed). *Commentary on the Catechism of the Catholic Church*. Collegeville, MN: Liturgical Press.

Van Hove, A. (transcribed by Douglas J. Potter) (1913). Diocese. *The Catholic Encyclopedia*. Retrieved from the World Wide Web: http://www.newadvent .org /cathen/TheCatholicEncyclopedia

Vatican II on Mary and the Church. *Lumen Gentium* (1964). Vatican Council II, Dogmatic Constitution on the Church. Excerpts from Chapter VIII: Our Lady, section 60–65. Retrieved from the World Wide Web on July 14, 2001: http://www.ewtn.com/faith/teachings/teachframes.htm

ADDITIONAL RESOURCES

Books

Castillo, A. (Ed.). (1996). *Goddess of the Americas (La diosa de las Americas): Writings on the Virgin of Guadalupe*. New York: Riverhead.

Dolan, J. and Figueroa-Deck, A. (Eds.). (1994). *Hispanic Catholic culture in the U.S.: Issues and concerns.* Notre Dame, IN: University of Notre Dame.

Dolan, J. and Hinojosa, G. M. (Eds) (1994). *Mexican Americans and the Catholic church, 1900–1965.* Notre Dame, IN: University of Notre Dame.

Espin, O. (1997). *Latina realities.* Boulder CO: Westview.

Stevens-Arroyo, A. M., and Pantoja, S. (Eds.) (1995). *Discovering Latino religion: A comprehensive social science bibliography.* New York: Bildner Center for Western Hemisphere Studies.

Vila, P. (1996). *Catholicism and identity on the U.S.-Mexico border.* El Paso, TX: University of Texas at El Paso, Chicano Studies Program. (Occasional paper series no. 8).

Web Sites

Center for the Study of Latino/a Catholicism, University of San Diego Department of Theology and Religious Studies: http://www.acusd.edu/theo/latino-cath.html

The Handbook of Texas, Texas State Historical Association and The Center for Studies in Texas History, University of Texas at Austin: http://www.tsha.utexas.edu/handbook/online/articles/view

Videos

Images of Faith (1992). Discusses the creation and use of santos in Christian worship in Puerto Rico.

La Ofrenda: The Days of the Dead. In a rich mosaic of festive and warmly intimate scenes, La Ofrenda takes a nontraditional look at the Mexican tradition of Days of the Dead, evoking Mexican and Mexican-American attitudes toward death. It celebrates living by cultivating the awareness of death and capturing the intensity and plentitude of the Mexican and Chicano soul.

La Pastorela (1991). A Christmas fantasy musical retelling of the sheperds' journey to Bethlehem (in Spanish).

Latinos: The Life of the Spirit (1993). Latinos and Catholicism are no longer synonymous. This program explores the recent trend among Latinos to leave the Catholic Church for Evangelical or Protestant religions, the rediscovery by Chicanos of native spiritual and religious rituals that predate the arrival of Columbus, and the traditional Good Friday pilgrimage to the sanctuary at Chimayo, New Mexico, which shows that traditional spirituality is alive in modern times.

Mundo Milagroso (Miraculous World) (1995). Examines the blend of Spanish Catholicism and indigenous religion that flourishes among Mexican Americans living along the Texas–Mexico border.

Spirit Doctors (1996). Examines the folk healing practices of Mexican-American curanderas living in the lower Rio Grande Valley of Texas (in Spanish).

Tradiciones Navidenas (1991). With the former Convent at the Desierto de los Leones as the backdrop, this program lets viewers take part in a traditional posada. The songs, the piñata, the litany, the lights, and the candlelit walks through the historic buildings and grounds bring this Christmas fiesta to life (in Spanish).

List of Video Distributors of Hispanic-related Videos

Cinema Guild
1697 Broadway, Suite 506,
New York, NY 10019
Phone: 800-723-5522,
212-246-5522
Fax: 212-246-5525
http://www.cinemaguild.com/

The Cinema Guild web site is organized into five broad directories: The Arts and Humanities, Health, The Sciences, Social Studies, and World Cultures. There are separate sections for New Releases and Special Selections. This site includes a separate "Latino Studies" catalog (http//www.cinemaguild.com/docs/latino.html#LATINO).

Films for the Humanities & Sciences
P.O. Box 2053,
Princeton, NJ 08543-2053
Phone: 800-257-5126
Fax: 609-275-3767
http://www.films.com/

First Run/Icarus Films
153 Waverly Place,
New York, NY 10014
Phone: 212-727-1711
Fax: 212-989-7649
E-Mail: info@frif.com
http//www.echonyc.com/~frif/

Library Video Company
P.O. Box 580,
Wynnewood, PA 19096
Phone: 800-843-3620
Fax: 610-645-4040.
http://www.libraryvideo.com/

The National Latino
Communications Center (NLCC)
3171 Los Feliz Boulevard, Suite 200,
Los Angeles, CA 90039
Phone: 213-663-8294
Fax: 213-663-5606
http://www.nlcc.com/
To order videos: 1-800-722-9982
NLCC Educational Media
P.O. Box 39A60,
Los Angeles, CA 90039

New Day Films
79 Raymond Avenue,
Poughkeepsie, NY 12601
Phone: 914-485-8489
http://www.newday.com/

University of California Extension
Media Center/Center for Media
and Independent Learning
2000 Center St., 4th Floor,
Berkeley, CA 94704
Phone: 510-642-0460
Fax: 510-643-9271
http://www-cmil.unex.berkeley.edu/media/

Other Distributors

Ambrose Video Publishing Inc.
28 West 44th St, Ste 2100,
New York, NY 10036
Phone: 800-526-4663,
212-768-7373
Fax: 212-768-9282
http://www.ambrosevideo.com

Collision Course Video Productions
PO Box 347383,
San Francisco, CA 94134-7383
Phone: 415-587-0818
Fax: 415-587-0818

GLOSSARY

Brother A member of a religious order (Franciscan, Dominican, Jesuit) who has taken vows.

Capirotada Pudding made with bread, raisins, cinnamon, nuts, cheese, and sometime onion and eaten during Lent.

Curanderos Individuals in the Latino community believed to have been blessed with the gift of healing.

Eucharist One of the seven sacraments. During mass, bread and wine are consecrated, and Catholics believe that at that moment Christ becomes present in the bread and wine.

Hispanic Title assigned by the Bureau of the Census to persons of Spanish origin, including Puerto Ricans, South Americans, Central Americans, Mexican Americans, Cuban Americans, and others.

Mandas A promise to go on pilgrimage to give thanks at a shrine of the Virgin or saint by whose intercession a favor or healing was granted.

Mexican Americans Hispanics of Mexican descent.

Nopales Cactus eaten during Lent.

Nuestra Senora de Guadalupe (Our Lady of Guadalupe) The Mother of God who appeared to a young Mexican Indian in Tepeyac in the 1500s. She is venerated as the patroness of the Americas.

Nuestra Senora de San Juan de Los Lagos (Our Lady of San Juan) A statue of the Immaculate Conception made in 1521 and given to the Mexican Indians of San Juan de Los Lagos Jalisco, Mexico. The statue took on the name of the town where it was located. Its fame spread as a result of the miraculous recovery of a young woman who fell to her death but came back to life when the image was placed on her chest. Ever since then persons who have received favors come to this shrine to give thanks.

Padrinos Baptismal sponsors who maintain close ties with their godchild and family throughout the child's life. The Catholic Church teaches that the sponsor is responsible for the Christian formation of the child if the parents are unable to provide this.

Posada A Novena (nine day period) beginning on the 16th of December in preparation for the birth of Christ. Forming a procession headed by two people portraying Mary and Joseph, families walk to each of three homes singing and praying. They ask for hospitality and are turned away at two homes and admitted to the third, where festivities are held.

Priest A person ordained for ministry in the Roman Catholic religion.

Quinceañera The celebration of coming of age or the debut of a girl into society at the age of 15. The family attends mass, and in a short ceremony the parents consecrate their daughter to Mary and ask God to bless her.

Reconciliation One of the seven sacraments, sometimes referred to as the sacrament of forgiveness or confession. It is the ritual in which Catholics confess their sins and receive forgiveness.

Sister (nun, woman religious) A member of a religious order (Franciscan, Dominican, Carmelite, Sister of Charity, Sister of Mercy) who has taken vows of poverty, celibacy, and obedience.

8 CHAPTER

ISLAM

ANEESAH NADIR
SOPHIA F. DZIEGIELEWSKI

INTRODUCTION

Awareness of Islam and its teachings is essential to ensure culturally sensitive practice with Muslim clients by social workers and other helping professionals. This chapter will discuss the traditions, basic beliefs, and obligatory duties of those who practice Islam, as well as misconceptions about this faith. Traditions, children, youth, family life, social relationships, occupational concerns, and the role of Islam in the life of the practicing Muslim will be addressed. Professionals are encouraged to identify, acknowledge, and anticipate the struggles faced by clients of the Islamic faith. We hope that the information in this chapter will sensitize readers regarding Islam and Muslims in North America.

MASTER STORIES: CONVERSION TO ISLAM

According to Islam, all human beings are born Muslim, which is an Arabic word that means "one who submits his or her will to God's will." So, when people become Muslim, regardless of where they are in the life cycle, they are considered to be reverting to their original state of being, as everyone is born pure and free of sin in submission to the will of God.

Before an individual can become Muslim, he or she must take the *shahadah*—that is, state the Declaration of Faith. The taking of the shahadah can be done at any time. The shahadah is often taken in front of at least two witnesses, although the primary requirement is that the individual make this commitment to God. The shahadah may be performed formally, in a small ceremony in which the *Imam*, or leader of the mosque, is also present, or informally among friends. People who accept Islam declare that "there is no God but Allah and Muhammad is His Messenger." The new Muslim is immediately welcomed into the community. Witnesses are excited to have a new brother or sister in faith. Most new converts to Islam were raised in a different faith. Yusef Islam (formerly Cat Stevens), Muhammad Ali (formerly Cassius Clay), and Nancy Ali (formerly a Catholic nun) are some of the more famous of the many individuals who have come to Islam. We are gaining greater awareness about the conversion experience as famous Muslim converts share their experiences with us.

Taking the shahadah erases the new believer's previous sins and gives him or her a fresh start in life, but developing an Islamic personality presents various challenges. Each convert needs to learn to carry out the norms and traditions of the faith and to use appropriate etiquette for relating to non-Muslim friends, relatives, and coworkers. Conversion to Islam is a process that occurs over varying lengths of time, depending on the individual and his or her life circumstances.

Many mosques, which are the Muslim places of worship, have begun the practice of presenting the new Muslim with a document that is signed by witnesses, attesting to the person's Declaration of Faith (M. Misri, personal communication, April 16, 1998). This document can be used for various personal purposes, such as obtaining leave of absence for Islamic holidays or applying for a visa to perform the pilgrimage to Makkah. The document is not a requirement for a person to accept Islam; simply making the statement of the Declaration of Faith is sufficient.

ANEESAH NADIR'S PERSONAL STORY

I embarked on my journeys toward an Islamic way of life and toward a career in social work at about the same time. As a sophomore in undergraduate school in the mid-1970s, I decided to major in social work because I believed it was important to become an instrument of social justice, having seen so much injustice as a young African American woman in the inner city. My interest in helping people had surfaced as early as age 13, when in the eighth grade I served as a mentor for incoming high school freshmen and later as a summer camp counselor. I remember my oldest brother and his friend identifying with the role models portrayed in the *Superfly* films, and I vowed to find other role models for them to follow.

At about this time, I was introduced to a community of African American students on campus who identified themselves as Muslim. These schoolmates provided answers to questions that I had been pondering. These young people were strong, confident, involved in the community, interested in economic development, and striving for social justice. They were active in redefining their existence and demanding their share of the economic pie. As a 19-year-old African American I discovered that this group helped to provide answers that I had not received as a Christian, along with an opportunity to engage in achieving greater social justice.

So, after considerable pondering and discussions with my family, especially my father, I declared that I was a Muslim in May of 1975. But this was only the beginning, for I discovered that I had yet to learn what it really meant to be a Muslim. The Nation of Islam was in the midst of change, as Elijah Muhammad had died in February of that year, and his son Warith Deen Muhammad had become the leader of this community. When Warith Deen Muhammad took the leadership, he began to move the community from exclusion to inclusion, continuing to place a value on social and economic justice within the context of the Sunni, or orthodox, traditions of Islam. He opened up the then Nation of Islam to a whole new way of thinking and a source of knowledge that the members of the community had not been familiar with: the Qur'an and the traditions of the Prophet Muhammad of Arabia.

For the next 20 years, I was involved in the remarkable work of learning what it meant to be Muslim, while I completed my B.S.W. and then later my M.S.W. My husband and I moved our young family from New York to Arizona in search of a better way of life as well as the safety and security of a smaller city. To be a Muslim in Arizona in the early 1980s was a struggle, as the Muslim community there was still very small and growing in its understanding of Islam. I found myself trying to make sense of who I was as an African American, a Muslim, a wife and mother, and a social worker. For the next 10 years, my identity as a social worker strengthened. I was an active member of the social work community and the African American community, learning from my mentors Clay Dix and Carole Coles Henry. In retrospect, it is clear that Allah placed in my life the people I came in contact with at Arizona State University and in the Phoenix social work community so that I would learn and grow as a social worker.

In 1986, with the support of some of the Muslim community leaders, I was blessed to start the Arizona Muslim Youth Group of Greater Phoenix, and together these young people and I learned and grew. Although I had been involved in Muslim community activities in New York, this was my first real opportunity to combine Islam and social work. The youth group provided opportunities for social support, self-esteem and self-confidence building, leadership development, and Islamic education. Involvement in the youth group led to my teaching young people in the weekend Islamic school and to involvement in women's study groups.

It was not until 1995 that I truly connected what it meant to be a Muslim and a social worker. This occurred at the Sixth Regional Training Program of the Dawah Academy in Orange County, California, when Dr. Anise Ahmed, one of the Academy's instructors, taught us about Sura (Chapter) 2 verse 177 in the Qur'an. This verse is a mandate for Muslims to engage in the elimination of oppression and to care for orphans and the poor and needy. Although I knew that was part of the responsibility of a Muslim, I never realized just how much importance it had. It was at this point in my career that I understood what it was to be a Muslim social worker, someone who practices spiritually and culturally sensitive social work and is involved in the development of Islamic social services.

I began to travel and speak about social work issues at national Islamic conferences. I met Mrs. Shahina Siddiqui, who became my mentor. Identifying herself as a layperson and volunteer, she provided me with wonderful insights about spiritual counseling from an Islamic perspective. In 1996, I embarked on my doctoral studies while co-founding the Arizona Muslim Family Health and Social Services, the first Islamic social services agency in Arizona and one of only a few in the country. Later that year, I was asked to serve as a member of the advisory board for the social services department of the Islamic Society of North America. When the department folded, Shahina Siddiqui, Dr. Belkis Altareb, Maryam Funches, and I founded what is now known as the Islamic Social Services Association of the United States and Canada. It is amazing to me how God works, supporting me through my journey from a young girl in the inner city of New York to a career in social work. With the opportunity to embrace life as a Muslim and to make a commitment to serve God, I believe I have been called to be a Muslim social worker.

ISLAM AND THE MUSLIMS: SOURCES OF POWER

Historically, when Scripture has been revealed, it arrives in the language of the people who receive it. This was what happened with the Qur'an, which was revealed in the language of the Arabs. Muslims therefore believe that the Arabic people were the first of humanity to receive the final word of God. *Islam,* an Arabic word, means "submission" (Barboza, 1994; Sarwar, 1989) and "obedience/peace" (Sarwar, 1989). To Muslims, Islam is more than a religion; it actually provides a framework for human living and development. Arabic is the language of Islam, and *Allah* is the Arabic word for God. According to Islam, a Muslim is one who submits his or her free will to Allah. A Muslim's purpose in life is to serve God by enjoining the good and forbidding evil. The objective of a Muslim is to live a righteous moral life that will lead to eternal life in Paradise. Muslims are taught that everything they do should be in the name of God and that the Creator's blessings should be sought with every action they take. The primary sources that guide the faith of Islam are the Holy Qur'an, considered by Muslims to be the final revelation of God, and the Hadith, the collection of traditions of Prophet Muhammad.

According to the teachings of Islam, Prophet Muhammad, a member of the elite Quraish tribe and a descendant of the Prophet Abraham, was born in

Makkah, a city in Saudi Arabia, in 570 C.E. Muhammad was kind, trustworthy, and concerned about the evils and immoral behavior of his society. In 610 C.E., while pondering his purpose in life and the concerns of society, Muhammad was visited by the angel Gabriel (Jibra'il), who revealed that Muhammad was God's last messenger to humanity. Muhammad was instructed to carry the message of the oneness of God to all of humanity. His life as a prophet lasted 23 years and influenced the spread of monotheism. Although Prophet Muhammad could not read or write, he recited the words of God, which have inspired millions over the last 14 centuries. After hearing his teachings, his companions committed the Scripture to memory and put it in writing. With the success of his teachings on both the religious and secular levels, Prophet Muhammad is considered one of the most influential individuals in history, and his teachings represent the seal of the prophets—that is, Muhammad is considered the last of the prophets, and the role of prophet was sealed (or closed off) after him.

The six basic beliefs in Islam are grouped in three categories: Oneness of Allah (*Tauheed*), Prophethood (*Risalah*), and life after death (*Ahkirah*) (Sarwar, 1989). The first basic belief is that all Muslims believe in one God, Allah, and recognize that Allah is the Creator of all things. Second, Muslims believe in angels, the most famous of which is the angel Gabriel. Third is the belief in the prophets of God, including Adam, Abraham, Noah, Lot, David, Solomon, Jacob, Issaac, Ismael, Jonah, Joseph, Jesus, Moses, and Muhammad. Fourth is the belief in the revealed books of Allah, which Muslims identify as the Scrolls of Abraham, the Psalms of David, the Gospel of Jesus, the Torah of Moses, and the Qur'an revealed to Muhammad. Fifth is the belief in *Qadr,* or Divine Destiny, whereby everything is pre-determined by Allah and whereby humans actually have limited free will. Sixth is the belief in life after death and Judgment Day, when obedient believers will go to heaven and those who do not believe will go to hell (Sarwar, 1989).

In addition to these six basic beliefs, there are five duties that are obligatory for Muslims. These duties are referred to as the Five Pillars of Islam. The Declaration of Faith (the shahadah) is the first of the five pillars. To accept Islam as one's way of life, one must state and continuously reaffirm that there is "no god but Allah and Muhammad is the last messenger of God." Muslims are obligated to pray five prayers (*salat*) each day. Salat, the second of the Five Pillars, is performed facing the direction of the Ka'aba, the house of worship built by Abraham and his son Ismael in Makkah. The obligatory prayers provide Muslims with five formal opportunities to remember God and ask for forgiveness, patience, and steadfastness in the face of trial and adversity.

Muslim men are also obligated to attend congregational prayer services on Friday when the noonday, or *zuhr,* prayer would normally be performed. While women are not obligated to attend Friday, or *Jumah,* services, they are encouraged to attend, especially in countries in which Muslims are considered a minority. This service is a time for spiritual development, fellowship, nurturance, and support and for obtaining community news about upcoming events and activities.

Alms-giving, or charity (*zakat*), the third of the Five Pillars, is a system of contribution to the welfare of the needy members of the Muslim community. A Muslim is instructed by God to give 2.5% of his or her annual wealth, after his or her expenses are paid, to care for the orphaned, widowed, and impoverished. Zakat is a form of purification of the Muslim's wealth, which is considered a blessing and a loan from God. Fasting, or *sawm,* during Ramadan, the ninth month of the Islamic calendar, is the fourth of the Five Pillars. According to Islamic teaching, fasting teaches self-restraint and helps Muslims empathize with those less fortunate.

The Fifth Pillar of Islam is the pilgrimage, or *Hajj,* to Makkah. The Hajj is a once-in-a-lifetime obligation for Muslims. Approximately 2 million Muslims a year accept the "invitation to Allah's House" and make the trip to Islam's holiest site to fulfill this duty. The Hajj symbolizes the day when everyone will return to Allah for final judgment, and Muslims from every walk of life, ethnicity, and socioeconomic status participate in the rituals of the Hajj. The Hajj is also a demonstration of the diversity in Islam, as each Muslim is judged before Allah for piety and God consciousness—regardless of whether the individual is male or female, black, white or any other race, Arab or non-Arab, young or old, rich or poor, able-bodied or physically challenged, educated or illiterate.

RITUALS AND PRACTICES: DIET AND DRESS

Islamic practices often involve dietary and dress guidelines. Like Jews, Muslims are not permitted to eat pork, pork by-products, or any meat killed for or sacrificed for any deity other than God, the Creator of all things. When Muslims slaughter an animal, they say, "In the name of Allah." Muslims are permitted to eat meat slaughtered by devout Christians and Jews, and no restrictions are placed on seafood, vegetables, or fruit or the mixing of dairy and non-dairy products. Muslims are forbidden to consume alcohol or any drugs that have the potential of impairing normal functioning. Although Muslims acknowledge the benefit of some of these products, their use is forbidden because of the harm to the individual and society that results from substance addiction and abuse.

Modesty is very much a part of Islamic tradition for Muslim women and men, and both are taught to adhere to Islamic dress guidelines. Traditionally, Muslim women show nothing but their face, hands, and feet when they are in the company of those not part of their *mahram* (close family members, those who are not eligible to marry the woman, including her father, grandfather, brothers, sons, uncles, nephews, sons-in-law, and father-in-law). The women's clothing is opaque, loose-fitting, long-sleeved, and ankle length. The Qur'an (Chapter 24, verse 31) tells women to draw their veil, or *khimar,* over their head, ears, neck, and bosom so as not to show their adornments. This manner of covering is also known as a *hijab*. In the presence of close family members, dress requirements are relaxed.

Muslim men must also adhere to a dress code. They are required to cover from their navel to their knees. Their garments must be loose-fitting. Traditionally Muslim men wear a shirt, which covers their private area, and loose-fitting slacks. In accordance with the *sunna,* or traditions of Prophet Muhammad, Muslim men may wear a beard and a small cap known as a *kufi.* Muslim men are forbidden to wear gold or silk.

CHALLENGES FACED BY CONTEMPORARY MUSLIMS

It is difficult to discuss the issues and challenges Muslims face in North America comprehensively in the limited space of a single chapter. However, Muslims' primary concerns are related to the challenges of practicing Islam and maintaining an Islamic identity in a non-Muslim society. Because Islam is a total way of life, Islamic teachings are at the foundation of and permeate every aspect of daily living. Despite surveys that indicate that 96% of Americans believe in God or a universal spirit, 90% pray, and 43% attend religious services either weekly or more often (Hastings and Hastings, 1996; Princeton Religion Research Center, 1996), U.S. society values a secular way of life that relegates religious affairs to the private domain, separate from public life. This difference in perception regarding the role of religion in society affects the Muslim's experience and presents challenges at work, at school, and in the family.

Family

Family is considered to be the cornerstone of Muslim society, and parents are expected to raise children who will work for social justice. Obedience to parents is a divinely ordained value. Many Muslims value filial piety; however, many parents may find it difficult to recognize the conflicts their children can experience when they are exposed to the more secular American society. Muslim youth, like children everywhere, are subject to peer pressure. For the young, peer pressure is intensified when they are part of a community that is not accepted by the larger society. Immigrant and indigenous, those raised as Muslims and more recent converts, all face the challenge of raising Muslim youth in a non-Muslim environment.

Mate Selection

Mate selection presents significant challenges, because of the Islamic guidance that prohibits Western-style dating. Dating by unmarried persons who spend time alone, risking a premarital sexual relationship, is forbidden in Islam. Arranged, not forced, marriage is the tradition in Islam. Chaperoned courtship provides opportunities to meet one's future spouse and discuss concerns and plans for the future. As individuals become more identified with mainstream U.S. culture and less religious, traditional practices meet with resistance from young people, who participate in mixed-gender activities and live in isolated communities far from other Muslims.

Marital Stability and Success

Muslims have traditionally been a group with low rates of divorce and high marital stability and success. The Qur'an reminds Muslims that marriage is an institution that provides tranquility and comfort. The Prophet Muhammad told his followers that the best among them are those who are kindest to their wives. Unfortunately, marital stability and success have become increasingly threatened, as Muslims in North America have begun to see their divorce rates escalate. According to a U.S. Department of Education study, the overall divorce rate among Muslims is 31.14%, significantly higher than the Muslim world's two highest rates of divorce: Turkey and Egypt, with 10% each (Ba-Yunus, 2000). This suggests that the divorce rate among Muslims is fast approaching the divorce rate of the mainstream culture. Many of the marital problems could be resolved with family support, basic life skills, and knowledge of Islamic family law. Abandonment of traditional mate selection practices, lack of family and community support, and loss of Islamic identity and knowledge of Islamic teachings are to blame for this problem.

The Self-Image of the Muslim in North America

The psychological impact of being Muslim in a society that misunderstands and devalues one's way of life can be extremely negative. This devaluation can cause low self-esteem. The Muslim client may want to hide his or her identity so as not to stand out. Muslims may feel pressure to lead a dual existence, wanting to be viewed as non-Muslims by day and practicing Muslims during the evening and weekend. The fear of becoming the victim of a hate crime is ever-present but is exacerbated by media reports that link terrorist acts with Islam, Muslims, and Arabs. Women and girls who wear the hijab become immediate targets. Men who don the beard and kufi or in any way resemble media stereotypes also become targets of hate crimes. Xenophobia and media-generated fear of Islam promote a climate of hate and fear among Americans toward Islam, which are internalized by many Muslims.

Like those in other cultural groups, individual Muslims are often asked to represent and serve as spokespeople for their group, as if all Muslims were the same and held the same views on every issue (Dziegielewski, Leon, & Green, 1998; Leon & Dziegielewski, 2000). Such activity, often proposed by well-meaning educators and friends, can place unrealistic expectations on a Muslim. Many Muslim individuals feel that they often have to defend their faith and clarify their beliefs to strangers, friends, and non-Muslim family members. At times, Muslims feel as though they are expected to be able to respond to everything that is negative regarding Islam and Muslims in books, movies, and television. Feeling as though one has to defend one's way of life and educate those around one in regard to the religion can be quite stressful. Acknowledgment of the sheer amount of mental and physical energy it takes to deal with such issues on a day-to-day basis is essential in understanding the Muslim experience.

Muslim Children in Public School

Muslim children in the public schools, in general, receive negative messages about Islam from their textbooks and their teachers. Organizations like the Council on Islamic Education work closely with schools and textbook publishers to eradicate the misinformation and provide teachers with accurate information about Islam and Muslims.

Islamic practices of separation between genders, praying five times daily, modest dress, and dietary restrictions receive little, if any, support. Muslim students often feel penalized for attendance at Friday religious services and the Islamic holidays of the Feast of Fasting (*Eid ul Fitr*) and the Feast of Sacrifice (*Eid ul Adha*). They are put in the position of having to choose between Islamic duties and school activities. During Ramadan, the month of fasting, Muslim students are challenged to maintain a balance between their Islamic obligations of extra worship and their school workload.

Public school tends to socialize children into accepting common societal practices like dating, drinking, questioning parental authority, attending dances, and socializing with the opposite sex and attitudes that promote secularism and country above God. These practices and attitudes are in direct conflict with Islamic teachings and often lead either to conflict in the family or to assimilation and a loss of Islamic values and identity.

Women and Islam

Most Muslims who accept Islam as adults are women (Granger & Portner, 1985). The book *Daughters of Another Path,* by Carol Anway (1996), recounts one woman's personal experience as the mother of an American convert as well as the experiences of American women who have converted to Islam. Because of media stereotypes and sensationalism, many non-Muslims perceive Islam as oppressive to women. Many Muslim women, however, do not agree, as they see Islam as a way of life that provides them with a sense of purpose, peace, and freedom not common in Western society. As Muslims, they believe that "most of the disabilities Muslim women suffer have nothing to do with the Qur'an," but rather "they come from the humdrum circumstances of time, place and economics" ("Islam and the West," 1994, p. 11). It is important to recognize that many of the inequities Muslim women face are the result of cultural or political traditions that have nothing to do with and are not sanctioned by the teachings of Islam.

According to the Qur'an, moral and legal duties and responsibilities, as well as spiritual and legal consequences and rewards, are the same for both men and women (Chapter 3, verse 195; Chapter 4, verse 124; Chapter 33, verse 35; Chapter 57, verse 12). Islam does not blame Eve (*Hawwa*) for the fall of man, and both Adam and Eve are held accountable for their disobedience to Allah (Qur'an, Chapter 2, verse 36). In fact, in one passage, Adam alone is blamed (Chapter 20, verse 116–122).

The duties of Muslim women are similar to those of men. Muslim women are expected to worship Allah, enjoin good and forbid evil, and do good deeds in their quest for a place in heaven. Women have the right to vote in community matters, to own property, to work outside the home, to conduct business and sign contracts, to spend their money as they determine, to choose or refuse their marriage proposals, to divorce, to attend the mosque, to keep their family name, and to pursue higher religious and secular education (Badawi, 1995). Women also have the right to be provided for by their spouse, father, or brother(s). They are not obligated to spend their money, even if they are rich, in order to maintain themselves or their families. Women have the right to kind treatment (Badawi, 1995). The prophet Muhammad told his followers to be kind to women. He also told them that Paradise lies at the feet of the mother and that a degree of honor should be extended to the mother above the father, though both should be well cared for and respected. Basically, Islam teaches that women are to be highly respected.

One of the foremost scholars in the early days of Islam was Aisha, one of the wives of the Prophet Muhammad. Khadijah, the Prophet Muhammad's first wife, and his only wife for 25 years, was a business owner and the first convert to Islam. Women also participated in the defense of Muslims against their oppressors and were among the early martyrs and refugees.

Elder Muslims

The Muslim community is a largely youthful one: 49% of U.S. Muslims are under 20 years old, 50.5% are between 20 and 65 years old, and the remaining 0.5% are over 65 (Ba-Yunus and Siddiqui, 1998). Among these senior citizens are the parents of those who came with the wave of Muslim immigration to the United States in the 1960s and 1970s; those who converted to Islam in the 1930s and 1940s; and refugee elders who were displaced as a result of the wars that occurred during the 1990s in countries such as Bosnia and Somalia. As the Muslim community ages, the challenges of caring for its elder members increase. Traditionally, elder parents are cared for as part of the extended family. Muslim children are taught to care for their elder parents and to value and respect their wisdom.

The Muslim community is faced with the difficulty of ensuring that its elders receive the care they have a right to as part of Islam's tradition. The challenge is related to the conflict between Muslim values and American cultural values that prefer youth to the elderly. The desire of devout Muslims to adhere to the Islamic teachings and maintain a strong sense of community helps them remain committed to care of the elders. But as Muslims become less devout in their faith and begin to acculturate into the American mainstream, problems such as elder abuse and neglect have become more prevalent. Also, middle-aged Muslims experience the challenges of the "sandwich generation" faced by those in mainstream American culture. Trying to raise children and care for elder parents becomes very stressful for this generation. Muslims face the real possibility that they may have to place elder parents and relatives in nursing homes because of an inability to take care of them when they experience diseases like Alzheimer's or become disabled and frail. American society just does not facilitate the care of the elderly in the home that is possible in communities in which the extended family is the norm. Many devout Muslims may interpret their own decision to place an elder in a nursing home as a sinful deed that goes against the Qur'anic mandate to care for their parents. As social workers provide services to the Muslim family unit, they need to consider the extreme guilt and conflict that many adult Muslims experience as a result of such a decision.

Muslims in the Workplace

The work environment presents its own issues and challenges. Most employers and supervisors lack the cultural sensitivity necessary to create an environment that includes and values Muslim employees. Muslim employees often feel threatened with the loss of their jobs if they reveal that they are Muslim. The American Muslim Council and the American Muslim Alliance are nationally based organizations that work to promote political representation of Muslims and to pass laws like the Religious Freedom Act which reflect and support Muslim concerns. The Council on American Islamic Relations (CAIR), a non-profit Muslim civil rights organization, intervenes in workplace issues affecting Muslim employees. Women who wear the religiously mandated head covering experience harassment, ridicule, and loss of employment. Muslim men who don the traditional beard and kufi and attend Friday congregational prayers also risk demotion and unemployment. Because the Islamic holidays do not coincide with those traditionally celebrated in the United States, Muslim employees have to use vacation time or develop some creative way of attending their services. Many opt not to attend services rather than risk being perceived as different and making waves with their employer. Perhaps more than the experiences during regular work hours, after-work and extra-work gatherings, meetings, and "happy hour" business sessions present challenges to Muslims. Oftentimes these activities interfere with the practicing Muslim employee's opportunity to obtain the support, nurturing, and reinforcement needed to function in a non-Muslim environment. The after-hour activities may also conflict with Islamic etiquette regarding mixed-gender socialization, pork-free dietary guidelines, and not drinking alcoholic beverages. The stressors presented by after-hours activities, the scheduling of meetings and conferences on Fridays, the requirement for unaccompanied overnight travel, especially for Muslim women, add to the pressures of managing work, family, and personal obligations.

Economic Issues

Economic issues affect the life of the Muslim American. While the median income of Muslims in the United States is $39,700 per year, and while a significant portion of Muslims are in medicine, engineering, business, finance, and higher education (Ba-Yunus and Siddiqui, 1998), the community also experiences its pockets of poverty both among U.S.-born Muslims and among new arrivals. Many well-educated Muslims are underemployed because of immigration issues and racism that present challenges to full participation in the work force.

Managing life in an interest-based economy is also challenging and presents conflicts for the Muslim American. The Qur'an strictly forbids the giving, taking, or witnessing of interest-bearing contracts. This, however, is almost impossible to avoid for most Muslims who travel or want to own a home or purchase a vehicle. Some religious scholars have interpreted the situation in the West as extreme—which allows Western Muslims to make an "exception" for the purchase of a home or car. Still, many devout Muslims feel their religious beliefs are compromised when they have to make this choice. The Muslim Housing Coop, and organizations such as La Riba and Amana Trust, are working to develop interest-free alternatives for loans, mortgages, and investing.

CONCEPTIONS OF HEALTH: ISLAMIC TRADITION AND THE STRENGTHS-BASED PERSPECTIVE

According to Islam, a healthy individual is one who leads a balanced life spiritually, physically, emotionally, intellectually, and socially. One tradition of Prophet Muhammad reminds followers that time should be given to work, spiritual development, and leisure activities. Muslims are reminded not to spend so much time in the pursuit of spiritual fulfillment that they forget the practicalities of life. Likewise, too much time should not be given to the worldly matters without attending to spiritual concerns and activities that soften the heart, such as pondering and reflecting on the wonders of Allah's creation and providing community service. Muslims are prohibited from drinking alcohol, eating pork, or overeating. Another tradition of Prophet Muhammad reminds Muslims to allow one-third of their body space for food, one-third for water, and one-third for air. Given the high rate of obesity, alcoholism, and depression in U.S. society, these traditions serve to promote healthy living and prevent many of the health problems often faced by non-Muslims.

Muslims are empowered and better able to withstand the hardships of life when they develop a strong relationship with God, commit themselves to adhering to the Qur'anic commandments, and model the teachings of Prophet Muhammad. Muslims believe that God knows what is best for them, that in every challenge there is ease, and that God places no burden greater than the individual can bear. When a tragedy strikes, Muslims remind themselves and each other that everything happens as part of God's ultimate plan. They say, "from Allah we come to Allah we return." Regular obligatory prayer, extra non-obligatory prayer, fasting for the sake of God, and regular remembrance of God through informal supplications are considered preventive measures. These are also suggested strategies when clients are experiencing life's problems. The stories of the struggles Prophet Muhammad and his companions faced during the early days of Islam also empowering for Muslims.

A strong sense of belonging to a community that includes over a billion people throughout the world from different walks of life is empowering for the Muslim. Acknowledging a shared belief in God and a connection to a fellowship in faith provides an immense source of strength. Many converts are awed by the relationship that they develop with other Muslims purely because of their mutual love of God and commitment to the tenets of Islam. To know that brothers and sisters in faith all over the world are praying for each other in whatever trials they may experience and wanting the best for each other enables Muslims to get through very tough times. Being able to count on one's brothers and sisters in faith to fulfill their religious duties, including sharing their wealth so that no needs go unmet, is powerful.

Because Islam is the framework on which practicing Muslim clients base their lives, professionals may find it helpful to consider Qur'anic teachings and the traditions of Prophet Muhammad as they seek ways to address the social concerns of Muslim clients through professional interventions. These primary texts can provide the foundation for counseling strategies that are important for practicing Muslims. Islamic traditions provide adherents with strategies for addressing most daily concerns as well as steps to prevent abuse, manage anger, eliminate poverty and oppression, and address the concerns of the spiritually bankrupt.

CULTURALLY SENSITIVE PRACTICE WITH MUSLIM PEOPLE

For helping professionals, being aware of cultural heritage, beliefs, and mores can aid in developing an understanding of why clients feel and act as they do (Irving, 1982). It is impossible for counseling professionals to help Muslims without understanding the similarities and differences between religious traditions, cultural practices, and stereotypes of Islam and Muslims. Further, some believe that much so-called knowledge of Islam and the Middle East has been based "on ignorance or prejudice" (Irving, 1982, p. 6), and Islam is often blamed unfairly for problems wrongly assumed to have been caused by Muslims (as in the cases of the Oklahoma City bombing and the crash of TWA Flight 800) (Fedarko, 1996; Friedman, 1995; Hitchens, 1995; Shammas, 1995).

ACCULTURATION AND RELIGIOUSNESS AMONG MUSLIMS

Among Muslims, just as among other religious groups, there are varying degrees of religious practice or devotion to the way of life. Because Muslims are a minority religious group in some countries, particularly the United States and Canada, it is important to explore individual clients' degree of acculturation and level of religiousness in order to gain an understanding of their relationship to the larger society and to their own community. A typology of Muslims in North America has begun to emerge as those who work with Muslims attempt to gain an understanding of important intragroup factors, but much more research needs to be conducted. To date, five types, or categories, of Muslims have been identified:

- Traditional–strongly practicing
- Bicultural–moderately practicing
- Acculturated–marginally practicing
- Assimiliated–nonpracticing
- Recommitted–strongly practicing

The extent to which an individual's assimilation and acculturation in society and knowledge and practice of the religion influence his or her sense of identity, decision making, and life as a Muslim in America provides the basis of this framework.

Muslims who are *traditional–strongly practicing* do not see religious and secular affairs as separate. They are active in mosque and community affairs and find support in their relations with other Muslims. They are devout in maintaining the six Articles of Faith and the Five Pillars of Islam. Their worldview and decision-making process are based on the Qur'an and the traditions of Prophet Muhammad.

Bicultural–moderately practicing Muslims believe in the Articles of Faith and the Five Pillars of Islam. They have a strong Islamic identity and are active in the Muslim community as well as in the dominant society as much as time and distance allow. Their worldview and decision making are based on both Islamic teachings and secular knowledge, with Islamic teachings having greater influence.

An *acculturated–marginally practicing* Muslim is likely to be identified as Muslim by his or her name but exemplifies little Islamic identity and adheres to few Islamic traditions and practices. This person's worldview and decision making are largely based on the cultural traditions of the mainstream society. Acculturated–marginally practicing Muslims are not committed to their five obligatory prayers and are rarely involved in regular mosque activities, but do celebrate the Islamic holidays of the Feast of Fasting and the Feast of Sacrifice. Ba-Yunus and Siddiqui (1998) also refer to this group of Muslims as "Eid Muslims" or "cultural Muslims."

Those in the fourth group in the continuum, *assimilated–non-practicing* Muslims, are very private about their identification as Muslims. They are likely to Americanize their name and dress. They do not practice the Articles of Faith and Five Pillars of Islam even though they have been raised Muslim or come from practicing Muslim families. Their worldview is largely secular, and their decision making is largely based on cultural tradition and the values of the mainstream society.

Finally, the *recommitted–strongly practicing* Muslim is similar to the traditional–strongly practicing Muslim in many ways, except that this individual has reclaimed the Islamic teachings and recommitted himself or herself to the Five Pillars and the Articles of Faith after having been marginally practicing or non-practicing. Decision making is once again based on the purpose and worldview of Islam. Individuals in this group adopt dress, decision-making processes, and associations similar to those of the traditional–strongly practicing and bicultural–moderately practicing Muslims.

Because of the importance of modesty between the genders, traditional–strongly practicing Muslims are observant of the practice of preventing physical contact between non-mahram men and women. Therefore men and women are likely to limit eye contact and prefer to lower their gaze, as prescribed in Qur'an. Private meetings between a man and woman are avoided. According to the traditions of Prophet Muhammad, when a man and woman are alone, the Devil is the third party, beckoning them to engage in unlawful sexual activity. According to Islamic tradition, religious Muslim men and women refrain from shaking hands with people of the opposite sex. In counseling settings, private meetings between a man and a woman should be prevented and avoided.

Religious Muslims are also likely to be hesitant about seeking help from a professional who is not a Muslim because of fears that stereotypical information may be used to their detriment. Therefore, religious Muslims are more likely to seek the counseling of family, close friends, a community member, or a trusted imam or scholar. Nakhaima and Dicks (1995) recommend the use of consultation, or link counseling, with religious families. This strategy places the social work professional in the role of a consultant sharing social work strategies and interventions with an informal counselor while supporting faith-based strategies. This allows for collaboration between the professional helper and the family or religious leader.

THE MUSLIM SOCIAL WORKER

Social work is prescribed as a laudable work and a religious obligation for Muslims. Many passages throughout the Qur'an (e.g., Chapter 2, verse 177, Chapter 107, verses 1–7) and in the Hadith highlight the importance of caring for the poor, the needy, the orphaned, the widowed, and the oppressed. The obligation to pay 2.5% of one's wealth annually promotes social justice by redistributing wealth and narrowing the gap between the haves and the have-nots. The institutionalized collection and distribution of this zakat forms an Islamically based social welfare system. Muslims are encouraged to give generously above and beyond the obligatory 2.5%. Throughout the history of Islam there have been periods when poverty among the residents of a given geographic location was eliminated through the distribution of zakat.

The mutual aid system that developed in colonial America and the neighborliness of the settlement house movement are similar to the Islamic tradition of addressing neighborly needs. The Qur'an (Chapter 107) reminds Muslims of the importance of attending to the needs of their neighbors. Refusing to bestow small kindnesses or to meet neighborly needs (*al ma'un*) is highly frowned on in the Qur'an. A tradition of Prophet Muhammad says that one who allows his neighbor to go hungry while he is satisfied is not a believer. The care and kind treatment of orphans is also behavior that is considered among the good deeds and could earn the faithful a place in heaven, according to Islamic tradition.

Islam also establishes a foundation for social action, the appreciation of cultural diversity, and the provision of counseling services, which serve as primary intervention strategies. In the Qur'an and the traditions of the Prophet Muhammad, Muslims are directed to fight against oppression and tyrannical leadership, and to provide *naseeha,* or advice, to those experiencing marital problems or facing other day-to-day problems of life. The Qur'an (Chapter 49, verse 13) reminds Muslims that they were developed into nations and tribes to know and appreciate one another. In his last sermon, Prophet Muhammad told those who gathered to hear him that neither race, ethnicity, nor tribe was a criterion for superiority, and that kind treatment and observance of the rights of women were divinely ordained and must be adhered to. Mosques in North America have assisted immigrant Muslims in the resettlement and readjustment process. Relief organizations just as the Red Crescent Society, the Holy Land Foundation, and Islamic Relief have a long history of providing help to displaced and needy Muslims throughout the world.

Even though care of those in need is an inherent religious obligation, the Muslim social worker's job is not an easy one. Muslim social workers experience the difficulty of advocating for an oppressed, underserved, often misrepresented, and culturally diverse religious community. Further, because non-Muslim social work professionals have little awareness of Islamic traditions and practices, clients experience a "blaming of the religion" for the social problems of the individual. Therefore, it is easy for misinterpretation or inaccurate information about Islam and generalizations about Muslim people to lead to inappropriate assessments and intervention or treatment plans. For this reason, practicing Muslims are usually reluctant to meet with or seek the assistance of mainstream providers. When they do meet with non-Muslim social workers, Muslims want someone who is sensitive and aware of their religious teachings (Kelly, Aridi, & Bakhtiar, 1996).

Further, the North American Muslim community in general has not fully recognized the extent of the social problems it faces. The consequence of living in an environment that lacks the community supports to sustain a growing population is only now being acknowledged. Only in the last 20 years have the institutions needed to support this community—civic organizations, businesses, schools, and media—been firmly established (Council on Islamic Education, 1995). Even though Islam has a long tradition of social service and charitable efforts and Muslims were in the Americas before the arrival of Columbus (Haddad, 1986), most community-based Islamic social service organizations in the United States are less than 10 years old. This leaves the Muslim social worker facing the challenges of working with a community that is reluctant to believe that it cannot handle its own problems and is often in denial about the type and nature of the problem being encountered. At the same time, this resistance can be misunderstood, as the mainstream social service system is unaware of the Muslim community's traditions and practices or, even worse, bases its interactions with Muslims on media stereotypes. The Islamic Social Services Association (ISSA) of the United States and Canada was recently established to bring Muslim social service providers together to devise ways to address the various social problems its members see.

CONCLUSION

The issues, changes, and challenges faced by Muslims in North America are unique to this population and at the same time are very much like the experiences of other cultural and religious minorities. To facilitate the problem-solving process, social workers need to be aware of their own perceptions, stereotypes, and assumptions about Islam and Muslims. Questioning Muslims about the validity of their beliefs is disrespectful of their religion and may bring the therapeutic relationship to an end prematurely. As Altareb (1996) states, "most American Muslims are sensitive to the biases in the larger society and may see non-Muslim counselors as representing the views of that society." Therefore, social workers need to be familiar with their own values and those of the Muslim client in order to better understand that client (Altareb, 1996).

Muslims are a growing minority in North America, as well in as the rest of the world. Like those of most minority groups, the problems Muslims face can differ depending on whether the individuals are first- or second-generation members of immigrant families or recent converts, on how religiously or culturally entrenched they are, and on the community with which they identify. Social workers may need to advocate on behalf of the client or know where to refer the client for help in matters such as taking time off from work to observe religious holidays or perform obligatory prayers. Advocating for change and sensitivity in programs that were not designed to take the beliefs and practices of Muslims into account requires knowledge of Islam and Muslims.

To achieve culturally-sensitive practice, social work professionals must be exposed to the beliefs, needs, issues, and challenges of the minority group and to maintain constant awareness of their own cultural mores and preconceived notions. Sensitivity training regarding Islam and Muslims can provide the basis for better understanding. Workshops, curricula, and training that focuses on ethnic groups and minorities are essential.

REFERENCES

Ali, A. Y. (1999). *The Qur'an Translation.* New York: Tahrike Tarsile Qur'an, Inc.

Altareb, B. Y. (1996). Islamic spirituality in America: A middle path to unity. *Journal of Counseling and Values, 41,* 29–38.

Anway, C. L. (1996). Daughters of another path: Experiences of American women choosing Islam. Lee's Summit, MO: Yawna Publications.

Badawi, J. (1995). Gender equity in Islam. Indianapolis, IN: American Trust Publication.

Barboza, S. (1994). *American jihad: Islam after Malcolm X.* New York: Doubleday.

Ba-Yunus, I. (2000). Divorce among Muslims. *Islamic Horizons, 29*(4), 52–53.

Ba-Yunus, I., & Siddiqui, M. M. (1998). *A report on the Muslim population in the United States of America.* New York: Center for American Muslim Research and Information.

Council on Islamic Education. *Teachings about Islam.* (1995). CA: Author.

Dziegielewski, S. F., Leon, A., & Green, C. (1998). African American children: A model for culturally sensitive group practice. *Early Child Development and Care, 147*(3), 83–97.

Fedarko, K. (1996, July 29). Who wishes us ill? *Time,* p. 41.

Friedman, R. I. (1995, May 15). One man's jihad. *The Nation,* pp. 656–657.

Granger, J. M., & Portner, D. L. (1985). Ethnic and gender-sensitive social work practice. *Journal of Social Work Education, 21*(1), 38–47.

Haddad, Y. (1986). *A century of Islam in America.* Washington, DC: Islamic Affairs Programs.

Hart, M. H. (1989). *The 100: A ranking of the most influential persons in history.* New York: First Carol.

Hastings, E. H., & Hastings, P. K. (Ed.) (1996). *Index to international public opinion,* 1994–95. Westport, CT: Greenwood Press.

Hitchens, C. (1995, May 22). Minority report. *The Nation,* p. 71.

Irving, T. B. (1982). *The tide of Islam* (rev. ed.). Cedar Rapids, IA: Ingram.

Islam and the West. (1994, August 6–12). *The Economist,* pp. 3–18.

Kelly, E. W. Jr., Aridi, A. & Bakhtiar, L. (1996). Muslims in the United States: An exploratory study of universal and mental health values. *Journal of Counseling and Values, 40*(3), 206–218.

Leon, A., & Dziegielewski, S. F. (2000). Engaging Hispanic immigrant mothers: Revisiting the psychoeducational group model. *Crisis Intervention and Time-Limited Treatment, 6*(1), 13–27.

Nakhaima, J., & Dicks, B. (1995). Social work practice with religious families. *Families in Society, 76*(6), 360–368.

Princeton Religion Research Center. *Religion in America, the Gallup poll, 1996*. Princeton, NJ: Author.

Sarwar, G. (1989). *Islam: Beliefs and teachings*. London: The Muslim Educational Trust.

Shaikhr, M. A. (1995). *Teaching about Islam and Muslims in the public school classroom: A handbook for educators*. Fountain Valley, CA: Council on Islamic Education.

Shammas, A. (1995, January 30). Presumed guilty. *The New York Times*, p. A25.

ADDITIONAL RESOURCES

Books

Abdalati, H. (1975). *Islam in focus*. Indianapolis, IN: American Trust Publications.

Ahmad, K. (Ed.). (1990). *Towards understanding Islam*. London: The Islamic Foundation.

Bucaille, M. (1979). *The Bible, the Qura'an, and science*. Indianapolis, IN: American Trust Publications.

Congress, E. P. (1994). The use of culturagrams to assess and empower culturally diverse families. *Families in Society, 75*(9), 531–540.

Congress, E.P. (1997). *Multicultural perspectives in working with families*. New York: Springer.

Devore, W., & Schlesinger, E. (1981). *Ethnic Sensitive Social Work Practice*. St. Louis, MO: C. V. Mosby Co.

Haneef, S. (1993). *What everyone should know about Islam and Muslims*. Des Plaines, IL: Library of Islam.

International Institute of Islamic Thought. *Islam: Source and purpose of knowledge*. (1988). Herndon, VA: Author.

Kamal, A. A. (Ed.). (1991). *The meaning of the Qur'an*. Lahore, Pakistan: Islamic Publications, Ltd.

Matar, N. I. (1992). *Islam for beginners*. New York: Writers and Readers Publishing.

Siddiqui, S. (1999). The senior citizens of our ummah. Soundvision. http://sound vision.com/misc/elderly/senior.shtml

Tarazi, N. (1995). *The child in Islam*. Indianapolis, IN: American Trust Publications.

Web Sites

Links to information about Islam: www.islamic-religion.com
Information on the Islamic religion: www.islamworld.net

GLOSSARY

Allah The Arabic word for God, used by all Arabic speaking people whether Muslim or Christian.

Aqiqa The celebration of a baby's birth. The occasion is commemorated by slaughtering a lamb to share with members of the community and by asking the community to pray that the child grows to be a good Muslim.

Arabic The language of Islam and the people of Arabic speaking countries. While the majority of Arabic speaking people are Muslim, only 18% of Muslims around the world speak Arabic.

Council on American Islamic Relations (CAIR) A non-profit Muslim civil rights organization that intervenes in workplace issues affecting Muslim employees. CAIR also works to promote accurate information about Islam by eliminating misconceptions and media stereotypes.

Hadith One of the two primary sources that guide the faith of Islam. This source provides a collection of traditions of the Prophet Muhammad.

Hajj One of the Five Pillars of Islam, an obligatory pilgrimage to Makkah made at least once in his or her lifetime by every Muslim who is healthy and financially able to travel. Hajj symbolizes the day when all Islam followers return to Allah for final judgment. The Hajj is also a demonstration of the diversity in Islam, as before Allah each Muslim is judged for piety and God consciousness.

Hijab The Islamic tradition of covering the body. Hijab commonly refers to the obligatory headscarf worn by Muslim women. The obligatory covering worn in the company of a man varies depending on the degree of relationship between the man and the woman.

Holy Qur'an One of the two primary sources that guide the faith of Islam. According to Islam, the Qur'an is the final revelation of God.

Islam An Arabic word that means "submission" and "obedience/peace." For the followers of this religion, Islam constitutes a complete way of life that provides adherents a framework for human living and development.

Islamic holidays Two primary Islamic holidays are the Feast of Fasting (Eid ul Fitr) and the Feast of Sacrifice (Eid ul Adha).

Janazah Islamic funeral. Deceased Muslims are washed and shrouded for burial. A prayer is said for the deceased before he or she is buried.

Khimar A veil that Muslim women wear to cover their head, ears, neck, and bosom so as not to show their adornments.

Kufi A small cap worn by Muslim men.

Mosques Muslim places of worship.

Muslim beliefs There are six basic beliefs in Islam that are grouped into three categories: Oneness of Allah (Tauheed), Prophethood (Risalah), and life after death (Ahkirah).

Muslim dietary restrictions Muslims are prohibited from drinking alcohol, eating pork, or overeating.

Pillars of Islam The five duties of Islam, including the declaration of faith, obligatory prayers, alms-giving, fasting, and the pilgrimage to Makkah.

Prophet Muhammad The prophet of Islam who was born in Makkah, a city in the Hijaz (known today as Saudi Arabia) in 570 C.E. Muhammad received the commandment to carry the message of the oneness of God to all of humanity. Through his prophethood, which lasted 23 years, many were influenced to believe in the message of monotheism.

Ramadan The ninth month of the Islamic calendar in which fasting, or sawm, is practiced.

Salat The second of the Five Pillars of Islam, the five obligatory prayers Muslims are expected to complete each day. Salat is performed facing the direction of the Ka'aba, the house of worship built by Abraham and his son Ismael in Makkah, Saudi Arabia.

Sawm One of the Five Pillars of Islam. Healthy Muslims past the age of puberty are required to fast for 29 or 30 days each year during the month of Ramadan.

Shahadah Declaration of faith. There is no baptismal process in Islam. To become a Muslim, one merely openly declares his or her belief in one God and that Muhammad is the last prophet.

Zakat The third Pillar of Islam; obligatory alms-giving or charity. In this way a Muslim contributes to the welfare of the needy in the community. Zakat is a form of purification of the Muslim's wealth, which is considered a blessing and a loan from God.

Zuhr prayer The midday prayer Muslims perform shortly after noon.

PROTESTANTISM: AN OVERVIEW

CHAPTER 9

MARY P. VAN HOOK

Protestantism encompasses a wide variety of religious groups, or *denominations,* within the Christian tradition. One recent list of denominations in the United States included about 130 groups that could be considered Protestant (Lindner, 1999). These groups are distinguished by their beliefs, organizational structures, or historical, regional, and ethnic differences. There is also a growing trend for groups to establish themselves as non-denominational, or independent, churches organized around a specific leader or set of beliefs and practices. While there have been ecumenical efforts to unify various Protestant denominations, these have met with limited success. In recent years there has been an increase in more fundamentalist groups (which believe in the literal interpretation of the Bible) and Pentecostal groups (which emphasize the active working on the Holy Spirit) and a decline in traditional mainline Protestant groups. The current trend toward individualism and away from denominational loyalties complicates the picture further, because many Protestants readily switch their affiliation despite differences in the official belief systems of the organizations involved (Lindner, 1999). The decision to join a specific

The author would like to thank Thomas Brunkow, Donald Lindskoog, Marlin Vander Wilt, and Jay Van Hook for reviewing the manuscript.

Protestant church may be based on an appreciation of the church's youth program, the welcoming nature of the congregation, or the music rather than on understanding and acceptance of the historical traditions of the denomination. As a result, the official beliefs of a denomination might not represent those of many members, and a social worker cannot make assumptions about a client's understanding of or agreement with a particular religious tradition.

Because there are substantial differences within and among Protestant groups, this chapter will attempt to strike a balance between discussing common themes and describing some important differences. In the interest of a more complete discussion, the chapter will discuss both mainline and more conservative groups. It will also describe some general themes in Protestantism. To give a richer picture of the diversity within Protestantism, later chapters cover Baptists (the largest set of denominations within Protestantism) and Seventh-Day Adventists (a major group with several distinctive views). There is also a chapter on the African American Baptist tradition, to reveal the complex interplay between beliefs and practices and racial and ethnic traditions. The chapter on Mormonism (Church of Latter-day Saints) discusses another large Christian group whose identity as a Protestant denomination is controversial.

My own life reflects the tendency of many Protestants to participate in several different denominations. When I was a child, my family was active in two denominations (Presbyterian USA and Christian Reformed). As an adult, I have belonged to four denominations (Christian Reformed, United Methodist, Reformed Church of America, and Presbyterian USA), and my grown children are currently active in three different ones (African Methodist Episcopal, Christian Reformed, and United Methodist). While some of of my moves to different denominations were in response to my views on religious matters, others reflected a sense of being welcomed by a particular church within a community. Unlike some of my colleagues within other traditions represented in this book, growing up Protestant for me meant being part of the majority culture. Even though I had close friends who were Jewish, Roman Catholic, and atheist, and my family later joined a church group that had a strong sense of being a minority religious group, my earlier experiences continued to give me and my immediate family the sense of being part of the broader world of Protestantism and the mainstream culture.

Much of my motivation for entering social work arose from how I learned to view myself and the world around me. Several themes in the Protestant tradition played an important role for me, as they have for fellow Protestant social workers. The concept of the family of God, which underlies both attempts to establish social justice and efforts to respond to individuals in times of need, has been a central one. I grew up learning stories from the Bible that demonstrated God's protective care as well as his expectations for people. I heard the words of the prophets of the Old Testament speaking of the need for people to show love and justice. I learned about the life and teaching of Jesus, who stressed the importance of caring for others, including those who are marginalized because they are poor or do not belong in some way. These views have been echoed in the writing of fellow Protestant social workers (Hugen, 1998; Keith-Lucas, 1996; Sherwood, 1997). I was taught that my Christian faith should be reflected in the way I treated other people and the way in which I lived my daily life. The actions of my parents and my religious training influenced the way I was brought up to think about people. Since people are created as children of God, they deserve to be treated with respect and dignity and cannot be viewed primarily as means toward an end.

The doctrine of grace also shaped my thinking about social work. This doctrine is a constant reminder that all of us are recipients of the grace of God. Thus, differences between us and others are not due primarily to any inherent goodness on our part, but arise from the actions of the grace of God within us. This does not mean that I am not responsible for my decisions, but that much of the positive side of my being results from God's working within my life through grace. The doctrine of grace also means that no one should be "written off" because of the life that he or she has led so far, because God can work in the heart of anyone. I realize that my clients are not alone in being dependent in certain situations, because I recognize that all of us are dependent on God.

I was brought up to believe that being loved by God means that there is a purpose for each of us. It also means that the gifts we have (our talents, our time, our energy) are given to us for a purpose. From this perspective, social work for me and for many other Protestant social workers represents a "calling," a reflection of the purpose of God in my life.

The concepts and views that set me and many of my colleagues on the path toward social work also prompted many Protestant groups to be active in beginning social work programs that addressed social and personal needs. Among these efforts were homes for children, family counseling agencies, centers for the elderly, hospitals, and emergency services. Many current social welfare programs began in this way and continue to have strong ties to various Protestant groups.

As a life-long Protestant, I have experienced or witnessed the support and welcome that can be blessed parts of the tradition, as well as the divisiveness and judgmental attitudes that can make people feel isolated and alienated. I have seen how the gifts that people have may be appreciated and nourished or disregarded because of gender or other personal characteristics that marginalize them. As a result, I have learned both to draw upon the resources of the Protestant tradition in helping people and to recognize that people can be carrying scars related in some way to their religious background and the ways in which important people in their lives interpreted it.

HISTORICAL BACKGROUND AND MASTER STORIES

Historically, Protestantism began in 1517 with the work of Martin Luther, who was followed by other European theologians who broke away from the teachings and practices of the Roman Catholic Church. Some of these leaders established their own traditions within Protestantism. Although the specific beliefs, practices, and concerns of the early Protestant leaders and their subsequent followers differed in some respects, several common themes emerged. These, which have been characteristic of Protestantism over the years, include salvation by faith as a gift of grace and the priesthood of all believers. These beliefs are set within the basic religious paradigm of a God who encourages personal relationships between the divine and human beings.

Salvation as a Gift of Grace

Protestants, along with all traditional Christian groups (including Roman Catholic and Orthodox), believe that God created the world. Human beings were created as children of God and are therefore good and of great value. Unfortunately, sin soon entered into this perfect world. Consequently, human beings must contend with the struggle between good and evil within themselves and in the world around them (McGrath, 1997). The noted Protestant theologian Reinhold Neibuhr described the paradox of human beings. They are elevated because they are created in the "image of God," and at the same time they are sinners struggling with evil in the heart of the personality—the will (Niebuhr, 1941). Sin represents a wrong use of the human capacity for self-determination and freedom of choice. The consequence of sin is a broken quality in a person's relationships with God and with other human beings. To save people from these consequences, God demonstrated redemptive love for them by sending Jesus—God in human presence—to live, to teach, to die, and then to be resurrected. God's act of saving people from their sins does not mean that people will not do anything wrong or will not suffer, but that they can live with the knowledge of God's love and forgiveness in their lives (Smedes, 1982). God's actions also give people the hope that they will live again after death in fellowship with God in heaven. God continues to act in the lives of people through the Holy Spirit.

Salvation by grace means that salvation is a gift from God rather than something earned by good deeds. This belief is echoed in the words of the creeds and the confessions of the mainstream denominations—for example, the Augsburg Confession of Lutherans and the Westminister Confession of Presbyterians and Reformed (Kerr, 1966). Living according to the commandments of God and carrying out religious practices represent expressions of thankfulness for the gift of grace, not efforts to earn salvation. God strengthens people in their efforts to live in this manner (Kerr, 1966). John Wesley, founder of Methodism, especially emphasized how God's grace helps people grow in spiritual maturity as they are not only cleansed by grace of the guilt of sin but also enabled to contend with sin in their lives (Kerr, 1966, pp. 194–200). This belief reflects the Holiness tradition within Protestantism that is characterized by the emphasis on the power of grace to change the lives of people during life on earth (Marsden, 1991). The Holiness tradition was carried on by groups that gradually separated from the already existing denominations to stress not only personal purity in life but also responsibilities toward the poor. The Salvation Army exemplifies these groups (Marsden, 1991).

Individual Protestant denominations vary in their relative emphasis on the sinfulness of human beings and the love of God. The related beliefs held by individuals or their families, either currently or in the past, can have a profound impact and can be pertinent when people are struggling with issues of guilt, problems in relationships with others, and their sense of the meaning of events in their lives. Consequently, information about clients' beliefs about sin and God's love can sometimes be important in understanding how they experience life events and the resources available to them.

Priesthood of All Believers

The concept of the priesthood of all believers refers to the ability of all laypersons to relate to God directly rather than through intermediaries. Protestants have been encouraged to pray directly to God rather than through saints or others. They have also been encouraged to read the Bible, the sacred text of Christians, because it represents the basis for Christian religious beliefs. As a result, Protestants have stressed the need to have the Bible in the language of the people and have been active in efforts to translate and disseminate the Bible.

Because the Bible is so central to Protestantism, major religious struggles have occurred regarding not only what it says, but also what it represents. Views of Scripture within Protestant traditions vary from those that stress a literal understanding of the Bible and its absolute freedom from error (its inerrancy) to those that view the Bible as an essential guide to matters relating to salvation and faith, but not to other issues. Some are more willing than others to consider the cultural context in which the Bible was written in interpreting its meaning (Marsden, 1991; Marty, 1992; McGrath, 1997). Fundamentalist groups and some conservative Protestant groups hold very strongly to the literal, error-free nature of the Bible, whereas mainline Protestant groups have typically been willing to look at the cultural context of the Scriptures in drawing implications for current life. Current struggles within some denominations regarding the role of women in the church and the age of the Earth reflect these differing interpretations of the Bible. While some conservative groups take a passage from the Bible such as "Women should keep silent in the church" (I Corinthians 14: 34) as forbidding women's taking leadership roles within the church as pastors and teachers, other groups have argued that this statement was in response to specific cultural issues that were relevant when the passage was written. Some groups take the word *day* in the story of God's creation of the world to mean literal 24-hour days, and thus believe that the world is about 6000 years old; other groups view the term as a metaphor and can accept scientific data that argue for an older earth. As a result, Protestants vary not only in terms of what they currently believe but also in what evidence they are willing to accept in changing their views. These differences in interpretation can have profound influences on how people view issues, including gender roles within the family and the church, divorce, the role of science, and more recently, homosexuality.

Meaning of Life Events

One of the most profound questions is "What is the purpose of my life?" In the Reformed/Presbyterian tradition, the Westminster Catechism answers this question with "To glorify God and enjoy him forever" and the Heidelberg Catechism describes belonging to God as the only comfort in life and death. As expressed in the Book of Common Prayer, the Episcopalian tradition emphasizes an "incarnational" theology (the living out of one's faith in the world in response to the life, death, and resurrection of Christ) that gives meaning to life (Wacome, K., August, 1999, personal conversation). Speaking from the Lutheran tradition, the 14th-century German scholar Philipp Melancthon cited the gift of eternal life as something that helps gives one's life a sense of value and purpose (Kerr, 1966). These attempts to answer this question share the belief that there is a profound and transcendant purpose to the life of each person. The meaning of specific events in life is set within this broader context.

Answers to the question of life's purpose represent a comfort, a challenge, and a dilemma for Protestants. The comfort is in knowing that one is a beloved child of God. The Bible (John 3:16) asserts that God loved human beings so much that Jesus was sent into the world to die for them. Children learn to sing songs such as "Jesus loves me, this I know, for the Bible tells me so" and "Jesus loves the little children of the world. . . all are precious in his sight." As a result, people learn that they are valued for themselves and that God has a purpose for their lives.

The belief that we are children of God's family also represents a challenge, because it implies that we are responsible in some way for other members of that family. What is my obligation when I am comfortable financially and others are suffering (Sider, 1984, 1999)? On the one hand, these concerns have prompted many of the charitable efforts of Protestant groups, such as the One Great Hour of Sharing, Church World Service, Lutheran Social Services, and other efforts that promote social justice and charity. Churches currently make major contributions to the social welfare of others (Cnaan, 1997; Staral, 1998) and traditionally have been active in caring for those in need and improving the lives of others (Kreutziger, 1998). On the other hand, some religious groups and individuals have emphasized the personal rewards of prosperity, victory, and other benefits that accrue to believers. Prosperity in various forms is thus viewed as a side benefit of faith (Ellingsen, 1988).

Protestant denominations also vary in their perspective on their mission relative to the nature of human beings. Some groups emphasize almost exclusively the spiritual part of the person and his or her personal relationship with God; others take a broader view of the whole person and his or her life circumstances, including economic as well as spiritual aspects. Church groups and individuals vary widely in emphasizing either the broad family of God, with accompanying responsibilities to others, or a sense of individualism and the individual's own personal relationship with God. The individualism of some churches mirrors the emphasis on individualism in U.S. society (Sider, 1999). As indicated earlier, there is also variation in the emphasis on the sinfulness of human beings or the grace of God.

A dilemma also arises from the question of life's purpose: why is there suffering in a world governed by a loving God? Tragedies happen to the children of God—their children die, they get cancer, their businesses fail. Headlines are replete with the tragedies and injustices of life—refugees caught up in the vortex of war, people suffering from AIDS, young people being disabled for life by someone driving while intoxicated. Social workers often become involved with people during difficult and painful times in their lives. Sometimes the difficult circumstances and times are the results of problematic behaviors of the individuals (for example, financial ruin caused by excessive gambling). All Protestant denominations believe that individuals have free will to act counter to how God would wish them to live. Yet many tragedies do not occur as a result of such acts. When such tragedies occur, belief in the love and protection of God can be shaken, and people must contend with how to reconcile God's love and human suffering. As a result, believers must struggle with the role of God in the midst of suffering.

Protestant denominations have answered the question about suffering in various ways. The Reformed/Presbyterian tradition has emphasized the sovereignty of God—the belief that God is in control of everything that happens—while at the same time recognizing that God grants people the gift of freedom, including the freedom to sin. While this tradition does not go so far as to say that God is the author of the evil that creates suffering, it emphasizes the larger plan of God, even though the meaning of a given event might not be apparent to the people involved. The Reverend Robert Schuller, in his book *What Happens to Good People When Bad Things Happen* (1995), emphasizes the redemptive actions of God through the hurt people experience as God helps them gain resiliency and depth of character. Groups in the Methodist and Lutheran traditions have not emphasized the control of God but have instead viewed God as suffering with and caring for people during difficult times. As indicated earlier, some denominations stress that God will bring good things and prosperity to Christians who believe, and they emphasize the need for people to be fervent in their beliefs and religious practices even during bad times. Despite these differences, Protestant groups hold that God remains a support during the difficult times of life and encourage members to turn to God for help. As indicated earlier, however, official church answers might not represent those of their members, because people tend to switch groups and are often ignorant of official church positions. Thus, it is important to explore how individuals themselves are seeking to answer this question.

Like other Christians, Protestants view death and suffering in the context of their belief that life continues after death. Thus, the purpose of life is not limited to what happens on earth; life also has a transcendent and eternal dimension. In this context, suffering is sometimes viewed as having a purpose linked to this transcendency.

SOURCES OF POWER

One of the key sources of power within Protestantism is the belief in a God who loves and protects. The Heidelberg Catechism, an early Protestant creed, asks the critical life question "What is my only comfort in life and death?" and answers it with "That I belong to God." John Wesley, founder of Methodism, wrote: "The Spirit of God . . . witnesses to my spirit, that I am a child of God; that Jesus Christ hath loved me, and given Himself for me" (Kerr, 1966). A popular Christian hymn asserts, "What a friend we have in Jesus." Another describes God's concern in these terms: "His eye is on the sparrow and I know he cares for me." These statements reflect the belief that God cares what happens to people and seeks personal relationships with them. God's protection is described in a hymn by Martin Luther, "A mighty fortress is our God." While the language is more modern, many of the contemporary praise songs and Christian rock songs express similar themes.

Protestantism has encouraged people to turn to God through prayer in times of trouble as well as of joy. Prayer, either in formal public arenas or in private, represents an important way of relating to and speaking to God. People are also encouraged to pray for the welfare of others, out of a belief that prayers of others can be helpful. Many people describe the strength they received because others prayed for them and tell how these prayers made it possible for them to get through a tragedy in life.

Reading the Bible is also viewed as a source of power. This is particularly true of some of the stories and Psalms that describe the abiding presence of God, for example, Psalm 23, which asserts "The Lord is my shepherd, I shall not want."

There is also a growing body of inspirational literature written by Protestants from various traditions to help give comfort and advice. These books and articles vary widely and appeal to different groups.

Participation in worship services in a church is another source of power. These experiences are viewed as opportunities to relate to God and to experience fellowship with others. Religious services vary widely in their level of emotional expression and degree of formality. Pentecostal groups especially have stressed the importance of religious experience in the form of the "outpouring of the Holy Spirit" as part of the worship as well as of the daily life of believers (Marsden, 1991). Many of the churches that are currently growing emphasize the emotional expressiveness of worship, and this type of worship service has been increasing in prevalence, even in groups that have typically had a more formal service. Although denominations traditionally were characterized by specific patterns of the worship service, this uniformity has been diminishing. Even within the same denomination, worship services can now range from those that are highly emotional to those characterized by formal rituals.

The sacrament of Communion (also called The Lord's Supper) represents another source of power in the Protestant tradition (as well as in other Christian groups). While the specific interpretation and frequency of this event vary depending on the religious group, Communion is a ritual consisting of eating bread and drinking wine or grape juice in celebration of the love of God through the death and resurrection of Jesus. In celebrating this sacrament, people are not only communing with God personally but also experiencing fellowship with others.

Small groups are also important in many Protestant churches and enable people to experience fellowship as well as explore the meaning of their faith. These groups are increasingly important to people seeking a sense of community while living in a fragmented world (Wuthnow, 1994).

The Protestant tradition encourages people to turn to other church members and their prayers for support. The belief that church members are fellow children of God encourages a view of the church as a family whose members support each other. As a result, church services typically include information about illnesses, problems, or joyful events in the lives of members of the church family. Prayers are usually offered for healing and thanks. Churches have traditionally collected funds for people in financial distress (both within the church and in the community at large) and encouraged giving by members.

The belief in sin and grace theoretically helps promote a "level playing field" before God; however, churches have had to struggle to make this sense of family and community real. Depending on the specific church, community, and period of time, experiences such as divorce, homosexuality, birth of children out of wedlock, or AIDS have been sources of stigma and distance from the fellowship. As a result, it can be useful to explore how the relevant religious support system views the particular life situation of an individual or family in order to understand the nature of the potential resources or the burdens people experience.

The minister in a Protestant church is also viewed as a source of comfort and help during difficult times. The term *pastor* used in many Protestant circles reflects this role of a minister. While the minister is a potential resource, it can sometimes be difficult for people to turn to their minister with concerns that might be viewed as problematic by the church.

RITUALS AND PRACTICES

Protestantism has several rituals that play key roles in religious life. While some of these, like Baptism, occur only once, others, like prayer, can be part of daily life.

Baptism or christening, is one of the important sacraments in the Protestant tradition. Both children and adults can be baptized. Baptism uses water to symbolize the washing away of sin and the nature of a special covenantal relationship between the person who is baptized and God. Parents bring infants and children for Baptism and make their commitment to raising the child in the Christian faith. For adults, Baptism is part of a public commitment to becoming a Christian. Baptism is not essential for salvation and does not ensure it, but it is a visible sign of God's love.

Communion, or the Lord's Supper, is the sacrament that symbolizes God's love and sacrifice through Jesus for human beings. Some churches celebrate Communion weekly; others celebrate it only a few times a year. Communion provides participants with a sense of the special presence of God in their lives.

Prayer is another important ritual in the Protestant tradition. Prayer can take place silently and in private or can be a public ceremony in which people repeat a prayer in unison. Some families pray together before eating their meals. These prayers represent efforts to turn to God for guidance and help as well as to express appreciation for gifts that have been received. Prayers for healing are offered in both individual and group contexts. Prayer can be used to help develop a sense of solidarity among people as they turn to God together.

LIFE-CYCLE EVENTS AND THE PROTESTANT TRADITION

The birth of a child is the arrival of an infinitely precious gift from God. While Protestants share this view of children, denominations and individuals disagree about abortion. Some members have been in the forefront of the anti-abortion, or "right to life," movement, believing that the sanctity of life begins very early when the child is in the womb, perhaps even at conception. Other groups have been willing to accept abortion when the health of the mother is at risk or when she has been a victim of rape or incest or to grant the mother the right to make this difficult choice. Although typically more fundamentalist and conservative groups have emphasized the "right to life" position and more mainstream groups have granted women the right of choice, individual members vary in their own positions on this issue. Most Protestant groups accept birth control methods that prevent conception.

As mentioned, Baptism is a meaningful ritual in most Protestant traditions for children as young as infants. (See Chapters 10 and 11 on the Baptists for alternatives.) In many churches, members are asked to promise to help in the teaching and care of the child. Sometimes godparents, who have accepted a special responsibility to care for the child, participate.

Sunday school, now often called church school, is held on Sunday to teach children and adults about the Bible and the religious beliefs, practices, and implications of the faith. Sunday school has also been used as a means of church outreach and evangelism to the community. Parents may be interested in sending their children to Sunday school even though they themselves do not attend church services.

Separate schooling has traditionally characterized only a small number of Protestant groups (for example, Lutherans, Christian Reformed), but this is a growing trend, especially among conservative groups. Historically, the division between church and state seemed a less pressing issue to Protestants because they dominated the institutions of society (Lindner, 1999; Marty, 1992). As the United States has become more pluralistic, the movement among some conservative Protestant groups to establish their own schools has grown. These schools also attract other families who have become disenchanted with public education in their communities.

Most Protestants eventually move to the stage in life when they affirm their own faith through the act of Confession of Faith and become members of the church. This frequently occurs during the early teenage years, but the age can vary depending on the individual and the specific group. Traditionally people became eligible to participate in Communion after they make their confession of faith, but a growing number of churches permit younger baptized children to participate in Communion.

Marriage is an important life event but is not a sacrament in Protestant circles. While many couples are married in a church or chapel by a minister, there is great flexibility about these arrangements. Marriage represents the establishment of a new family (which the church of course hopes will be a Christian family). Attitudes vary toward intermarriage—marrying someone from a different religious tradition. Attitudes depend somewhat, of course, on the nature of the tradition and on how self-conscious the group is about its distinctiveness. Given the importance of children, one of the key concerns is whether the children born of such marriages will be raised with the appropriate beliefs.

There is a growing acceptance of the reality of divorce, with a consequent inclusion of divorced individuals in most Protestant groups, but the degree of acceptance varies among specific congregations. Some congregations deliberately reach out and minister to divorced individuals, who might feel left out in other congregations where divorce still carries a stigma. Fellowship groups provide specific support and programs to make divorced people feel included.

When people become too frail to attend church services and programs and to participate with others in the sacrament of Communion, they can feel increasingly isolated from the important support of church services, community, and fellowship. The challenge in many congregations is sustaining the needs of the elderly while reaching out to the youth who are the future of the church. Many large churches have a pastor with special responsibility to visit the sick and elderly, but pastors in small churches are also charged with this responsibility.

Death can come at any age but becomes more of a concern as people get older. While people grieve when loved ones die, there is comfort in the belief that the person continues to live with God after death. Church members use phrases such as "joined the Church triumphant," which means that the person has joined God and other believers in heaven. Yet grief and a sense of loss can still be very real. Efforts by some to comfort with platitudes such as "she is in a better place" can make people feel misunderstood, because they feel that their grief is minimized.

HEALTH AND SOURCES OF HELP

Health in the Protestant tradition encompasses physical, emotional, and spiritual aspects. Illnesses that have traditionally been viewed as physical, such as cancer, heart disease, and pneumonia, have been attributed to physical causes. The support of most Protestant denominations for traditional forms of healing for physical illnesses is reflected in their establishment of hospitals. Seeking help from the medical community and using medicine are viewed as appropriate. In this context, God is viewed as working through the scientific knowledge and actions of health professionals.

At the same time, Protestantism has recognized a spiritual aspect of the healing process, in which God's power of healing is evoked more directly through prayers. People are strongly encouraged to pray directly for their own healing, and the circle of prayer widens to include the prayers of family members, friends, and fellow church members. Many church groups have times during the religious service in which people are encouraged to request prayers for healing for themselves or others. Healing services are also becoming institutionalized in many Protestant churches. Historically, these services were typically limited to groups belonging to the wings of Protestantism called fundamentalist, charismatic, or Pentecostal; in recent years, however, a wider range of Protestant churches have instituted healing services. The nature of these services varies, of course, depending on the religious tradition. They are typically not viewed as substitutes for traditional medical care but as parallel aids to healing that evoke the power of God in some profound manner. Protestants generally combine a belief in the possibility of miracles by God with willingness to use the means of modern medicine.

Mental health problems and services have been more problematic for Protestants. The recognition that mental health problems can sometimes have a physical cause or can be related in some way to a person's life circumstances has been growing. Along with this has come an increasing acceptance of mental health services. For some time, there was a lingering belief among some conservative Protestant groups that mental health problems were due to spiritual problems or were reflections of inadequate religious faith. As a result of this heritage, some people who experience mental health problems tend to feel that there is something wrong with their faith and that they have failed in some way as Christians. These belief systems can be particularly burdensome when combined with the sense of worthlessness experienced by individuals suffering from depression. Such belief systems can also be reflected in the types of advice given individuals with mental health problems by others within their religious communities. While it would be very atypical for a Protestant to be told that he or she should rely entirely on prayer to cure cancer, such advice might be forthcoming for depression or other mental health problems. It can be worthwhile for the social worker to explore how clients and those in their support system view mental health problems.

IMPLICATIONS FOR SOCIAL WORK PRACTICE

Potential Resources

The Protestant tradition offers members the assurance of a personal relationship with a loving God, a relationship that holds a promise of great comfort and strength. This belief can also provide a sense of meaning for both the immediate experiences and the transcendent experiences in people's lives. In addition, Protestantism also potentially offers the resource of a surrounding church family that can be a support at difficult times in life.

Social workers can help clients draw upon these strengths and tap the supportive network available through the pastor, fellow church members, and small fellowship groups. They can elicit from clients statements about their religious beliefs that will support them during difficult periods. Religious beliefs can help people gain a sense of dignity and value as children of God. When a person's sense of self-worth has been based on his bank account, appearance, employment, or some other aspect of social status, financial reversals or other problems can threaten that self-worth, but these changes do not diminish the person's role as a child of God. As various treatment models increasingly stress the role of the meanings that individuals and family members attribute to life events and the importance of helping clients create narratives that heal and empower, social workers and other counselors can help clients draw on their Protestant religious beliefs in creating such healing interpretations. In addition to the idea of being a child of God, these interpretations can draw on religious concepts such as grace, love, and purpose in life.

Social workers can explore religious rituals that are meaningful to clients, the barriers to using these rituals, and the ways clients can draw strength from the rituals, to help clients use the rituals of their faith in healing ways.

As indicated previously, the social support of the congregation can also be helpful in terms of financial and other material resources. Protestant churches have typically joined forces to help members during times of crisis. Churches have also been instrumental in developing support programs for the community at large, for example, family support programs that provide clothing and food, programs for the homeless, or youth outreach. President Bush's emphasis on faith-based efforts as alternative sources of support within communities would suggest that these programs are likely to increase. Social workers can be instrumental in linking individual clients with such services and can work with church groups to recognize and respond to community needs through services and advocacy. Although churches have historically been active in addressing institutionalized social injustices, the strength of churches typically has been in responding to cases of individual need (Van Hook, 1996).

Potential Tensions and Social Work Responses

Protestant beliefs can also create some tensions that social workers should recognize. When tragedy strikes, people can sometimes struggle with their anger toward God. They must contend with this anger and potentially a sense of alienation from their religious tradition. It can be important to help clients recognize and accept the normalcy of feelings of anger in the process of dealing with their pain. Mr. A., for example, could not really find peace with God until he was able to express his anger toward God for letting his son die. As he shared how he felt angry toward God at this time, he lifted the burden of guilt from the shoulders of several other individuals who were struggling with their own sense of guilt over their anger at God. An elderly woman, Mrs. H., was afraid of losing her faith as she struggled with serious depression. She was helped to understand that when people are depressed, they fear losing what is most important to them. This understanding helped her accept treatment for depression without the additional burden of feeling she was a bad Christian for being depressed at all. People may also feel that God is punishing them when things go wrong. Mr. S. was facing financial ruin as a result of the farm crisis that was creating financial and emotional havoc for many families and communities in the 1980s. He wondered if his actions were perhaps God's judgment for his sin in losing his temper with his animals when he was feeling stress. He and the social worker explored the broad economic problems that were hurting him and many of his neighbors and what he really believed about God. He was able to recognize that his interpretation did not really fit with his religious views.

Despite the emphasis on the doctrine of grace, people can feel burdened by their own sense of falling short of God's expectations and can internalize this as guilt and alienation. The situation becomes intensified when pastors and other church members are moralistic and judgmental. People can find it very difficult to accept the implications of the gift of grace for themselves and others, as they live in a world that continues to calculate what people deserve and are owed (Yancey, 1997). The cognitive behavioral tool of asking people to describe the advice they would have for others can be a useful strategy for a social worker. People can be asked what the gift of grace would mean for a friend in a situation similar to their own. This strategy can be helpful in permitting people to forgive themselves and to accept forgiveness and grace.

People can also feel the need to demonstrate the actions of God and grace in their lives through major life changes. When these changes do not materialize or people revert to old patterns, they can begin to doubt and to feel discouraged, or they can distance themselves from others rather than seeking their support. This tendency can be especially strong for members of groups within the Holiness tradition (characterized by the belief in the possibility of and need for major changes during life on earth) but can be present in others also. The Bible is replete with stories of "heroes of faith" who acted in sinful ways, and clients can be asked to reflect upon the significance of some of these stories to help them realize that they are not alone. The message of grace means that God works in our lives. Clients can be asked to reflect upon ways in which God demonstrated grace and thereby be helped to turn to their faith for strength in their efforts to make constructive changes in their lives. When clients feel unsure of their ability to change, social workers can help them reconnect with the strength of their religious tradition by asking what kind of relationship God wants to have with them—one characterized by distance and discouragement or a close one in which the individual is open to God's love.

It is also important to explore how a client's particular religious group views specific actions and circumstances. These views can be powerful in determining what supports are available as well as in influencing how individuals view themselves. Because religion can influence early paradigms that shape how people view themselves and the world around them, people sometimes must contend with beliefs that were part of their early life experience, despite current efforts to distance themselves from such beliefs. As a result, it can be important to explore the beliefs of a client's family of origin, as well as the client's own current beliefs.

Gender Issues

Protestant groups vary widely in their views of the roles of women. Some groups nourish the gifts of women in all the areas of the life of the church; other groups stress male dominance within the church and the home. In working with women and families, it can be important to learn about these gender role expectations, both as they are currently experienced and in the client's childhood. At the same time, it is important for counselors to remember that their own perspective on gender roles may be quite different from that of the client, so what appears as suppression to the counselor could be viewed as protection by a female client and her family members. In religion, as in other cultural issues, understanding how beliefs and patterns are experienced by the parties involved is an important and sometimes complex process.

CONCLUSION

Protestantism represents a diverse set of traditions within the Christian religion and historically stresses the role of grace and the ability of human beings to establish a personal relationship with God. The beliefs and social support system represented by Protestantism can provide important support for individual clients and family members during difficult times and can help to establish a basic sense of worth. At the same time, these beliefs and support systems can create tensions that can be important in understanding how people view themselves and others. Understanding the nature of these tensions can help in identifying healing interventions.

REFERENCES

Cnaan, R. (1997). *Social and community involvement of religious congregations housed in historic religious properties: Findings from a six-city study.* Philadelphia: University of Pennsylvania School of Social Work.

Ellingsen, Mark (1988). *The evangelical movement.* Minneapolis, MN: Augsburg.

Hugen, B. (1998). Calling: A spirituality model for social work practice. In B. Hugen (Ed.), *Christianity and social work* (pp. 91–105). Botsford, CT: North American Association of Christians in Social Work.

Keith-Lucas, A. (1996). The church and social welfare. Philadelphia, PA: Westminster.

Kerr, H. (1966). *Readings in Christian thought.* Nashville, TN: Abington.

Kreutziger, S. (1998). Social work's legacy in the Methodist settlement movement. In B. Hugen (Ed.)., *Christianity and social work* (pp. 27–40). Botsford, CT: North American Association of Christians in Social Work.

Lindner, E . W. (1999). *National Council of Churches 1999 yearbook of American and Canadian churches.* New York: National Council of Churches.

Marsden, G. (1991). *Understanding fundamentalism and evangelicalism.* Grand Rapids, MI: Eerdmans.

Marty, M. (1992). *Modern American religion, Vol 2.* Chicago: University of Chicago Press.

McGrath, A. (1997). *Christian theology: An introduction (2nd edition).* Oxford, England: Blackwell.

Niebuhr, R. (1941). *The nature and destiny of man. Vol 1.* New York: Charles Scribner & Sons.

Schuller, R. (1995). *What happens to good people when bad things happen.* Grand Rapids, MI: Zondervan.

Sherwood, D. (1997). A Christian view of social justice in a pluralistic world: Freedom, responsibility, and the common good. *Social Work and Christianity: An International Journal, 24*(1), 19–33.

Sider, R. (1984). *Rich Christians in an age of hunger.* Downers Grove, IL: Intervarsity Press.

Sider, R. (1999). *Good news and good works: A theology for the whole Gospel.* Grand Rapids, MI: Zondervan.

Smedes, L. B. (1982). *How can it be all right when everything is all wrong?* New York: Harper and Row.

Staral, J. (1998). Community practice: Lessons for social work from a racially mixed central city church. In B. Hugen (Ed.), *Christianity and social work* (pp. 41–54). Botsford, CT: North American Association of Christians in Social Work.

Van Hook, M. (1996). Rural poverty: Christian charity and social justice approaches. In S. Carlson-Thies & J. Skillen (Eds.), *Welfare in America: Christian perspectives on a policy in crisis* (pp. 348–367). Grand Rapids, MI: Eerdmans.

Wuthnow, R. 1994. *Sharing the journey: Support groups and America's new quest for community.* New York: Free Press.

Yancey, P. (1997). *What's so amazing about grace?* Grand Rapids, MI: Zondervan.

ADDITIONAL RESOURCES

Books

Balmer, R. (2001). *Religion in twentieth century America.* New York: Oxford University Press.

———. (1989). *Mine eyes have seen the glory: A journey into the evangelical subculture in America.* New York: Oxford University Press.

Noll, M. (2000). *Protestants in America.* New York: Oxford University Press.

Marty, M. (1992). *Varieties of Protestantism.* New York: K.G. Sauer.

———. (1992). *Protestantism and social Christianity.* New York: K.G. Sauer.

Mardsden, G. (1991). *Understanding fundamentalism and evangelicalism.* Grand Rapids, MI: W.B. Eerdmans.

Web Sites

African Methodist Episcopal: www.ame-church.org

Assemblies of God: www.ag.org/top

Charismatic/Pentecostal: www.iphc.org/pccna/

Church of Christ: www.church-of-christ.org/

Episcopal: www.anglican.org

Lutheran: www.elca.org/

Mennonite: www.mennonites.org/

Presbyterian: www.pcusa.org/

Reformed Church in America: www.rca.org/

United Methodist: www.umc.org/

GLOSSARY

Baptism/Christening A ritual in which a child or adult either receives a sprinkling of water on the head or is immersed in water to symbolize the washing away of sins and the promise of a special relationship with God. When children are baptized, their parents promise to raise them in the belief in God. Church members also agree to support the child in the Christian life. For adults, baptism is part of a personal acknowledgment of faith in God and commitment to the Christian life.

Bible The sacred text of Christians.

Charismatic groups Religious groups that emphasize the emotional aspect of the religious service and individual subjective experiences of the Holy Spirit of God.

Communion/Lord's Supper The ritual of eating bread and drinking wine or grape juice that celebrates the love of God through the death and resurrection of Jesus.

Confession of faith A ceremony in which people publicly indicate that they believe in God and the doctrines of the church. This step represents joining the church as an adult (as distinct from childhood baptism).

Fundamentalist groups Religious groups that emphasize the literal interpretation of the Bible.

Grace The doctrine that salvation from sin and the care of God are gifts based on the love of God rather than being rewards for good deeds by people. Grace is not something that is earned.

Heaven Where people live after death in fellowship with God. Christians also believe that the earthly world will end eventually and then people will live with God in a new heaven and earth. There are differing interpretations of the exact meaning of this doctrine.

Holiness tradition The tradition of groups that stress the process of becoming holy when a person accepts Jesus. Accepting Jesus is viewed as being "born again" and is accompanied by growth in holiness through the grace of God and the activity of the Holy Spirit of God.

Inerrancy The doctrine that the Bible is absolutely error-free in all matters.

Pentecostal groups Religious groups that emphasize the emotional, mystical nature of religion and the active working of the spirit of God in the worship service and life of Christians. The religious services of such groups tend to be rather emotional.

Prayer Communication with God. Prayer can be either silent or spoken, individual or in a group.

Priesthood of all believers The doctrine that ordinary believers can relate directly to God rather than through intermediaries.

BAPTISTS

T. LAINE SCALES

CHAPTER 10

INTRODUCTION

When I took on the task of writing about Baptists and social work, I thought it would be quite easy to describe what it means to be Baptist. After all, I was born to parents who met one another in a Baptist student organization, and I was reared in an active Southern Baptist family involved in church leadership. I graduated from a Baptist seminary, practiced as a social worker in Baptist congregations, wrote a book about Baptist women, and teach social work in a Baptist University. However, I have found the task surprisingly difficult. The astounding diversity among Baptists makes it quite impossible to describe the full range of deeply held convictions and often conflicting practices of this group of Christians. As one Baptist writer points out, ". . . one of the hallmarks of being Baptist is a diversity that is hard to describe" (Campbell-Reid, 1998, p. 4). There are over 80 different Baptist groups in the United States, with the Southern Baptist Convention (SBC) representing the largest group, having over 16 million believers (Leonard, 1994, p.1). While there are some core beliefs and doctrines basic to Baptists, traditionally there have been no official written creeds or policies that determine practices for all Baptist churches. Each individual congregation has the freedom to act on the beliefs of its members. This accounts for a great deal of difference among Baptist churches.

Although I find it virtually impossible to describe a definitive "Baptist view," I will attempt to describe some basic features of Baptist life, while cautioning the reader that these generalizations will apply to many but not to all Baptists. I will describe how my own experience in a Baptist family and church influenced me as a social worker and suggest guidelines for workers involved with Baptist individuals, families, organizations, and communities. While many of the beliefs and practices described span a variety of Baptist groups, the focus of this chapter will be on the Southern Baptist Convention.

A BRIEF HISTORY OF BAPTISTS

Baptists in England and the Colonies

Baptists emerged in 17th-century England amid the various dissenters who turned away from Catholic and Anglican traditions. Baptists championed the cause of religious liberty, claiming the freedom of each person to approach God without interference from secular or religious authorities. The doctrine of "the priesthood of all believers" emerged from an emphasis on corporate decision making and mutual responsibility within the body of believers rather than dependence upon a priest (Baker, 1974, pp.18–19). Rejecting infant baptism and, by 1641, insisting on full immersion as the appropriate mode of baptism of believers, these groups worked out a distinct identity among Protestants. Like other religious dissenters, English Baptists were persecuted for their beliefs (Ammerman, 1990, pp. 20–21; Torbet, 1950, pp 33–43).

By the middle of the 17th century, English Baptists were seeking religious freedom and migrating to the colonies, first to New England and later to the Southern colonies. As the 18th century came to a close, Baptists turned to the task of missionary expansion, both on the American frontier and overseas. In response to a plea for contributions to support missionaries, 33 Baptist men convened in Philadelphia in May of 1814 to form the first national organization of Baptists in America: the General Missionary Convention of the Baptist Denomination in the United States for Foreign Missions. Planning to meet every 3 years, the group became more commonly known as the Triennial Convention, made up of male delegates from mission societies, churches, and other groups. Enthusiasm for missions, both domestic and foreign, spurred the creation of Baptist colleges as a means of furthering this cause (McBeth, 1987).

Southern Baptists

The number of Baptist churches in the South grew rapidly as a result of evangelism. But by the middle of the 19th century, Baptists in the South came to reject the national alliances they had formed. As Baptists in the North became involved in the national movement to abolish slavery, Baptists in the South worked to defend the institution of slavery. Each side used Scripture and Baptist doctrine to defend its position (Torbet, 1950, pp. 282–291). On May 8, 1845, 328 delegates gathered to organize the Southern Baptist Convention (SBC) to ensure that Baptists in the South could hold slaves, particularly slave-holding missionaries who had been refused appointment by Northern Baptists. They created two mission boards (foreign and domestic) and invited existing missionaries to work for the new denomination (McBeth, 1989, pp. 388–391).

The new body inherited an ecclesiastical structure with four levels of organization, which had been developing since 1707. At the base was the local church; churches within the geographical area consisting of a county or two formed an association. Baptists within a state organized state conventions, while the Southern Baptist Convention, at the apex, coordinated denominational efforts throughout the South. However, as Spain points out, the organization was not hierarchical. Each church and each individual member retained a high degree of independence within the framework of a generally accepted body of beliefs and practices (Spain, 1967, pp. 7–8). Women and Blacks could not hold any positions of power within the denomination until the late 20th century. However, women learned leadership skills in their own Woman's Missionary Union, created in 1888 as an auxiliary to the male-run SBC (Allen, 1987).

Other Baptist Groups

The SBC was formed to allow White Baptists in the South to maintain their oppression of Blacks through the institution of slavery. After the Civil War, Black Baptists separated from White Baptists to form their own local churches. These churches eventually joined together to form conventions at the state level, and finally, in 1895, the National Baptist Convention, U.S.A. was created. Higginbotham (1993) notes that the movement to formulate a national denominational body was an important means of Black empowerment during an era of profound discrimination in the South. Today, Baptists number over 7 million nationwide (Leonard, 1994, p. 198). The group from which Southern Baptists split became known as the Northern Baptist Convention (1907–1950), changed its name to the American Baptist Convention (1950–1972), and then became the American Baptist Churches in the USA. ABC-USA claims over 1.5 million members (Leonard, 1994, pp. 21–22).

Conflict and Division in the SBC

By the late 19th century, Southern Baptists were in the mainstream of Southern society. Like other Southerners, the majority of Southern Baptists lived in rural areas and were "of humble birth and modest means." By 1900, theirs was the largest White denomination in the South (Spain, 1967, p. 10). In the 1920s, as other Protestant denominations split in fundamentalist–modernist controversies, Southern Baptists were held together by what Baptist historian Bill Leonard calls "a Grand Compromise in which idealogues on the right or the left were not allowed to control the center" (Leonard, 1990, pp. 8–9). But by the late 1970s, the synthesis that had held a great diversity of Southern Baptists together began to break down, and conflict and fragmentation emerged within the SBC. In 1979, following a planned strategy organized by fundamentalists who claimed that the SBC had grown too liberal, the SBC was divided into two camps: fundamentalists and "moderates." Leonard describes fundamentalists as "those persons within the SBC who accept a doctrine of biblical inerrancy [the belief that the Bible contains no errors] as the only method for defining biblical authority and who seek to participate in a concerted movement to make that doctrine normative. . . ."[1] The adjective "moderate" came into use in the early 1980s to describe opponents of the fundamentalist movement. Often referred to as "liberals" by their fundamentalist critics, the moderates hope "to affirm what they view as traditional Baptist doctrine—biblical authority, missions, evangelism, soul competency, and religious freedom—while resisting fundamentalist dominance" (Leonard, 1990, p. 7).

The Emergence of New Baptist Groups

Throughout the 1980s and 1990s, fundamentalists gained control of the SBC agencies and the six Southern Baptist seminaries, firing employees they considered to be liberal or to be obstructing the change process. Moderates began separating from the SBC and organizing themselves into groups to work together toward common goals. Two of the moderate organizations that emerged in the late 1980s and early 1990s were the Cooperative Baptist Fellowship and the Alliance of Baptists. The new entities strongly asserted that they were not new denominations, but rather were designed to facilitate partnerships of local congregations that were coming together to meet common goals such as the funding of missionary efforts and the education of church leaders (Leonard, 1994).

BASIC BAPTIST BELIEFS

The heart of recent controversies among Baptists is not the Baptist *distinctives,* or core beliefs; rather, conflict has erupted over differing interpretations of how these beliefs should be implemented. Each side claims that it upholds the beliefs that define what it means to be Baptist. In contrast to some other denominations, Baptists have no written creed to define their beliefs. However, two formal confessions of faith have been written since the founding of the SBC. In 1925, the Memphis Articles, formally titled the Baptist

---

[1]I'm using the term "fundamentalist" as a neutral descriptor, but social workers should be aware that some consider the term pejorative. See Leonard, 1994, p. 7 for a more complete discussion of the terms "fundamentalist" and moderate."

Faith and Message, were written after controversy in which Baptist fundamentalists accused the SBC of being too liberal, teaching biological evolution and modernistic views of Scriptures in Southern Baptist seminaries and colleges. A second confessional statement, the 1963 Baptist Faith and Message, was composed in the wake of controversy in which a seminary professor was fired after publishing a book, *The Message of Genesis*, which supported the historical-grammatical method of biblical study (McBeth, 1989, pp. 674–678). Although the 1963 document contains a preamble stating that it is not to be considered a binding creed, McBeth notes that in recent years, the SBC has used the document to discipline and exclude and "has gone far toward hardening it into a creed" (McBeth, 1989, pp. 685–686). In 1998, the SBC drew national attention by amending the 1963 document to include a statement on family that denounces divorce and same-sex marriages and requires women to be submissive to men in the home and in church.[2]

While the absence of creeds allows for doctrinal diversity among Baptists, historians have identified basic distinctives that have unified Baptists through the centuries:

- *The priesthood of all believers.* This is perhaps the overarching principle at the heart of being Baptist. Each believer approaches God without the aid of clergy. Laypersons and clergy cooperate, and church members are "priests" to each other.
- *View of the Bible as the authoritative word of God and the only foundation for Christian faith and practice.* Baptists believe that people can read and interpret the Scripture for themselves.
- *Baptism (by immersion) of believers who are called to personal faith in Christ.* This is known as the principle of "regenerate church membership."
- *The autonomy of each local congregation in decision making and direction for mission and ministry.*
- *Religious liberty and the separation of church and state.* The state cannot control matters of faith; each person is responsible to God for religious choices. (Campbell-Reid, 1998, pp. 10–11; Leonard, 1990, p. 73; Leonard, 1994, p. 4).

BAPTISTS AND SOCIAL ISSUES

Social problems of the early 20th century sparked the Social Gospel movement, which challenged Christians to consider racial and economic inequalities. This movement emerged among Northern Baptists under the leadership of Walter Rauschenbusch, who described the movement as "humanity

[2]For a copy of the amendment, see the SBC website: www.sbc.net

organized according to the will of God" (Leonard, 1994, p. 13). The theological premise behind the Social Gospel movement is that believers can "bring about the kingdom of God" through their efforts to create social and economic justice. A few Southern Baptist leaders, both men and women, did join the Social Gospel movement, working with the Southern Sociological Congress for prison reform, passage of child labor laws, compulsory education, and solutions to racial conflict (Sumners, 1975, p. 17). However, most Southern Baptists did not support the movement, claiming that it was too concerned with political and economic matters, rather than with the more important evangelical mission (Leonard, 1994, p. 13).

Though they debated whether social services or evangelism to the individual was primary, Southern Baptists of the 20th century developed a remarkable network of social services. For example, in the Progressive Era, Southern Baptist women organized settlement houses to address social problems of immigrants and others in poverty. However, in contrast to other settlements, the goal was religious conversion of the individual, rather than societal reform (Scales, 2000, pp. 185–190). The Baptist child welfare network began at the turn of the 20th century with traditional orphanages. Today, it is one of the largest private networks for children's services in the nation. Other social services were established in the latter part of the 20th century. Baptist hospitals provide top-of-the-line health care. Urban community centers and emergency relief programs utilize many Baptist volunteers and funds. The well-known and respected Habitat for Humanity program, which provides housing for low-income families around the world, was created by a Baptist and was initially supported by Baptist groups before becoming a national volunteer program. Through their agencies and churches, Baptists are involved in nearly every aspect of serving those in need from birth to death.

Baptists demonstrate a variety of responses to social issues. For example, the National Baptist Convention and other Black Baptist groups were at the center of the civil rights movement of the 1960s, led by Dr. Martin Luther King, a Baptist preacher. A few Southern Baptist churches supported Black Baptists in the movement, although the majority of Southern Baptists militantly opposed it. Today, Baptists have diversified responses to social issues such as abortion or women's rights. It is helpful for social workers attempting to enlist Baptist churches in community projects to be aware of Baptist debates surrounding social issues.

MY JOURNEY AS A BAPTIST SOCIAL WORKER

Because of this remarkable network of social services, Baptists have opportunities to volunteer through their churches, even from a very early age. My experiences growing up in a Baptist family and church that viewed social service as a necessary part of sharing the love of Christ led me to be a social worker. I was born in the South and into a family that had been Southern

Baptist for many generations. Our family attended church several times each week, and as a young girl, I was involved in many missions activities, either in groups sponsored by my church or with my family. We defined "missions" as both proselytizing and providing food or cash assistance to those less fortunate. My family often delivered Thanksgiving dinners to the poor; my Sunday school class "adopted" an elderly couple in poverty to visit and to help with cash assistance. As a child, I had an opportunity to interact with those who were suffering, and I was moved to find ways to help. Now, as I look back on these activities, I see them as quite limited in light of the demanding and often radical work that churches are mandated to do in the name of Christ. However, they provided an important foundation for my commitment to social justice.

This foundation in home and church prompted me to explore a variety of ways of helping others. I earned a B.A. in Psychology and planned to pursue a career in counseling, envisioning myself as a Christian counselor. I was called to ministry, as I believe all Christians are called. I had yet to find the profession that would allow me to bring that calling and my professional training together into a vocational ministry, but I was following these leadings on my career path.

In 1984, after completing my undergraduate degree, I entered the Southern Baptist Theological Seminary in Louisville, Kentucky. The seminary was developing a new M.S.W. program in the Carver School of Church Social Work, which prepared social workers to work in congregations or in church-related agencies. At that time, the Carver School was the only seminary-based social work school in the nation to be accredited by the Council on Social Work Education (CSWE). After a year of theological studies, I earned an M.S.W. I was fortunate to study a unique curriculum specifically designed to integrate Christian faith with the knowledge, values, and skills of the social work profession.

At the Carver School, I developed a dual identity as a social worker and a minister, and I saw my professional work as an attempt to fulfill a calling to ministry. I completed a field placement in a Baptist congregation, leading the congregation to reach out to its community. I was able to bring social work skills such as needs assessment, planning, intervention, and evaluation to my efforts to assist this congregation in caring for its community. While gathering social work experience in a church-related setting, I pursued a Ph.D. with the hope of teaching new professionals at the Carver School.

Conflicts between fundamentalist and moderate Baptists escalated through the late 1980s and early 1990s, with fundamentalists gaining control of the seminaries by the mid-1990s. Fundamentalists in the SBC began to limit the focus of that group to evangelism and the conversion of individuals while greatly reducing financial and other commitments to social work ministry. By the time I completed my Ph.D. and was ready to teach, the Carver School had been closed by the Seminary president, who stated that social work had no place in the work of the Seminary (Garland, 1999). Because of this denial of social work as a valid activity in the work of Christian ministry and the limitations the "post–1979" SBC has placed on women, both in the home and in the church, I have ceased identifying with the SBC and now refer to myself as a moderate Baptist.

After a brief time teaching social work in a state university, I have returned to teaching in a program that integrates faith and social work practice at a Baptist university: Baylor University in Waco Texas. I find my calling as a professional social worker and my calling to ministry to be inseparable. I believe we are commanded to be transformed and to transform our broken world into one where peace and social justice reign. This is the work that Jesus did on earth and the church is to continue this work until Jesus comes again. My goals as a social work educator come out of my experiences as a Baptist woman committed throughout her career to integrating faith and social work practice.

LIFE'S BIG QUESTION

For Baptists, as for many others in evangelical groups, the biggest question in life is that of salvation. The SBC addresses the question in this way: "Life's Greatest Question is 'Do you know for sure that if you were to die you would go to heaven?'"[3] This question is often framed as "Are you saved?" meaning "Are you saved from Hell?"or "Are you born again?" The term "born again" refers to Scripture (John 3) describing the conversion experience as a rebirth. For Baptists, the greatest purpose in life is evangelism: sharing the "good news" of salvation. Baptists have a diversity of approaches to this task, but "spreading the Gospel" is a mandate for every Baptist believer. Some may embrace the social justice aspects of sharing the good news, focusing on compassionate action and providing help beyond the spiritual, transforming whole persons, whole groups, whole nations. Others may emphasize spiritual conversion only.

The Gospel message that Baptists are mandated to share is that sin is breaking God's Law and everyone has broken God's Law. Sin separates us from God. God loves us, though we are sinners, and has provided a way, through belief in Jesus Christ, for us to receive forgiveness and eternal life.

The notion of eternal life encompasses not only an endless life for the individual, but also participation with God in God's eternal existence. Each person must decide to "receive Christ" personally into his or her life and make this decision public. This act is known as a "profession of faith." This profession is made among a community of believers. After making a profession of faith, Baptists are expected to join a church and to attend regularly.

---

[3]For a complete discussion of this question from an SBC point of view, see: http:www. sbc.net/godseternal.cfm

The matters of sin and forgiveness are important ones for social workers to understand in working with Baptist clients who are experiencing shame or feeling unloved or unlovable. The concept of eternal life is important when working with Baptist clients facing their own death or the death of a loved one.

SOURCES OF POWER

Baptists rely on the power of prayer and the power of daily reading of Scriptures. Many churches encourage members to schedule a devotional time each morning for prayer and Bible reading. Some families join together for devotions each day.

The Bible

The Bible is an extremely important holy book, which Baptists are expected to read and reflect upon. The Bible provides a guide for living, and its stories are a narrative portrait of God's relationship to humanity. Worship services may include two or three Scripture readings. Baptists are quite diverse in their beliefs regarding the Bible. While most affirm Biblical authority, stating that the act of writing Scriptures was inspired by God, some Baptists are "Biblical inerrantists." The doctrine of inerrancy states"that "the Bible is without error in all matters of faith, history, theology, biology, or any other issue that can be discussed in its light" (Leonard, 1990, pp. 7–8). Inerrantists are also literalists, believing that the Bible should be taken at face value. The doctrine of Biblical inerrancy was at the center of the conflicts among Baptists of the 20th century, particularly in the 1920s and the 1980s. Social workers may introduce biblical stories or parables to illustrate principles for living. However, in order to maintain a good rapport, the social worker should avoid arguing about the doctrine of inerrancy or about the client's interpretation of certain biblical passages.

Prayer

Baptists use prayer as a daily tool for living. In contrast to some religions that prescribe a certain number of prayers each day, Baptists decide for themselves. While some may read a prayer from a book, there are no communal written prayers, as in the Anglican or Catholic traditions. Many Baptists prefer to have a "free style" prayer, which is a simple conversation with God. Some families pray together. Like persons of many different religions, Baptists may either cease or increase their prayer activity in times of crisis. Typically, Sunday church services include prayers, but there may also be a special meeting during the week (often on Wednesday evenings) called "prayer meeting," when Baptists gather specifically to pray together about the needs of the congregation, the community, and the world. Social workers may utilize the prayer meeting to announce needs and opportunities for service in the community.

Devotional Materials

Like many Protestants in the United States, Baptists have published a great deal of devotional literature. These writings can be comforting for an individual or family, particularly in times of crisis. There are several large Baptist publishing houses, such as Broadman/Holman and Smyth and Helwys, that produce instructional and devotional literature for Baptists of all ages. A survey of recent titles by Baptist publishing houses indicates the wealth of devotional books that may be comforting for a Baptist in hard times: Titles such as *A Faith to Meet Our Fears, Light for the Path,* and *He Restores My Soul* indicate that faith may be a source of strength as clients struggle through the problems of life.

Pastors, Church Staff Members, and Deacons

Pastors are ordained ministers called by God to preach and to provide leadership to a local church. In providing "pastoral care," a pastor may visit sick persons at home or in the hospital or even provide counseling. Social workers should be aware that some pastors are trained and certified to provide pastoral counseling, while others have no special training. In larger churches, other staff members such as an associate pastor, a minister of education, a minister of senior adults, or a minister of social work may also visit the sick or provide counseling. Deacons are laypersons who are elected by the congregation to lead in decision making and in service to the congregation and community. Deacons are ordained by their churches. A deacon may visit with a family during times of crisis to pray and talk. A few churches in the Southern Baptist tradition ordain both men and women as deacons, but the majority ordain only men. Deacons are excellent resources for social workers when dealing with clients in crisis or when attempting to introduce new community projects to a congregation.

RITUALS AND PRACTICES

Corporate Worship

Baptists come together on Sundays (and sometimes also on weekdays) to worship as a gathered community of believers. There is a great deal of variety in style and presentation, but most Baptist worship services include a sermon, reading aloud from the Bible, hymns sung by the congregation, musical presentations by a choir or soloist, and corporate prayer. Many Baptist churches hold a special worship event once or twice a year called a "revival." Revival meetings span several consecutive nights and often focus on an evangelistic message, urging non-members to join the church.

Sunday School

Sunday school provides an opportunity for Baptists of all ages to study the Bible together in smaller groups. Typically, students are divided according to age and sometimes according to gender. A study guide provided by a Baptist publishing house guides the students and their teachers through the lessons for the week. Sunday school classes typically meet for about an hour prior to the corporate worship service, though some classes may meet during the week (in which case they are known as Bible Study classes). The large numbers of Baptists of all ages who are involved in Sunday school demonstrates the Baptist commitment to reading, studying, and attempting to understand the Bible.

Baptism

Immersion Baptism is the ritual by which a Baptist believer declares his or her faith in Christ. In contrast to some other Christian denominations that practice infant Baptism, Baptists believe that a person should wait until he or she is old enough to experience a conversion and to declare his or her faith publicly. Immersion Baptism has been practiced for centuries. The ritual of Baptism is not what brings salvation; rather, it symbolizes the salvation experience that has already occurred when a person claims Jesus Christ as Savior. With the aid of a minister, the baptized person falls from a standing position back into the water and then is lifted to stand upright again. This action symbolizes the death and resurrection of Jesus. It also symbolizes the figurative death of a person's sinful self and and the start of a new life. While rural or overseas churches may use natural water sources such as a creeks or rivers for Baptisms, most churches in the United States use a constructed pool that is incorporated into the architecture of the worship facility.

Baptisms are typically performed by an ordained minister. The ritual of Baptism marks a person's new membership in the church. If a baptized member moves to a new city, he or she need not be rebaptized to join another Baptist church. However, persons from other denominations who may have been baptized by sprinkling or other methods may not be full members of a Baptist church without a Baptism by immersion. Some Baptist churches may allow such a person to be an associate member, while others may exclude the person from membership unless he or she is rebaptized by the immersion method.

The Lord's Supper (Communion)

The ritual of the Lord's Supper is celebrated by Baptists to reflect upon the death and resurrection of Christ. There is no uniform procedure for administering communion, and no rule as to how often the Lord's Supper is to be commemorated. The Lord's Supper celebration is often led by the pastor or deacons, but if no ordained person is present, some churches allow another baptized member to administer the ritual. Typically, a small piece of bread and a small sip of grape juice are offered to each participant, either by passing them around to each member of the congregation, or by asking members to come to the front of the church and be served by deacons. Some churches use unleavened bread, as Jesus would have eaten at Passover. Other churches use ordinary loaf bread. Grape juice is traditionally used, as many Baptists refrain from drinking alcoholic beverages, a prohibition that emerged in the early 20th century.

The Lord's Supper is often integrated into the usual Sunday morning worship service, though it can be celebrated at any time or place, such as at a wedding or on a retreat. Some churches celebrate the Lord's Supper together four times per year, while others celebrate once a month.

LIFE-CYCLE TRANSITIONS

Baptists and Birth

Birth is a time of great celebration for Baptist families and an opportunity for parents and the church to make commitments to one another concerning the nurturing of the child in the Baptist faith. Baptist churches have a tradition called "Baby Dedication" in which the new parents and the baby are presented to the church. In this brief ceremony, during the regular Sunday worship, the parents are asked a series of questions to affirm their commitment to rear the child within the faith. The congregation is asked to confirm its commitment to support the parents and the child. There is no standard written service, and no set age at which the dedication must occur, but it is typically within the first year of life. Some churches dedicate many infants at one time, perhaps on a Mother's Day Sunday, while others dedicate a baby during a Sunday worship service close to the birth date. This ritual highlights the importance of family and the expectation that the Baptist community will assist the parents in rearing the child in the Baptist faith.

Baptists and the Age of Accountability

"Age of accountability" is an expression used to mark the age at which a person is considered mature enough to understand the concept of salvation. This is a time of identity formation for a Baptist person, often in pre-adolescence. At this time, the person either makes a decision to accept Christian beliefs or rejects them. If the person chooses to become a Baptist, he or she is baptized, joins the church, and is eligible to participate in the Lord's Supper for the first time. In the early part of the 20th century, young people typically were baptized at 18 or 19 years old (Foreign Mission Board, 1926). In the 1950s and 1960s, the typical age for baptism was about 9 or 10. Nowadays, many children are being baptized as early as 5 or 6 years old. There is no set standard for the "age of accountability." Some parents may worry that if a child is old enough to be "accountable before the Lord" but has not been baptized, he or she will not have eternal life. Generally, however, Baptists believe that infants or other children who die before reaching the age of accountability will gain eternal life, because God would not condemn a child who was not old enough to understand the concept of salvation.

Adolescent Baptists

Baptist teenagers have opportunities at church to interact with other young people and to learn about Baptist principles. Programs for Baptist young people provide a strong positive peer group and supportive relationships with mentors and other positive role models throughout the adolescent years. There are many educational programs for teenagers, such as mission study organizations in which students earn tokens of achievement for mission activities in church and community. Since the 1920s, Baptist churches have been bringing their young people together for youth camp experiences in the summer. These originally were gender-segregated camps, but from the middle of the 20th century, camps included both young men and young women. Youth camps offer outdoor recreation, worship services tailored for teenagers, and fellowship with other Baptist young people. Many Baptists remember youth camp experiences as times of intense spiritual growth as well as important times for building a peer support group. Baptists who attend college may choose from over 50 Baptist-affiliated schools around the nation. Students who attend state universities may join student organizations such as Baptist Student Union and gain support from a Baptist campus minister. Throughout the adolescent years, Baptist young people may find positive supporting relationships among other Baptist youth and adults.

Marriage and the Family

Baptists consider marriage a sacred commitment. Baptist young people are encouraged to marry other Baptists or, at the very least, to marry another Protestant. However, there is diversity of belief among Baptists about what constitutes a Christian marriage. The SBC made national headlines in the summer of 1998 by stating its position on marriage and the family, which mandated submission of wives to their husbands. In its revision of the Baptist Faith and Message of 1963, the SBC declared that marriage is "the exclusive, permanent, monogamous union of one man and one woman." The document continues, rejecting what it calls "the perversion of homosexuality" and stating that "Jesus clearly did not advocate divorce." The statement calls on husbands to love their wives and for wives to "forsake the resistance to the authority of their respective husbands and to practice, willing, joyful, submission to that leadership" (Southern Baptist Convention, 1998).

These statements issued by the fundamentalist-controlled SBC were written in reaction to recent events taking place in moderate churches. Throughout the 1980s and 1990s, some Baptist churches ordained women as deacons. In 1992, the Pullen Memorial Baptist Church of Raleigh, North Carolina sanctioned a union ceremony between two gay men; in the same year O. T. Binkley Memorial Church in Chapel Hill, North Carolina licensed a homosexual member for ministry (Cornell, 1992). These examples demonstrate the diversity of practice among Baptists concerning homosexuality, marriage, divorce, and authority and equality in the home.

Older Baptists

Like most older persons, older Baptists hope to live life to its fullest with dignity and purpose. Many older adults find a community of caring in their church, and Baptists are no exception. Some larger churches employ a staff member who is responsible for organizing Bible classes, activities, and field trips for seniors. Baptist church members may make visits, provide taped church services, or bring the Lord's Supper to older persons who are unable to leave their homes. There are also Baptist-affiliated agencies, such as the Buckner Retirement Services of Texas, which offer residential facilities for independent living, nursing care, and other community services. Many of these Baptist-affiliated agencies have professional social workers on staff to provide services.

Death

Baptist beliefs concerning death are tied to the concept of eternal life. Because human beings are fallible and sinful, we must die. However, a Baptist believer will be resurrected to eternal life. Baptists turn to their faith for comfort in times of death, believing that death has "no victory" over Baptist believers who, after death, will be resurrected and live eternally in heaven. Baptist rituals for death are like those of other mainstream Protestant groups. A religious funeral service is typically held in a church or funeral home. The pastor may deliver a sermon of comfort, with friends and family offering eulogies and music. The message typically emphasizes the eternal life of the Baptist believer and the hope of resurrection. Death and resurrection of a believer are also associated with common Baptist beliefs surrounding "Last Things," or the end of the world. The Baptist Faith and Message of 1963 defines these beliefs in this way:

> God in His own time and in His own way, will bring the world to its appropriate end. According to his promise, Jesus Christ will return personally and visibly in glory to the earth; the dead will be raised; and Christ will judge all men in righteousness. The unrighteous will be consigned to Hell, the place of everlasting punishment. The righteous in their resurrected and glorified bodies will receive their reward and will dwell forever in Heaven with the Lord. (Hobbs, 1971)

The Baptist community provides support and encouragement for individuals and families throughout the life cycle. A Baptist believer may be cradled in the love of community through good times as well as challenging times. Social workers can encourage clients to draw upon an appropriate Baptist network of support at every stage of life.

HEALTH AND HEALING

Baptists believe that God heals individuals, and they ask God for healing in prayers. In prayer meetings, Baptists often report specific health needs of people in their community. There is no written traditional prayer for healing; rather, Baptists pray in their own words for the specific needs of the one who seeks healing. Prayer is also a reminder to members to provide more tangible services to sick persons, such as visiting them in the hospital or providing food for families experiencing illness.

Many Baptists believe that God may work through medical professionals and others to bring healing. In fact, Baptist philanthropists have founded many hospitals, and the network of Baptist health care agencies is quite strong. When working with a Baptist hospital, social workers will find that not all employees are Baptists, and at first glance, the hospital may look like any other. However, members of the Boards of Trustees are often Baptists, and denominational politics may be at play behind the scenes. Social workers may be able to draw on the resources of a Baptist chaplain in a hospital setting to pray with a patient or talk with the family. Chaplaincy requires licensing or ordination as a minister. Both men and women serve as chaplains. In fact, since pulpits in Baptist churches are usually closed to women ministers, chaplaincy has become one of the fastest-growing areas for Baptist women in ministry (Anders, 1995). Since Baptists hold a diversity of beliefs regarding the place of women in ministry, a social worker should explore whether a Baptist client will accept services from an ordained woman chaplain before making such a referral.

Mental Health

Baptists typically support the use of social workers, psychologists, psychiatrists, and others who provide mental health services. Social workers trained in clinical practice, particularly those associated with faith-based organizations, are considered important resources for those in need of counseling. Baptists from both extremes of the theological spectrum support the use of pastoral counseling, a field that emerged in the 1960s to address the relationship between faith and healing. Pastoral counseling draws on the disciplines of psychology, psychiatry, and theology. Baptist pastor and educator Dr. Wayne Oates is considered the founding patriarch of pastoral counseling (Wingfield, 1998). Pastoral counselors are typically seminary-trained ministers who have taken courses in counseling methods and practiced under supervision. Many may be certified by the American Association of Pastoral Counseling. However, a social worker should not assume that every pastor who offers counseling is trained in delivering mental health services or licensed or certified to do so.

SOCIAL WORK PRACTICE WITH BAPTISTS

The larger community of Baptists can provide many strengths and resources for individuals and families who are struggling with life's problems. In addition, a strong network of Baptists working together can provide help for marginalized groups and communities. Social workers who are able to empower clients to utilize these resources may find that the Baptist community will provide a helping network to address almost any concern. Here are a few suggestions for working with Baptist individuals, families, organizations, and communities.

Social Work with Individuals and Families

- *Be aware of and sensitive to the diversity of beliefs and practices among Baptists.* When working with a client who states that he or she is a Baptist, a social worker must never assume that the client embraces a particular set of beliefs or practices. Following the principle of "priesthood of all believers" leads to a great diversity of belief. For example, some Baptist clients may want to discuss biblical passages or stories. One client may assign a literal meaning to the stories, while another client may view the verses as authoritative but not to be interpreted literally. When assessing a client's resources or exploring the client's potential involvement in a church community, social workers must not assume that one Baptist congregation is just like another. It is best not to bring up denominational politics or ask clients to label themselves in order to discover their beliefs. It is not always necessary to discover the denominational allegiances of a Baptist client. Some folks in the pew do not enter into denominational controversies and may not have an answer for a social worker who asks, "Are you a fundamentalist or a moderate Baptist?" Instead, as the client begins to discuss his or her religious beliefs, the social worker may simply inquire about particular beliefs that are relevant to the issue at hand. The important question for the social worker is not how to label a client, but, whether the client is in a context that affirms his or her beliefs, allowing him or her to live congruently and genuinely.
- *Do not directly challenge or attempt to change a client's religious beliefs.* The social worker must be comfortable with his or her own religious beliefs and be aware of any biases he or she may have toward Baptists (Denton & Denton, 1994, p. 11). The wise social worker will "start where the client is" and avoid stereotyping the client's religious views.

- *Consider soliciting the support of a Baptist minister.* When working with individuals or families who strongly value their minister's opinion, the social worker might contact the minister, with the family's permission. This may give credibility to the social worker by demonstrating her or his respect for the beliefs of the client (Denton & Denton, 1994, p 13).
- *Like other people of faith, Baptist clients often feel strengthened by the power of prayer, hymns, the Lord's Supper, and frequent gatherings with other Baptists.* Denton and Denton (1994) suggest that prayer may be used if it is appropriate to the situation, especially if the client requests it. If the social worker is not comfortable praying with clients, he or she can recommend that clients pray on their own, or that clients ask others in the Baptist community to pray for them. Baptists believe that an individual has direct access to God through prayer and that everyone's prayers are heard by God, For some, the ritual of prayer can be very comforting. Baptists who would like for others to pray for them, but who do not want to reveal their problem or dilemma, can announce state to the community that they have an " unspoken request" for prayer. This means that the community will pray that God will aid the person with his or her need, but the nature of the problem remains confidential.
- *Utilize Baptist networks as a resource.* Baptists maintain a remarkable social network, from cradle to grave. Churches provide activities throughout the week for people of all ages. Families can spend their summer vacations attending Baptist camps or doing mission projects. Wherever they go in the world, Baptists can find other Baptists to commune with and share the joys and the burdens of life.
- *Social workers can help recreate social support when a Baptist has been marginalized by his or her community.* Unfortunately, some congregations may judge that a person is engaged in behaviors that cause him or her to be living outside of God's grace. These Baptists may believe that the person does not deserve to be a member of the worshipping community until those behaviors are changed. In addition to exploring the feelings surrounding this exclusion, social workers may need to be proactive in helping the client rebuild a torn social network or create a new one. In these cases, it is important for the social worker to remember that Baptist churches are diverse in belief and practice. The same client who was excluded by one Baptist church may be readily embraced by a different one.

Social Work with Congregations and Organizations

Like other Christians, Baptists are biblically mandated to help others. Social workers will find a ready network of compassionate volunteers who feel called by God to help others. Volunteers may benefit from having a professional social worker point out the needs and guide their helping efforts.

- *Baptists have created an extraordinary network of social service agencies.* Typically, one does not need to be a Baptist to receive services, but Baptist clients may readily draw from resources provided by their own faith tradition. Many of these agencies employ professional social workers.
- *Some social workers are uneasy about working with Baptist churches.* Some may be uncomfortable with the strong Baptist tradition of evangelism. However, many Baptists are able to view "sharing the Gospel" as an activity that involves deeds rather than simply words. Some approach people with a more wholistic perspective, viewing them as persons with physical and emotional needs, as well as spiritual needs. Social workers need to educate themselves about a particular Baptist congregation or organization and its approach to evangelism and what is often called "social ministries." The wise social worker will carefully assess a Baptist congregation or agency and openly discuss these issues.
- *Social workers may partner with Baptist groups for community change.* A Baptist church may take on the client role by seeking consultation with a social worker about grant writing, working with volunteers, or other types of service. Or, social workers may partner with Baptist churches or Baptist agencies for community change. In light of the diversity among Baptist churches, it is important that social workers understand the congregations and agencies with which they are working. In forming a community coalition that includes more than one Baptist church, the social worker must assess the ability of several different Baptist churches to work together as partners. Is it possible that the theological differences between the Baptist churches would become an obstacle to partnership? Or can the churches put aside their differences for a common goal? My own church, whose membership is predominantly White, has been in partnership with a historically Black church for over 30 years, meeting together for worship and engaging in a variety of social ministries together. However, my church maintains that women and men have equal roles in the life of the church, ordains women deacons, and invites women into the pulpit to preach, while our partner church maintains a male-only deacon board and invites only men into the pulpit to preach. Each church is quite adamant in its stance on gender and worship but puts differences aside in the interest of the larger goal of a communal and interracial partnership of worship and service. Both sides happily compromise when we attend one another's churches. As a social worker encounters Baptist churches with such differences, he or she might talk with the pastors and a few members of the churches to assess how well particular Baptist churches may work together in partnership.

As social workers, we must be knowledgeable and respectful of our clients' religious traditions. Those who work with Baptist clients, whether individuals, families, organizations, or communities, will find many strengths and resources to empower thems. The successful social worker will acknowledge the diversity among Baptist believers and utilize the strengths of this important religious tradition.

REFERENCES

Allen, K. (1987). *A Century to celebrate: History of the woman's missionary union.* Birmingham, AL: Woman's Missionary Union.

Ammerman, N. T. (1990). *Baptist battles: Social change and religious conflict in the Southern Baptist Convention.* New Brunswick, NJ: Rutgers University Press.

Anders, S. F. (1995, June 5). Role of women worth celebrating. *Louisiana Baptist Message.*

Baker, R. (1974). *The Southern Baptist Convention and its people: 1607–1972.* Nashville, TN: Broadman.

Campbell-Reid, E. (1998). *Being Baptist.* Macon, GA: Smyth and Helwys.

Cornell, G (1992, March 7). An absolute departure: Homosexuality proposal called attack on autonomy. *St. Louis Post Dispatch,* 9A.

Denton, R. T., & Denton, M. J. (1994). Treating religious fundamentalist families: Therapists' suggestions from a qualitative study. *Human Services in the Rural Environment, 17*(3/4), 9–14.

Foreign Mission Board. (1926). *Album of Southern Baptist foreign missionaries,* Richmond, VA: Foreign Mission Board of the SBC.

Garland, D. (1999). When professional ethics and religious politics conflict: A case study. *Social Work and Christianity, 26*(1), 60–76.

Higginbotham, E. B. (1993). *The women's movement in the Black Baptist Church, 1880–1920.* Cambridge, MA: Harvard University Press.

Hobbs, H. H. (1971). *The Baptist faith and message.* Nashville, TN: Convention Press.

Leonard, B. (1990). *God's last and only hope: The fragmentation of the Southern Baptist Convention.* Grand Rapids, MI: Eerdmans.

Leonard, B. (Ed.). (1994). *Dictionary of Baptists in America.* Downer's Grove, IL: Intervarsity Press.

McBeth, L. (1987). *The Baptist heritage.* Nashville, TN: Broadman Press.

Scales, T. L. (2000). *"All that fits a woman": Training Southern Baptist women for charity and mission, 1907–1926.* Macon, GA: Mercer University Press.

Southern Baptist Convention. (1998), *Report of the Committee on the Baptist Faith and Message, approved at SBC, June 9, 1998.* Retrieved [date] from the World Wide Web: www.sbc.net

Spain, R. B. (1967). *At ease in Zion: Social history of Southern Baptists, 1865–1900.* Nashville, TN: Vanderbilt University Press.

Sumners, B. F. (1975). *The social attitudes of Southern Baptists toward certain issues, 1910–1920.* Unpublished master's thesis, University of Texas at Arlington.

Torbet, R. (1950). *A history of the Baptists.* Valley Forge, PA: Judson Press.

Wingfield, M. (1998, November 3). Pastoral counseling's pioneer recalls his experiences." *Western Recorder, 172*(43).

ADDITIONAL RESOURCES

Books

Leonard, B. (Ed.). (1994). *Dictionary of Baptists in America.* Downers Grove, IL: Intervarsity Press.

Southern Baptist Convention. (1998). Report of the Committee on the Baptist Faith and Message. Approved at SBC June 9, 1998. www.sbc.net

Web Sites

Homepage for all persons of the Baptist faith: www.baptist.org/

Baptist Church Directory: www.prairienet.org/temple/churches.htm

GLOSSARY

Age of accountability The age at which a person is considered mature enough to make a decision to become a Christian; the typical age has varied across generations.

Biblical inerrancy The belief that the Bible contains no error and should be taken literally. This doctrine was at the center of Baptist conflicts in the 20th century, particularly in the 1920s and 1980s.

Fundamentalists Those within the Southern Baptist Convention (SBC) who accept biblical inerrancy as the only model of biblical authority and participate in a political movement to make their position normative for all within the SBC.

Moderate Baptists A term that came into use in the 1980s to describe opponents of the SBC fundamentalist movement. Moderates affirm traditional Baptist doctrines such as biblical authority, evangelism, priesthood of all believers, and religious freedom; they are sometimes called "liberals" by their opponents.

Priesthood of all believers Core Baptist belief that stresses the competence and responsibility of the individual believer to relate to God directly, rather than depending on a priest or other intermediary.

Profession of faith Term used by Baptists to describe the public declaration that one is a follower of Christ.

Social Gospel Movement Emerging among Northern Baptists of the early 20th century, and led by Walter Rauchenbusch, this movement challenged Baptists to consider and address racial and economic injustices.

THE AFRICAN AMERICAN BAPTIST TRADITION

CHAPTER 

DARLENE GRANT

INTRODUCTION

In July 1944, my maternal grandfather, Reverend E. C. Vester, an African American Baptist minister, gave an inspirational address before a gathering of other ministers, in which he focused on the importance of the teaching ministry within the church. A yellowed and worn copy of this sermon is one of my most prized possessions, as is the 1921 edition of the *Gospel Pearls,* a small stapled paperback hymnal published by the Sunday School Publishing Board of the National Baptist Convention, U.S.A., in Nashville, Tennessee. The hymnal belonged to his wife, my grandmother Jennie Inge Vester. My maternal aunt Vera mailed me the copy of his address during a particularly difficult period during my doctoral studies, with the following note:

> Sorry you feel you won't graduate in May. I have faith that you'll come through. I shall fast for 1 week for your strength to overcome all obstacles that will befall you from now until May. I am sending you this inspirational sermon to let you know where we come from. Even when Whites thought Blacks were not thinkers, your granddaddy was thinking of you and all Black children of the future. With God's help you can do it. Never think you can't. Our family was never rich monetarily, but as a loving and Christian family that will

look out for each other, we are as rich as anyone in the world. (February 1993)

In his address, my grandfather stated that "[Our] race goes forward on the feet of little children. The youth express it, carry all the memories and achievements and hopes of the race down through the centuries. Without the conserving of the child of today we lose tomorrow, for whatever you wish the knowledge and strength of the coming generation to be must be implanted within the child of today."

So, my Aunt Vera fasted, my entire family prayed, and I stayed the course and earned my Ph.D. in November 1993. This story is one of many examples of how race and religion coalesce and manifest themselves in daily life in the African American family and community. This coalescence is evident in my grandfather's 1944 inspirational address, in which he talked about the church as the foundation upon which the spiritual and material advancement of African Americans was built since emancipation from slavery and after the Civil War. He went on to emphasize that without teaching as a way to combat "popular reading of magazines and movies reeking with rot and vulgarity, we will fail." His message of freedom, hope, and advancement resonates in the messages African Americans hear from the pulpit today.

Born in 1960, I remember my family's annual summer trips from Cleveland, Ohio to Demopolis and Forkland, Alabama to visit my grandparents, a yearly sojourn made by thousands of African Americans who had, in the early 1900s, migrated to the North seeking jobs and better conditions. Church was an integral part of every trip "down South."

I remember Springhill and Shilo Baptist Churches—small whitewashed clapboard buildings, windows open wide and congregants praying for a cross-breeze while waving hand-held cardboard fans displaying a white Jesus and advertisements on the back for funeral home services; hard uncomfortable pews; and the harmonic moaning of the "old mothers" of the church all dressed in white. I remember the ritual dressing up to go to church: Vaseline on children's ashy legs and faces, pink frilly dresses, patent leather shoes, and tiny purses, each holding a hankie, a few coins for the offering plate, and Lifesavers to keep me and my sisters quiet and awake during the long hot services. And after morning service there was cool sweet water from the boat-well, dinner on the church grounds, adults talking about the past and catching up on news of the present, and children running and playing. Occasionally, we would stop playing long enough to listen to the stories that would later become important to the values and beliefs we would hold as adults; just as the history told through these stories would gain academic and social legitimacy.

The tradition of service to family and the broader world community and the messages of freedom, equality, and social justice that I was born into come directly from African American Baptist tenets. The African American Baptist heritage is "significantly oral" (Fitts, 1985), tremendously spiritual, essentially congregationally controlled, grounded in a sociopolitical pedagogy, and generally accompanied by rhythmic music and dance. After examining the history of the African American Baptist tradition, the discussion here will focus on how this faith tradition influenced my motivation to enter the social work profession and how that influence extends to my current role as a college professor teaching about human behavior and the social environment, cultural diversity, research, and practice theory and methods.

It is not possible to present *all* African American Baptist history, perspectives, beliefs, values, and experiences in this chapter. This limitation should not obscure the existence of a diversity of beliefs and practices across and within the African American Baptist church, nor does it imply that beliefs or practices not discussed here are unimportant. My experience is not stereotypical, nor are my beliefs and interpretation absolutely correct—and I have take great pains in the chapter to clarify what is my experience in relation to what may be the broader African American Baptist experience. The reader is referred to the references provided at the end of this chapter and encouraged to explore this topic even further. I encourage social work practitioners and counselors from other disciplines never to depend solely on one resource for their understanding of a person or group of people.

PREVALENCE OF AFRICAN AMERICAN BAPTISTS

In 1998, there were an estimated 100 million Baptists in the world (in 200 countries) (Adherents.com, 1999). African American Baptists make up the fourth-largest religious denomination in the United States and the largest religious group among African Americans, with over 8 million members affiliated with the National Baptist Convention, U.S.A. (Murphy, 1993; Newsome, 1995). The African American Baptist church is generally governed congregationally; a broader organization of Baptist associations and state conventions unites individual churches. These broader associations and state conventions facilitate the pooling of support and resources, thus enabling churches to support each other, schools, indigents, and other sociopolitical causes. Murphy (1993) notes that there are "four predominantly African American Baptist associations that report a membership in the millions: the National Baptist Convention, U.S.A.; the National Baptist Convention of America; the National Missionary Baptist Convention of America; and the Progressive National Baptist Convention" (p. 64). The *1999 Yearbook of American and Canadian Churches* (Lindner, 1999, p. 87) provides the following statistics on African American adherents or congregants: National Baptist Convention, U.S.A., 8,200,000; National Baptist Convention of America, 3,500,000 (in 1987, the most recent statistic available); National Missionary Baptist Convention of America, 2,500,000; and the Progressive National Baptist Convention, 2,500,000.

A BRIEF HISTORY OF THE AFRICAN AMERICAN BAPTIST CHURCH

It is generally understood that most African Americans who claim any religious preference are Christians. Although there are an increasing number of African American Roman Catholics and a few African American members of the Eastern Orthodox Church, as well as African American adherents of Buddhism, Islam, Judaism, and other non-Christian religions, (Crim, Bullard, & Shinn, 1981), the vast majority of African Americans are Protestants, primarily Baptist and Methodist.

Slavery was maintained in the United States until 1865. But as Brown (1998) points out, with regard to African American religions, "belief in God did not begin when enslaved [Black] people were "Christianized" by plantation preachers. [Prior to the introduction of Christianity] there was an established belief of God in everything" (p. 46). Most African slaves in the United States came into contact with the Christian practices of their owners and traders, later merging what they learned in their new land with what they recalled from their African and African Caribbean religious and spiritual belief systems. And as cruel and dehumanizing as the oppressive use of religion by plantation owners was, it gave expression to the ancestral and spiritual ethos of the African American—the expression of her and his humanity, strength, and resilience.

Encouraged by their owners (who interpreted the Christian Gospel to them) to view God as their "White master in heaven" and to see heaven essentially as a place where they would receive their "rewards" and as a more cheerful place to "serve" God, slaves and freedmen privately worshipped a God whom they saw in a much different light. The slaves' God did not view them as property, but rather "recognized them as equals to Whites, and was on their side as powerful medicine for sick souls and frustrated hopes. Slaves and freedmen believed and preached that although the slave master might be more powerful than the slave, he was not more powerful than their God, [giving them] a feeling of psychological and spiritual advantage over the slave master" (Martin & Martin, 1985, p. 28).

The view of God and God's power as more powerful than any oppressor or oppressive system is evident throughout the history of African American Baptists in the United States. During the civil rights movement of the 1960s, for example, Martin Luther King, Jr., Ralph Abernathy, Adam Clayton Powell, Sr., and other African American Baptist clergy made frequent reference to the power of God over systems of oppression and inequality, asserting that these institutions would not stand forever. And as African American churches spread, they responded to growing rural and urban problems by providing aid and social services, many in cooperation with entities such as the NAACP and the National Urban League.

In relating the early history of African American Baptists in North America, Fitts (1985) emphasizes the paradox of the "accommodation to slavery on the part of [White] Baptists" (p. 24) and the stress and controversy the issue caused among the White ministers, church leadership, and members. There were, however, both proslavery and antislavery Baptists, as well as slave owners who allowed their shaves to hear Black mission preachers whose work was the precursor to organized African American Baptist churches.[1] Although the evangelization of slaves was generally accepted, "Black slaves were not permitted to have their own churches, pastors, and preachers. It was the common practice throughout the slave territory to permit them to attend preaching services in the White churches at a time designated by and under conditions prescribed by their masters" (Fitts, 1985, p. 31). Fitts notes that "there is some discrepancy among historians relative to the establishment of the first plantation mission for Black Baptists" (p. 37) and subsequently the first African American Baptist church. The First Colored Baptist Church, in Savannah, Georgia and the Silver Bluff Baptist Church, in Aiken County, South Carolina appear to vie for the position of the first African American Baptist church in the United States.

Most frequently, however, the rise of the free Black church is often credited to Richard Allen, a Delaware slave who bought himself from his owner and established the African Methodist Episcopal (A.M.E.) church sometime between 1773 and 1794 (Asante & Mattson, 1991; Melton, 1996). Ingram (1998) reports that "by the end of the Civil War, there were perhaps a million Black Baptists in the South." Freed from slavery, and dissatisfied with the "segregational and discriminatory policy of most White Baptists" and other institutions (Fitts, 1985, p. 43), African Americans sought to establish their own churches and other social and social service institutions.

During the 1960s and later in the 1990s, race consciousness resulted in the incorporation of Afrocentric images of Christ and the Virgin Mary, symbols, ornamentation, and attire into many African American churches (Asante, 1988; Crim, Bullard, & Shinn, 1981). Asante (1988) suggests that "the Black church is among our most authentic contact with the gods of our ancestors" (p. 74) and highlights the role of hymns and spirituals, and the syncopated and polymetric beats of pianos, organs, drums (in some churches), handclapping, and foot-tapping used in place of the drums of those ancestors. As Asante suggests, it is as if the internal strivings of our souls are physically manifest in the music, resulting in rhythmic catharsis. Although "hymns are

---

[1]Ingram (1998) notes "neglect of prophetic ministry among Southern Baptists. . . . [Instead] the churches reflected the surrounding culture rather than challenging it. . . . But in 1995 the SBC adopted a resolution apologizing and asking forgiveness for their history of racial prejudice and discrimination" (p. 41).

an important part at all Baptist services" (Bishop & Darton, 1988), the fervor and charisma of the preached sermon and prayers, the ritual of "call and response" between minister and members of the congregation, and the execution and performance of music in the African American Baptist church all seem significantly different from services in White Baptist and other churches—particularly in the extent to which music taps and elicits the God-force/Holy Spirit in the church congregation.

Organizational Structure of the African American Baptist Church

There is no clearly defined or uniform organizational structure distinguishing African American Baptists from other Baptists. Each Baptist church is autonomous, self-financing, governed by the congregation (which is presided over by a minister and lay deacons who are elected by the members), involved in relationships with other local and state Baptist churches, and affiliated with a national union and/or convention (Bishop & Darton, 1988; Brandon, 1970; Crim, Bullard, & Shinn, 1981; Ellwood & Alles, 1998). Crim, Bullard, and Shinn (1981) suggest that this autonomous organizational structure and the historical lack of a requirement of formal education for the ministry are the reasons many African Americans formed Baptist churches. Subsequently, the Baptist church has become a major force in the African American community. Billingsly (1992) describes the African American Baptist church as "perhaps the most decentralized and democratic of the large, national, African-American organizations" (p. 350).

"In 1895, three groups met in Atlanta to form the National Baptist Convention of America. A dispute over adoption of the charter in 1915 led to a split and the formation of the National Baptist Convention, U.S.A." (Ingram, 1998, p. 40). National Baptists have historically been active in the moral, spiritual, material, and political progress of African Americans, and well-known National Baptist ministers include civil rights leaders Martin Luther King, Jr., Ralph Abernathy, and Jesse Jackson (Ingram, 1998).

GENERAL DOCTRINAL BELIEFS OF AFRICAN AMERICAN BAPTISTS

Although African American Baptist associations differ in their approach to educational, political, and social issues, there is general agreement on basic Baptist doctrinal beliefs. Melton (1996) highlights two basic Baptist doctrines: (1) "people are given free will so they can choose whether or not to follow the Gospel" (p. 97); and (2) membership requires a "personal experience of regeneration (in modern terms, the "born again" experience involving an awareness of Jesus as personal savior)" (p. 97). Montgomery (1993) notes that following the experience of "regeneration," the person is baptized by total immersion in water. Baptism serves to dramatize the death of the person as a sinner and her or his rebirth as a Christian. Similarly, Bishop and Darton

(1988) suggest that Baptism by immersion is "an outward and visible sign of identification with Christ in His death and resurrection." Montgomery (1993) emphasizes that "Christian Baptism resonated with ancient West African water rites that were embedded in African-American culture" (p. 3). Once baptized, a person receives Communion. In the Baptist church, "Communion is most generally celebrated fortnightly, alternately in the morning and in the evening" (Bishop & Darton, 1988, p. 128).

McBeth (1987) delineates seven doctrinal beliefs:

- Making a confession of faith in God is key to the Baptist faith.
- Belief in God, who is revealed as the Father, Son, and Holy Spirit Trinity, wherein the Holy Spirit serves as "inspiration, comfort, and illumination of scripture" (p. 69).
- Belief in the final authority of Scripture and refusal to accept human authority unless it agrees with Scripture (p. 70).
- Belief that Christ died for every person and that whoever believes in him can be saved. This belief in atonement is central to the Baptist faith. Belief in atonement is coupled with the belief that people are free to choose their eternal destiny, and that children dying in infancy are secure in the love of God (p. 73).
- Belief that Baptism by total immersion after the confession of faith is the outward manifestation of the inward acceptance of the faith and evidence of starting a new life in Jesus Christ. In other words, Baptism symbolizes the death and resurrection of Christ. Infant baptism is not practiced, because Baptism requires a prior confession of faith.
- Belief that Communion or the Lord's Supper is a memorial supper to recall and reflect upon the death of Christ, his resurrection, and hope for humanity.
- Belief in the return of Christ and his subsequent judgment as revealed in the book of Revelation in the New Testament.

In his *Introduction to the Baptists,* Hulse (1973) lists the following additional beliefs as definitive of the Baptist faith:

- A strong emphasis on the separation of church and state
- A strong emphasis on evangelism, i.e., responsibility to witness to, and pray for, the unconverted
- Belief in the sovereignty of God
- Belief that God created the universe, the heavens, and the earth
- Belief in man's free will to become a Christian or to fall into a state of sin
- Belief in repentance and salvation
- Belief in the moral law of God as laid out in the Ten Commandments and throughout the Bible
- Belief that God's judgment is inscrutable, for He was willing to have His Son suffer and die for our sins

African American Baptist church doctrine has historically been conservative with regard to the role of women in the church and home and with regard to homosexuality. Although women have risen to significant status in their roles as ministers' wives and "auxiliary" chairs, their role in the pulpit, with very few exceptions, remains limited to speaking on Women's Day or at women's conferences (Brown, 1998; Montgomery, 1993). The same holds true for the few courageous gay or lesbian church members who dare to be "out" in the African American church—their roles remain limited to musicians and choir directors. Women in the African American church traditionally sing in the choir, teach children, serve the pastor, give financial support, keep the building clean (Brown, 1998, p. 45), welcome visitors, and cook elaborate meals for the congregation on special occasions.

Outside of theological doctrine, African American Baptists exhibit a range of views regarding educational, familial, political, and social issues. While there are religious traditions that may be considered "universal" to Baptists of every race, African American Baptist churches have historically and continue today to view themselves as bastions against social and institutional threats to African Americans, including racism in all its forms. This is counter to the more "universal" Baptist belief in the separation of church and state. One of the predominant emphases of this chapter is that the oppression that has shaped the African American Baptist tradition has compelled these churches to become voices in the socio-political arena.

Billingsly (1992) sees the uniqueness of the African American church as its commitment to being "at the leading edge of the African-American community's push to influence the future of its families" (p. 349). By and large, African American churches continue to fight for race consciousness, the right to vote and other civil rights, the preservation of the African American family, and equality in education and employment opportunities, and against drugs, gambling, organized crime, and gang involvement.

MORAL AND ETHICAL VIEWS ON SOCIAL ISSUES

"There is no clearly defined moral code that is a means of distinguishing Baptists from other Christians" (Hays & Steely, 1981). Further, Baptists "have not required formal education for the ministry and [have] allowed for autonomy of local congregations" (Crim, Bullard, & Shinn, 1981). "The beliefs and teachings of different groups of Baptists differ widely" (Ellwood, & Alles 1998). For example some Baptists believe in the "laying on or imposition of hands" (Bishop & Darton, 1988), others in the ordination of women as deacons and/or ministers, and yet others believe in "speaking in tongues," while still other groups of Baptists do not hold any such beliefs. Groups of Baptists vary in how sophisticated or worldly they are, and, as mentioned earlier, there may be distinct differences in beliefs and teachings about the personal and public responsibilities of Baptists.

Hays and Steely (1981), in their discussion of Christian ethics, however, provide some insight into broadly accepted areas of personal and public responsibility for African American Baptists, including the use of alcoholic beverages, gambling, observing the Sabbath, marriage and divorce, and taking responsibility for others "by keeping private and corporate greed and graft in politics in check, and standing up against social inequality and injustice" (p. 91), including racism.

As an African American female, I would be remiss if I didn't point out the clearly sexist and paternalistic language of most Baptist discussions in the literature. The impact of paternalistic interpretations of Baptist teachings within African American Baptist churches is of particular concern to me. Such doctrine can and does distance a significant number of African American (and other) women from God's word and the supportive community of the church. In my experience, male African American Baptist ministers are adverse to addressing the gender inequity issue and the role of their own interpretation of the Scripture in maintaining gender inequity—a stance that seems to relate directly to the overall doctrinal belief that the Bible is infallible and, by definition, immutable.

Substance Abuse, Drunkenness, and Gambling

While drunkenness is frowned upon, the Christian church demonstrates a broad tolerance of the use of alcoholic beverages. The Christian "ideal," however, is total personal abstinence (Hays & Steely, 1981). Baptists show more unanimity in their denouncement of gambling as an evil vice. Further, Christian churches in general are divided on the question of disciplining members for drinking, illicit drug use, and/or gambling. Reactions to these actions range from ignoring the problem, to prayer vigils asking God to take away the individual's taste for the substance or behavior, dismissal from any position held in the church, and referral to outside medical and/or social service agencies for help.

It is not unusual for an African American minister to profess a calling to the ministry following a life involving alcohol and/or other substance abuse, gambling, crime, or other personal and/or public problems. These ministers are often deemed to have a gift of life experience that provides invaluable insight into the needs of the "ordinary" church member battling similar temptations and problems. The minister's counsel in these areas, whether he is a trained counselor or not, is given significant credibility, and more likely than not his advice falls on the more lenient end of the discipline continuum. It is important to note that the processes these ministers used to turn their own lives around are often then what they suggest to members of their congregations. So, if a minister experienced spontaneous sobriety following a personal spiritual experience, he might encourage constant prayer and vigil rather than participation in Alcoholics Anonymous, Al-Anon, or Gamblers Anonymous or checking in to a drug rehab program. On the other hand, churches that count among their members social workers, addiction counselors, and recovering addicts and gamblers often can enhance such ministerial responses to chemical and other dependence by establishing supports, referrals and other services for the members.

Marriage, Divorce, and Cohabitation

"Baptists take seriously Biblical teachings concerning marriage and divorce. . . . The most common position is that divorce is permissible only on 'Scriptural grounds'—that is, that the 'innocent party' may sue for divorce on the grounds of marital infidelity" (Hays & Steely, 1981, pp. 92–93). Acknowledging the psychosocial stressors experienced by couples and families today, Baptist churches are increasing their efforts to provide preventive and intervention-focused educational programming and counseling regarding marriage and the family to members and training to teachers, deacons, other leaders, and pastors. Requiring marital counseling prior to marriage is becoming a common practice as divorce rates escalate within congregations.

The social worker and other professional counselor should note that evidence of strict, lax, or uneven adherence to disciplinary actions in the case of marital dissolution or divorce, teen pregnancy, and/or cohabitation does not suggest that African American Baptists are "less Christian" than other denominations or racial or ethnic groups. The context of decades of life adjusting to, negotiating, surviving, and in many instances thriving in a society fraught with institutionalized inequities and oppression suggests that flexibility in family structure and roles has had to be the rule more often than the exception. This raises an important question: Does this context make cohabitation, for example, "acceptable" or "right" in the Christian tradition? Numerous authors, academicians, and theologians have presented their answers to this and other questions, but no singularly definitive conclusion has been reached (Fitts, 1985; Hays & Steely, 1981; Hulse, 1973; McBeth, 1987; Montgomery, 1993).

Practitioners in general, and African American Christian practitioners more specifically, must be careful to avoid (1) pathologizing normative responses to surviving in oppressive systems, and (2) defining behavior that is dysfunctional even in its cultural context as behavior that is typical of the culture itself. From this perspective then, cohabitation without marriage in the African American community is not a "cultural thing" it is, instead, a response to negotiating an entrenched system of oppression that requires flexibility in family roles and functions.

These issues are complex, and there are no easy answers. Simplistic models of cause and effect will only serve to keep us entrenched in ineffective ways of understanding and intervening both through the church and through the social service system.

Social and Economic Injustice and Inequality

Baptists in general have traditionally held individual and corporate greed, systems of social inequality and injustice, graft in politics, and, in some instances, racism, in lofty disdain (Hays & Steely, 1981). At the same time, religious truth and actual practice across the decades have often conflicted, as in the case of preaching and teaching about Christian brotherhood while supporting slavery prior to the Civil War or tolerating segregated church membership since that time. Within the broader Baptist context, the African American Baptist church has striven for self-sufficiency, via ownership of the physical structures of the church, and social rehabilitation, in order to take care of its own members and those in the broader African American community and to reduce dependency on institutions run predominately by Whites, who may have negative views of African Americans in troubled situations.

Often the primary entity leading fights against inner-city gentrification, drug infestation, gang violence, illiteracy, lack of affordable and clean housing for the elderly, hunger, and more, the African American church has focused on establishing economic strength (Billingsly, 1992). The success of these efforts is demonstrated in Billingsly's 1992 book *Climbing Jacob's Ladder,* in which he lists over two dozen exemplary social programs supported by church fund raising and matching grants, focusing on teen pregnancy prevention, housing, health education, recreation, art, music, nursing homes, free lunch programs, prison outreach, child care centers, displaced worker programs, drug rehab programs, and inner-city housing renovation projects.

Issues of racism, sexism, ableism, and homophobia continue to be controversial in the Baptist church in general, especially where there is conflict between Biblical teachings, ministerial interpretation, and practices across membership groups. These issues pose significant challenges to the African American church during the 21st century.

MY PERSONAL NARRATIVE

1

I want Jesus to walk with me.
I want Jesus to walk with me.
All along my pilgrim journey,
I want Jesus to walk with me.

2

In my trials Lord, walk with me.
In my trials Lord, walk with me.
When the shades of life are falling,
I want Jesus to walk with me.

3

In my sorrows, Lord, walk with me.
In my sorrows, Lord, walk with me.
When my heart within is aching,
I want Jesus to walk with me.

—American Negro Spiritual

I am an African American Baptist woman with a Ph.D. in Social Work. After 9 years of working in direct practice with sexually abused children, adolescents in in-patient psychiatric treatment, and drug addicts and alcoholics, I am now as a professor at a large, predominately White, research-oriented university in the Southwest. Like many social work practitioners, I have seen the worst and the best of human beings, and I rely on my religious beliefs to help me remain optimistic about the possibility of change and the elimination of seemingly intractable human and social problems.

I grew up with a maternal grandmother who hummed old Negro spirituals as she cooked, washed, cleaned, and did just about everything else. And when she wasn't humming, she was telling stories about her seven children, her religion, days gone by, and survival with some modicum of happiness. The story telling and the singing have always been the parts of my Baptist experience that cause something to well up inside of me. This something is variously called the "Spirit" or the "Holy Ghost." I like that. The link between this welling up inside of me with my subsequent choice of profession as a social worker and teacher has been quite natural.

I believe that social work values, if taken seriously, are not values to put on and take off at one's leisure. Morales and Sheafor (1995) state that "social workers tend to believe that society has the responsibility to assist people in meeting their needs, that people should be included in making decisions (i.e., empowered) that affect their lives, that positive change in people's lives can be attained through professional help, and so on" (p. 161). My personal and professional lives have been spent adhering to these values while assisting people, young and old, Black, White and Brown, men and women, in freeing themselves from their pain, problems, and limited vision, so that they too can experience the unspeakable freedom and joy that come with being involved in something that provides them a sense of being alive and important in this world. (For me, that something is my Baptist tradition and personal connection to God.) I hope my grandparents approve.

In my work, I seldom if ever reveal my religious background or beliefs. I've never offered to pray with a client, for example, and feel most comfortable and professional when supporting clients' efforts to enhance their religious and spiritual lives and support systems by encouraging them to talk to their minister or establish a relationship with their religious or spiritual institution. When asked point-blank if I am a Christian, I respond honestly and succinctly, "yes," and maintain my focus on the client's problem and the task at hand—finding and exploring solutions using the client's own strengths as the basis for the change process.

The ability to avoid demanding perfection in clients and to create opportunities for honest self-examination and commitment to growth-enhancing beliefs and lifestyle is one consequence of the coalescence of my religious beliefs and my social work values. While writing this chapter, I heard wonderful reminiscences from my maternal aunt Delilah, about the nonjudgmental, nonpunitive process of "gettin' religion," back in Alabama when a revival was held once a year and ended with the Baptism of everybody who "got religion," repented their sins, and professed to "have the Holy Ghost."

> We'd have Revival every July or August. Everybody who wasn't saved sat on the front two pews, called the "mourner's bench," and that's who the preacher would really preach to. There was one week of preaching and one week of praying. Sitting on the mourner's bench meant you were in mourning because you were repenting for your sins and praying that your sinner self would die and your Christian self would be born. The mourner's bench was mostly filled with younger people from the age of 9 or 10 on up. You were considered "old" if you were 15 or 16 and still sittin' on the mourner's bench.
>
> It was about Thursday and Friday when the unrepentant would really start to get religion. Sometimes a mourner would fall out right there during the prayin'—just a-shaking and moaning the words "I got Jesus. I got Him all in my soul." And the people in the congregation would cry and shout in celebration right along with them. Everybody from miles around would attend Revival 'cause you never knew who'd get the spirit and repent. Sometimes an old person would sit on the mourner's bench. Maybe he'd be about 17 or 18 or even as old as 20 or 30, having returned to the bench after many years not sitting on it during Revival. Parents put you on the mourner's bench when you were about 9 or 10 years old and you'd return every year during Revival until you got religion or you turned 18 and just decided for yourself not to sit there anymore.
>
> There was no pressure to repent. You just sat on that bench year after year until you got religion or decided not to sit there. Other than the obvious pressures of being seated out front with one's peer mourners, it was such a normative part of our lives, we felt more supported and loved than pressured and coerced. And when you got religion, you had to share it. You would go house to house and tell how you got religion and sing "I got Jesus. I got Him all in my soul." Sometimes people from the houses you visited would follow you to the next house and on to the next, celebrating, shouting, and singing right along with you.
>
> The last event of Revival was Sunday Baptismal service. African American Baptist churches were built close to creeks where these yearly baptisms would take place. Oh, and we had a time! Women would be dressed up in the only new dress they'd get that year. And since each of the six Black Baptist churches in the county had their own separate Revival Sunday, everybody from the other churches would be in attendance too. We'd start early in the morning and sometimes we'd have 10 or 12 and sometimes as many as 16 people to baptize. Onlookers would be lined up on the creek bank and hillside crying and shoutin' for joy. The row of new repentants would be dressed all in white and taken out into the water by helpers to the preacher to be baptized. After the baptism we'd have a big church picnic and recall the highlights of the two weeks, looking forward to the next year's Revival.

I am committed to working from a perspective that integrates social work and religious values to derive an ethical, boundary- and value-driven approach to people and social problems. Using this practice approach, I have not stumbled on definitive answers that are immutable, given the diversity of people, problems, and perspectives encountered in social work practice. I do, however, maintain and encourage a personal and professional commitment to avoiding premature closure on any subject or a judgmental attitude—by reading, questioning, learning, exploring, discussing, and debating social issues for the purpose of greater understanding.

This stance, it should be noted, occasionally runs counter to what more orthodox African American Baptists believe—those whose opinions and biblical and religious interpretations I honestly consider and respect. My mother, Vernece, for example, might say "Some of our values are just plain God's truths that we don't need to question or understand or overinterpret. We just need to believe and take what is written on faith." My sister Regina might add, "A little bit of higher education (drenched, of course, in the White man's perspective) is dangerous. It keeps you from taking as truth the stuff that African Americans have taken as truth as long as we've been surviving and being resilient in our growth and development in this country. We may have adjusted our family structure, sexual practices, and attitudes about divorce to survive living in an oppressive system, but that doesn't mean we can't hold ourselves to a standard of marriage and intact families, abstinence until marriage, etc." And she's right.

PHYSICAL AND MENTAL HEALTH

The theoretical paradigms used to define the type of physical and psychological treatment African Americans received prior to and following emancipation and until recently in U.S. history include the biological determinism, inferiority, and cultural and social deprivation paradigms (Carter, 1995). Considered biologically, genetically, and intellectually inferior, African Americans were assumed to be mentally disturbed when they protested their enslavement and oppression. Faithful acceptance of oppression was a sign of mental health, which was used as an argument for continued paternalistic domination by Whites (Carter, 1995). African Americans have been assumed to be psychologically unsophisticated people who could be protected from mental illness if taken care of by biologically, genetically, intellectually, and psychologically superior Whites. Racist characterizations of African Americans were used in the assessment of mental health and illness, and culturally specific and contextually normative survival behaviors were pathologized. Precursors to mental illness in African Americans included "laziness, impulsivity, lack of reasoning ability, and suspiciousness" (Carter, 1995, p. 36).

Little has occurred to convince African Americans that social service, psychological, and mental health paradigms have changed into culturally sensitive, empowerment-oriented, and strengths-based paradigms, as new jargon and propaganda suggests. This suspicion extends equally to African American social workers and psychologists, who have been trained and who practice using White mental health paradigms. Traditional physical and mental health services continue to be perceived as "repositories for negative projections, distortions, and destructive myths about [the African American] race and cultures" (Carter, 1995, p. 42), even as African Americans have internalized these same racist myths and beliefs. Consequently, African American religion has continued to provide the venue for empowerment and strengths-based assessments and interventions for physical and mental health problems.

As reflected in my grandfather's inspirational address to his peer ministers, discussed earlier, and as evidenced in the African American Baptist church today, the church's beliefs, rituals, and teachings have evolved to serve as protection against the ravages of oppression, poverty, neglect by state-funded public education, alcohol and other drug abuse, and various other forms of individual, familial, and social problems. Church tradition affirms and promotes the family, and more particularly the health, growth, and development of children. By offering youth and family involvement in church school, youth church, summer vacation Bible school, and mentoring by church deacons, parents, and other elders, the African American Baptist church serves as a stabilizing community resource. The church's overall goal is to facilitate effective social functioning and minimize the damage that might result from exposure to secular or worldly pressures and lead to damage to one's relationship with God, the dissolution of the family, or self-destructive behaviors.

In the African American Baptist tradition, profession of belief and faith in Jesus Christ, Baptism by immersion, having a personal relationship with God, being "good," having a deep spiritual conviction, giving tithes, and actively participating in and serving the church are the ingredients for transcending everyday suffering and pain on this earth and receiving rewards in heaven. Physical and emotional illness, then, are seen as a punishment for the lack of adherence to the above ingredients for transcending pain and suffering, a punishment for one's own sin or sin committed by one's father (i.e., generational sin), or simply as a way of testing one's faithfulness. Since slavery, the paradigm of pain, suffering, and sin has been accompanied by an attitude that might be expressed as "God won't put more on you than you can bear," or "Just keep on believing and praying and working in the church and that'll help you through—it won't necessarily take the pain and suffering away, but it will help you through." Further, this paradigm has influenced the initiation and use by African American congregants of social service, mental health, and medical systems outside of the church.

Years ago, as a neophyte social worker, I viewed this view of pain and suffering as a breeding ground for martyred African American women and angry rebellious African American men. Today, I am more likely to interpret this view of pain and suffering as a contextually driven way to deal with problems and to hold the church to a standard of psychosocial sophistication that focuses on educating congregants about mental and physical health issues as well as civil rights, educational, employment, and family issues. Given the history of the African American church as the preeminent source of social services when traditional programs and institutions were weak or error-prone or just plain failed, the new millennium finds the church establishing social service centers that combine faith, spiritual conviction, and church involvement with traditional social service, counseling, education, and referral. These service centers are established and administered by members with specialized education in such areas as addiction counseling, family and mental health counseling, social work, psychology, and nursing. Emulating the church's social service programs of the early 20th century and the civil rights era, these modern-day in-church social service centers reflect the variety of issues confronting the African American family and community and pragmatically seek to "stand in the gap."

SOURCES OF POWER, HELP, AND HEALING WITHIN THE AFRICAN AMERICAN BAPTIST TRADITION

Historical Considerations

Historically, African American ministers have been the "interpreters of Black social and political agendas, placing themselves between the White man/oppressive sociopolitical policies and the membership" (Asante & Mattson, 1991, p. 49). Further, ministers helped interpret the Bible using an oral storytelling tradition familiar to the African American experience. In this context, religion became the major avenue for power, help, and healing—by resisting discrimination, challenging inferior treatment, caring for the mental, physical, and social welfare of African Americans, and providing education and leadership development. Church leaders emphasized African Americans' faith in God's omnipotence and their ethos of hard work, frugality, industriousness, education, and sobriety as their sources of power (Martin & Martin, 1985).

The African American Baptist tradition is a "self-help" tradition. With minimal resources, and consistent with the principles of self-help and "love thy neighbor," the church historically provided the foundation, impetus, and leadership for the development of institutions for supporting and uplifting the race. The system of legalized discrimination, segregation, and oppression that African Americans faced forced them to establish their own social, political, and economic institutions. Seeking and securing aid, education, and even legal and political help from their churches became a way of life for African Americans. By working with African American churches and institutions that were outgrowths of them, African Americans maintained power over their lives that they did not have when dealing with White institutions.

While establishing separate institutions for advancement of the race, the African American church also worked to make the nation more responsive to the moral dimension of its own grand vision that "all men are created equal and endowed by their creator with certain inalienable rights," as announced in the Constitution. Martin Luther King, Jr.'s work focused on raising national consciousness about racial inequality, inclusiveness, and the broadening of the meaning of America to including all American people, regardless of color (Asante & Mattson, 1991). As the civil rights movement led to the Montgomery bus boycott, the ordering of U.S. troops into Little Rock, Arkansas to enforce court-ordered desegregation, and the selection of Thurgood Marshall to the Supreme Court in 1967, African Americans increasingly demanded to be educated, treated, and served as any other U.S. citizen.

During and after the civil rights movement of the 1950s and 1960s, much of the African American self-help movement was interpreted by many White

Americans and some African Americans as "separatist" and thus counter to the goals of the movement. After the late 1960s, an interesting paradox evolved as African Americans were increasingly assimilated into the "broadening of the meaning of America" and the institutions created to uplift the race began declining—or even disappearing. This is unfortunate, in that although "there has been a gradual improvement in the health of African Americans since [emancipation], African Americans still have one of the highest mortality rates of any ethnic or cultural group in the United States" (Asante & Mattson, 1991, p. 167). Poverty, poor nutrition, unequal access to and utilization of medical and mental health care, and discriminatory service delivery are all factors related to this dismal situation (Asante & Mattson, 1991).

Sources of Help and Healing Today

God is "powerful medicine for sick souls and frustrated hopes." Considering the African American Baptist value and belief system, this may logically be translated as "God is more powerful than illness, can take away pain and mental or emotional confusion—but only in his own time." So, the believer must have faith and wait for deliverance, which may come in this life or in the next life (in heaven). Deliverance from physical, mental, and/or emotional pain and problems can come in a number of forms, including through mysterious spontaneous remission or through the ministrations of a teacher, physician, social worker, or other helper who is being used as God's instrument for healing.

Given that God is believed to work through others, the social worker should not be surprised to be asked about her or his own religious or spiritual beliefs and tradition. African American Baptist clients who ask may want to reassure themselves that they are in a client–social worker relationship in which they can get honest, direct answers. The social worker is encouraged to consult with colleagues if necessary and establish her or his own personal bounds and limits on religious or spiritual self-disclosure—with the understanding that some self-disclosure is important to gaining credibility with African American clients, while too much self-disclosure is considered offensive.

IMPLICATIONS FOR SOCIAL WORK AND COUNSELING PRACTICE

Some African American clients may enter the social work or counseling relationship with a number of defenses related to race as well as religion; others may not. Further, it cannot be assumed that a Black client's ancestry and religious tradition is rooted in slavery. A Black client may have, for example, Afro-Caribbean roots—and although West Africans were also involuntarily shipped to and enslaved in the Caribbean, history and religious traditions there evolved quite differently from those of people enslaved in the United States. In other words, it is important for social workers and counselors not to assume anything about the African American client's experience with race, oppression, and religion, yet to be aware of the paradoxical role religion in particular has played historically and continues to play in the lives of both religious and non-religious African Americans. The client must be allowed to tell her or his story. The social worker is further encouraged to investigate a client's degree of adherence to religious traditions and the extent to which Scripture is interpreted in the legalistic vein, based on ministerial teachings, especially since these may vary widely across church affiliations.

Historically, religion was used to keep slaves docile and obedient and to convince them to accept their lot in life. The Baptist and other Christian religions were used to advance the interests of slavery (Martin & Martin, 1985). Social workers and counselors are encouraged to avoid a deficit or deviance-based assessment of African Americans who criticize and/or turn away from religion for these reasons. A sample case record note made by a social worker using a deficit-based assessment is illustrated below, followed by a more empowerment/strengths-based case record note.

> *Deficit Model Case Note:* The fact that Mr. Jones does not attend church services with his wife and daughters suggests that he is unwilling to participate in an important aspect of family life that would help toward alleviation of their oldest daughter's problems with depression.

> *Empowerment Model Case Note:* While Mr. and Mrs. Jones hold different beliefs regarding church attendance and participation, they are willing to discuss the various spiritual roles they might take individually and as a couple to help toward alleviation of their oldest daughter's problems with depression.

Conversely, the African American church has played and continues to play a significant role in social change and the uplifting of the race. Religion has proven to be one way for African Americans to express traditional African consciousness, identity, self-worth, humanity, and morality (Martin & Martin, 1985). The history of African American Baptists is one of resiliency, resourcefulness, struggle, and self-help, cooperation, identity- and community-building, the socialization and education of children, the fight for civil rights, and the provision of social services.

Application of Knowledge about African American Baptists: A Case Example

Helping, flexible family roles, the inclusion of blood relatives and non-relatives in the family, and the high value placed on religion, education, and work are all characteristic strengths of African American families (Carter, 1995). Placing these types of behavior in the context of the history of psychosocial and economic oppression and related role adaptations is critical to effective assessment, problem delineation, and intervention.

For example, consider an impoverished, physically frail, single, African American grandmother who is rearing her children's children and even one or two of her great-grandchildren. This woman might be assessed as "co-dependent and enabling" if her situation were to be considered outside of the context of her religious beliefs, which place a high value on "taking care of one's own." In fact, this grandmother is likely preoccupied with doing whatever it takes to help her wards avoid the predominantly White-administered social service, foster care, and juvenile and adult justice systems. She may present to the social worker as smiling and constantly referring to "the Lord makin' a way somehow," or "the Lord don't put more on us than we can bear," or "I'm not going to be on this earth much longer so I've got to do what I can now." She and others like her, by and large are not enablers, or martyrs in the classic sense of these terms, but strongly religious and committed to the survival of their families. Her belief system abhors selfishness and individualism, and admires as heroines and heroes those who hold their own well-being second to the survival of children—thus, the survival of the race.

A strengths-based perspective that defines this grandmother's behavior and commitment as heroic is recommended. Normalizing her experience is important—for example, by providing her with relevant information, such as the fact that in 1990, U.S. Bureau of the Census data showed that two-thirds of African American children under age 18 lived with their grandparents (Grant, 1999). Creating a therapeutic environment that permits this grandmother to tell her story will provide the social worker with in-depth information regarding her values and beliefs, support system, and the barriers she faces. Then the social worker and the grandmother can cooperate in the therapeutic and/or case-management process and utilize old and new resources in ways the grandmother may not have previously considered. The social worker will also want to consider encouraging this grandmother to permit God to work through others to help her maintain her physical and mental health and quality of life, which will help the children survive and thrive. Reframing the introduction of the social worker, psychologist, and other resources and agencies into her life, when many of these systems have failed her in her efforts to raise her own children successfully, will prove a challenging endeavor. Ideally, the social worker should not simply refer the grandmother elsewhere and then discontinue involvement in the case. The chance of an encounter with an insensitive worker in another agency will make the grandmother's need to remain in contact with the social worker and to receive encouragement to "press on toward her goal" all the more important.

It should be noted that the application information presented in this chapter does not preclude considering clients' socioeconomic status, level of acculturation, family structure, and similar characteristics when defining and addressing problems.

CONCLUSION

Historically, African American Baptists and other religious African Americans have worked for the educational, social, civil, and economic advancement of the race. As we continue into the new millennium, it seems logical that African American Baptists will expand their role and challenge prejudices and biases that impede *any* people's advancement. Increasing socioeconomic stratification of African Americans may decrease their involvement in the church, resulting in decreased membership, particularly in inner-city churches. But the African American Baptist church can still remain the dominant cohesive institution in the community, providing for socioeconomic, educational, and political advancement. For this to happen, we must pursue an African American Baptist theology that is intimately connected to community life and people's real everyday problems and achievements—building programs, organizing, and empowering.

REFERENCES

Adherents.com (1999). *Adherent statistics and religious geography citations.* Retrieved June 21, 2001 from the World Wide Web: http://www.adherents.com

Asante, M. K. (1988). *Afrocentricity.* Trenton, NJ: Africa World Press.

Asante, M. K., & Mattson, M. T. (1991). *Historical and cultural atlas of African Americans.* New York: Simon & Schuster Macmillan.

Billingsly, A. (1992). *Climbing Jacob's ladder: The enduring legacy of African-American families.* New York: Touchstone/Simon & Schuster.

Bishop, P., & Darton, M. (1988). *The encyclopedia of world faiths.* New York: Facts on File.

Brandon, S. G. F. (1970). *A dictionary of comparative religion.* New York: Charles Scribner's Sons.

Brown, T. F. (1998). An African American woman's perspective: Renovating sorrow's kitchen. In C. M. Smith (Ed.), *Preaching justice: Ethnic and cultural perspectives* (pp. 43–61). Cleveland, OH: United Church Press.

Carter, R. T. (1995). *The influence of race and racial identity in psychotherapy: Toward a racially inclusive model.* New York: John Wiley & Sons.

Crim, K., Bullard, R. A., & Shinn, D. (Eds.). (1981). *Dictionary of living religions.* Nashville, TN: Abingdon.

Ellwood, R. S., & Alles, G. D. (1998). *The encyclopedia of world religions.* New York: Facts on File.

Fitts, L. (1985). *A history of black Baptists.* Nashville, TN: Broadman.

Grant, D. (1999). Effective therapeutic approaches with ethnic families. In C. Franklin & C. Jordan (Eds.), *Family practice: Brief systems methods for social work* (pp. 259–297). Pacific Grove, CA: Brooks/Cole.

Hays, B., & Steely, J. E. (1981). *The Baptist way of life* (2nd ed.). Macon, GA: Mercer University Press.

Hulse, E. (1973). *An introduction to the Baptists.* Cambridge, England: Carey Publications.

Ingram, L. (1998). Baptists. In W. H. Swatos, Jr. (Ed.), *Encyclopedia of religion and society* (pp. 40–41). Walnut Creek, CA: AltaMira.

Lindner, E. W. (1999). *1999 yearbook of American and Canadian churches.* Nashville, TN: Abingdon Press.

Martin, J. M., & Martin, E. P. (1985). *The helping tradition in the Black family and community.* Washington, DC: NASW Press.

McBeth, H. L. (1987). *The Baptist heritage.* Nashville, TN: Broadman Press.

Melton, J. G. (1996). *Encyclopedia of American religions* (5th ed.). Detroit: Gale.

Montgomery, W. E. (1993). *Under their own vine and fig tree: The African American church in the south, 1865–1970.* Baton Rouge: Louisiana State University Press.

Morales, A. T., & Sheafor, B. W. (1995). *Social work: A profession of many faces* (7th ed.). Boston: Allyn and Bacon.

Murphy, L. (1993). Religion in the African American community. In L. G. Murphy, J. G. Melton, & G. L. Ward (Eds.), *Encyclopedia of African American religions* (pp. xxxi–xxxv). New York: Garland.

Newsome, C. G. (1995). A synoptic survey of the history of African American Baptists. In W. J. Payne (Ed.), *Directory of African American religious bodies: A compendium by the Howard University School of Divinity,* (2nd ed.), (pp. 20–31). Washington, D.C.: Howard University Press.

ADDITIONAL RESOURCES

Books

Appiah, K. A., & Gates, H. L., Jr. (1999). *Africana: The encyclopedia of the African and African American experience.* New York: Perseus Books. Also available at http://www.africana.com/civitas/order.htm

Cleage, A. B., Jr. (1972). *Black Christian nationalism: New directions for the Black church.* New York: Morrow.

Davis, G. L. (1985). *I got the Word in me and I can sing it, you know: A study of the performed African-American sermon.* Philadelphia: University of Pennsylvania Press.

Franklin, J. H., & Moss, A. A., Jr. (1994). *From slavery to freedom: A history of African Americans* (7th ed.). New York: McGraw-Hill.

Paris, P. J. (1991). *Black religious leaders: Conflict in unity.* Louisville, KY: Westminster/John Knox Press.

Web Sites

The African American Mosaic:
http://www.lcweb.loc.gov/exhibits/african/intro.html

African American Perspectives:
http:/lcweb2.loc.gov/ammem/aap/aaphome.html

Africans in American: http://www.pbs.org/wgbh/aia/

African-American Religion in the Nineteenth Century:
http://www.nhc.rtp.nc.us:8080/tserve/nineteen/nkeyinfo/nafrican.htm or http://afroamculture.miningco.com/culture/

National Association for the Advancement of Colored People:
http://www.naacp.org/

National Urban League, Inc.: http://www.nul.org

PBS Teachers Guide to General Resources:
http://www.pbs.org/wgbh/aia/tguide/tggeneralresources.html

Schomburg Center for Research on Black Culture:
http://www.nypl.org/research/sc/sc.html

Videos

Guida, L. (Producer and Director). (1992). *Saturday night, Sunday morning: The travels of Gatemouth Moore* [Video]. San Francisco, CA: California Newsreel. This 70-minute video documents, through interviews and early photographs, the life of Arnold Dwight "Gatemouth" Moore, a prominent blues singer who left the stage at the height of his career to reach and sing Gospel music. Among those interviewed are Moore himself, Rufus Thomas, Andrew Chaplin, B. B. King, and Benjamin Hooks.

Kearns, L., Marquis, D. (Producers), & Kearns, K. (Director). (1988). *In remembrance of Martin* [Video]. This 60-minute video made for PBS is a tribute to Martin Luther King, Jr. composed of testimonies by his family, associates, and government leaders and documentary footage.

Willis, J. (Producer). (1966). *Lay my burden down* [Video]. Location: National Educational Television. This 59-minute video surveys the accomplishments of the civil rights movement during the year after the dramatic Selma-to-Montgomery march and the passage of the Voting Rights Act of 1965, as observed in the status of tenant farmers with average earnings of less than $1000 per year.

GLOSSARY

Abernathy, Ralph (1926–1990) Baptist minister who earned a master's degree from Atlanta University, worked with Martin Luther King, Jr., in coordinating the Montgomery bus boycott (1955) and during the civil rights movement, and assumed presidency of the Southern Christian Leadership Conference (1968–1977) following King's death.

African Methodist Episcopal Church Church founded in 1816 by Richard Allen, in response to an unbending policy of segregated seating in Philadelphia's White Methodist church.

Allen, Richard (1760–1831) Born a slave, Allen converted to Christianity in 1777, bought his freedom, and formed the African Methodist Episcopal Church in 1816. Allen was consecrated as the church's first bishop.

Baptism by immersion A sacramental rite that admits a candidate to the Christian church, involves submersion in a pool of water (in contrast to the baptismal practice of *affusion,* having sacred water poured or sprinkled on the head). Baptists assume that those wishing to join the church require sufficient maturity to make a religious decision; thus, there is no infant baptism in the Baptist faith.

Confession of faith A declaration of religious belief.

Father, Son, and the Holy Spirit Trinity In Christian theology, God has three cosubstantial, coequal, and coeternal parts.

King, Martin Luther Jr. (1929–1968) Civil rights leader, Baptist minister, prime mover of the Montgomery bus boycott of 1955, and youngest Nobel Peace Prize laureate (1964). Attended Crozer Theological Seminary in Chester, Pennsylvania and was granted a doctoral degree in 1955. First president of the Southern Christian Leadership Conference.

National Association for the Advancement of Colored People (NAACP) Interracial organization established in 1910 with the merging of the Niagara Movement of W. E. B. DuBois and a group of concerned Whites (including social worker Jane Addams). Early efforts focused on eradicating lynching. Primarily created to work for the abolition of segregation and discrimination in housing, education, voting, and transportation; to oppose racism; and to ensure African Americans their constitutional rights.

National Baptist Convention of America One of the two largest African American Christian denominations in the United States, established in 1915 as the result of a schism within the National Baptist Convention U.S.A.

National Baptist Convention U.S.A., Inc. Formed in 1895, one of the two largest African American Christian denominations in the United States.

National Urban League Established in 1910, an interracial, nonprofit, nonpartisan community service organization that uses tools of social work, economics, law, and other disciplines to secure equal opportunities in all sectors of society for African Americans and other minorities.

Powell, Adam Clayton Sr. (1865–1953) Baptist minister and father of the late Harlem Congressman, Powell Sr. attended the Yale University School of Divinity and later pastored Abyssinian Baptist Church in Harlem.

Regeneration The spiritual rebirth which, according to traditional theology, is effected in the soul by Christian baptism.

Resiliency The ability to spring back or rebound after adversity or deformation; irrepressible life and liveliness.

Revival A type of religious worship during which religious ferver and confessions of faith are stimulated by intensive preaching and prayer.

Self-help tradition In the context of the African American Baptist Church, efforts to achieve social and political gains for African Americans.

12 CHAPTER

SEVENTH-DAY ADVENTISTS

CURTIS J. VANDERWAAL
DARYL McMULLEN

HISTORY AND DESCRIPTION OF THE RELIGIOUS TRADITION

The Seventh-day Adventist church was officially organized in 1863, although its roots can be traced back to the Protestant Reformation and the great American religious awakening of the early 19th century. This religious renewal grew out of a renewed interest in Bible prophecy. A New England Baptist farmer named William Miller, founder of the Millerite Movement, began preaching about the prophecies in the books of Daniel and Revelation. His detailed study convinced him that the prophecies foretold the end of the world and the return of Christ to earth. He determined that this event would occur on October 22, 1844. As the date approached, "Crops were left unharvested; potatoes undug. Shops were closed; workers resigned from their posts. Nothing was important except that Christ was coming in a few days" (Schwarz, 1979, p. 50). However, October 22, 1844 came and went without the return of Christ. To those who had joined the Millerite Movement and placed their faith in the "blessed hope" that the end was near, the day was simply known as The Great Disappointment. Confusion and embarrassment followed, and many gave up their faith in God all together. Among those who continued to believe, one group returned to the Biblical prophecies to discover what had gone wrong. They concluded that this date did not signify the end of the world, but rather the day when Jesus was beginning a new phase of his heavenly ministry on behalf of all believers. This understanding led to the development of five distinctive Adventist doctrines: the Sabbath, the Remnant, the Sanctuary, the Investigative Judgement, and the Health Message (described below). The church quickly spread to over 3000 members by 1863.

Among this new group of believers was a woman named Ellen G. White. Born in 1827, she had become a Millerite at age 12 and endured The Great Disappointment at age 17. She remained with the small group of believers who felt that the Bible prophecies had been misunderstood. She began to experience visions, which she believed came from God. Her first vision occurred in December of 1844, and hundreds more followed. In these visions, she received what was considered to be divine instruction from God regarding doctrine, church organization, and personal behavior. She also wrote prolifically on other topics such as education, health, the life of Christ, the importance of the church community, and the Great Controversy between God and Satan. Although she never referred to herself as a prophetess, the Adventist church affirms her in this status. The official church position on her writings is that they "enhance our appreciation of the Bible" (Rice, 1997, p. 223), but some church members have argued that her writings have taken a position equal to, and sometimes greater than, the Bible. Indeed, quotations from "Sister White" form a large part of the basis of the beliefs of many church members and are used to defend behavior and doctrinal positions. Until her death in 1915, White's leadership was crucial to the development and growth of both the structure and doctrines of the Seventh-day Adventist church. Ironically, despite the fact that White was a woman, the highly hierarchical organizational structure of the church is predominantly male.

UNIQUE ADVENTIST BELIEFS AND INSTITUTIONS

With respect to core doctrines regarding the creation of the world, the natures of God and humanity, the life, death, and resurrection of Jesus, and the nature of salvation, Adventists have a great deal in common with other Christian denominations, particularly those within an evangelical tradition (see Dederen's *Handbook of Seventh-day Adventist Theology,* 2000, for more detailed explanations of these doctrines). The five uniquely Adventist doctrines referred to earlier (and described below) help to better explain why Adventists think and behave as they do. Education and evangelism are also important to Adventists' core mission of spreading "the end-time message" to the world.

The name "Seventh-day Adventist" identifies two of the central beliefs of the denomination. Members worship on the seventh day of the week—that is, on Saturday (the Sabbath)—and believe in the imminence of the Advent, or second coming of Christ. The seventh-day Sabbath is perhaps the most important and unique Adventist belief. Early Adventists believed that sin was the direct violation of one or more of the Ten Commandments and so sought to understand the true meaning of each. Their study led them to agree with the Jewish and Seventh-day Baptist traditions, which taught that the Sabbath mentioned in the Fourth Commandment ("Remember the Sabbath day, to keep it holy," Exodus 20:8–11) was to be observed on the seventh day of the week—Saturday. In addition to weekly church attendance, most Adventists keep the Sabbath by engaging in fellowship with family and friends, enjoying nature (since the Sabbath is seen as a memorial of God's creation), and shunning activities that take their minds off God. On the Sabbath, Adventists generally avoid working at all but the most necessary jobs, making any purchases, traveling unnecessarily, or participating in most forms of entertainment and media. (The definition of "appropriate Sabbath behaviors" is hotly debated among Adventists.) These beliefs are closely tied to the "Remnant" message.

The Remnant doctrine is the belief that Adventists, at the end of earthly time, will be the church that "keeps the commandments of God, and the faith of Jesus" (Revelation 14:12). Adventists believe it is their mission to spread this Gospel about the commandments of God (including keeping the Sabbath as a unique sign of loyalty to God), and the faith in Jesus (that he will soon return). They do not believe that they are the only ones in the Remnant, but that they will be part of it in a special way, because of their unique perspective on the Sabbath.

A related doctrine is that of a literal sanctuary in heaven, where Christ reviews the records of the dead to determine who will be included in heaven at the end of time. Adventists believe that Christ finished this job on October 22, 1844 (see above) and then entered another portion of the sanctuary, where he is currently reviewing the records of the living for inclusion or exclusion from heaven. This period, called the Investigative Judgement, is thought to be a prelude to the Time of Trouble, when Christ will make his final decisions about the eternal salvation of the living. During the Time of Trouble, all believers will be left without his intercession on their behalf in the Heavenly Sanctuary, and unbelievers will persecute the faithful. Believers must be "right with God" and judged perfect prior to this Close of Probation, or they will not be saved. Many Adventists have a great deal of fear about this Time of Trouble because they believe that they may be judged unworthy of salvation because of their inability to live up to God's laws and demands perfectly.

Another large part of the Seventh-day Adventist belief system concerns the Health Message. Inspired by both the temperance movement of the late 19th and early 20th centuries and Ellen G. White's visions, church members began to search the Bible for suggestions on healthful living, which they considered essential to the development of a perfect body, mind, and spirit. Healthful living was (and for many, still is) believed to prepare one for heaven. The verse "Or do you not know that your body is the temple of the Holy Spirit who is in you, whom you have from God, and you are not your own?" (I Corinthians 6:19) became the driving force behind such healthful living habits as a vegetarian diet, and abstinence from tobacco, alcohol, illegal drugs, coffee, tea, and caffeinated carbonated beverages. Many Adventists refrain from eating meat; a minority are strict vegetarians (vegan), who do not eat eggs or dairy products. Some Adventists do eat what the Bible calls "clean" meats (beef, chicken, fish, and lamb), while avoiding pork and shellfish.

John Harvey Kellogg, who, along with his brother, W. K. Kellogg, helped establish Kellogg's breakfast cereals, pushed to get the church health movement started, through his work at the Western Health Reform Institute. Later at the Battle Creek Sanitarium, founded in 1866, he and other early church pioneers developed a place where people could come to learn how to stay well. Hydrotherapy and other natural remedies were used to increase physical well-being. The sanitarium was a first link in a network of health care provided by the Seventh-day Adventist church that continues to this day, with over 600 hospitals, clinics, retirement homes, and orphanages around the world (General Conference of Seventh-day Adventists, 2000a).

The Seventh-day Adventist church also determined to provide Christian education as part of its wholistic training of children and youth. The Adventist system of education serves as a method of raising children in the doctrines of the church as well as "protecting" them from the larger, secular educational systems. Today, the church operates over 5500 schools (elementary grades through high school) and over 80 colleges and universities (Adventist News Network, 1997).

International evangelism began early in the history of the church. The church currently operates many publishing houses and translates books, magazines, pamphlets, quarterlies, and other devotional material into 229 languages. Adventist media in the form of television and radio programs have also grown. The church uses television, radio, and the Internet to increase the spread and availability of the Gospel. Other major programs include community service initiatives in many U.S. locations and worldwide disaster relief and development in foreign countries. The evangelistic nature of the church has resulted in relatively modest growth in North America but dramatic increases internationally. The church as a whole grew from roughly 2 million members in 1970 to well over 11 million members in 2000, with established churches in 205 countries (General Conference of Seventh-day Adventists, 2000b).

The church's current structure is highly centralized, with the Washington, DC-based General Conference (GC) being the highest governing body. This organization coordinates the world church's growth and stability and ensures consistency in doctrine. There are four levels under the GC: 12 worldwide geographical divisions, 90 medium-sized unions, 483 even smaller conferences, and almost 45,000 individual churches (General Conference of Seventh-day Adventists, 2000b). The leadership of the top three levels is made up of individuals who have been democratically elected by proportional member representation. Pastors of individual churches are educated through the worldwide network of Adventist colleges and universities (bachelor's, master's, and Ph.D. degrees are available) and are selected by the leaders of the individual conferences. Pastors are expected to uphold church doctrines and to seek counsel from the local conference in important church matters. Pastors are generally men, because a majority of church representatives have remained unwilling to allow women to be ordained. The pastors of individual churches (within each division) are paid equally by their conference (throughout each division), regardless of the church's size or membership (Neufeld, 1976). Individual churches pay tithes (10% of their gross earnings) to the local conference, which sends a portion of the money up to the GC for world church projects and proportionally redistributes the rest to the churches throughout the conference.

Combined, these initiatives and beliefs create a uniquely Adventist lifestyle, internally known as "being in the world, but not of the world." This Biblical phrase refers to living in the world without adopting "worldly" values and behaviors. Though the verse speaks more of attitude and behavior, the church has created an environment in which a person can also live physically apart from the world, in Adventist communities. A person can be born in an Adventist hospital, go to school in the Adventist school system (kindergarten through graduate school), work for an Adventist business or organization, retire in an Adventist retirement center, and finally, come full circle by dying in an Adventist hospital.

Another reason for these lifestyle differences is the belief in the Seventh-day Sabbath. With most Protestant Christians worshiping on Sunday, the Sabbath becomes yet another peculiarity that places an unseen barrier around the church. These factors, along with the conservative behavioral standards held by most Adventists (described in the following section), all combine to make Adventists feel "peculiar," the Biblical term that Adventists have applied to describe themselves as being set apart from the world (General Conference of Seventh-day Adventists, 1988).

CURT VANDERWAAL'S JOURNEY AS AN ADVENTIST SOCIAL WORKER

I grew up in a third-generation Seventh-day Adventist home. My upbringing was typical of that of many Adventists, which meant that certain behaviors were automatically forbidden. I could not dance, wear jewelry or "immodest" clothing, listen to rock, jazz, or other modern forms of music, eat "unclean" meat, have sex without being married, gamble or play cards, go to movie theaters, or watch "unwholesome" TV programs. The Sabbath, which lasted from sundown on Friday night to sundown on Saturday night, was meant to be spent attending church, walking quietly in nature, reflecting upon God's goodness, doing good for those who were less fortunate, and witnessing to others about the Truth of Adventism. We were not allowed to swim, ride bikes, watch television, shop, go out to eat, or, in general, "do our own pleasure" during the Sabbath hours. While it had many restrictions, Sabbath was also a special family time that my parents spent entirely with us kids. During those hours, we read religious stories, played religious games, went to church, and took nature walks.

I grew up feeling different from non-Adventists because of these beliefs and behaviors, but was mostly shielded from discomfort because I went to an Adventist school and an Adventist church and had only Adventist friends. Like many other Adventists, I felt a lot of guilt about not being good enough to merit God's favor, because our church taught that a person must eventually become perfect in order to get to heaven. I remember occasional dreams in which Jesus returned in the Second Coming, only to find that I wasn't good enough to make it into heaven. I was especially scared of the Time of Trouble.

Growing up Adventist has also meant living with the occasional notoriety that comes when institutions or church members make the news. On the positive side, I was proud but also a little embarrassed to be associated with the Loma Linda University Medical Center, where the first heart transplant from a baboon to "Baby Fae" took place. On the negative side, I was ashamed to be distantly associated with the Branch Davidians, a radical offshoot of Adventism led by David Koresh. The group made headlines in 1993, starting with a shootout with FBI agents in Waco, Texas and ending in an inferno as members were incinerated in a self-fulfilling apocalyptic tragedy. While this group had many extremely strange beliefs and practices and had no direct connection to the formal church, some have estimated that 90% of those who died at Waco came directly from Seventh-day Adventist families (Branson, 1993). I personally went to an Adventist church school with one of those who died in the fire and was taught typing by another. While Adventists don't condone weapons stockpiling, polygamous marriages, or drinking in bars, persecution and other Time of Trouble themes remain common in Adventism, despite our attempts to distance ourselves from the bizarre and tragic branches of our family tree.

I also remember many positive things about growing up as an Adventist. There was a sense of assurance and belonging in believing that I knew the Truth (although this can also result in Adventists' having a sense of superiority over those of other religions). I had the security of being surrounded by a community of people who believed the same things I did. My identity was clearly defined, and I felt I had clear answers to life's big questions. Because I felt very strongly about keeping up a good relationship with God, I worked as hard as I could to always do and say the "right thing." My strict religious belief system kept me from experimenting with alcohol, drugs, or tobacco, which I believed would have caused me physical or emotional damage. I also liked my experience of a personal connection to God. That connection was empowering and reassuring to me since I felt connected with a God who cared about all my needs and problems.

Our church has a strong mission and outreach emphasis, which continues to influence my social work career. I grew up hearing and reading thrilling stories of missionaries in exotic locations who had miraculous experiences and brought about dramatic conversions while serving God. Although we were not normally expected to interact with non-Adventists ("non-believers," we called them), we regularly participated in a number of "outreach" activities, which were designed to either influence non-Adventists to join our church or help someone less fortunate. A good activity accomplished both. For instance, our school classes regularly chose outreach projects such as going to local nursing homes to sing religious songs and socialize; raking and doing yard work for the elderly; collecting food door-to-door at Thanksgiving; or collecting money for disaster-relief projects in front of neighborhood stores and around the community (a yearly project, which we called Ingathering). These local mission projects undoubtedly influenced my decision to become a social worker.

Whenever I was in the company of non-Adventists, I felt embarrassed about my differences. This discomfort became particularly acute when I attended my first non-Adventist school for my M.S.W. degree. I remember feeling like I didn't fit in a secular environment, and when I was invited to Friday night or Saturday activities, I would make vague excuses or stumbling explanations about my faith. I developed most of my friendships with other Adventists in a local church, but also started some friendships with non-Adventists. During that time, I started to understand and appreciate other worldviews and was also forced to balance my personal faith with my professional social work values. This was quite a struggle for me, but I was helped on my journey by another social worker at my first job, who helped me process and integrate my beliefs into a more coherent framework. I was thrilled when I found out that my religious values could, in many ways, be reconciled with social work values. In talking with social workers from other faith traditions, I now realize that this search for an integration of religious and professional values and beliefs is a common experience, which often requires modifications in both belief and value systems.

While many of my friends have left the Adventist church, I have remained a member. I no longer have the same childhood sense of the exclusive superiority of my belief system, but my community provides me with a number of other things. First, Seventh-day Adventism is a major part of my personal identity. Despite my feelings of embarrassment over growing up in a religious tradition that was out of the mainstream, Adventism has shaped who I am and what I believe. Second, Adventism creates a shared sense of community. There's something reassuring about knowing that I have so much in common with others who have had similar feelings, experiences, language references, history, and beliefs. This connectedness radiates out to people and places all over the world. Any Adventist, particularly in North America or Northern Europe, can go into any Adventist church and almost always find someone with whom he or she has a mutual acquaintance. Third, I appreciate many of my church's behavioral standards. For example,

I like the health-related benefits that come from being a teetotaler and a vegetarian. I especially appreciate the benefits of the Sabbath. Our family lights candles on Friday night and spends time reading, playing games, working on craft projects, or just talking. Sabbath is a time of worship, eating leisurely meals with family and friends, walking in nature, or resting. This sort of weekly ritual offers a wonderful break from the pressures of work, school, and the consumer culture. Finally, I like my church's commitment to improving social conditions around the world. The Adventist Development and Relief Association has often worked shoulder-to-shoulder with the Red Cross and other humanitarian relief agencies to ease the suffering of disaster victims, develop micro-enterprises in poor countries, and create more humane social policies in international settings. In the United States, Adventists work through local churches to collect and distribute food and clothing, respond to national and local disasters, and develop comprehensive community centers to meet the physical, social, emotional, and spiritual needs of the local community. This sort of practical Christianity inspires and motivates me to act with compassion, relieve suffering and pain, and make the world a better place. Overall, although my church is far from perfect, it offers me a sense of identity, community, lifestyle, and social mission. For these reasons, I stay in and feel nurtured by my community of faith.

MEANING OF MAJOR LIFE EVENTS

Adventists share much in common with other conservative Christians in matters concerning the big questions in life: "When and where did life begin?" "Who are we?" "What is the meaning and purpose of life?" and "How do you explain suffering and death?"

The Origins of Life and Human Identity

Adventists believe that the Trinity (God, Son, and Holy Spirit) has existed forever in heaven. Most Adventists believe that God created the world and human beings in 7 literal days, approximately 6000 years ago. God created humans, Adam and Eve, perfect and in his image. While they were created to live forever, he gave them free will so that they could choose to serve and love him. On the seventh day, the Sabbath, God rested to commemorate his creation and proclaimed the day to be one for rest and worship.

At some point, the angel Lucifer (now known as Satan) waged a war on God and was banned from heaven. He was able to come to the earth, where he tempted Adam and Eve to commit the first sin. Upon learning of this disobedience, God banned the couple from the garden and cursed the land. In addition, humans were forever required to work for their survival and inherited sinful human natures, thus making them prone to selfish and evil behaviors.

The Purpose of Existence

Adventists believe that God created intelligent, sinless life forms on other planets in the universe. They believe that, since the big battle between Lucifer and Michael (an archangel who fought for God), Lucifer (Satan) has tried to convince the rest of the sinless universe that God is unfair. Adventists call this ongoing conflict The Great Controversy. In essence, the earth has become a showcase designed to reveal Christ's love to sinful human beings. Adventists believe that Jesus proved his goodness and Satan's evil when he became human, lived, and died on the cross. However, God allows human suffering to continue in order to give as many people as possible a chance to accept Jesus' sacrifice on the cross as an atonement for their sins. Adventists also find special meaning in their personal relationship with God. It is this personal relationship that gives strength and motivation to live holy lives and also inspires Adventists to tell others about Jesus' love for them.

Adventists' primary goal is to tell as many people as possible about Jesus before he returns. Religious meaning and purpose are found in sharing the special end-time message of the Sabbath and Jesus' imminent return.

The Meaning of Suffering and Death

Because of Adam and Eve's Original Sin, suffering and death became a natural part of the human condition. Adventists believe that God cares deeply about human suffering and has the power to stop bad things from happening. However, he does not usually intervene, for two reasons. First, Satan brought evil to the world and continues to try to create as many problems for God and his creation as he possibly can, because this brings pain to God. Bad things continue to happen to people who believe in God because he cannot give special protection to those who believe in him. If he did, Satan would accuse God of playing favorites and people would only follow God because they wanted special treatment or were afraid of the consequences if they did not follow him. Above all, God must prove that he plays fair with the universe. He must also convince humans to serve him out of love, not fear. Second, God created humans with the free will to make their own decisions. This means that sometimes people make poor choices and end up suffering the natural consequences of those choices. However, even though God cannot always intervene and protect his people, the Holy Spirit is always with us in our suffering, offering comfort and assurance of God's love.

Ultimately, all humans die as a natural consequence of Original Sin. They can be raised again in a final resurrection at Christ's Second Coming by asking forgiveness for their sins and accepting Jesus' substitutionary death on the cross. Satan will then be judged guilty and destroyed, while those who have accepted Christ into their lives will live forever. In keeping with an Adventist interpretation of hell, those who choose not to accept Jesus will be quickly and forever destroyed by fire in an action that will cause great pain to God (for a more complex explanation of this doctrine, see Dederen, 2000).

SOURCES OF POWER

The sources of power for an Adventist are very similar to those enjoyed by members of other Protestant churches. This section and those that follow will describe those sources and offer suggestions that may help clinicians better understand their clients' perspectives and help them to tap into these sources of power, hope, and comfort.

Prayer, the Holy Spirit, and Reflection

Prayer permits direct communication with God. It can be offered either publicly or privately. The Holy Spirit helps people know what to pray, advocates on their behalf before God, and gives believers spiritual gifts to help in church ministry. Reflection should not be mistaken for Eastern-style meditation or New Age visualization or relaxation. Rather, reflection can be described as turning one's thoughts to spiritual things. This may include contemplating how God has worked in one's life, how he is working in the lives of others, and how he has worked in the past through Bible stories or nature. For example, a person may read the Bible and then reflect on the meaning of a particular verse for her own life.

Although it is often helpful and important to refer a client to his or her church pastor, this approach may not always be feasible or helpful. There are times when the clinician may find it useful to discuss with a client the role of prayer or the Holy Spirit in the client's life. Clients may think they are not praying "correctly" or that they are not worthy enough to pray. In such cases they may find it reassuring to hear that there is no special formula for prayer, and that it is as easy as talking to a friend on the phone. They may also be encouraged to know that the Holy Spirit interprets their prayers and presents them to God as a special message from one of his children. Similarly, a client may not have an understanding of what reflection is, or may be "out of practice." A clinician might help the client to discuss how reflecting on God's promises can lead to a more meaningful life. This is similar to cognitive restructuring, whereby a clinician would help a client focus on positive thoughts.

Bible Study

Adventists gain strength and comfort by reading the Bible. It provides assurance of God's leading, as well as strengthening faith and promoting character development. Adventists believe that those who wrote the Bible were inspired by the Holy Spirit. The Bible is therefore believed to be an infallible guide for Christian belief and experience. As a person reads the Bible, the Holy Spirit opens his mind and helps him understand and apply what he is reading. There are many verses in the Bible that offer assurance of God's love and include promises and suggestions for daily living. A clinician with little background in the Bible can still ask if there are verses that are meaningful to the client and suggest that these verses can be sources of power and strength in the client's life. If these verses seem to create doubt or fear, it is important to involve a pastor who will bring credibility to the dialogue and balance to the client's interpretations of Scripture.

The Writings of Ellen G. White

The writings of Ellen G. White are another source of power for Adventists, particularly for conservative or older church members. These writings are useful in interpreting the Bible and offer helpful information on living the Adventist lifestyle. Many who read her books find hope, comfort, and guidance when depressed, anxious, or confused. Her writings cover a broad range of topics, including parenting, health, money management, education, evangelism, medicine, spirituality, and extensive commentary on the Bible. These writings have, at times, been misused to make people feel guilty for their behavior and their failure to "measure up" to the standards of the church (Bull & Lockhart, 1989). Clinicians might question clients about the role these writings have played in their lives. They may be a source of power for some and pain for others. Some clients may feel they can never measure up to the behavioral expectations of these writings, so it is important to help them understand that perfection is the work of a lifetime and that God's grace covers their imperfections.

Lesson Study and Church Service

Adventists place a high value on attending Saturday morning church services. These services are seen as a way to worship God, connect with other believers, and strengthen one's faith. The service includes a "Sabbath School," where a General Conference-selected Bible lesson is discussed. The Lesson Study Guide containing the Bible lesson is a tool to help in daily Bible study, and also ensures consistency of doctrinal belief and study throughout the world church. Many Adventist Christians use this source of power daily. Sabbath School is followed by church, a worship service that includes the pastor's sermon.

Some Adventists can become estranged from the church as a result of guilt over their behaviors or a relationship problem with another church member. Clinicians might find it helpful to question a client about church attendance and the use of the Lesson Study, to determine if they are sources of power. If so, clients should be encouraged to make use of these resources.

Denominational Magazines, Books, Media, and the Internet

Publishing has allowed the Adventist church to reach large portions of the world with its unique message, ensure continuity of the belief system, and nurture spiritual growth among members. In addition to publishing a large number of books, the church provides several weekly publications designed to provide news, inspiration, and doctrinal support to its members. Clinicians may also suggest that clients access the Internet, where they can find the official home page of the Seventh-day Adventist church (www.adventist.org) as well as unofficial sites, chat rooms, and links to other Christian resources.

Pastors

In the Adventist church, the pastor has always played the dual roles of preacher and spiritual guide/counselor. For most people, the pastor is the primary person to call when they need advice, when someone has died, or when a child has run away from home. Although largely untrained in counseling, the typical pastor provides marriage counseling before a wedding, and marriage advice for troubled couples and performs baby dedications, commencement services at graduations, and eulogies at funerals. Because many people view a pastor as God's earthly ambassador, there are times when no one but a pastor can reach a person in his or her time of need. Clinicians should find out who a client's pastor is and to what extent support in the client's life. The pastor not only can be contacted for additional help with doctrinal questions, but may also be a key contact person for the client in mobilizing a support system.

RITUALS AND PRACTICES

Potlucks, Prayer Meetings, and Camp Meetings

After the church service, many churches invite members and visitors to a traditional "potluck," or church lunch, to which every family brings a favorite dish. This tradition is a fun way to welcome visitors and also builds a sense of community among church members.

Another tradition is the midweek service (usually referred to as Prayer Meeting), a time dedicated to in-depth Bible study and prayer. Prayer meetings are often small, making them a good way to spend more time with the pastor and improve one's relationship with God and other members.

Camp meetings were a traditional way for Adventists to meet for a week of spiritual revival, socialization, and summer vacation. While camp meetings are still conducted, they have gradually become shorter and less well-attended and are now often held in gymnasiums at Adventist secondary schools or colleges rather than in large fields and huge meeting tents.

Children's Traditions

Vacation Bible School (a 10-day period of Bible study and activities) and Pathfinders (similar to the Scouts) teach children and adolescents about Jesus through nature and craft activities. Adventist elementary and secondary schools also encourage children to participate in health and temperance clubs, where they learn about the adverse effects of drugs and alcohol. Pathfinders and temperance clubs were established by Adventists to educate youth about beliefs and lifestyle and also reinforce Adventist social networks.

Sabbath School also has a separate component for children and youth. The General Conference has developed a curriculum of age-appropriate Bible education materials to be used in Sabbath School.

The Lord's Supper, Foot Washing, and Anointing

The Lord's Supper (also referred to as Communion) and the ritual of Foot Washing are traditions held every quarter (every 13 weeks) to commemorate the death of Jesus and his acts of service to his followers. Foot Washing (which takes place just prior to Communion) is the time when a believer can make amends to someone he or she has wronged. Two people wash each other's feet in pans of warm water (a symbolic act of humility) and pray that God will help them maintain their friendship and commitment to God. After Foot Washing, church members take Communion. The unleavened bread and grape juice are taken as symbols of Jesus' body that was broken and his blood that was shed for the believer.

The church also has a tradition of "anointing" a person when an illness or accident becomes lifethreatening. At times like this, a pastor and a group of elders (church-appointed leaders) lay their hands on the sick person, pray, and pour a small amount of oil on the person's head. The pastor may offer a prayer such as "Lord, if it is your will, we ask for your healing hand to be on this person. If it is not in your plan for healing to occur, we ask that you give us the strength to accept it and to give this person into your care." This tradition is a powerful way for church members to show support for the ill person and also provides comfort to the other family members. While this ceremony is typically done by the church pastor or elders, a chaplain or other church pastor might also fill this role if Adventist church members are unavailable.

FAMILY LIFE-CYCLE TRANSITIONS

Birth and Childhood

Adventists believe that God creates everyone for a purpose. Consequently, each new life is celebrated as a gift from God. When a baby is born, the entire church family rejoices with the new parents by holding a baby shower to show material and emotional support for the family. Within the first year, the baby is dedicated during a regular church service. During this service, the pastor prays for the baby and briefly talks with the parents about their role in raising the child within the church. Because of its strong emphasis on healthy family life, the Adventist church has created books and videos to help new parents plan for and adjust to the stresses of bringing a new life into the world. Some larger churches offer support groups for women with new and very young children.

The next transition, Baptism by immersion, takes place when the child becomes old enough to understand the meaning of Jesus' death on the cross, usually around age 11 or 12. Baptism allows a person to publicly affirm his or her belief in Jesus' salvation and forgiveness. In each ritual, the church community is encouraged to do all that it can to support the children and keep them faithful to the church. Adventists believe that children who die before Baptism will be judged mercifully by God.

Adventists believe in using contraception. While they generally disapprove of abortion ("Abortion," 1989; Winslow, 1988), they also believe that each woman must make the decision that she thinks is best. Most Adventists are strongly opposed to laws that ban abortion, or any other state attempts to control personal behavior, primarily because of their strong beliefs about the need for a strong separation between church and state (Dudley & Hernandez, 1992).

Marriage

The Adventist church supports a sacred, lifetime commitment between heterosexual partners. The marriage ceremony should be conducted by an ordained Adventist minister. This service binds the couple together before God and the community. Rings are generally not exchanged in the service because these are considered to be jewelry, which is an unacceptable physical adornment. (This standard has been relaxed somewhat in recent years.) Alcohol and dancing are not part of the wedding reception.

Young people are strongly counseled to remain celibate before marriage. For many Adventists, one of the primary functions of Adventist colleges and universities is to provide a place where young people can meet other Adventists. Those who are caught having sex without being married are sometimes publicly shamed in the church (although this varies greatly from church to church) and are usually forced to withdraw from the school they are attending, particularly if the girl becomes pregnant. Separate dormitories are maintained for men and women.

Divorce

Divorce is tolerated, but strongly discouraged, within the Adventist church. The more traditional view holds that divorce is not permitted except in the case of confirmed adultery by one of the spouses. If a divorce occurs without proof of adultery, neither partner is expected to re-marry. Within traditional Adventist congregations, divorced persons are not permitted to hold church leadership positions and often live with a sense of shame for their actions. Because of a relatively recent rise in divorce rates among Adventists, some churches are broadening the church-sanctioned grounds for divorce to include domestic violence and emotional abuse. In areas with large concentrations of

Adventists, divorce support groups are becoming popular. In addition, divorce-recovery literature is now being published by the church.

Making Major Life Decisions

Most Adventists believe that God has a plan for each person's life. That plan includes divine guidance on choosing a marriage partner, a career, and even a major purchase such as a house or car. Church members are advised to turn their lives and will over to God's care and leading. They are expected to pray about all major decisions and to rely on God's leading when making those decisions. Divine direction might come through Bible study, prayer and meditation, or through the counsel of a godly friend or church leader. Many believe that following this approach will result in good decisions and blessings from God. Those who make decisions without using such methods can expect disappointment and heartache. Clinicians may need to address the pain of clients who have done all the "right" behaviors, yet are still experiencing personal hardships. Discussions about God's gift of free will as well as personal misfortunes can be helpful.

Personal Misfortunes

Personal misfortunes such as car accidents, miscarriages, unexpected deaths, and other tragedies are not considered to be part of God's plan. The evil in the world is considered to be a natural result of sin, often initiated by Satan. However, some conservative church members consider all misfortune to be part of God's divine plan, even though he does not create the evil. They might try to comfort those who are hurting or grieving by saying things such as "God never gives us more than we can bear," "It is God's will that this has happened," "God allowed this to happen to strengthen (or test) your faith," or "Have faith that this tragedy happened for a reason that will become clear at the Second Coming." Clinicians might find it useful to help the client determine the meaning of such statements in the context of the loss. They might also help the client to understand that a loving God would not directly cause pain and suffering and that he is big enough to handle any anger or pain directed toward him.

Death

Death is an enemy and is not considered to be a part of God's original creation. When a death does occur, the church family is expected to support those who are grieving through expressions of condolence, prayers, gifts of food, or other practical assistance. Men and women are expected to grieve with dignity. Those who are grieving are generally expected to maintain faith in God's divine wisdom and love throughout the grief process. Adventists do not believe that souls go to heaven at death, but rather that death is a form of unconsciousness, described in the Bible as "sleep." The funeral service is usually held in the church. The service traditionally includes a eulogy, reminiscences by family and friends, religious hymns, and a sermon from the pastor. The pastor reminds the mourners that, while death has been temporarily victorious, Christ's death on the cross means that all who die "in Christ" are temporarily sleeping (referred to as the First Death) but can look forward to a bodily resurrection at Christ's Second Coming. The pastor also generally uses this time to encourage those who have not "made things right" with God to do so, because of the uncertainty of life. This is particularly true if the person who has died was not known to have given his or her life to Christ before dying.

A short memorial service at the graveside generally follows the church service. At that time, the body is committed to God and buried. A potluck dinner in the church basement or fellowship hall traditionally follows the service. Larger churches are beginning to develop grief seminars and support groups for grieving family members and friends. In addition, the church publishes a number of resources designed to give hope and comfort to grieving individuals.

CONCEPTIONS OF HEALTH AND APPROPRIATE SOURCES OF HELP

Physical Health

Physical health is extremely important to Adventists. A large proportion of Adventists are vegetarians, and most Adventists believe that the Health Message is one of the Adventism's major contributions to society. Many churches use cooking classes and the numerous Adventist medical centers and hospitals as evangelistic tools to attract new members to the church. Adventists not only believe that the physical body is God's temple, they also believe that healthful living prepares them for heaven. Some within the church have more recently criticized this belief as an attempt to achieve perfection through "works" rather than relying on God's grace and acceptance.

Mental Health

Most Adventists believe that Satan is constantly seeking to gain control of a person's will and allegiance and that these evil influences can enter the mind through impure television and movies, rock or rap music, novels, and other sources. Because God gives humans free will to make good or bad choices, it is important to "guard the avenues to the soul" by avoiding these influences. Prayer, Bible study, and willpower are the three primary methods used by Adventists to resist evil impulses.

Adventists have much in common with other conservative churches with regard to ideas about mental health and illness. Many Adventists, particularly those with minimal education, do not believe in a physiological basis for mental illness. Problems such as depression, anxiety, or drug addiction are believed to be manifestations of Satan's attempts to control a person's will. They are best solved through Bible study, prayer, and, in more extreme cases, counseling with one's pastor. It is widely believed that God is able to offer victory over these problems if a person truly wants to change the behavior and asks God for the power to change. Many Adventists are suspicious of mental health professionals, believing that they are using Godless, mind-controlling methods to combat what could be more appropriately accomplished through God's power. Most Adventists are also extremely suspicious of techniques such as hypnosis and psychoanalytic therapy, based on fears of giving control of their minds over to someone other than God. Most are also deeply suspicious of New Age philosophies, including channeling, yoga, tai chi, use of crystals, Eastern-style meditation, affirmations, and use of guided imagery. Many of these suspicions have to do with fears that activities that "clear the mind" or bring in secular viewpoints will allow Satan an entry point into the mind. Institutions such as Alcoholics Anonymous and non-Christian psychiatric facilities are often viewed skeptically as well, although some churches are beginning to make referrals to these organizations.

IMPLICATIONS FOR SOCIAL WORK PRACTICE

Wide variations ranging from ultra-conservative to liberal exist within the Adventist church. (In general, North American Adventists are gradually moving away from fundamentalist doctrinal positions toward more evangelical perspectives.) Many younger Adventists who have left the church or who no longer actively attend a church still consider themselves to be "cultural Adventists," even though their relationship to the organized church may be tenuous at best. Thus, the social worker should not make assumptions about a person's belief system, since each person perceives events and situations differently. Garland (1991) maintains that "Faith identifies what events may mean to the client, a meaning quite unlike what others would experience in similar situations" (p. 77). It is likely that even clients who no longer actively attend church will continue to feel Adventism's impact in areas of personal identity, beliefs, morality, and basic worldview. It is important to explore these differences with each client in order to gain a sense of his or her personal beliefs and behaviors.

Similarly, it is important not to openly challenge a client's religious belief system. To begin where the client is, it is important to have the client describe what being an Adventist means to him or her. In addition, it is wise to get a sense of the client's beliefs about an intervention before attempting it. For example, while working with a depressed client, you could say "I know that some Adventists are suspicious of using medications to deal with depression. How do you feel about it?" While there may be times when the social worker views particular clients' beliefs as dysfunctional, attempts to share alternatives will not be heard unless they are related to the client's questions and concerns (Garland, 1991).

The church's view of women may also have implications for social work practice. Because of the church's conservative theological beliefs, women are often viewed as having a subordinate role to men. While many younger Adventists in the United States no longer subscribe to this view, older or more conservative members are likely to believe that the roles of men and women are different and mutually complimentary. (At a recent General Conference policy review session, representatives from the United States voted to allow women to become ordained ministers, but the much larger number of world delegates voted this motion down, resulting in an unchanged policy.) While this belief is comfortable for many, it often serves to make women feel like "second-class citizens," while more tangibly excluding them from participating in many positions of leadership within the church. In addition, within some dysfunctional families, this belief can be grossly misused to justify male domination and oppression of women (see below).

As a clinician, you may first wish to contact a client's pastor or another local Adventist pastor and get a sense of his openness to your form of intervention, as well as his willingness to assist you in helping the client. If he can become an ally, he will legitimize your work with the client. Showing a basic knowledge of the Adventist church and its beliefs will prove helpful in forming this relationship. These relationships should be formed carefully, since, in some cases, the support system could do more harm than good. For example, the Adventist support person may deny the importance of medications to deal effectively with various mental illnesses.

Clinicians may suggest that a client use prayer to cope with her or his concerns. If he or she has a similar Christian background, a clinician might even offer to pray with a client. However, the social worker must recognize that prayer is cultural as well as denominational. Garland (1991) argues for caution in approaching such prayers. It is important to know the client's understanding of prayer and its meaning so as not to frighten, alienate, or anger him or her. Garland also maintains that prayers should not be used to exert influence over the client, to prove the clinician's spirituality, or to serve as an escape when the clinician does not know what to say or do.

Many Adventist churches have small Community Service Centers, which can provide tangible resources such as food, clothing, and sometimes money. In addition, there are a number of Adventist hospitals, outpatient centers, and clinics around the United States that address specific issues such as addiction, mental illness, and crisis situations. Many of these resources can be located by calling Columbia Union PlusLine, a church-sponsored telephone directory (1-800-SDA-PLUS). An Adventist Web site, PlusLine (http://www.plusline.adventist.org/), offers a wide variety of helpful resources and links for addressing social, emotional, and church-related issues through Adventist-based support organizations. Several Internet chat rooms can also be accessed through this site. In addition, many non-Adventist Christian resources have been created to address psychosocial and emotional problems.

While most Adventists are suspicious of non-Adventist sources of help, they do have a high respect for medical professionals, particularly Christian physicians, so a physician can be one avenue for possible interventions. Christian counselors are gradually becoming accepted, particularly among younger Adventists, and church-based support groups are starting to become popular in some larger urban churches. On the macro level, Adventist physicians also provide a possible source of cooperation in community-change activities. Their involvement is often essential in convincing other church members to participate in community projects.

Community leaders and change agents who wish to enlist the help of Adventist churches in their communities may be viewed with suspicion by many pastors and other church leaders who want to avoid associations with "the world" and to avoid becoming distracted from the church's evangelizing mission. In addition, many Adventists believe that social problems can only be addressed at the individual level through a "change of heart." As mentioned previously, however, many churches manage Community Service Centers, which can be called on in times of community crisis to help with basic personal needs. Some Adventist pastors also belong to local interfaith church organizations. These individuals are often more willing to participate in activities aimed at community change.

One final implication for social work practice involves a disclaimer about this chapter. The authors, both Caucasian males, have offered one broad perspective on the Adventist church. Although theirs is a reasonable representation of the Caucasian Adventist reality, it is important to note that there are many Adventist churches in North America for people of color. For example, Asian and Latino Adventists comprise more than 11% of the North American Division membership (General Conference of Seventh-day Adventists, 2000b), and their numbers are expected to grow rapidly into the next century (Hernandez, 1995). African American churches, which comprise almost 24% of North American church membership (General Conference of Seventh-day Adventists, 2000b), have their own denominational structure, including separate churches and pastors, which operates within the North American Division. In addition, Adventism's global networks mean that many large cities in various countries around the world have small groups of Adventists. While many Caucasian churches show little or no membership growth, churches of color are often growing and vibrant places. Although doctrinal beliefs and sources of strength are similar for most Adventists, such cultural variations mean that there is wide variation in interpretation of some behavioral standards, worship styles, relationship patterns, and even some Biblical passages. Consequently, great care must be taken in exploring what the Adventist experience means for these various groups.

Issues That May Surface in Counseling

Because of the church's relatively strict behavioral code, most Adventists struggle with issues of guilt over failure to rigidly maintain these strict codes of conduct. Themes likely to emerge in counseling sessions include fears of personal inadequacy and damnation of and rejection by God, family, and the

Adventist community. Cognitive and behavioral manifestations might include anxiety, well-hidden anger, depression, and suicidality. Although attempts to engage clients in discussions about loosening up these behavioral codes are likely to be met with great suspicion, clinicians may find it helpful to explore issues of God's grace, forgiveness, and unconditional acceptance in spite of personal failures and shortcomings. As mentioned previously, attempts to use any techniques that could, in any way, be associated with mind control or New Age interventions will generally be viewed with great suspicion.

Many Adventists also have traditional, conservative views on gender roles. Men are generally expected to be the head of the household and the church, while women are to play support roles within the family, church, and society. Issues of domestic violence and sexual abuse are largely suppressed, but these problems are very real among Adventist families (Tinker, 1996). Similarly, the church's opposition to pregnancy outside of marriage and to abortion may propel Adventist girls and women into counseling (Spectrum, 1989). In addition, gay and lesbian Adventists have little in the way of formal church support, although a non–church-sponsored support network called SDA Kinship International (http://www.sdakinship.org/) affirms and supports Adventists or ex-Adventists who are gay, lesbian, or bisexual, without attempting to change their orientation.

CONCLUSION

Religious beliefs powerfully shape how Adventists view the world and relate to those outside their own community. Several unique doctrines have often shielded Adventists from regular interaction with non-Adventist service providers, but this separation has created a strong internal community of faith. Adventist doctrines and beliefs provide meaning, strength, are hope, and guidance throughout the life cycle, but particularly during times of distress. Among Adventists' unique internal sources of strength, are a shared sense of community, a healthy lifestyle, an internally integrated and consistent belief system, and a commitment to improve social conditions. Clinicians can draw on a wide variety of Adventist traditions, rituals, and practices in their provision of services. By drawing on such community resources as prayer, Bible study, church attendance, and the writings of Ellen G. White and other denominational literature, it is possible to give support and assistance to Adventists who are struggling with mental, physical, spiritual, or social concerns. Respect for and sensitivity to the sometimes wide variations within Adventist belief and practice will help clinicians to offer more effective services to those who require assistance.

REFERENCES

Abortion (special issue). (May 1989, May). *Spectrum, 19*(4).

Adventist News Network. (1997). *A quick look at Seventh-day Adventists.* Silver Spring, MD: General Conference of Seventh-day Adventists.

Branson, R. (May 1993). We didn't start the fire but the tinder was ours. *Spectrum, 23*(1), 2.

Bull, M., & Lockhart, K. (1989). *Seeking a sanctuary: Seventh-day Adventism and the American Dream.* New York: Harper & Row.

Dederen, R. (Ed.). (2000). *Handbook of Seventh-day Adventist theology.* Hagerstown, MD: Review and Herald Publishing Association.

Dudley, R. L., & Hernandez, E. I. (1992). *Citizens of two worlds: Religion and politics among American Seventh-day Adventists.* Berrien Springs, MI: Andrews University Press.

Garland, D. (1991). The role of faith in practice with clients. *Social Work and Christianity, 18*(2), 75–89.

General Conference of Seventh-day Adventists. (1988). *Seventh-day Adventists Believe . . . : A biblical exposition of 27 fundamental doctrines.* Hagerstown, MD: Review and Herald Publishing Association.

General Conference of Seventh-day Adventists. (2000a). *Seventh-day Adventist church world statistics.* Retrieved December 27, 2000 from the World Wide Web: http://www.adventist.org

General Conference of Seventh-day Adventists. (2000b). *Seventh-day Adventist yearbook 2000.* Hagerstown, MD: Review and Herald Publishing Association.

Hernandez, E. I. (1995). The browning of American Adventism. *Spectrum, 25*(2), 29–50.

Neufeld, D. F. (Ed.). (1976). *Seventh-day Adventist encyclopedia.* Hagerstown, MD: Review and Herald Publishing Association.

Rice, R. (1997). *Reign of God: An introduction to Christian theology from a Seventh-day Adventist perspective* (2nd ed.). Berrien Springs, MI: Andrews University Press.

Schwarz, R. W. (1979). *Light bearers to the remnant.* Boise, ID: Pacific Press Publishing Association.

Tinker, C. M. (1996, March-April). A call to truth. *Adventist Today, 4*(2), 2.

Winslow, G. (May 1988). Abortion and Christian principles. *Ministry, 61,* 12–16.

ADDITIONAL RESOURCES

Books

Bull, M., & Lockhart, K. (1989). Seeking a sanctuary: Seventh-day Adventism and the American dream. San Francisco: Harper & Row.

General Conference on Seventh-day Adventists. (1988). Seventh-day Adventists believe: A Bible exposition of 27 fundamental doctrines. Hagerstown, MD: Review and Herald Publishing Association.

Rice, R. (1997). *Reign of God: An introduction to Christian theology from a Seventh-Day Adventist perspective* (2nd ed.). Berrien Springs, MI: Andrews University Press.

Web Sites

General Conference of Seventh-day Adventists. (1999). *Fundamental beliefs of the Seventh-day Adventists.* Information posted on the World Wide Web at http: www2.advensit.org.beliefs

Seventh-Day Adventists homepage: www.sda.org

GLOSSARY

Advent, The The doctrine that the return of Jesus Christ to this world will be literal, personal, visible, and worldwide. Seventh-day Adventists believe that the second coming of Christ is the grand climax of the gospel, when the righteous dead will be resurrected, and together with the righteous living will be glorified and taken to heaven. The unrighteous will die a rapid, final death after God's judgment is completed.

Anointing of the sick A special prayer for healing conducted by Seventh-day Adventist elders at the bedside of someone who is gravely ill.

Doctrine of the Investigative Judgment Seventh-day Adventist belief that a final judgment takes place when Jesus enters the heavenly sanctuary (see Doctrine of the Sanctuary) and makes decisions about the final fate of the living and the dead.

Doctrine of the Sanctuary Seventh-day Adventist belief in a literal sanctuary in heaven where Jesus ministers on behalf of his believers before God to atone for their sins (based on the ancient Hebrew belief in a Day of Atonement) (see Doctrine of the Investigative Judgment).

General Conference of Seventh-day Adventists The central governing organization of the World Seventh-day Adventist Church.

Great Controversy, The Seventh-day Adventist belief that Christ and Satan are involved in a great controversy regarding the character of God, his law, and his sovereignty over the universe. Originated by Satan, and observed by the entire universe, this controversy takes place on earth. At the conclusion of the controversy the God of love will ultimately be vindicated.

Great Disappointment, The Members of the Millerite movement believed that Jesus would return to the earth on October 22, 1844. The failure of this prophecy was met with great disappointment, but bore the seeds of Seventh-day Adventism.

Health Message Seventh-day Adventists believe that Christians have a responsibility to preserve their health (particularly abstaining from alcohol and meat), since by doing so they can better serve others and keep their bodies pure as temples of God.

Ingathering An annual worldwide appeal by the Seventh-day Adventist church for funds from the general public, which is a way to both evangelize and collect money for medical, educational, and welfare projects in the community.

Lord's Supper The eating of the symbolic emblems of the body (unleavened bread) and blood (grape juice) of Jesus as an expression of faith in him as Lord and Savior, based on the original Communion service Jesus had with his disciples prior to his crucifixion.

Millerite Movement Doctrinally, Seventh-day Adventists are heirs of the interfaith Millerite movement of the 1840s. Between 1831 and 1844, William Miller, a Baptist preacher and former Army captain in the War of 1812, launched the "great second advent awakening," which eventually spread throughout most of the Christian world. When Jesus did not appear on October 22, 1844, Miller's followers experienced what came to be called The Great Disappointment.

Pathfinders Seventh-day Adventist organization, similar to the Scouts, that provides a character-building program of Christian activities for children between the ages of 10 and 15.

Remnant Seventh-day Adventists believe that the universal church is composed of all who truly believe in Christ, but in the last days before Christ's return, a Remnant will be called out to keep the commandments of God, including the Seventh-day Sabbath.

Sabbath Saturday, the Seventh-day Adventist day of rest, worship, and ministry, as required by God in the Fourth of the Ten Commandments.

Sabbath School The Seventh-day Adventist equivalent of Sunday school. A regular part of Sabbath School is the fostering of interest in missions through reports of worldwide mission work. It is intended to be a school not only for children and young people, but also for adult members of the church. All 10 million members worldwide study the same age-appropriate lesson each week.

Time of Trouble Seventh-day Adventist belief that, at the conclusion of the Investigative Judgment, God will remove his protective hand from the earth and allow Satan to bring the seven last plagues upon the earth just prior to Jesus' Second Coming.

Vacation Bible School A 10-day program offering games, crafts, and stories for children between the ages of 4 and 14, conducted as an evangelistic endeavor of the Seventh-day Adventist church during summer vacation.

White, Ellen G. One of the central founders of the Seventh-day Adventist church, Ellen G. White is considered to be a prophetess who received many visions from God regarding the Bible and the Adventist Christian lifestyle.

MORMONISM

DENNIS T. HAYNES

CHAPTER 13

INTRODUCTION

I am grateful that the editors chose to include Mormonism as one of the religious traditions to be examined in this book. I should note at the outset that I am not authorized as an official spokesperson of The Church of Jesus Christ of Latter-day Saints, commonly referred to as the Mormon Church.* I am pleased, however, to write as a professional social worker about my own spiritual and religious experience within the Mormon faith.

Mormonism is often stereotyped as a religious cult. Its teachings are misunderstood and misinterpreted, as they differ from those of mainstream Christian denominations. Mormons' beliefs in the Godhead, scriptures in addition to the Holy Bible, living prophets

* The official name of the church is "The Church of Jesus Christ of Latter-day Saints." This name appropriately recognizes that Jesus Christ is the center of church theology and worship. The church is commonly referred to in society as the Mormon Church because of its use of *The Book of Mormon: Another Testament of Jesus Christ,* in addition to the Holy Bible. However, although I acknowledge the inaccuracy of this terminology, I, prefer to not confuse the audience for whom this chapter is written, who typically refer to my religion as Mormonism.

and apostles, and continuing revelation, temple building, and welfare work, and health and moral practices are a few of the unique aspects of their faith. Many erroneously view the church as a provincial Utah sect. However, the church has a worldwide membership of more than 10 million, with more members residing outside of the United States than within (Hinckley, 1997). Mormonism is not a Sunday religion; it is a way of life. It encompasses every facet in the life of a member of the church. It is not possible to provide social work assessment and intervention with persons of the Mormon religious tradition without understanding the pervasiveness of their spiritual beliefs, as well as the resources and comprehensiveness of the church as an organized system and religious institution.

A BRIEF HISTORY OF MORMONISM

The master stories of Mormonism began before the formal organization on April 6, 1830 in Fayette, New York of The Church of Jesus Christ of Latter-day Saints. They form the core of all that is Mormonism and the doctrines on which our faith is based. In 1820, Joseph Smith was a 14-year old boy living in Palmyra, New York and searching for religious truth. He was schooled in the Holy Bible, and in confusion about the diverse religious denominations vying for converts in his day, he decided to follow the counsel found in the New Testament: "If any of you lack wisdom, let him ask of God, that giveth to all men liberally, and upbraideth not; and it shall be given him" (James 1:5). Joseph Smith testified that he saw a vision of heavenly beings, even God the Father and his son Jesus Christ, telling him to join none of the churches. This is referred to as the account of the First Vision (*The Pearl of Great Price,* Joseph Smith–History).

Joseph Smith also testified of other heavenly visitations from John the Baptist and the Apostles Peter, James, and John, who restored to Smith the keys of priesthood authority of Jesus Christ that had been lost. Smith stated that he was also visited by an angel who in time delivered to Smith an ancient scriptural account recorded on gold plates. Smith translated this record, which is the account of the visit Jesus Christ made to the peoples of the Americas following his resurrection from the dead. It is known as *The Book of Mormon: Another Testament of Jesus Christ* (from which members of the Church receive the nickname Mormons). All of these events occurred prior to the organization of the church.

Basic beliefs of Mormonism that flow from these accounts include the belief in God the Father and his Son Jesus Christ as two distinct, glorified personages, continuing divine revelation, additional scriptures, and the necessity of priesthood authority to administer the restored ordinances (rites) of the Gospel. Mormons believe that the church that Jesus Christ established during his mortal ministry was lost, as prophesied by Paul (II Thessalonians 2:3; II Timothy 4:3–4). This church has been restored to the earth with the same organization that existed in the ancient church. Mormons believe that the living prophets and apostles of the church possess the same authority bestowed by Jesus Christ on the original twelve apostles. Jesus Christ stands as the head of the church; thus its name, the Church of Jesus Christ of Latter-day Saints, to distinguish it from the ancient church of Christ's day.

These beliefs differed from those taught by mainstream American religions and those common in the frontier communities where Mormons built settlements. Suspicion about Mormons' beliefs on the part of their neighbors fed an atmosphere of extreme agitation and distrust. Swelling ranks of Mormon converts immigrating from Europe and the eastern United States also added fuel to opposition to Mormonism. Mobs attacked Mormon settlements, burning crops, destroying homes, murdering, raping the women, and threatening to exterminate the people. To escape the intense persecution, the church headquarters moved from New York to Ohio, then to Missouri. Mormons pursued legal redress for their suffering. When government officials ignored their appeal for protection from the extermination order issued by the governor of Missouri, Mormons fled to the Mississippi River swamplands of Illinois. Joseph Smith and his brother Hyrum were themselves martyred in Carthage, Illinois in 1844.

Another master story of the Mormon people is their pioneer exodus to the Great Salt Lake Valley in 1847. Brigham Young, as the senior apostle of the church, led the migration to a refuge outside of the United States in an untamed wilderness, now known as Utah. Some 70,000 Mormons made the 1300-mile trek across the plains. The Mormon pioneer heritage is extolled in values still held by members of the church: faith, work, perseverance, sacrifice, and deliverance. But persecution also followed the Mormons to Utah. Shortly after their arrival at the Great Salt Lake, at the end of the war with Mexico, the United States received title to much of the Southwest, including Utah. Rumors of plural marriage practices within the church in the 1840s were confirmed when the church publicly announced polygamy in 1852. Mormons believed that their religiously based practice of plural marriage, also practiced in Old Testament times, was protected by the U.S. Constitution. Anti-polygamy legislation, however, stripped Mormons of their rights as citizens, disincorporated the church, and permitted the seizure of church property. The church was brought to the brink of extinction, but then church president Wilford Woodruff announced as a revelation in 1890 the abandonment of polygamy as a church doctrine (*The Doctrine and Covenants,* Official Declaration 1). Today, no member of the church can practice polygamy without being excommunicated from the church.

Ironically, one of the basic tenets of Mormonism is "obeying, honoring, and sustaining the law" (*The Pearl of Great Price.* Articles of Faith 12), the very law that failed to protect them from religious oppression. Mormons are strong advocates of religious freedom and respect religious diversity. "We claim the privilege of worshipping Almighty God according to the dictates of our own conscience, and allow all men the same privilege, let them worship how, where, or what they may" (*The Pearl of Great Price.* Articles of Faith 11).

MY PERSONAL STORY

I remember my first job interview for a position as an entry-level social worker. I had just graduated with honors from my undergraduate program at Brigham Young University where I majored in family relations and minored in social work. I had prepared a resume of my experiences, including volunteer service as a missionary in Mexico. After glancing at my resume, the first question the interviewer asked was, "Dennis, with your background, how could you work with individuals having values different than your own?" I was taken aback by the question. It was a critical incident for me. I still remember my response, over 25 years later: "I feel solidly grounded in my own value base and do not feel a need to impose it on others." I was surprised that my religious affiliation would be our beginning focus and that it was assumed, because I come from a conservative religious background, that I could not work with people whose values differed from mine. Would nonreligious applicants be asked the same question? Why not? Doesn't the question apply to all of us, regardless of our religious backgrounds?

I grew up in the South as a member of a religious minority. There were only five Mormon students in my high school of 3000. My grandmother's family had been some of the first people converted to Mormonism in Florida. They had joined the church in 1899 when Mormon missionaries in the South were still being martyred for their beliefs. I experienced the prejudices and ridicule of my adolescent peers regarding my different standards. I was the outsider who would not join in, despite social pressure to smoke, drink alcohol, use drugs, or have sex. I remember instructors in my high school teaching false information about the Mormons and my standing up before the class to correct the errors. I remember my mother giving birth to my two youngest siblings, her eighth and ninth children, when I was in high school and having a teacher label her a Mormon "baby factory."

I also remember the strength, support, and fellowship of my religious community. In those days, with so few members of the Mormon faith in the South, we stood together. I was given early leadership experience as I visited the homes of the members, traveled as a speaking companion around the state with adult church leaders and as a summer companion with full-time Mormon missionaries, taught classes, and served in presiding capacities in the youth auxiliary organizations of the church. I attended religious instruction classes each morning at 6:00 A.M. with my Mormon peers before high school and developed knowledge of church doctrine beyond my years. My grounding was solid; my belief moved toward a personal conviction and faith that continue to sustain me.

It was my Mormon volunteer service that led me to social work. I interrupted my college education after my freshman year to serve a church mission for 2 years in southeastern Mexico. My international service experience changed my life. It laid the foundation of my commitment to the core values of the social work profession: dignity and worth of the person, importance of human relationships, service, integrity, competence, and social justice

(National Association of Social Workers, 1996). I had never experienced the oppression of poverty or the strength of the human spirit to confront inequities. I had never realized that there were other cultural worldviews that were as valid, or more so, than my own. Before my volunteer experience, I had planned to become a marriage and family therapist. I discovered, however, that therapy had little relevance to those who lacked the basic necessities and rights of life. I had gone to teach the Mexican people, but it was I who came away a changed man.

My religious identity is the framework of my life's experiences as much as race or ethnicity might be for other individuals. It flows through my very being. I cannot separate being a Mormon and a professional social worker, any more than can my social work colleagues who identify themselves as female, black, gay, or lesbian. I love my chosen profession; I also love my Mormon faith. To be a social worker with integrity, I strive to integrate the values and principles of my personal faith and my profession.

THE PURPOSE OF LIFE

Mortality, as viewed by Mormons, is the second estate of human existence and is part of the eternal life of each person. Prior to physical birth, we lived with God in heaven as his spirit children; thus, members of the church refer to each other as brothers and sisters. We believe that all human beings, regardless of race and ethnicity, are children of our Father in heaven and are literally spirit brothers and sisters. Mormons believe that there was a war in heaven (Revelation 12:7) in which all born into mortality chose to follow Heavenly Father's plan, as advocated by his Firstborn Son, our elder brother Jesus Christ, known in the Old Testament as Jehovah. Another brother, Lucifer, who became known as Satan, rebelled against God's plan to provide each person the right of free will and choice, referred to by Mormons as "free agency." Satan was cast out of heaven along with a third of the children of God, who followed him. He and his angels continue to tempt men to rebel against God and his laws.

The remaining two-thirds of the children of God stayed true to their first estate by following Jesus Christ, and therefore they were rewarded the blessing of obtaining a physical body, which empowers the spirit body. Mormons view the physical body not as evil but as necessary in order to have a fullness of joy. Mortality is a probationary period in which we, as the children of God, are tried and tested to prove our faithfulness to God. Heavenly Father prepared this plan for our growth, development, and learning. Mortality is a school in which each of us, by experience, learns to distinguish and choose between good and evil. We were not sent here without direction and guidance. Since the beginning of time, prophets have received revelation from God to lead us in the right way. Mormons believe that God continues to guide his children through his prophets, who serve as his spokespersons, even as Moses did in times of old.

The greatest goal of mortals is to become like their Father and return to his presence, referred to in the Scriptures as attaining eternal life. God has shown us how to do so by sending his son, Jesus Christ, who was chosen from the Councils in Heaven to be the Only Begotten of the Father and the Redeemer and Savior of humankind. Mormons consider themselves Christians because they worship Jesus Christ as the literal son of God and the only means by which people may be saved in the kingdom of God (*Living Christ,* 2000). Mormons believe that death entered the world through the transgression of Adam and Eve, who are esteemed as the first parents. Mormons do not believe that children are conceived in sin, but that through Christ, humankind is cleansed from Adam's transgression. Through Christ, the death of the physical body is overcome; all humanity, regardless of worthiness, receives the gift known as immortality through the miracle of resurrection. All will be resurrected to stand before God to be judged for their deeds, whether good or evil.

Mormons make a distinction between the free gift of immortality given to all and the gift of returning to live in the presence of our Heavenly Father, known as eternal life. As God's children, we receive the full benefit of Christ's atonement in our lives through "obedience to the laws and ordinances of the Gospel" (*The Pearl of Great Price.* Articles of Faith 3). When we disobey the will of God, his Holy Spirit withdraws from us. This distancing from his light and truth is known as "spiritual death." To again draw close to God, we must exercise faith in Jesus Christ and repent of our wrongdoing, not only by abandoning wickedness, but also by doing good works. Contrary to false stereotypes, Mormons do not believe that they can lift themselves to heaven by their own good works, but that it is good works that truly manifest their faith. "Faith, if it hath not works, is dead" (James 2:17). A basic teaching of *The Book of Mormon* is that "we know that it is by grace that we are saved, after all we can do" (2 Nephi 25:23). It is only through the atoning sacrifice of Jesus Christ, who took our sins on himself, that we have hope of eternal life.

Mormons believe that following the sojourn on earth, the spirit being continues to live when the physical tabernacle is laid in the grave. Prior to resurrection and judgment, our spirits reside in the "spirit world." Those who are righteous are received into paradise, a state of peace and rest from the troubles and cares of the world. The spirits of the wicked, are imprisoned by their evil desires and remain captives of the devil (*The Book of Mormon* Alma 40–42). Only through their repentance and faithfulness to the principles of the Gospel can they be freed from their spirit prison. Mormons believe not only in life after death, but also in eternal progression even beyond the grave in preparation for the universal resurrection and judgment of the dead. All will be judged according to their own level of knowledge and understanding. Prior to resurrection and judgment, all humankind will be granted the same opportunity: to be taught Gospel truth, whether in mortality or in the spirit world, and to exercise free choice in deciding whether to live according to these Gospel principles. Persons with disabilities in mortality, such as those with mental retardation, will be free in the spirit body of previous mortal barriers to learning and progress. Mormons believe Jesus Christ is the only door by which to enter into the Kingdom of God (John 10:9). "I am the way, the truth, and the life: no man cometh unto the Father, but by me" (John 14:6).

Although Mormons believe in a universal resurrection, they believe in more than one resurrection and that humankind will be resurrected with varying degrees of glory. This belief arises from the teachings of Paul, who asserted that "there is one glory of the sun, and another of the moon, and another glory of the stars; for one star differeth from another star in glory. So also is the resurrection of the dead" (I Corinthians 15:41–42). Based on their degree of obedience to Gospel principles, individuals will be resurrected to a celestial, terrestrial, or telestial glory of heaven (Mormons refer to "celestial" glory as the glory of the stars). Only those who have stood in the fullness of truth and light and then become enemies of God by fighting against light and truth will be cast out of heaven to dwell with the devil and his angels in what is referred to as "perdition." God is just and merciful; people will be rewarded and pay the consequences of their deeds.

SOURCES OF POWER

Self, family, and community are emphasized as sources of power for members of the church. The individual is encouraged to develop from his or her early years a testimony of Gospel truths through individual prayer and Scripture study. The accepted Scriptures include ancient and modern-day revelation, as recorded not only in The Holy Bible (The Old and New Testaments), but also *The Book of Mormon: Another Testament of Jesus Christ, The Doctrine and Covenants,* and *The Pearl of Great Price.* No one is asked to follow church teachings blindly. The true source of power in the Church does not rest with the leaders or the organization. It rests with the personal spiritual witness of each member of the truthfulness of its teachings. *The Book of Mormon* teaches:

> And when ye shall receive these things, I would exhort you that ye would ask God, the Eternal Father, in the name of Christ, if these things are not true; and if ye shall ask with a sincere heart, with real intent, having faith in Christ, he will manifest the truth of it unto you, by the power of the Holy Ghost. And by the power of the Holy Ghost ye may know the truth of all things. (Moroni 10:4–5)

The second source of power, the family, is considered to be the basic unit of the church and of society. Family relationships provide the foundation for individual growth and support. Parenting is considered to be the most important responsibility of a mother and father. "No other success can compensate for failure in the home" (McKay, 1964).

> Parents have a sacred duty to rear their children in love and righteousness, to provide for their physical and spiritual needs, to teach them to love and serve one another, to observe the commandments of God and to be law-abiding citizens wherever they live. Husbands and wives—mothers and fathers—will be

> held accountable before God for the discharge of these obligations. (Family Proclamation, 1995)

The church community is the third source of power for members of the church. The church is based in a lay clergy organization, whose members are "called" to carry out church responsibilities such as preaching sermons, teaching classes, and other service assignments. Service to families and communities is believed to bring spiritual power into members' lives. Members are organized into local congregations known as "wards" and "stakes," based on geographical residence and presided over by bishops or presidents ordained to these priesthood callings. Members have not only the support of this priesthood leadership, but also the support of auxiliary organizations for different peer groups: the Primary for children, Young Men and Young Women for youth, Relief Society for women, and Priesthood quorums for men. Priesthood home teachers and Relief Society visiting teachers visit church families in their homes at least once a month. In times of personal or family struggles and difficulties, members are encouraged to seek the counsel of home teachers, visiting teachers, and priesthood leaders. Church members are also encouraged to seek special priesthood blessings of spiritual comfort, counsel, and guidance. They are encouraged to live so as to be worthy of the Gift of the Holy Spirit to comfort, influence, and direct their lives.

RITUALS

Rituals of the Church of Jesus Christ of Latter-day Saints include those common to Christianity, as well as rituals that have been restored to the earth. Mormons believe in the ritual of Baptism by immersion for the remission of sins and in the laying on of hands for the gift of the Holy Ghost. What is unique is that Mormons believe that these rituals can only be performed by those who have authority to preach and administer the ordinances of the gospel (*The Pearl of Great Price,* Articles of Faith 5). Bearers of the restored priesthood are believed to possess this divine authority. All male members of the Church who are worthy, without regard to race or color, may be ordained to the priesthood by the laying on of hands (*The Doctrine and Covenants,* Official Declaration 2). The exercise of this priesthood power by the bearer is predicated on his adhering to principles of righteousness (*The Doctrine and Covenants* 121:36–37).

Mormons do not believe in infant Baptism or in Baptism for those who cannot understand, such as persons with mental retardation; they do believe that

> . . . little children are alive in Christ, and also all they that are without the law. For the power of redemption cometh on all them that have no law; wherefore, he that is not condemned, or he that is under no condemnation, cannot repent; and unto such baptism availeth nothing. (*The Book of Mormon.* Moroni 8:22)

Mormon, a prophet, taught that Christ's words regarding children include "all children are alike unto me; wherefore, I love little children with a perfect love: and they are all alike and partakers of salvation" (Moroni 8:17). Baptism and repentance are for those who are accountable and capable of committing sin. Young children and persons with mental retardation are not in need of Baptism for the remission of sins, as they are "alive" in Christ. Children are believed to reach the age of accountability at 8 years old (*The Doctrine and Covenants* 68:25–28).

Other rituals of the church spoken of in the Holy Bible include the naming and blessing of children, administering to the sick through the anointing of oil and laying on of hands, and the blessing and administration of the sacrament. The Lord's sacrament, as described in The New Testament (the Last Supper), is an ordinance that is administered each Sabbath Day in chapels or meeting houses, during what Mormons call sacrament meeting. Members of the church promise to always remember Christ, to take his name upon them, and to keep his commandments. In doing so, they have the opportunity to renew the covenants they made at Baptism on a weekly basis. Alma, another prophet, taught that the baptismal covenant also includes bearing one another's burdens, mourning with and comforting those in need, and standing as "witnesses of God at all times and in all things, and in all places" (*The Book of Mormon*. Mosiah 18:8–9).

Ordinances that are part of Mormon rituals but not of those of other Christian denominations include those performed in Mormon temples. Mormon temples are distinguished from chapels or houses of prayer, where all are welcome to attend worship services and activities. Temples, by contrast, are holy edifices that are dedicated as Houses of the Lord. After open house, when the public is welcomed, only the faithful members of the church may attend the temple. Mormon temples are similar to the temples of the Old Testament, where only the priests of Levi were authorized to enter the holy sanctuary to officiate in sacred ordinances.

One of the purposes of Mormon temples is to be places where saving ordinances can be performed for the living, eternal spirits of those who are deceased and did not receive Baptism while in mortality. The Mormon belief in baptism for the dead, known as "work for the dead," is based in the belief in eternal progression and in the perfect justice and mercy of God (I Corinthians 15:29). If Baptism by water and the bestowal of the Holy Spirit are prerequisites to enter into the kingdom of God (John 3:5), all humankind must be granted the same opportunity, or else God is an unjust and unfair God. Mormons believe that they have an ongoing and personal responsibility to see that saving ordinances are provided for their ancestors. The Baptism ordinance is performed in Mormon temples by faithful members who stand as proxy for their ancestors. It is believed that the spirits of the deceased still have agency and can accept or reject the ordinances provided. Members of the church also believe that salvation of one's ancestors is essential to one's own personal salvation (*The Doctrine and Covenants* 128:15). This is why such emphasis is given by the church to family history research. The church sponsors the world's largest on-line genealogy site, with access to over 640 million name entries (Family Search, 1999).

Sacred eternal ordinances for the living, which include religious instruction, eternal marriage, and the sealing together of parents and children, are also performed in the temples by those holding the sealing keys of the priesthood. Mormons believe that temple ordinances are crucial to preserve the family unit in the eternities. Individuals make covenants in the temple and commit to be obedient to the Gospel; to sacrifice and consecrate their time, talents, and resources to build up the kingdom of God on earth; to live chaste and virtuous lives; and to lose themselves in service to family and community. Mormons believe in being "honest, true, chaste, benevolent, virtuous, and in doing good to all men; . . . if there is anything virtuous, lovely, or of good report or praiseworthy, we seek after these things" (*The Pearl of Great Price.* Articles of Faith 13).

Mormon doctrine holds that the highest ordinance is eternal marriage between a man and woman. The highest ordinances of temple worship are "received by husband and wife together and equally—or not at all" (Nelson, 1999, p. 39), consistent with Paul's New Testament teaching ". . . neither is the man without the woman, neither the woman without the man, in the Lord" (I Corinthians 11:11). The president of the Mormon Church, Gordon B. Hinckley, in September, 1995 issued "The Family: A Proclamation to the World" reaffirming the Church doctrine on the family, which states in part:

> We, the First Presidency and the Council of the Twelve Apostles of The Church of Jesus Christ of Latter-day Saints, solemnly proclaim that marriage between a man and a woman is ordained of God and that the family is central to the Creator's plan for the eternal destiny of His children. . . . We warn that individuals who violate the covenants of chastity, who abuse spouse or offspring, or who fail to fulfill family responsibilities will one day stand accountable before God. Further, we warn that the disintegration of the family will bring upon individuals, communities, and nations the calamities foretold by ancient and modern prophets.

In light of these doctrinal beliefs, the church holds as one of its primary purposes the teaching of family ideals and the preservation of family relationships into the eternities.

LIFE-CYCLE CONSIDERATIONS

For members of the church, individual development across the life cycle is framed within a patriarchal family order. Sexual relationships are considered sacred and divinely reserved for legal marriage between a man and a woman.

> By divine design, fathers are to preside over their families in love and righteousness and are responsible to provide the necessities of life and protection for their families. Mothers are primarily responsible for the nurture of their children. In these sacred responsibilities, fathers and mothers are obligated to help one another as equal partners. Disability, death, or other circumstances may necessitate individual adaptation. (The Family, 1995)

Children are viewed as endowed with Christ-like spiritual qualities such as faith, humility, and love. Infants are not born in sin, nor are children prior to the age of 8 capable of sin. Mormons believe that Satan does not have power to tempt little children prior to the age of accountability and that the years from birth to age 8 are of particular significance in preparing children spiritually for the challenges of mortality.

Social and moral development are considered life tasks not only during adolescence but throughout life. Schooling and ongoing education for school-age children, adolescents, young adults, mature adults, and the elderly are encouraged. Mormon doctrine teaches ". . . yea, seek ye out of the best books words of wisdom; seek learning, even by study and also by faith" (*The Doctrine and Covenants* 88:118). Labor and work are valued and considered to be not a curse but a blessing, bestowed by God on Adam, the first man. Mormons are taught to avoid idleness "that your bodies and your minds may be invigorated" (*The Doctrine and Covenants* 88:124). But, they are also encouraged to enjoy life and to seek wholesome entertainment. Mormons value uniqueness and differences across cultural groups and embrace wholesome art, music, theater, and dance of all kinds. All humans are children of Heavenly Father, who is "no respecter of persons" (Acts 10:34). Mormons "repudiate efforts to deny any person his or her inalienable dignity and rights on the abhorrent and tragic theory of the superiority of one race or color over another" (Quorum of the Twelve Apostles, 1987).

The elderly in the church are revered as possessors of wisdom acquired through lifetimes of learning, service, and experience. As an example of this principle, the succession to church president is restricted to the senior apostle, as presiding church authority. The current president of the Mormon Church, Gordon B. Hinckley, is over 90 years old. Mormons teach that family has primary responsibility to care for its elderly members.

Finally, Mormons are taught that they are empowered to be engaged in good causes, that they should wear out their lives in service to their fellow beings, which is synonymous with being in service to God (*The Doctrine and Covenants* 58:27–28; 123:13; *The Book of Mormon*. Mosiah 2:17). Members of the church throughout the world are encouraged to be actively involved in the civic and political affairs of their respective communities. The church does not endorse any political candidate or political party affiliation, but encourages its members to seek to elect and uphold in office the honest and wise (*The Doctrine and Covenants* 98:10). The church does speak out as a religious institution on social issues that are viewed to have moral implications, such as gambling, abortion, and homosexuality, which are considered contrary to the laws of God recorded in his Holy Scriptures (Mark 10:19; Romans 1:26–27; I Timothy 6:10).

HEALTH

Faithful Mormons adhere to a strict health code, known as the Word of Wisdom. It cautions against the use of alcohol, tobacco, tea, coffee, and other substances harmful to good physical health and against the misuse of drugs. The Word of Wisdom is accepted as revelation received by the Prophet Joseph

Smith long before the health hazards of these substances were known. Recent research has documented that the population of Utah is ranked among the nation's healthiest. Mormons who follow their religious health code have one of the lowest death rates from cancer and cardiovascular diseases and enjoy a life expectancy 8 to 10 years longer than the U.S. average (LDS Health Code, 1997; Utah Health Profile, 1994).

Mormons are taught that every commandment obeyed brings a blessing and a promise. Obeying the Word of Wisdom comes with this promise:

> And all saints who remember to keep and do these sayings, walking in obedience to the commandments shall receive health in their navel and marrow to their bones; and shall find wisdom and great treasures of knowledge, even hidden treasures; and shall run and not be weary, and shall walk and not faint. And I, the Lord, give unto them a promise, that the destroying angel shall pass by them, as the children of Israel, and not slay them. Amen. (The Doctrine and Covenants 89:18–21)

Mormons believe that there is an inseparable link between the body, the mind, and the spirit. Maintaining good physical health enhances mental and spiritual health.

WELFARE

Mormons are encouraged to be prepared to meet their own welfare needs. Living within one's means, staying out of debt, saving financial resources, maintaining health and life insurance, and incorporating physical exercise and proper diet are all part of provident living. Members are encouraged to take time to strengthen family relationships during what is institutionalized within the church as Monday night Family Home Evening. This allows time to build family and social relationships. Individuals are encouraged to foster emotional resiliency and self-reliance through ongoing exercise, relaxation, education, and skill development. Those who do not take care of their personal and family resources will not be able to assist others in need.

Disasters, of course, are part of life. Provident living prepares one for the unexpected. Mormons are encouraged to store a year's supply of food and emergency resources for such times. When personal resources are not adequate to meet needs, church members are encouraged to seek out family support, and then to call upon church resources. The church has established Deseret Industries operations to provide employment and training opportunities for persons with physical or mental disabilities, employment centers for the unemployed or underemployed, and social service agencies to assist in the areas of adoption, foster care, unwed parent services, and counseling. The Church Welfare Program has an extensive storehouse system stocked with produce and goods available for welfare distribution. These resources are administered through the bishops of the church and are not restricted to church members (Wirthlin, 1999). Assistance is given to people in need regardless of religious affiliation. Since 1984, Mormon humanitarian aid has reached 146 countries and is valued at tens of millions of dollars annually (Welfare and Humanitarian Services, 1999).

These financial and other temporal resources are paid for by voluntary donations made by church members. Mormons contribute tithes—10% of their income annually—to the church to cover costs of church development such as welfare work, temple and chapel building and the like. Mormon missionaries provide their voluntary church service at their own and their family's expense. They, like other lay clergy of the church, are not paid for their church service. In addition to tithing, church members also donate a fast offering to the church to assist the poor and the needy. On the first Sunday of each month, members are encouraged to fast for two meals and to donate the money that they would have spent on food to those in need. Those who can do so are encouraged to give a more generous donation.

Mormons believe that all truth comes from God, including scientific truth. They do call upon competent professionals and often choose those of Mormon faith. They also utilize community resources outside of the church, such as lawyers, doctors, mental health counselors, social workers, etc., but are encouraged to seek out those who will respect their religious beliefs and value system.

IMPLICATIONS FOR SOCIAL WORK PRINCIPLES AND PRACTICE

Practice Principle 1: Respect Client Beliefs

Mormon religious doctrine, principles, and practice pervade every aspect of the life cycle. In my own social work practice with Mormons, I have found that even individuals who no longer choose to actively participate in the church or who are estranged from it find it difficult to truly leave the church, because it is so all-encompassing. Believing as social workers that we must begin where the client is, it is important to not jump in too quickly to side with a client in criticisms of religion. The client might be critical of the religion while at the same time holding to it for strength and support. Seeing religion as a barrier to personal growth (a common bias of some social work professionals) undermines clients still struggling with their own spiritual journeys. Professionals should not undermine the beliefs of clients who choose to obey church doctrine.

Practice Principle 2: Tap Into Client Spiritual Strengths

Beginning from a strengths perspective, social workers should help clients tap into their own inner spiritual resources. It is possible for non-Mormons as well as Mormons to misinterpret basic church principles, doctrines, and practices. Encourage clients to tap into their religious sources of spiritual power such as individual prayer and Scripture study. Clients may need help in recognizing when their interpretations hinder or promote spiritual growth. Mormon clients can become misguided if they focus too much on one particular aspect of the Gospel and lose sight of the whole Gospel plan of faith, repentance, forgiveness, and love. Some clients may give extreme attention to their own weaknesses, and thus undermine their own spiritual strengths. Perfection is beyond the grasp of every human being; we have all sinned and are imperfect. Personal joy within the Mormon religion is impossible without Jesus Christ as the centerpiece of faith. Clients can be helped to view obedience in the context of the principles of both justice based on laws of obedience and the mercy, love and forgiveness afforded by the atoning sacrifice of Jesus Christ.

Practice Principle 3: Overcome Client Isolation

Clients of the Mormon faith may face obstacles that arise from the uniqueness of their religion. Many of the teachings of the church are different from mainstream religious beliefs and practices. Social pressure might lessen a Mormon client's spiritual commitment to live his or her religion. Mormons may also live in communities where they are a religious minority; they may feel isolated by their differences from other community members. Active involvement in church services and activities helps strengthen clients' spiritual resolve and offsets the differences and community alienation that might occur. Mormons are taught, however, to stand up for their beliefs and not to isolate themselves from social interaction in their communities. Clients should be encouraged to involve themselves in their communities and to interact with both Mormons and non-Mormons.

Practice Principle 4: Access the Resources of the Client's Religious Institution

The resources that the Mormon religion, as an institution, provides for its members are noteworthy. These resources often are accessed through the bishop of the local congregation. A client who has been inactive in the church, however, may be reticent to avail himself or herself of the resources and support available. Professional social workers are trained to be aware of community resources. The social worker should serve as a support to help Mormon clients link with church resources. Church leaders are also encouraged to collaborate with non-Mormon community resources and could be incorporated into a service team approach for the client and his or her family.

Practice Principle 5: Promote Informed Client Decision Making and Responsibility for Choices

The Mormon religion requires much of its members. Some may view the doctrines of the church as overbearing, restrictive, and limiting of personal choice. A key principle of Mormonism is that free agency and personal choice are key to spiritual growth and progress. People cannot fulfill their divine destinies as children of God without the freedom to choose when faced with alternative options. They also receive the consequences, whether positive or negative, of their choices. Resources of the church are readily available to assist and counsel members in difficult decisions and choices. Priesthood authorities within the church are called to receive inspiration to guide and direct the members of the church for whom they have jurisdiction. Once the counsel is provided, however, members are encouraged to seek their own spiritual inspiration and confirmation for personal choice, and not to base decisions solely on others' direction. They are encouraged to not follow blindly, but to assume personal responsibility for choices made.

Practice Principle 6: Confront Discrepancies between a Client's Religious Beliefs and Actions.

What if clients choose a course of action contrary to Mormon beliefs and practices, resulting in spiritual and religious disharmony? Clients may act contrary to church teachings because they do not fully understand the doctrine. If they are unsure of the doctrine, they should be encouraged to seek counsel with their local priesthood authorities. When willing, they should be encouraged to consult with the local bishop, even if they disagree with the teachings. Mormons who believe that they have a full understanding of the church position may be misinformed. If clients do not agree with the counsel provided by their local bishop, they can be encouraged to consult with a member of the stake presidency for additional clarification or counsel. A vast support system, including priesthood home teachers, Relief Society visiting teachers, and auxiliary officers and teachers, is available to assist clients of the Mormon faith in addition to the bishop. Professionals within the Mormon community may also be invited by bishops to give of their services to those in need at reduced cost or at no cost, if necessary. It is crucial that clients be encouraged to confront incongruencies between their religious beliefs and actions, or personal spiritual growth is hampered.

Practice Principle 7: Acknowledge Loss of the Present Ideal and Facilitate Hope in the Future.

Another potential challenge for clients of the Mormon religion are the high goals and ideals espoused by the church. In reality, no one lives up to the fullness of the ideal. We all fall short. Many individual circumstances and problems experienced in life are anything but ideal, including divorce, illness, alcohol or drug addiction, abuse, delinquency and crime, death, etc. The church will continue to uphold the ideal for which to strive; it is a goal to seek rather than a stick with which to beat oneself. An important principle of hope is that the fullness of the Lord's blessings are available to all who endure in their striving to live the gospel plan through the exercise of continuing faith, repentance, and obedience. No one is alone; the Holy Ghost is given as a gift of spiritual comfort and direction as one faces the crises, problems, and difficulties of mortality. At these times, Mormon clients should be encouraged to utilize the strengths of their religious and spiritual traditions, and not to pull away out of feelings of personal inadequacy and unworthiness. The mission of the church is to lift its members, give direction and support in time of need, and to hold out eternal hope through Jesus Christ.

The Church of Jesus Christ of Latter-day Saints identifies its primary mission as leading its members to Jesus Christ, the only true source of individual and family empowerment and happiness. Social workers are committed to a similar mission of enhancing client well-being through empowerment.

REFERENCES

The Book of Mormon: Another Testament of Jesus Christ (Alma 40–42; 2 Nephi 25:23; Moroni 8:17, 22; 10:4–5; Mosiah 2:17; 18:8–9).

The Doctrine and Covenants (Sections 58:27–28; 68:25–28; 88:118, 124; 89:18–21; 98:10; 121:36–37; 123:13; 128:15; Official Declaration 1; Official Declaration 2).

The family: A proclamation to the world. (1995). Retrieved June 26, 2001 from the World Wide Web: http://www.lds.org/

Family Search. (1999). Retrieved June 26, 2001 from the World Wide Web: (http://www.familysearch.org/)

Hinckley, G. B. (1997, October). *LDS General Conference Report,* p. 91.

LDS Health Code. (1997). Retrieved June 26, 2001 from the World Wide Web: http://www.athenet.net/~jlindsay/Wwisdom.shtml

The living Christ: The testimony of the Apostles. The Church of Jesus Christ of Latter-day Saints. (2000). Retrieved June 26, 2001 from the World Wide Web: http://www.lds.org/

McKay, D. O. (1964, April). *LDS General Conference Report,* p. 5.

National Association of Social Workers. (1996). Preamble. *NASW Code of Ethics* [Brochure]. Washington, DC: Author.

Nelson, R. M. (1999, May). Our sacred duty to honor women. *Ensign,* p. 39.

The Pearl of Great Price, The Articles of Faith of The Church of Jesus Christ of Latter-day Saints, (Numbers 3, 5, 11, 12, 13; Joseph Smith–History).

Quorum of the Twelve Apostles, Official Statement. (1987).

Utah Health Profile. (1994). Retrieved June 26, 2001 from the World Wide Web: http://www.ce.ex.state.ut.us/national/goodmed.htm

Welfare and Humanitarian Services. (1999). Retrieved June 26, 2001 from the World Wide Web: http://www.lds.org/

Wirthlin, J. B. (May, 1999). Inspired church welfare. *Ensign,* pp. 76–79.

ADDITIONAL RESOURCES

Books

The Church of Jesus of the Latter-day Saints. *The book of Mormon: Another testament of Jesus Christ.* Salt Lake City, UT.

The Church of Jesus of the Latter-day Saints. *The doctrine and covenants.* Salt Lake City, UT

The Church of Jesus of the Latter-day Saints. *The pearl of great price.* Salt Lake City, UT.

Web Sites

Official web site of the church: www.lds.org/

Links to other church sites: www.mormonlinks.com/

Family Proclamation, "The family: A proclamation to the world." (1995). Available at: http://www.lds.org

The living Christ: The testimony of the Apostles, The church of Jesus of Latter-day Saints. (2000). Available at: http://www.lds.org

GLOSSARY

Apostles The restored Church of Jesus Christ is built upon the same foundation of living apostles and prophets as existed in the Church established by Jesus during his mortal ministry. Members of the Church recognize apostles and prophets as authorized representatives of Jesus Christ who receive revelation to guide the Church and its members.

Articles of Faith Thirteen basic beliefs of the Church of Jesus Christ of Latter-day Saints written by the Prophet Joseph Smith, now included as part of modern scriptures referred to as the *Pearl of Great Price.*

Baptism The restored Church believes that the first ordinance of salvation is baptism by immersion for the remission of sins. Baptism follows faith in Christ and repentance from sin and is only administered by those in authority to administer the ordinances of the Gospel.

Baptism for the dead Christ taught that baptism is essential for one to be able to enter the kingdom of God. The baptism ordinance is performed in the temples of the restored Church by faithful Mormons who stand as proxy for their ancestors who did not receive the ordinances of salvation in mortality.

Bishop The pastor of the local geographical unit (ward) who, as the ordained priesthood authority, ministers to the needs of the congregation. Mormons believe that the Bishop is authorized to receive revelation at the local level of the Church, even as apostles and prophets receive revelation for the Church as a whole.

Book of Mormon One of the standard works of ancient scripture of the restored Church. This book was translated by the Prophet Joseph Smith from gold plates and contains the record of Christ's visit to the ancient inhabitants of the Americas following His resurrection from the dead. The *Book of Mormon* is a second witness of Jesus Christ and is companion scripture to the Holy Bible, the first witness of Christ. The *Book of Mormon* was first published in 1830.

Chapels Meeting houses or houses of prayer for local congregations of Mormons. Both members of the restored Church and non-members are welcome to attend Sunday services and other activities held during the week such as classes for instruction, family history research, sports events, dances, etc.

Church of Jesus Christ of Latter-day Saints The official name of the Church, established in New York in 1830, recognizes Christ as the center of Church theology and worship. Although nicknamed the "Mormon" Church by society because of our belief in the *Book of Mormon* as scripture, this nickname is inaccurate as it detracts from Jesus Christ as the head of the restored Church.

Degrees of glory Mormon doctrine includes the belief in differing times and glories of resurrection for the dead according to one's worthiness to the Gospel of Christ. Degrees of glories include the celestial, terrestrial and telestial kingdoms of heaven, as recorded by Paul in the New Testament.

Doctrine and Covenants One of the standard works of modern day scripture of the restored Church containing selections from the revelations, translations, and writings of the Prophet Joseph Smith.

Eternal life The greatest gift of God, as taught by the restored Church, is to be able to return again and dwell in the presence of our Father in Heaven. Eternal life is conditional upon one having faith in the atoning sacrifice of Jesus Christ, repenting of our sins, obeying the commandments of His Gospel, and enduring in faithfulness to the end of our lives.

Eternal marriage A unique doctrine of the restored Church is that marriage can be for eternity. Eternal marriages must be performed in a temple by one who has priesthood authority to seal families on earth and in heaven. For temple marriages to remain in effect, couples must not only make but also keep the covenants that they make with God in His Holy House.

Eternal progression The restored Church believes that life does not end with death but continues throughout eternity. As eternal children of Heavenly Father, we will be able to continue to progress throughout eternity.

Faith Faith in Jesus Christ is the first principle of the Gospel of Christ that leads to the fruits of repentance from sin and baptism by immersion for the remission of sins.

Family The restored Church teaches that marriage between a husband and wife is ordained of God and that the family is essential to God's plan for the eternal destiny of his children.

Family history research To help trace ancestors, the restored Church manages the largest genealogical resources in the world. These records are available to the public for research at no cost. Family history records may be accessed at Family History Centers located in Mormon chapels throughout the world and also over the internet.

Family home evening Mormons are encouraged to set aside Monday evening each week to spend time to strengthen family relationships through Gospel study, activities, service, and fun.

Fast offering Faithful members of the restored Church fast for two meals one day a month and donate the money they would have spent on these meals, or more, to fund help for the needy. These offerings of members enable the Church to finance welfare and humanitarian programs worldwide.

First vision Joseph Smith, as a youth of fourteen years, prayed for direction as to which church to join. His testimony is that Heavenly Father and His Son, Jesus Christ, appeared to him in vision in 1820 to instruct him and prepare the way for the restoration of The Church of Jesus Christ again to the earth.

Free agency According to doctrine of the restored Church, free agency is the right of free will and choice granted to each individual spirit child of God. This right of agency was preserved through a war in heaven led by Jesus Christ in which Satan and his followers rebelled and were cast out.

Godhead Members of the Church of Jesus Christ of Latter-day Saints believe in God the Father, in His Son Jesus Christ, and in the Holy Ghost. The three compose the Godhead as separate beings, but one in purpose.

Heavenly Father All humankind is believed to be spirit children of God, Who is addressed in prayer as Heavenly Father. God as the Father of our spirits, means that each of us is a daughter or son of God, with divine heritage and attributes. All humankind is related as spiritual brothers and sisters, regardless of race or ethnicity.

Hinckley, Gordon The current prophet and president of the Church of Jesus Christ of Latter-day Saints is recognized as the living spokesman of God, like the Prophet Moses of the Old Testament.

Holy Bible The King James Version of the Holy Bible, containing the Old and New Testaments, is considered to be the first witness of Jesus Christ, and companion scripture to the *Book of Mormon,* the second witness of Jesus Christ.

Immortality A free gift given to all who have lived, now live, or will live on the earth, made possible through the atoning sacrifice of Jesus Christ who overcame death through resurrection so that all could live again.

Jesus Christ The only Begotten Son of God in the flesh and the Firstborn of His spirit children, through Whom is made possible the free gift of immortality through the resurrection and the gift of eternal life through faith and obedience to His Gospel ordinances.

Laying on of hands Following baptism by immersion for the remission of sins, newly baptized members of the restored Church have hands laid upon their heads by those who hold priesthood authority to bestow the Gift of the

Holy Ghost. This Gift of the Holy Ghost, manifested through the gifts of the spirit, is the baptism of fire spoken of in the Holy Bible.

Lucifer A spirit son of God who rebelled against his Heavenly Father in our premortal estate and with one third of Father's spirit children were cast out of Heaven to the earth to tempt humankind in the struggle between good and evil.

Mormon A prophet who lived in the Americas in approximately 400 A.D. and compiled all the religious history from records of the ancient American civilizations, covering a period from 2200 B.C. to 421 A.D.

Mormonism See Church of Jesus Christ of Latter-day Saints.

Moroni A prophet, the son of Mormon, lived in the Americas in approximately 400 A.D. and recorded the final words in *The Book of Mormon.* Moroni appeared as a resurrected being to the Prophet Joseph Smith in 1823 and subsequently delivered the ancient record of the American inhabitants to Joseph Smith for translation.

Ordinances of salvation Ordinances of salvation of the restored Church that are administered by those ordained with priesthood authority include baptism by immersion, laying on of hands for the Gift of the Holy Ghost, priesthood ordination, eternal marriage, and sealing of children to parents.

Pearl of Great Price One of the standard works of modem day scripture of the restored Church containing selections from the revelations, translations, and writings of the Prophet Joseph Smith.

Priesthood ordination The authority to act in the name of Jesus Christ is bestowed through ordination by those in authority to administer the ordinances of the restored Church.

Priesthood home teachers Each family in the restored Church is assigned priesthood home teachers who visit their home at least once a month. Home teachers go in pairs as representatives of the Bishop of the Ward. They bring messages of spiritual inspiration, guidance, good will and render service as needed.

Prophets See Apostles.

Relief Society One of the oldest and largest women's organizations in the world. It was established in 1842 to help the sick, the poor, and others in need of compassionate service. During its weekly meetings, the organization provides instruction on a variety of topics, including theology, home and family education, compassionate service, social relations, and home management. The Relief Society also administers a literacy program in several countries.

Relief Society visiting teachers Adult female members called "visiting teachers" are assigned in pairs to render compassionate service as they assist with temporal and spiritual needs of every woman in the restored Church. Visiting teachers (along with priesthood home teachers) serve as representatives of the Bishop to every individual or family within the jurisdiction of the local congregation.

Revelation The Church of Jesus Christ of Latter-day Saints is founded on the doctrine of continuing revelation to those called and ordained with priesthood authority to administer the ordinances of the Gospel of Jesus Christ. Individuals and families are also able to receive revelation from God to assist them in personal matters, decisions and areas of stewardship to which they have been called.

Sabbath day Mormons are commanded to honor the Sabbath Day and to keep it holy. They are counseled to set Sunday aside as a day of worship, and to abstain, except for emergencies, from temporal work. Sunday is accepted as the Sabbath Day, to honor the first day of the week as the day in which Jesus Christ was resurrected from the dead.

Sacrament Mormons meet each Sunday in chapel services called "sacrament meeting" to partake of the Lord's sacrament in a renewal covenant of obedience to keep His commandments. Bread and water are used as emblems to represent the body and blood of Jesus' atoning sacrifice.

Sealing A unique ordinance of salvation of the restored Church is the sealing of spouses, parents and children as eternal families by those with priesthood authority to seal on earth and in heaven. This promised eternal family union is contingent on faithful obedience to the covenants made in the sacred temples of the Church.

Smith, Joseph The first prophet and president of the restored Church of Jesus Christ. Joseph Smith testified that in 1820 he saw in vision Heavenly Father and His Son, Jesus Christ. Through the Prophet Joseph Smith, the original Church established by Jesus Christ during His mortal ministry was restored again to the earth, along with priesthood authority and additional scriptures, both ancient and modern. Joseph Smith was martyred in Illinois in 1844.

Spirit world The restored Church believes that the eternal spirits of God's children await their resurrection in the spirit world. Spirit beings dwell in the world of spirits either in paradise or in spirit prison based on their faith and obedience during mortality. Spirits continue to exercise faith, repent and progress as they learn and obey gospel principles and accept ordinances of salvation, performed by proxy in their behalf in Mormon temples.

Stake A geographical unit of the restored Church consisting of a number of local wards and presided over by a stake presidency comprised of a president and two counselors. The stake president, having priesthood authority, is set apart to receive spiritual inspiration to shepherd and lead the members of his stake.

Temples Sacred edifices wherein spiritual instruction and eternal ordinances are provided for faithful members of the restored Church. Temple ordinances include baptism for the dead, eternal marriage, and sealing of parents and children for the dead and the living. Temples are not used for Sabbath day services nor are they open to the public once dedicated for their sacred purposes.

Tithing Faithful members of the restored Church embrace the biblical principle of tithing and contribute one-tenth of their income for the work of the Church.

Ward The local unit of the restored Church is composed of members who live in a designated geographical area and meet in chapels as a congregation on Sundays and also participate throughout the week in other activities and services.

Welfare program The restored Church welfare program is based on the principle of individual self-reliance. When individuals and their families are unable to meet their own personal needs after doing all they can, they call upon the Church for assistance. Recipients, within their ability, work for what they receive. Church welfare services include employment rehabilitation and placement, commodity assistance, education, and counseling. In addition, the Church sends welfare missionaries throughout the world, as part of their humanitarian effort, to share skills in agriculture, employment, education, social and medical services, and to assist in times of disaster and crisis.

Word of Wisdom Faithful members of the restored Church adhere to a strict health code, received through revelation by the Prophet Joseph Smith in 1833, that includes abstaining from alcohol, tobacco, tea, coffee, drugs and other harmful substances.

Work for the dead Ordinances of salvation provided for ancestors through proxy by faithful Mormon descendents in the temples of the restored Church. Ordinances provided for the dead include baptism, laying on of hands for the Gift of the Holy Ghost, priesthood ordination, eternal marriage, and sealing of children to parents. It is believed that the spirits of the deceased still have their agency to accept or reject the ordinances provided. Members of the restored Church also believe that this work for the dead is essential to their own salvation.

Young, Brigham The second modern-day prophet of the restored Church. Prophet Brigham Young led the first expedition in 1847 of Mormon pioneers 1300 miles across the plains from Illinois to the mountains of Utah in search of freedom from religious persecution. Under the direction of Prophet Brigham Young, over 600 communities were established throughout Canada, Mexico, and the western part of the United States.

HEALTH, RELIGION, AND SPIRITUALITY

CHAPTER 14

MARY VAN HOOK
MARIAN AGUILAR

There is growing interest within the health-related professions about the role that religion can play in promoting health. Health professionals are being encouraged to include religion in their view of the individuals and families they treat and to treat these clients in a wholistic manner (Cascio, 1998; Dossey & Dossey, 1998; Koenig, 1998; Mitka, 1998; Rolland, 1998). Since social workers frequently become involved with clients who are confronting health issues (broadly defined as both mental and physical health), this chapter reviews some of the research linking dimensions of religion with health. Recognizing that both religion and health are multidimensional phenomena, we will examine ways in which religion influences health from prevention through the treatment of disease: prevention efforts, the ways in which people experience their illnesses and symptoms, the coping strategies they employ, and the disease process itself. We will also draw upon information from earlier chapters on specific religious traditions.

In discussing religion, we recognize that people's religious beliefs and practices are influenced not only by the official belief systems of the institutionalized religion they affiliate with, but also by their cultural and ethnic backgrounds. Understanding clients' beliefs and practices as well as their cultural backgrounds can enable social workers to establish more effective collaborative relationships and to provide a wholistic approach to care (Rolland, 1998). Similarly, although we address the specific issue of religion and health, we do so with the understanding that these issues are part of a wider context—the social context of individuals, families, and communities—which plays a powerful role. Moreover, social policies influence the nature of health care available to community members. Poverty and related economic problems influence access to health care and treatment as well as risk factors for various environmental toxins. The physical environment can play a critical role, as children are exposed to lead poisoning or workers to asbestos. Technology brings new opportunities and challenges that may force society to redefine previous concepts. For example, what do life and death mean in a world in which technology can prolong life indefinitely?

Before we discuss specific ways in which religion can influence health and illness, it is useful to describe several concepts that can help to reveal the process by which religion can exert such an influence. Levin and Chatters (1998) use a model that draws on several frameworks to describe the process by which a healthy person becomes ill. In a "prepathogenesis" phase, factors related to agent, host, or the environment interact to produce pathology in healthy people, which at this stage is not symptomatic (p. 39). "Pathogenesis" follows, as the clinical signs of illness occur and are accompanied by the subjective perception of illness (and probably the social role of sick person). The opposing process is represented by protective factors that protect against illness and pathogenesis or even help reverse this process (p. 39). Levin and Chatters draw upon the concept of "salutogenesis" (developed by Antonovsky, 1987) to explain the role of religion in promoting health and well-being. Salutogenesis is a dynamic process based on several assumptions: health and disease are parts of a continuum rather than a dichotomy, and salutogenic factors may not be simply the "opposite" of risk factors for pathogenesis but can be entirely different constructs (p. 39). The concept of salutogenesis focuses attention on the potential mediating factors that explain why dimensions of religion can promote health and well-being.

RELIGIOUS AND SPIRITUAL MEDIATORS OF HEALTH

To help explicate the complex relationship between health and religion or spirituality, we have developed the model in Figure 1. This model attempts to demonstrate what we theorize as the relationship between aspects of religion and elements of health. In the following discussion, we recognize that spirituality, with its experiential component and search for meaning, is typically a component of religion, but it can also be experienced apart from formal religious traditions. Spirituality and/or religious beliefs and practices influence health in several ways:

- They encourage behaviors and interpretations of life (meaning) that promote well-being through prevention efforts.

FIGURE 14.1 | RELIGIOUS AND SPIRITUAL MEDIATORS OF HEALTH

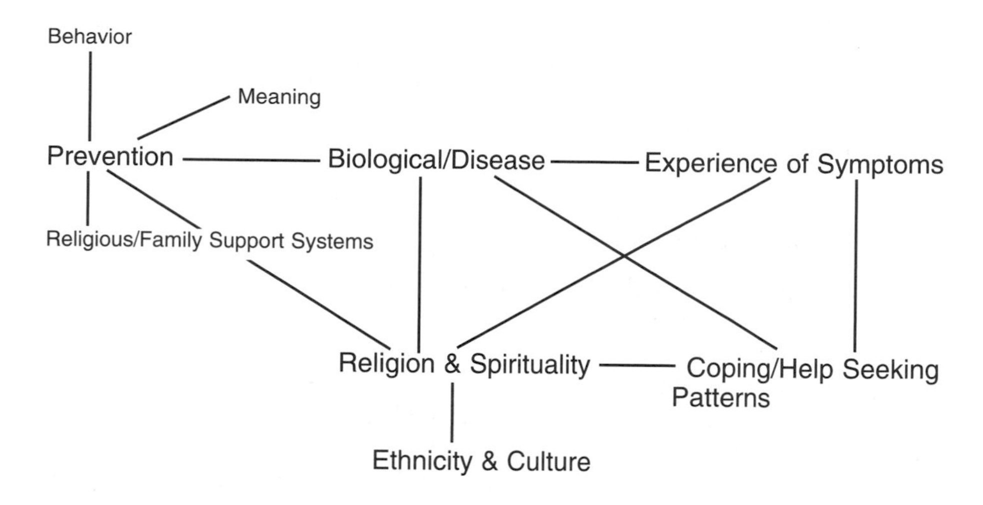

- They influence the perception of symptoms or illness.
- They promote coping and help-seeking patterns that influence how symptoms are experienced, the nature of the disease process, and the types of help utilized.
- They promote the healing process and reduce vulnerability to illness.

These influences represent a system of mutual interaction. Coping and help-seeking patterns both influence and are influenced by the experiencing of symptoms and the nature of the biological disease. The experience of symptoms, along with coping and help-seeking patterns, affect a person's religious practices, and vice versa.

In assessing the role of religion in clients' lives, it is important to remember that people who describe themselves as religious vary in the degree of their religious beliefs and participation, and thus the degree to which religion represents an important sense of meaning and purpose their lives varies as well (Gerwood, LeBlanc, & Piazza, 1998; Koenig, 1995). Views about religion and the role of religion in an individual's life can also change throughout the life cycle in response to life events (Koenig, 1995).

It is also important to acknowledge that even individuals with strong religious beliefs and those who are active participants in their faith communities can and do become ill and suffer from serious diseases. Thus, while religious beliefs and practices can help promote well-being, they do not represent any guaranteed shield of protection from illnesses. Any beliefs about such guarantees may add to the burden experienced by religious persons who are ill or have a family member with a serious illness.

RELIGION AND THE PROMOTION OF WELL-BEING

Perry (1998) suggested a schema for understanding the relationship between health and religion. In this schema, five factors contribute to the relationship of religion and health: Religion provides behavioral constraints, meaning systems, hope, a sense of community (belonging), and beliefs and practices that arm believers with tools to combat circumstances in their lives that lead to distress and disease.

Health-Promotion Behaviors

Religion can promote health by mandating, or at least encouraging, a lifestyle and behaviors that contribute to good health. Religious views that grant dignity to the body support these lifestyle prescriptions. Christian groups, for example, describe the body as the "temple of God" (Perry, 1998). As indicated in earlier chapters, the Lakota tradition holds that the body is a container for the spirit, a gift from the Creator (Chapter 2); Hindus view God as present in the bodies of human beings as well as other creatures (Chapter 3); and Buddists view the body as a precious vehicle for seeking enlightenment and helping others (Chapter 4).

Substance Abuse

People holding religious beliefs and participating in the organized life of a religious tradition generally are less likely to abuse alcohol and other drugs and to experience the related health problems (Booth and Martin, 1998). Abuse of alcohol and other drugs is noticeably absent among members of groups that proscribe the use of alcohol (for example, Mormons, Seventh-day Adventists, Hindus, Muslims, and some fundamental and evangelical Christian groups) (Booth & Martin, 1998; Sinha, 1998). Membership in groups that discourage excessive drinking but do not proscribe use of alcohol entirely is linked to lower than average incidence of substance abuse. Women are especially likely to demonstrate the link between reduced substance abuse and religious involvement and commitment (Booth & Martin, 1998). Adolescents from strong religious backgrounds who actively practice their faith through personal and communal rituals are less likely to drink alcohol, smoke, and use illegal drugs than are their nonreligious peers (Donahue & Benson, 1995; Koenig, 1999).

Several models can help explain how religion appears to reduce substance abuse. At the experiential level, people who feel loved by God can feel less need for mood-altering chemicals. At the cognitive level, the cognitive consistency model suggests that consistent exposure to religious teachings that discourage drinking can help reduce substance abuse. In addition, religious participation confers membership in a social group that supports and reinforces non-drinking behavior. If substance abuse is conceptualized as occurring in stages, religion can be viewed as preventing the onset of substance abuse through a combination of beliefs, social support, and alternative cognitive and social coping strategies (Booth & Martin, 1998).

Smoking is also less prevalent among members of some religious groups, which brings reduced health risks. Examples of groups that prohibit smoking are Seventh-day Adventists (see Chapter 12) and Mormons (see Chapter 13). Further, a recent study in North Carolina, whose residents are exposed to the competing messages of Bible Belt Christianity and the tobacco industry, found that people who were very active in their religion were substantially less likely to smoke than were their peers (Koenig, 1999).

Social Support Systems

The role of the support system provided by religious participation in promoting health has been studied extensively. In a recent meta-analysis of studies involving 126,000 participants, religious participation was associated with reduced mortality, especially for women (McCullogh, Hoyt, Larson, Koenig, & Thoresen, 2000). A social support system provides a peer group that may promote healthy behaviors and that offers the sense of being part of a community and of a larger family, which can be very meaningful (Koenig, 1999). Earlier chapters in this book describe the sense of belonging experienced by people in diverse religious communities. Participants in a study of Christians described the strength they received from belonging to the same body, the body of Christ (Perry 1998).

Social support from a religious community has also been found to be protective of mental health (Levin & Chatters 1998; Petersen & Roy, 1985). Participation in the life of the church has been associated with lower levels of anxiety (Petersen & Roy, 1985). Elderly persons living in deteriorating neighborhoods who participated in the religious life of a church community had an improved subjective sense of well-being despite an unchanged objective health status. (Krause, 1998), emphasizing the potential differences between perceived and objective health conditions. The church has been identified by African Americans as an essential source of support and resiliency in coping with stressors (Bagley & Carroll, 1998). Religious groups can offer members tangible types of help as well as role models. According to Perry (1998), the strength drawn from the community of faith reduces the stress of daily life that would otherwise threaten physical and emotional health.

A religion-based social support system can further promote well-being through effects on the immune system. Recent studies have found that elderly people who attend church regularly have healthier immune systems than those who do not. Researchers hypothesize that if religious commitment reduces stress, it might also lower the production of substances that impair immune function (Mitka, 1998).

Belief System/Meaning

Religious beliefs and associated cognitive frameworks can also promote well-being. Religion represents an orientating system—a way of perceiving and dealing with the world (Pargament & Brant, 1998). Such a system is described as giving a sense of coherence to life events (Perry, 1998), an important theme of spirituality. Several aspects of a belief system appear to be associated with an improved sense of well-being, including a sense of hope, a sense of purpose, and a perception of meaning.

Hope helps promote well-being and has several important religious dimensions. It can include the belief in life after death, either in heaven or as a series of reincarnations. As described in Chapters 3 and 4, for Hindus and Buddhists, life consists of a series of creations, dissolutions, and recreations that are influenced in turn by *karma*. Every action of a human being, as well as internal emotions such as desire, affects what the person becomes in the next re-creation. Since the quality of the rebirth is based on the merit acquired by the soul because of its actions, or karma, Hindus strive for the unity of the individual soul (*atman*) with the universal soul, or godhead, through works, knowledge, and expiation. Buddhists teach that sickness and death can be used as means to grow spiritually and to inspire others.

Hope can also include faith in the healing power of God (Allah) in the Christian, Islamic, and Jewish traditions, along with an assurance of God's care and ability to control what is happening (Koenig, 1999; Levin & Chatters, 1998; Perry, 1998). Catholics hold that God's love is healing in itself. The sacraments of Reconciliation, Eucharist, and Anointing provide means for healing. Catholics believe in miracles, including the intercession of the Virgin and the saints in times of sickness or distress. Many shrines dedicated to Mary have been the sites of healings.

Religious beliefs also instill life events with meaning (Koenig, 1994; 1999). A sense of purpose and meaning arising from a spiritual life contributes to vitality and promotes well-being (Todd, 1996). Religious beliefs also influence the extent to which the mind is viewed as contributing to well-being. Belief in the importance of the mind for well-being is reflected in spiritual exercises such as meditation, yoga, and guided imagery (Canda & Furman, 1999; Rolland, 1998; Todd, 1996; also see Chapters 4 and 5).

As earlier chapters in this book demonstrate, the precise meaning given to life events varies considerably from one religious tradition to another. Exploring how family members understand events relating to illness, death, substance abuse, or other health matters can be productive and also help establish a sense of collaboration (Cascio, 1998; Rolland, 1998). Understanding these meaning systems can help the social worker respect and appreciate a client's understanding of suffering as an inevitable part of life, especially as this understanding relates to coping with difficult life experiences and health problems (Levin & Chatters, 1998; Dancey & Wynn-Dancy, 1994; Thomas, 1997). Eugene describes how the spiritual community, the rituals of faith, and the emotional release provided by the church help Black women forge a sense of meaning in life and cope with the suffering associated with oppressive social structures (Eugene, 1995). Suffering in the Hindu tradition also has meaning, in that control of suffering by the mind strengthens the soul for the next life (Sinha, 1998). Chapter 4 indicates how suffering can be a means for growing spiritually within the Buddist tradition. In the Jewish tradition, everything that one experiences has meaning. Historical events such as the Holocaust have provided the Jews with symbols of death and rebirth that are profoundly religious (Microsoft Encarta 98 Encyclopedia). Pain and suffering are seen as experiences that may not be fully understandable. Although evil exists in the world and must be overcome, it does not come from God. For Mormons, suffering is not in itself redeeming, but how one responds to and deals with it can be redeeming. In the Islamic tradition, pain and suffering can be considered tests from God. While patience in the face of pain is important, Muslims are expected to use the knowledge God has given humankind to ease pain and suffering. Suffering can also be the result of not following God's teachings.

THE IMPACT OF RELIGION ON THE EXPERIENCE OF SYMPTOMS AND THE DISEASE PROCESS

Religion can also influence the mode and course of treatment of disease symptoms. Koenig (1999) found that people whose religious orientation was a primary influence on their life decisions were more likely to recover from depression. Many individuals in a subsequent study attributed their recovery from depression to religion or their faith (Koenig, 1999).

Religion can also promote healing through reductions in stress hormones. People who participate actively in religious life typically have lower levels of stress hormones and stronger immune systems (Koenig, 1999; Mitka, 1998). Religious involvement is also linked with improvements in other health conditions, including blood pressure (Koenig, 1999). Oxman (1995) found that a strong religious faith was associated with reduced mortality following surgery for serious heart problems. Orthodox Jews in Israel were found to experience less heart disease than non-Orthodox Jews (Koenig, 1999). A study of gay men infected with HIV revealed that men who were actively involved in religious practices had higher resistance to the virus. Those who used religious coping were less likely to be depressed (Koenig, 1999). In a study of residents of the Christian Bible Belt, elderly individuals who used religion as a coping mechanism were less likely to be hospitalized, and their hospital stays were shorter than those of elders who did not use these coping strategies (Koenig, 1999). Although studies link elements of religion with improvements in recovery, we must reassert that religion should not be viewed as guaranteed protection against the ravages of illness; nor should signs of illness be taken as reflections of a weak religious faith.

COPING WITH ILLNESS: COPING/HELP-SEEKING PATTERNS

Coping efforts used to promote well-being and to respond to symptoms of illness link behavior, social participation, and beliefs. Coping strategies represent more specific ways to deal with life events and are better predictors of positive response than a client's general religion orientation.

In the study of elderly persons in North Carolina, reliance on religion emerged as the most important coping strategy, especially among women (Koenig, 1999). An analysis of 40 studies examining the statistical relationships between various types of religious coping and outcomes of negative life events revealed that 53% of the relationships between religious types of coping and positive outcomes were statistically significant (Pargament, 1997). These studies recognize that religion is a multidimensional phenomenon. Consequently, it is useful to explore the specific nature of coping strategies and the nature of the problems being addressed (Pargament & Brandt, 1998).

One helpful religious coping mechanism is viewing oneself as being in a relationship with God and believing in the control of God. A perception of support and a sense that God is a source of guidance and a partner in times of need are helpful in coping and lead to greater sense of well-being and ability to handle stressful events. The belief that a loving God is in control of illness and life events is associated with an increased sense of well-being and sense of self-worth (Koenig, 1999; Pargament & Brandt, 1998). Being able to use prayer to call upon God gives a greater sense of control over a situation (Koenig, 1999; Perry, 1998).

Studies of religious coping reaffirm the value of social support that arises from participation in a faith community (Eugene, 1995; Koenig, 1999; Pargament & Brandt, 1998). While people may typically think of a social support network in terms of what they themselves can receive, Pargament and Koenig (1999) found that one of the most effective coping strategies is to reach out to help others. Those who coped with their physical illness by offering spiritual support and comfort to others were less likely to be depressed and more likely to report a higher quality of life. As Koenig (1999) suggests, social workers can help clients find ways in which they can contribute to the spiritual lives of others, even when they do not have the physical strength or economic resources to help in other ways. Pargament and Brandt (1998) conclude that religious coping adds a further dimension to non-religious coping strategies. They cite especially the sense of a spiritual support that exceeds the benefits of general social support.

At the same time, some types of responses to problems are associated with decreased sense of well-being and can increase the level of stress people who are religious experience. These include a sense of alienation and dissatisfaction with the religious community, a feeling that God has abandoned one, and a sense of being punished by God with accompanying guilt and fear (Pargament & Brandt, 1998). Perceptions of a punitive God can be associated with increased anxiety (Trenholm, Trent, & Compton, 1998).

Although the emphasis of this section has been on coping with physical health problems, religious coping can also help prevent the mental health complications experienced by persons with severe physical illness. In a study of seriously ill elderly persons, including some with severe disabilities, individuals who scored highest on the Religious Coping Inventory demonstrated the lowest levels of depression both at the time they completed the inventory and in the subsequent 6-month period. This pattern was especially likely for individuals who were severely disabled (Koenig, 1999). Some empirical evidence demonstrates that the belief that God plays a role in controlling health and illness may be important to psychological adjustment (Wallston, et al., 1999). Visits from chaplains have been associated with more rapid recovery for mental health patients (Koenig, 1999). In a study on religious coping and physical illness, Koenig (1995) found that the use of religion as a coping behavior increased with the severity of the illness (though it may be less helpful when a depressive disorder is severe). He concludes that religious cognitions may provide a powerful intrapsychic mechanism to help people who are physically ill or disabled alter their appraisal of the situation in ways that enable them to adapt more successfully. To attest to this phenomenon, one only need to examine the belief of Catholics in miracles. Chapter 7 points out that Hispanic Catholics believe in miracles and that they often go on pilgrimages to a shrine of the Virgin or of the saint to whose intercession miracle is attributed, to give thanks for healing or favor.

Fallot (1998) analyzed how spiritual and religious narratives influence an individual's view of his or her illness, ability to cope with mental illness, orientation to self, and recovery process. Fallot identified five themes: First, spirituality as a core of one's identity provides an "antidote to mental illness as a core identity" (p. 38). People who are able to view themselves as being children of God or an essential part of a larger world rather than being defined by their illness often adopt a more hopeful view of their lives. Second, recovery is viewed as a long-term process and a journey that requires effort. Religion provides the metaphor of pilgrimage rather than immediate healing. Third, there is the vital element of hope that reminds people of God's presence in their lives despite great obstacles. This lets them take hope from knowing that there is a source of power allied with good and opposed to evil. Fourth, there is a belief in the reality of a loving relationship with God and the need to find ways to establish loving relationships with others. Fifth, the Serenity Prayer encourages people to accept what cannot be changed and to focus their efforts on what can be changed in their lives.

In answer to why religious coping is effective, Pargament and Brandt (1998) suggest that religion offers a response to the "problems of human insufficiency." When we are pushed beyond our resources and recognize our fundamental vulnerability, religion offers some solutions in the form of spiritual support, explanations for puzzling and difficult life events, and a sense of control.

The death of a loved one represents a time of vulnerability to mental health problems. Several studies indicate that religious people who have lost a spouse or a child are less likely to suffer depression than are those who do not have religious faith (Koenig, 1999). It is unclear the extent to which specific religious beliefs play a role here, since religious traditions vary widely. Angel, Dennis, and Dumain (1998) suggest that there is value in drawing upon spirituality and spiritual connections with God when dealing with the death of a parent.

The preceding discussion points out ways in which religious coping can reduce the likelihood that symptoms of illness will be experienced as disabling or will contribute to further problems and ways in which such coping can promote healing. Although the literature generally reflects the positive role of religion in this process, research also indicates that people's coping strategies can sometimes increase the level of stress. In working with individual clients, it is important to explore their current religious beliefs and support systems in terms of whether they are perceived as helpful or contributing to the burden experienced by the client.

RELIGIOUS TRADITIONS AND HEALTH AND HEALING

Ethnographic research on spirituality and palliative care indicates that two dominant themes are "making the most of the now and making sense." As reflected in earlier chapters of this book, the meaning of life is a central theme in most religions (O'Connor, Meakes, McCarroll-Butler, Gadowsky, & O'Neill, 1997). Addressing these themes with clients can help reinforce their coping in times of illness. In addition to religious traditions, race and ethnicity play a role in shaping the nature of coping strategies. Ethnicity influences both the likelihood that one will be a member of a specific religious group and the unique ways in which one's religious convictions will be expressed. Studies indicate some of the profound differences within specific religious traditions based on ethnicity (for example, the discussion by McGolderick, Giordano, and Pearce, 1996 regarding differences among Roman Catholics from Irish, Italian, Polish, and Chicano backgrounds).

Ethnicity and Culture

All religion is practiced in a cultural context, and one's culture defines one's beliefs about the relationship of healing to the supernatural. Religion is often a conduit for spirituality, because it provides the cultural structure in which a person can grow spiritually. Culture and ethnicity inform religion and spirituality and influence the expression and practices of religion. For a large percentage of the population, ethnicity and religion are intertwined. Many Americans of Western European origin are, for example, either Protestant or Catholic. Americans whose country of origin is Laos, Thailand, Sri Lanka, Cambodia, India, China, Japan, Taiwan, or Vietnam are more likely to espouse Buddhism. Among the 5.5 million Jews living in the United States are German Jews, Polish Jews, and South American Jews yet all share certain beliefs in common. The various religions share common beliefs that influence the experience of health and illness, coping mechanisms, and beliefs about healing; at the same time, there can be differences in practices and the meanings attributed to aspects of the tradition.

A religious tradition provides certain structures: a set of common beliefs (doctrines), practices (cultural and religious rituals), a written word (the Bible, Koran, Vedas, or Torah) or an oral tradition, a code of conduct, and fundamental principles that define an individual's relationship to God, to others, and to the world (Perry, 1998).

All religions provide a form of social support, but the specific manifestation depends on the cultural group. People's practice of their religion falls along a spectrum ranging from conservative to traditional to liberal. A person may accept some, all, or few of the principles of his or her religion.

Folk Healing

In addition to the institutionalized avenues of well-being, many ethnic groups also utilize folk healing methods, most of which have spiritual and religious connotations or elements. Most cultures have a folk healing system, which, according to Wing (1998), "is a set of beliefs that has a shared social dimension." Most of the knowledge of the folk healing system is passed on through tradition or orally. Traditional cultures have some key concepts in common: the origin of illness, balance, motion, colors, symbols, and the union of body, mind, and spirit (Wing, 1998). For example, illness occurs when one does not follow the law of nature or when there is a lack of harmony in one's life. Race and ethnicity influence these interpretations: Southeast Asians believe that natural illness is the result of an imbalance of *chi* (energy), while Afro-Caribbean people attribute a natural illness to defying the laws of nature. Illness that is considered unnatural is generally attributed to an outside force, such as a person who has the power to inflict evil. Native Americans believe that the evildoer makes "bad medicine" to bestow illness or misfortune on a victim. Magicians in Afro-Caribbean cultures practice hexes, and hexes are placed by *brujas* in Central and South American countries. The Hmong believe that angry spirits can be called upon to punish people. Malevolent desires rooted in envy cause unexplained illnesses. Wing (1998) found that among some Native American and Hispanic cultures, alcoholism is perceived as an unnatural illness inflicted on a victim by an evildoer. Mediterranean cultures believe in "the evil eye," which can be countered with a prayer to restore balance and harmony.

Latin Americans and people from many Asian cultures believe that foods, medicine, and illnesses have hot and cold properties that create balance or imbalance by affecting bodily heat loss (Wing, 1998). Energy or motion is another element common to folk healing traditions. In China, energy is referred to as *chi*; in India, it is called *prana;* it is known as *doshas* in the Vedic tradition and as *Spirit* in the Native American culture. Native Americans believe that dancing is a way of communing with the Creator. Balanced energy brings about mental alertness, spiritual realization, enthusiasm, and balanced bodily rhythms. People in various cultures believe that energy is harnessed through such activities as meditation, diet, avoidance of negative emotions, and acupuncture. Powerful healing symbols and colors are also used by many cultures (Wing, 1998).

Many Native American, Latin American, and Asian American people share the belief that there is no separation between body, mind, and spirit. Islam stresses the balance of the spiritual, emotional, physical (including diet), and intellectual in supporting health. Recognizing that people are made of body, mind, and spirit, the Roman Catholic Church has supported the use of culturally relevant rituals, dance, and song by African American, Hispanic, and Vietnamese Catholics.

Culture also influences beliefs about God's role in controlling health and illness, which can help in adjusting psychologically (Wallston, et al., 1999). Further, one's culture influences one's view of one's own role in coping with stressors. The self may be perceived as passive, placing the responsibility for coping under God's control; a person may see himself or herself as self-directing and God as passive; or the person may perceive a collaborative relationship in which God and self work together to deal with a stressor. The stance one takes will influence one's adjustment to stress (Wallston et.al., 1999).

Cultural Specificity in the Experience of Symptoms of Illness

Help seeking and responses to symptoms are influenced by culture. A study by Li, Logan, Yee, and Ng (1999) found that among the major barriers preventing Chinese people from seeking professional help were language, perceptions of symptoms, and lack of knowledge about services. In another study on culture and illness management, Henry (1999) found that responses to illness among the Hmong ranged from an orientation to an animistic cosmology to the acceptance of Western theories. The study suggested the use of Hmong disease metaphors to interpret Western medicine.

Not only is the experience of symptoms of illness culturally specific, but attitudes toward death also vary with culture. People have differing views of advanced directives, organ donation, suicide, and euthanasia (Braun & Nichols, 1996). For example, Chinese and Japanese people who are Buddhists perceive death not only as part of life but also as an extension of life (Char, Tom, Young, Murakami, & Ames, 1996).

IMPLICATIONS FOR SOCIAL WORK PRACTICE

The preceding discussion demonstrates ways in which the religious beliefs and practices of individuals and families may help promote health, reduce the progression of disease, and aid in the healing process—thus helping people cope with illness, disability, and death. While the goal of the social worker or other counselor is not to proselytize for religion, it can be appropriate to encourage clients to identify the help that is potentially available and to help them capitalize on the resources present within their religious tradition. In doing so, the social worker needs both to draw upon an understanding of the tradition and to enlist the client in identifying his or her own precise meaning of life events and the relevant practices that can be sources of strength. Recognizing that social workers and many other counselors are not trained as religious counselors, this section discusses how they can work with clients to draw upon the strengths of the client's religious and spiritual tradition.

First, in spite of the differences that emerge among religious traditions, the supportiveness of the religious community transcends these differences. Helping clients identify the types and sources of help available within this network is a first step. As described in earlier chapters, religious traditions have differing interpretations of the types of help that are appropriate for specific problems. Religious views may encourage giving help for some types of problems while discouraging people from responding in a supportive way to other problems, events, or situations. The tension surrounding homosexuality, for example, has certainly been an issue within some religious traditions. Social workers can work with religious groups to develop supportive networks and to promote understanding for people who need help.

Rituals represent another source of help within religious and spiritual traditions. Rituals that mark life-cycle transitions (becoming an adult, marriage, birth, death) can be important to the individuals' sense of identity and their role within the family and the larger community. These rituals can confer status and a sense of belonging to the family, the religious or spiritual community, and the wider community. Some rituals and related ceremonies are designed to promote healing (for example, prayer, the laying on of hands, specific offerings). Rituals that encourage reconciliation with the Divine or with other individuals can help people deal with a sense of alienation in their lives. Rituals can help promote forgiveness and reconnection. Counselors can help clients identify potentially important rituals and encourage them to draw on these resources.

It can also be helpful with some clients to identify the tensions that are preventing them from being able to participate in religious rituals. Mr. C, for example, was a married Roman Catholic who had not participated in Confession or Communion for many years. Earlier in his life, he had been involved in an affair. Although he broke off the affair, he continued to feel guilt-ridden and alienated from his religious tradition. He began to have a growing number of anxiety-related symptoms that finally culminated in his going to the emergency room for a panic attack. An essential adjunct to the brief counseling that he received was a meeting with his priest, which included the ritual of Confession and the resumption of participation in Communion. These rituals were very helpful in allowing him to move forward in reconciliation with God, with his wife, and with himself.

Closely related to rituals are the behaviors that are encouraged by religious traditions to promote a sense of health and well-being. Meditation is an important example and is a part of a variety of religious traditions. Earlier chapters describe the role of meditation as encouraged by Confucianism, Hinduism, and Buddhism. In Chapter 2, Brave Heart describes ways in which traditional Native American (Lakota) religious ceremonies can contribute to well-being by restoring harmony with the natural world.

Finally, religious and spiritual traditions all contain a set of interpretations of life that can give people a sense that their lives have a meaning and purpose, even in the face of the inevitable suffering that is part of life. Such views give people a sense of hope, help them feel that they are not alone, and can give them a sense of dignity and worth. Social workers can help clients draw on these meaning systems.

Again, we recognize that belief systems can also be a source of tension for individuals who are struggling with life issues that are viewed as unacceptable by their religious tradition. While sometimes tensions are unavoidable, there are also clients who can be helped to realize that they have burdened themselves excessively through misinterpretation of doctrine or policy or isolation from the variety of voices within their tradition. As one anxious man indicated, "I must be a bad Christian to view God in this way." It was helpful for him to realize that while his views were in disagreement with his particular denomination, they did fit with the mainstream thinking of the Methodist denomination.

In working with clients to get them to draw on their religious and spiritual traditions, counselors need to develop ties with leaders of religious and spiritual groups in the community. These individuals have the requisite knowledge and credibility. One of the authors worked with a woman who had divorced and then remarried without the permission of the church. She feared the day that she would be punished by God. When her son was born with a serious birth defect, she was sure that this was God's punishment for what she had done. She received essential help from an understanding leader from her church, who assured her that her child's health did not represent such punishment. These words from a credible source within her own religious tradition were extremely powerful and healing and represented an essential adjunct to her counseling.

CONCLUSION

Research provides evidence that individuals who seek the comfort of their religion in time of illness are more likely to survive surgery and related health concerns; that spirituality helps individuals cope with chronic and serious illnesses like cancer, depression, and addiction; and that spiritual comfort is beneficial for dying and grieving individuals. Social workers in health care settings must consider not only a client's religion, but also the role that religion plays in that client's life, as well as the interpretation of health and illness provided by that person's religion and by his or her culture. These factors will assist the social worker in assessing the person's assets, coping capacity, and approach to health and illness.

REFERENCES

Angel, G., Dennis, B., & Demmon, L. E. (1998, November-December). Spirituality, resilience, and narrative: Coping with parental death. *Families in Society: The Journal of Contemporary Human Services,* 615–629.

Antonovsky, A. (1987). *Unraveling the mystery of health: How people manage stress and stay well.* San Francisco: Jossey-Bass.

Bagley, C. A., & Carrol, J. (1998). Healing forces in African-American families. In H. McCubbin & E. Thompson (Eds.), *Resiliency in African-American families. Resiliency in families series,* Vol. 3. (pp. 117–142). Thousand Oak, CA: Sage Publications.

Booth, J., & Martin, J. E. (1998). Spiritual and religious factors in substance use, dependence and recovery. In H. Koenig (Ed.), *Handbook of religion and mental health* (pp. 175-199). New York: Academic Press.

Braun, K., & Nichols, R. (1996). Cultural issues in death and dying. *Hawaii Medical Journal, 55*(12), 260–264.

Canda, E., & Furman, F. (1999). Spiritual diversity and social work practice: The heart of helping. New York: Free Press.

Cascio, T. (1998, September-October). Incorporating spirituality into social work practice: A review of what to do. *Families in Society: The Journal of Contemporary Human Services,* 523–531.

Char, D., Tom, K., Young, G., Murakami, T., & Ames, R. (1996). A view of death and dying among the Chinese and Japanese. *Hawaii Medical Journal, 55*(12), 286–290.

Dancey, J., & Wynn-Dancy, M. (1994). Faith of our fathers (mothers) living still: Spirituality as a force for the transmission of family values within the Black community. In V. Jackson (Ed.), *Aging families and use of proverbs for values enrichment* (pp. 87–105). Binghamton, NY: Haworth Press.

Donahue, M. J., and Benson, P. L. (1995). Religion and the well-being of adolescents. *Journal of Social Issues, 51*(2), 145–160.

Dossey, B., & Dosey, M. (1998). Body-mind-spirit: Attending to holistic care. *American Journal of Nursing, 98*(8), 35–38.

Eugene, T. (1995). There is a balm in Gilead: Black women and the Black church as agents of a therapeutic community. In J. Ochshorn & E. Cole (Eds.), *Women's spirituality, women's lives* (pp. 55–57). Binghamton, NY: Haworth Press.

Fallot, R. D. (1998, Winter). Spiritual and religious dimensions of mental illness recovery narratives. *New Directions for Mental Health Series*, 80, 35–44.

Gerwood, J., LeBlanc, & Piazza, N. (1998). The Purpose-in-Life test and religious denomination: Protestant and Catholic scores in an elderly population. *Journal of Clinical Psychology, 54*(1), 59–53

Henry, R. (1999). Measles, Hmong, and metaphor: Culture change and illness management under conditions of immigration. *Medical Anthropology Quarterly, 13*(10), 32–50.

Koenig, H. (1995) Religion as cognitive schema. *The International Journal for the Psychology of Religion, 5*(1), 31–37.

Koenig, H. (1999). *The healing power of faith: Science explores medicine's last great frontier.* New York: Simon and Schuster.

Krause, N. (1998). Neighborhood deterioration, religious coping, and changes in health during late life. *The Gerontologist, 38*(6), 653–664.

Levin, J. S., & Chatters, L. (1998). Research on religion and mental health: An overview of empirical findings and theoretical issues. In H. Koenig (Ed.), *Handbook of religion and mental health* (pp. 33–50). New York: Academic Press.

Li, P., Logan, S., Yee, L., Ng, S. (1999). Barriers to meeting the mental health needs of the Chinese community. *Journal of Public Health Medicine, 21*(1), 74–80.

McCullough, M., Hoyt, W., Larson, D., Koenig, H., & Thoreson, C. (2000). Religious involvement and mortality: A meta-analytic review. *Health Psychology, 19*(3), 211–222.

McGolderick, M., J. Giordano, & J. Pearce (Eds). (1996). *Ethnicity and family therapy.* 2nd ed. New York: Guilford Press.

Mitka, M. (1998). Getting religion seen as help in being well. *Journal of the American Medical Association 280* (22), 1896–1897.

O'Connor, T., Meakes, E., McCarroll-Butler, P., Gadowsky, S., & O'Neill, K. (1997). Making the most and making sense: Ethnographic research on spirituality in palliative care. *Journal of Pastoral Care, 51*(1), 25–36.

Oxman, T. (1995). Lack of social participation or religious strength and comfort as risk factors for death after cardiac surgery in the elderly. *Psychosomatic Medicine, 57*, 5–15.

Pargament, K. (1997). *The psychology of religion and coping: Theory, research, practice.* New York: Guilford Press.

Pargament, K. I., & Brant, C. R. (1998). Religion and coping. In H. Koenig (Ed.), *Handbook of religion and mental health.* (pp. 111–128). New York: Academic Press.

Pargament, K., Zinnbauer, B., Scott, A., Butter, E., Zerowin, J., & Stanik, P. (1998). Red flags and religious coping: Identifying some religious warning signs among people in crisis. *Journal of Clinical Psychology, 54*(l), 77–89.

Parry, J., & Ryan, A. (1995). Introduction. In J. Parry & A. Ryan (Eds.), *A cross-cultural look at death, dying, and religion* (pp. ix–xxvi). Chicago: Nelson Hall.

Perry, B. G. F. (1998). The relationship between faith and well-being. *Journal of Religion and Health, 37*(2), 125.

Petersen, L., & Roy, A. (1985). Religiosity, anxiety, and meaning and purpose: Religion's consequences for psychological well-being. *Review of Religious Research, 27*(1).

Rolland, J. (1998). Belief and collaboration in illness: Evolution over time. *Families, Systems, and Health, 16*(1/2), 7–25

Sarason, R. (1998). "Judaism." Microsoft Encarta 98 Encyclopedia.

Sinha, P. (1998). Hinduism and medical practice. *Journal of the Medical Association of Georgia, 87*(4), 312–314.

Thomas, L. (1997). Aging, religion and spirituality. *Journal of Aging Studies, 11*(2), 97–100.

Todd, M. (1996). The SPRITual history. *Archives of Family Medicine, 5*(1), 11–16.

Trenholm, P., Trent, J., & Compton, W. (1998). Negative religious conflict as a predictor of panic disorder. *Journal of Clinical Psychology, 54*(1), 59–65.

Wallston, K., Malcame, V., Flores, L., Hansdottir, I., Smith, C., Stein, M., Weisman, M., & Clements, P. (1999). Does God determine your health? The God locus of health control scale. *Cognitive Therapy and Research, 23*(2), 131–142.

Wing, S. (1998). A comparison of traditional folk healing concepts with contemporary healing concepts. *Journal of Community Health Nursing, 15*(3), 143–154.

CONTRIBUTORS

MARIAN A. AGUILAR

Marian A. Aguilar has a B.S.W. with a specialization in religious studies and an M.S.W. from Our Lady of the Lake University in San Antonio, Texas, and a Ph.D. in social work from the University of Illinois at Champaign–Urbana. She is an associate at the University of Texas at Austin and is currently on leave to develop and direct a social work program at Texas A&M International University at Laredo.

During the last 30 years, she has participated in many spirituality and religious education workshops. She worked in parish ministry for 13 years and taught in Catholic institutions of higher learning for 9 years. She has been a member of a religious order since 1963.

Aguilar has conducted research in the area of culture, health, healing, and spirituality and has presented workshops on these topics as well. Her area of specialization is in health care delivery to people of color. She has published on topics ranging from women and health care to the educational achievement of young Mexican American women. Her most recent research is in the field of aging among minority groups. She has received numerous grants to research topics ranging from social work practice in Mexico to an evaluation of Medicaid managed care in Texas.

MARIA YELLOW HORSE BRAVE HEART

Maria Yellow Horse Brave Heart is a Hunkpapa/Oglala Lakota and member of the Wapaha Ska (the White Lance), a *tiospaye* (extended kinship network of Wounded Knee survivors and cousins of Sitting Bull). Brave Heart received an M.S.W. from Columbia University in 1976 and her Ph.D. in clinical social work from Smith College in 1995. She serves as the director of the Takini Network and an associate professor at the University of Denver Graduate School of Social Work.

Brave Heart specializes in trauma work for indigenous communities and is the historical trauma specialist for the Indigenous Law Institute. She is the author of 14 journal articles and book chapters and has delivered over 60 presentations and workshops on historical trauma and unresolved grief among the Lakota, the culmination of more than 20 years of work on the phenomenon of intergenerational transfer of indigenous traumatic history. She participates in traditional spiritual ceremonies in Kyle, South Dakota, on the Pine Ridge Reservation and at Sitting Bull camp at Standing Rock, South Dakota.

Brave Heart is a member of the editorial board of *Affilia, Journal for Women in Social Work*. She develops curricula on Indian research and substance abuse prevention projects and was the initiator and lead curriculum developer of the Wakanheja (Sacred Child) Lakota parenting project funded by the Center for Substance Abuse Prevention.

EDWARD R. CANDA

Edward R. Canda has degrees in anthropology (B.A., Kent State University), religious studies (M.A., University of Denver), and social work (M.S.W., Ph.D., The Ohio State University). He has also studied and conducted research in Korea as a Fulbright-sponsored graduate fellow in East Asian philosophy, as a visiting professor in Sung Kyun Kwan University, and as a fellow sponsored by the Korea Foundation and the Academy of Korean Studies. He is a professor and chairperson of the doctoral program in the School of Social Welfare at the University of Kansas.

Canda founded the Society for Spirituality and Social Work in 1990 and now works internationally to promote spiritual diversity in social work. He has given more than 100 presentations on spirituality and cultural diversity in the United States, Korea, Japan, Hong Kong, Croatia, the Netherlands, Germany, and Mexico. He is the author of more than 50 publications on related topics, including *Spiritual Diversity in Social Work Practice* (co-authored with Leola Dyrud Furman, Free Press, 1999) and *Contemporary Human Behavior Theory* (co-authored with Susan P. Robbins and Pranab Chatterjee, Allyn and Bacon, 1998). Canda is the editor of *Spirituality in Social Work: New Directions* (Haworth Press, 1998) and is the co-editor (with Elizabeth D. Smith) of *Transpersonal Perspectives on Spirituality in Social Work* (Haworth Press, 2001).

DOUGLAS K. CHUNG

Douglas K. Chung has a B.A. in English literature from Soochow University, an M.S.W. from West Virginia University, an M.A. in Public Administration, and a Ph.D. in Social Work from The Ohio State University. Chung is a professor in the School of Social Work at Grand Valley State University in Michigan.

Chung is the first social work scholar to introduce ancient Chinese Qigong principles and practices into human services. He has taught Qigong therapy courses to graduate students and served as a Qigong therapist and master since 1995. Trained as a researcher in mental health, community organization, and family therapy, Chung has extensive practice and teaching experience and has written about cross-cultural social work education and practice. He is engaged in building spiritually sensitive models for personal and social transformation through the integration of Qigong techniques and human services. He is the author of more than 40 papers and publications, including *Social Work with Asian Americans* (1993) and *Qigong Therapies* (2000).

Chung founded the Asian Center in Grand Rapids, Michigan, and serves as its president. He has obtained grants, conducted workshops in different countries, produced videotapes, and established the Asian Resource Center on the Asian Center's Web site. You are invited to visit the author at the Asian Center's Web site at http://asiancenter.8m.com

SOPHIA F. DZIEGIELEWSKI

Sophia F. Dziegielewski is a professor in the School of Social Work at the University of Central Florida in Orlando. She received her M.S.W. and her Ph.D. in social work from Florida State University in Tallahassee. Dziegielewski is a clinical social worker licensed in Tennessee, Georgia, and Florida.

Dziegielewski's professional interests primarily focus on health and mental health issues and on time-limited, empirically based practice strategy. She has over 65 publications and four books on health and mental health. Her practice interest centers on the establishment of outcome-based treatments in the health and mental health setting, with a special emphasis on recognizing human diversity in the health and mental health fields. She has served as the methodologist on numerous research and grant-writing projects. In addition, she has conducted over 200 workshops and community presentations on implementing medical and mental health-related counseling practice and strategy in today's managed-care environment.

BRUCE D. FRIEDMAN

Bruce D. Friedman is director of the social work program at the University of Texas–Pan American. He received his Ph.D. in social welfare from Case Western Reserve University's Mandel School of Applied Social Sciences in 1993. His doctoral dissertation was entitled *No Place Like Home: A Study of Two Homeless Shelters.* His M.S.W. is from Washington University's George Warren Brown School of Social Work, where he specialized in families and substance abuse; and his B.A. in Religion and Sociology is from Case Western Reserve University.

The author of *The Ecological Perspectives Cookbook: Recipes for Social Workers* (Brooks/Cole, 1999) and *The Research Tool Kit: Putting it All Together* (Brooks/Cole, 1998), Friedman has been doing research on integrating religious concepts into social work. He has also written a number of papers, including "Charity Concepts and the Relationship to Social Work Practice" (*Social Thought,* 2001) and "Building A Spiritual Based Model to Address Substance Abuse" (*Social Thought,* 2000). He has also presented a number of papers at CSWE APM and the Society of Spirituality and Social Work on integrating Old Testament text into social work practice.

DARLENE GRANT

Darlene Grant received her M.S.S.A. degree from Case Western Reserve University's Mandell School in 1984 and received her Ph.D. from the University of Tennessee, Knoxville, in 1993. Grant is an associate professor at the School of Social Work at the University of Texas at Austin, where she teaches courses on human behavior and the social environment, research methods, advanced social work practice, mental health and chemical dependency, cultural diversity, and women and addiction. Grant has won numerous teaching awards and is often invited to state, national, and international conferences and workshops to speak from her experience as a practitioner and researcher.

Avid in her efforts to provide practitioners with applicable research findings, Grant has authored a number of publications, including book chapters on substance abuse by African American children and effective therapeutic approaches with ethnic families. She is also editor of a government-sponsored monograph on delivering culturally competent services to women and children who are affected by drugs. Grant also served as one of three researchers to develop and disseminate a plan for the recruitment and retention of persons of color for careers in chemical dependency counseling for the Texas Commission on Alcohol and Drug Abuse. She has recently received a National Institute on Alcohol Abuse and Alcoholism award to study the impact of drug court on low-income drug users involved in the criminal justice system.

DENNIS T. HAYNES

Dennis T. Haynes is an Associate Professor and director of the M.S.S.W. program at the University of Texas at Austin School of Social Work. He received his B.S. in Family Relations from Brigham Young University (1973), his M.S.W. (1977) from California State University, Fresno, and his Ph.D. (1993) in social work at Florida State University. Haynes has taught courses and presented workshops on values and ethics, religion and spirituality, teaching effectiveness, international social work, and child abuse prevention. He has written several articles in the area of values and ethics.

Haynes has over 20 years of varied experience in social work practice. He has been a practitioner and administrator in both public and non-profit agencies. He also has extensive ecclesiastical service as an LDS bishop, a stake presidency counselor, and a missionary to Southeastern Mexico.

BERYL HUGEN

Beryl Hugen received a B.A. from Calvin College, an M.S.W. from Western Michigan University, and a Ph.D. from the University of Kansas. He is professor of social work and practicum coordinator in the Department of Social Work and Sociology at Calvin College in Grand Rapids, Michigan. He currently serves as a board member and publications editor for the North American Association of Christians in Social Work.

Hugen has published papers on mental health, the integration of Christian faith and social work practice, and social work history. He is editor of *Christianity and Social Work: Readings on the Integration of Christian Faith and Social Work Practice* (North American Association of Christians in Social Work, 1998). He was the principal investigator for the research project *Coming Full Circle: Devolution of State Delivery of Human Services to Faith-Based Human Service Organizations* (Council for Christian Colleges and Universities, 2000) and a research associate for the project *Service and Faith: The Impact on Christian Faith and Congregational Life of Organized Community Caring* (Lilly Endowment, Inc. 2000).

DARYL McMULLEN

Daryl McMullen graduated from Andrews University in 1999 with an M.S.W. and is currently licensed to practice in the state of Indiana. He provides individual, family, and group therapy to high school students in the South Bend, Indiana area. During graduate school, he pursued an interest in children and adolescents by completing internships in both outpatient and residential locations. Other interests include the use of computer/Internet technology in social work practice and the field of Christian Counseling. His future plans include working as a Christian counselor and writing books that help facilitate the growth, stability, and reputation of the Christian counseling field.

ANEESAH NADIR

Aneesah Nadir is on the faculty of the Department of Social Work at Arizona State University West. She received her B.S.W. from Adelphi University in Garden City, New York, and her M.S.W. from Arizona State University in Tempe, Arizona. She is a Ph.D. candidate at the Arizona State University School of Social Work. Her dissertation focuses on the experiences of young Muslim women in North America. She teaches diversity and social work practice courses. She also teaches an elective course, "The Muslim Reality," which focuses on the experience of Muslims in North America.

Nadir is the cofounder of Arizona Muslim Family and Muslim Community Services, both of which offer social services to Muslims, and currently serves as the President and cofounder of the Islamic Social Services Association of the United States and Canada. She provides diversity training for business, education, social work, and health care organizations and has been a speaker for national Islamic conferences as well as statewide NASW conferences. She was also a presenter for the 2000 Council on Social Work Education's Annual Program Management Conference. Nadir is a founding advisor for the Muslim Youth Group of Greater Phoenix and for Al Mu'minah, the Young Muslim Sisters Youth Group of Greater Phoenix, and is a dedicated advocate for Muslim youth and family concerns. She has taught Islamic weekend schools throughout Phoenix and helps teach the Islamic fundamentals class for new Muslims at the Islamic Cultural Center of Tempe, Arizona. She is a columnist for the newspaper *Muslim Voice* and has served as a panelist on social services for *Soundvision's Webcast Radio Islam.*

T. LAINE SCALES

T. Laine Scales is an assistant professor of social work at Baylor University, Waco, Texas. She received a Ph.D. from the University of Kentucky (1996), a certificate in theology from the Southern Baptist Theological Seminary, Louisville, Kentucky, an M.S.W. from the Carver School of Church Social Work (1986), and a B.A. from the University of North Carolina (1983).

One of Scales' most recent publications is *All That Fits a Woman: Training Southern Baptist Women for Charity and Mission,* 1907–1926 (Mercer University Press, 2000). She also recently contributed biographies of six Baptist women to *The Dictionary of Baptists in America.* She is currently writing teaching cases on spirituality and social work. Her research interests include social welfare history, rural social work, and spirituality and social work, and she has published and delivered presentations in these research areas.

RAM NARESH SINGH

Ram Naresh Singh, born in India, immigrated to the United States as a Fulbright scholar to obtain his Ph.D. in social work from Columbia University in 1968. He was also trained as a psychoanalyst and hypnotherapist. He taught at the

University of Tennessee at Knoxville, Valparaiso University in Indiana, and was a professor of social work at Grand Valley State University since 1988.

Singh was an active member in the development of a spiritual center for women in Ganges Town, Michigan. Based on Vedantic philosophy, the center is primarily an interfaith organization aimed at promoting female spirituality and providing psycho-educational programs for women. Sadly Ram died in August 2001. He is deeply missed.

CURTIS J. VANDERWAAL

Curtis J. VanderWaal received his M.S.W. from the University of Michigan in 1987 and his Ph.D. in social welfare from the Mandel School of Applied Social Sciences at Case Western Reserve University in Cleveland, Ohio, in 1995. He is currently the associate director of the B.S.W. program at Andrews University and the project director for ImpacTeen, a Robert Wood Johnson Foundation research project, which is examining the impact of state-level illegal-drug laws on teen drug use rates. He is an associate professor of social work at Andrews University in Berrien Springs, Michigan, where he teaches B.S.W. and M.S.W. courses in Christian values and ethics, grief and loss, and social work methods.

VanderWaal has published two articles in the journal *Social Work and Christianity,* but the majority of his research has focused on substance abuse treatment, prevention, and AIDS. He has published research findings in the *Journal of Drug Issues, The Journal of Behavioral Health Services and Research,* and *Substance Use and Misuse* (in press) and has co-authored a research monograph for the National Institute of Justice titled *Breaking the Cycle of Drug Use among Juvenile Delinquents.* He has also presented 17 professional papers at national and international conferences.

MARY P. VAN HOOK

Mary P. Van Hook has an M.S.W. from Columbia University School of Social Work and a Ph.D. from Rutgers University. She is currently the director of the School of Social Work at the University of Central Florida.

Van Hook has worked extensively in the areas of family and children and mental health in New York City, Maryland, and rural Iowa. She has taught social work at the University of Michigan, Northwestern College, Grand Valley State University, and the University of Central Florida. Her research has focused on services to families and children, rural mental health, linkages between mental health and general health, international issues and women, and religious issues and social work practice. She has more than 30 publications in the areas of services to families and children, rural mental health, linkages between mental health and general health care, international issues and women, and religious issues and social work practice.

INDEX